# BIOLOGICAL INFLUENCES
# on
# CRIMINAL BEHAVIOR

# BIOLOGICAL INFLUENCES on CRIMINAL BEHAVIOR

## Gail S. Anderson

Simon Fraser University Publications

CRC Press
Taylor & Francis Group
Boca Raton   London   New York

CRC Press is an imprint of the
Taylor & Francis Group, an informa business

CRC Press
Taylor & Francis Group
6000 Broken Sound Parkway NW, Suite 300
Boca Raton, FL 33487-2742

© 2007 by Simon Fraser University Publications
CRC Press is an imprint of Taylor & Francis Group, an Informa business

International Standard Book Number-10: 1-4200-4331-5 (Hardcover)
International Standard Book Number-13: 978-1-4200-4331-0 (Hardcover)
International Standard Book Number-10: 0-86491-283-8 (Hardcopy SFU)
International Standard Book Number-13: 978-0-86491-283-1 (Hardcover SFU)

---

**Library of Congress Cataloging-in-Publication Data**

---

Anderson, Gail S. (Gail Scott)
    Biological influences on criminal behavior / Gail S. Anderson.
        p. cm.
    Includes bibliographical references and index.
    ISBN 1-4200-4331-5 (alk. paper)
    1. Criminal behavior. 2. Human biology--Social aspects. 3. Criminal behavior--Genetic aspects. 4. Sociobiology. 5. Criminology. I. Title.

    HV6115 .A644 2006
    364.3--dc22                                                    2006049390

---

**Visit the Taylor & Francis Web site at**
**http://www.taylorandfrancis.com**

**and the CRC Press Web site at**
**http://www.crcpress.com**

# Dedication

---

*To my parents, Alec and Pamela Anderson, and*
*my brother, David Anderson, who have always supported me*
*in all my endeavors; and to Professor Thelma Finlayson,*
*my mentor and friend, who has led the way*
*for women in science.*

# Preface

In modern criminology, the main schools of thought focus on social, environmental, material, and psychological factors that can cause crime. Although excellent and persuasive studies have been eloquently presented, as a scientist, I have felt for some time that most studies neglect one important aspect of the equation: the physical persons themselves. Human beings are a complex mixture of upbringing, background, environment, experiences, social structure, *and* biology. My work with criminology has allowed me to see that much research has been done on this biological dimension of criminal behavior. Over the past 20 years, valuable work on genetic background, hormone and neurotransmitter levels, diet, and physical insults such as brain trauma has been accomplished. With few exceptions, most introductory works in criminology seriously neglect this research. It is my hope in writing this book to help right this imbalance. It was written in the hope that through an integration of the biological view with mainstream social, psychological, and environmental views, we can find a new way of studying criminality, and we might gain some positive and useful explanations for criminal behavior.

It must be said at the outset that I do not believe biology causes crime, any more than a particular background, experience, or social environment can cause a crime. However, one would be remiss not to at least consider the physical person when trying to see the entire picture. If we are ever to fully understand behavior, we must look at all the factors that influence it. This text, then, joins with current biological theorists such as Ellis and Walsh, Trasler, Rowe, Raine, Andrews, and Quinsey in introducing criminologists to a new area. Despite the increasing evidence for biological influences on criminality, the number of such publications for students of criminology is remarkably slight. It is almost as if studying this particular influence has been forbidden in criminological texts. Wright and Miller (1998), in their excellent article entitled "Taboo until Today," measured the amount of text written about biological explanations for crime versus other sociological explanations, and found that if biology was mentioned at all, it was given infinitesimal coverage. Although excellent biological studies have been conducted, especially in recent years, they have not been included in mainstream criminology. In part, this is due to a fear of biology as determinism, but it is primarily due to a lack of understanding. Few scholars have both a criminological and a biological background. If we are to truly understand these valuable studies, strong backgrounds in genetics, neuroscience, and endocrinology, as well as criminology, are an asset. These backgrounds are not often found together. This book was written, then, to help the criminologist navigate an additional and vital new area of study; one with its own complexities and challenges. It does not attempt to suggest that biology plays *the* major role in criminal behavior. It was written with the belief, grounded in research, that something vital can be discovered when we assess all the factors related to the causes of crime; with luck, through this and texts like it, biology will be included in the equation.

One other qualification is necessary before we begin. Although you might think of yourself as a student of social behavior and not a scientist, you should be able to gain much from this text. You do not need to be a biologist to understand the concepts developed in *Biological Influences on Criminal Behavior*; in fact, you are not required to have any scientific background. The basic biological principles you need are explained so that you can understand the concepts discussed. There is only one real requirement that you must have to read and get as much out of this text as you can: *you must have an open mind.* You must be ready to look at new ideas. If you possess this trait, you can gain much from this text.

**Gail Anderson**
*Simon Fraser University, 2006*

# Acknowledgments

This text has its own history of development. It began as a series of lectures in my fourth-year seminar classes in the School of Criminology at Simon Fraser University in British Columbia. It progressed from there to a study guide, and finally, after much editing and revision, to its current shape as an introduction to biological influences on crime. I must thank the many people who have helped me work on this text and the many students who have shaped its approach. This book would not have been possible without the assistance and engagement of my students, both graduate and undergraduate. Their critical comments and questions helped the formation of this book. I would also like to thank Dr. John Whatley of SFU Publications for encouraging me to write this book in the first place and for his continued enthusiastic support.

Gail Anderson
*Simon Fraser University, 2006*

# About The Author

Gail S. Anderson earned a B.Sc. (Honors) in zoology from Manchester University, England; and her Masters of Pest Management and Ph.D. from Simon Fraser University in medical and veterinary entomology. Her specialty is forensic entomology, the use of insects in death investigations. Dr. Anderson is one of only two full-time forensic entomologists in Canada. She is an Associate Professor in forensic entomology in the School of Criminology at Simon Fraser University, and Undergraduate Director, and a forensic consultant to the RCMP and city police across Canada. Her work has been featured on several television programs, including "Journeys — Grave Testimony" and "Forbidden Places — Silent Witness" shown on The Discovery Channel, Planet Education, and "The Nature of Things — Postmortem." She was a recipient of Canada's "Top 40 under 40 Award" in 1999, received a YWCA Women of Distinction Award for Science and Technology in 1999, and the Simon Fraser University Alumni Association Outstanding Alumni Award for Academic Achievement in 1995. She was listed in *TIME* magazine as one of the top five innovators in the world, this century, in the field of Criminal Justice in 2001 and received the Derome Award from the Canadian Society of Forensic Sciences.

# Table of Contents

# Introduction to Biology and Crime

1

## Introduction

We have tried to understand why people commit crime since prehistory. Innumerable explanations have been put forth over time — many ludicrous, some plausible. Medieval "biological" explanations, for example, found criminal character rooted in a system of humors, large-scale influences on behavior brought about by balances and imbalances within specific organs of the body and their secretions. Moral theories of crime as an evil influence have been historically predominant. In about BC 400, Plato thought criminality was caused by an obscurity of thought — the imprisoned human mind was blocked from enlightenment as if it were locked in a cave, and thus acted irrationally. In c. AD 46, St. Paul thought it was caused by sinfulness, our inability to fulfill the law of God. In the 19th century, Cesare Lombroso put forward a more modern biological theory, a concept of facial types, *atavisms*, by which one could identify the criminal; his findings were supposedly based in science. And, as we shall see, highly suspect uses of genetics were used in Germany to study crime during the Nazi regime. From the late 19th century on, with the works of Durkheim, Marx, Weber, Freud, and others, social and psychological explanations of crime have gained widespread acceptance. These and other strands of modern theory, research, and speculation have continued into present-day criminology. However, despite the history and the almost constant theory building, we yet do not fully understand why a person commits a crime. The reasons are both perspectival and factual — any theory, even the most substantive, will be a partial view, and any theory will leave out some of the facts or significant strands of motive and cause of this changing phenomenon. This book is no different. The approach

1

developed in the following text cannot begin to explain all crime. However, it does introduce you to an integrative method for considering criminogenic behavior. With luck it will take its place among the mainstream approaches in the wider effort to gain a better understanding of this most baffling of human behaviors.

We work on the principle that in an effort to understand a complex human phenomenon such as crime, all factors must be considered. And, in this introductory chapter, we first try some critical thought experiments to clarify this complexity. With luck these will give rise to a healthy skepticism about research in human behavior, and especially about scientific research that purports to explain crime. We next explore how many of the biological bases for particular criminal behaviors are, at least in potential, *treatable*. This is the promise of biological research into crime. While biology may offer a limited answer to larger, more philosophical questions about crime, the approach explained in this text has some distinct advantages. From this discussion, some further cautions about studying crime in general are explored. We, for example, evaluate scientific methods throughout this text, and we need to engage some of the problems that can occur in any scientific research: definitions of crime will be assessed, as will Trasler's critical template for evaluating biological approaches that purport to be scientific.

The chapter reviews some of the social history from which this approach to crime has arisen. Up until the very recent past, the topics discussed in this text were considered too controversial to discuss in criminology. One of the important areas of controversy is, of course, the use of genetics to explain criminality. When social scientists respond negatively to biological explanations, they often assume that they are based in genetics. Genetic explanations of criminality have been much out of favor because they were not understood and such misinformation has been used reductively (and dangerously) in the past. They are now often strongly associated with past mistakes such as the eugenics movements, or with the genocidal regimes of Nazism and Stalinism in which whole populations were denied human rights based on supposed genetic differences. There are, then, some very good reasons to be cautious of their use. In relation to the approach developed in this book, it is important for the reader to realize that any reduction of the causes of crime to genetics alone can be a serious and dangerous distortion. Through a critical look at the field's checkered past, we hope in following chapters to explore its much brighter future.

## The Question of Biology, Crime, and the Environment

What then is the general place of biology in an explanation of crime? To explore this question, we first consider a less controversial, but parallel, question about genetics. We could ask, for example, a good biology question: Do our genes govern how we write? One advantage we would expect in taking this "genetics alone" approach is that we should receive a clear and precise answer. This, after all, is what scientific research promises.

Both common sense and scientific evidence tell us that the way we write is affected by our physical ability — how dexterous we are, how well we can manipulate objects with our fingers. Dexterity could then be determined by genetic makeup, the facility with finger movements and hand–eye coordination we are born with. But without much effort one can probably find an important qualification. Our ability to write is obviously also governed by nongenetic influences. Conditions in the womb, for example, have an influence on the development of hands and arms and can, therefore, affect later dexterity and thus later writing skills. Another qualification: we are not born able to write; we have to learn how to write. We write in a particular way because we were taught this way. We incorporate and model the scripts of the people who are significant in our early lives — teachers, older siblings, and parents. It is not too difficult to find an increasing array of other clearly environmental influences. A hand injury in childhood could also affect the way we learn to write; and equally, an injury in adulthood can change the way we write as we learn to compensate for the injury. Considering this multiplicity of real and potential environmental influences, how much of handwriting can be considered truly genetic in origin? The answer is that not much of it is genetic — it is really almost all a *learned behavior.*

But we can now take our thought experiment a bit further and ask a question to which the reductive, genetic approach might provide a better answer. The ability to write might have evolved with the human species and perhaps there is a genetic influence on this level. We might now refine our original question to: What makes us as a *species* capable of writing? What abilities do we have that other species do not? Why, for example, can a dog *not* write?"

Part of the answer involves degree of *intelligence* — the relative size, organization, and ability of the brain. For this reason, most dogs probably could not figure it out (border collies may be an exception). In general, we would think dogs would not have the higher-level skills in abstraction, sensory focus, dexterity, and memory that are required for writing and reading. What else then do we (and perhaps chimps) have that allows us to write, while dogs cannot? Another part of the puzzle is that we have opposable thumbs, and dogs do not; it is difficult to hold a pen (or type) without an opposable thumb, although some birds manage to use sticks to get at insects and chimps can be trained to use many tools. As well, people who have lost hands can write and even paint using their toes or teeth. In general, however, dogs do not have this ability. Thus, if you go back far enough into any feature or skill involving the body, it does appear to come down to genetics. Genes produce the specific attributes of the physical body that make us capable of writing — that is, a hand with fingers and a thumb, and a relatively capacious and intelligent brain that can instruct that hand to learn how to write.

Is writing then "caused" by genes? The problem is that at this level the genetic argument produces a form of absolute certainty by what might be termed "reductive generalization." Such certainties bother scientists — they are always either untrustworthy or of no real use. Yes, we can strongly and confidently assert that the brain itself is inherited and under genetic control, and that opposable thumbs are likewise under genetic control. You have a brain because humans evolved one, and the trait of producing a big brain and opposable thumbs is certainly inherited. Such assertions cannot be really contested. But the problem with them is, again, that even on this more general level, they are reductive of actual behavior. You are born with a brain, but what you *do* with it is a complex mixture of the brain itself, the inherited part, and the social environment — the most important part. The inherited big brain, the finger dexterity we share with the great apes, and the social environment that trains you (for better or for worse) in the necessary skills of script production and interpretation are all vitally necessary for you to write well, to be understood, and to understand writing by others. Learning how to read and write is a highly complex social and biological matter, as any speech therapist will tell you. Genetics is certainly not the only factor in acquiring this ability.

Thus, if you go back to the evolutionary level, you can relate even writing to genetics as a cause. But you may be able to now see that it is a rather one-sided explanation as far as behavior is concerned. Social development, education, and many other environmental influences are utterly necessary as well. Unfortunately, genetics alone cannot give us the magic explanation we wish because so much more is involved in any aspect of our functional, social-interpretive, painfully learned, and all too human behavior.

The argument for purely genetic explanations of behavior, and thus crime, can be qualified in another way. Although genetics is part of biology, biology as the "science of life" covers much more physiological territory than genetics. In this text we certainly consider genetics, but also examine a host of other biological explanations, such as hormone levels, the effects of disease, diet, neurotransmitters, brain injury, and prenatal problems. Some authors also place such material under genetics, but I think such presentations can be confusing. Note again their tendency to reduction. Biology, when it is good science, cannot be reductive.

There remains much resistance to thinking through the issues involved in biological approaches to crime. In many cases, social scientists are still afraid even to conceive of biological causes for crime. As mentioned in the Preface,

Wright and Miller, in "Taboo until Today" (1998), show how even the highly educated have boycotted the possibility of considering genetic and biological explanations. According to the article, this reaction comes from the idea's association with the vicious prejudices of the past, including the horrors of ethnic cleansing, slavery, and the genocides of World War II. However, the fact that an idea has been misused does not mean it should be forgotten or that it is wrong. It is vitally important to realize that horrific though these atrocities were, they were *not* based on science. They were based on the prejudices and psychopathic policies of people in power who decided to misquote science to an uneducated public to fulfill their own immoral agendas. There is the danger of repeating the prejudices of the past if we do not understand the truth of the science. It was the public's ignorance of the true facts that allowed such people to use these misrepresentations as weapons.

Another reason for the resistance is that some also think that a biological explanation means there is no hope for treatment. That, for instance, the approach may lead politicians to make laws that require incarceration of people with a biological predisposition for anti-social behavior. They must be locked away because they can never "get better." This view is, again, far from the truth and underscores the weakness of this kind of criticism. The biological view actually offers much more hope for those afflicted with these predispositions than social explanations. For example, as a society, we now seem to accept that terrible abuse during childhood could predispose a child toward criminality in later life. But this explanation offers no "cure"; we can never take away that abuse. We can try to ameliorate it, we can try to change society for the better, but we can never change the fact that it has occurred. In contrast, the outcome is actually much more hopeful if the behavior has a biological basis, because there are many biological states that we can treat or change.

## The Promise of Biological Research

With these initial cautions in mind, a picture is emerging of careful testing of the areas where this research paradigm can be applied, where it cannot be applied, and where it might offer a positive benefit. Here are some further examples where biology certainly has a profound influence on behavior and in which successful treatment has been found. They are not all related to crime but they set the stage for our approach in that they can show biological conditions for which, through research and treatment, predicted outcomes changed dramatically. These examples should give us some hope that a similar change in biologically based types of crime could, with adequate research, be available and they could be arrived at in a similar way.

1. *Phenylketonuria (PKU)*. In the old days, a percentage of children were born with a disease called phenylketonuria. The disease is genetically based; children who have it are unable to digest or metabolize phenylalanine, an amino acid that is essential for life. We get some amino acids from a balanced diet and make others ourselves; phenylalanine comes from diet. In children with PKU, the amino acid builds up to toxic levels that cause severe mental retardation by age 5. In fact, most people with mental retardation in the past had this disease.

   The cause of the disease was discovered in the 1930s, and the genetic basis was finally understood by the 1950s (Mednick, 1987), making treatment easy: simply keep most phenylalanine out of the diet (a tiny amount is required, but no more) until children are at least 7 years old, at which point high levels can build up without damage. Once this was understood, children born with the inability to metabolize phenylalanine no longer showed brain impairment, and the level of mental retardation in the population dropped dramatically.

   Now, all babies are tested at birth (their toes pricked for tiny blood samples); those at risk are fed restricted diets. The dramatic result is that there are no more PKU children. Actually, that is not true; the disease is still prevalent. In fact, it is more prevalent than before because these children have grown up normally and had children themselves, passing the disease on. But their offspring do not show the effects of the disease because we have changed the biological outcome.

2. *Cystic fibrosis (CF)*. This terrible disease has been traced to just one gene (Rommens et al., 1989). People who have CF lack this gene and therefore develop serious lung problems that eventually result in early death.

   Scientists have been experimenting with ways to implant the missing gene in people. To simplify, it is possible to use a virus to place a gene somewhere. Scientists put the required gene into the virus, and the virus carries the gene into the person. A virus works by getting inside your cells. To kill a virus, one must kill the cell it is in. Unfortunately, in the process, the host is often killed; this is why the common cold is so difficult to cure.

   Scientists have experimentally placed the missing gene that causes CF into a flu virus, which is modified so that it is incapable of causing the flu but still capable of penetrating a cell (Moss et al., 2004). When a person inhales the impregnated flu virus, the way he or she might inhale an asthma medicine, the gene rides the virus straight into the mucosal tissue and the lungs, and thus directly into the target cells.

The gene only lasts in those cells for a few weeks because cells constantly die. While most of us produce new cells that have all the right genes, people with cystic fibrosis do not. The gene is missing from their original DNA, so the replacement cells do not have it either — but the person can inhale it again.

This is a very new technique and still experimental, but if it continues to show promise, it might help people with CF live beyond their mid-20s. Even more exciting, if people who are missing this gene are treated from birth, they might escape all the terrible side effects of the disease and enjoy long, normal lives.

Both of these examples are unusual because they each concern just one gene, which is rare. Behavior, on the other hand, involves many genes, and is, as we have discussed, heavily influenced by the environment. Here is a more crime-related example.

3. *Serotonin.* Serotonin is a substance the brain uses to facilitate communication among cells. Low serotonin levels have been found to result in impulsivity and violence. Low serotonin can result from genetics, alcoholism, and various other factors — and it can be corrected by something as simple as diet.

In sum, these three examples show us that DNA does not necessarily mean destiny. You might now be able to see that fear of reductionism and a potential repetition of the errors and moral outrages of the past should not blind us to the potential of modern biological research to help solve some parts of the puzzle of criminogenic behavior.

A second warning. We must remember that any potential biological influences we may find will result only in a *predisposition* toward a particular behavior. There is no gene for crime, and none will ever be found; as a scientist, this author knows that genetics does not work that way. Because even hair color is the result of multiple genes, there certainly could not be a single one for a behavior. And even if there is a genetic predisposition, that is all it is — a predisposition. It is likely that genes or hormones sometimes contribute to proteins that have effects on certain behaviors, which are then greatly affected by situations, environments, and social upbringing. The influences can also be indirect. For example, biological influences on intelligence might affect the chances that a person who commits a crime will be caught; and from the other direction, biological influences on impulsivity might have a bearing on whether the person will commit a crime in the first place.

To explore the idea of predisposition a little further, here is a third thought experiment. Let us once again propose a genetic basis for behavior, and one like those above that has a known genetic risk factor. This time, however, we can find an example of criminal behavior that is well documented as having a definite genetic predisposition. The *high-risk genotype* for this factor is detectable at birth and often before, and the person who has it is almost 100% more likely to be convicted of a specific crime than a person with the low-risk genotype. What crime are we referring to? Rape. And the genetic predisposition? Possession of a Y chromosome — that is, being male. A male is much more likely to commit rape than a female. However, maleness is a *predisposition* to the crime of rape only. If you think a predisposition means something *will* happen, you must believe that all men are rapists — and we know that is not true. Only a very small percentage of men are rapists. The Y chromosome is a predisposition only — nothing more, nothing less.

Thus, biology and social environment always work together and they do so in complex, subtle, nuanced ways. Almost all the research that indicates genetic or biological influences on criminal behavior also shows strong environmental components. But this is the beauty and challenge of most biological studies. By their nature, they must take into account both the genes and the environment. In trying to distinguish the effects of biology from those of the environment, scientists must study both; they thus accept both. Biological studies never exist in a vacuum. Much sociological research, on the other hand, does not take biology into account at all. Biological studies of crime must look at both environment and physiochemistry in order to compare the two and determine the effect of one versus the other. All biological studies fully recognize the importance of the environment and use it as a comparable variable. In fact, biological studies have done more to *prove* the existence of an environmental influence, particularly as an ameliorating effect, than sociological studies ever have. Biology, after all, as Rachel Carson's *Silent Spring* (1965) reminds us, gave us the basis for today's Green movement. Keep in mind that the basis of the stance in Carson's book, now a bible of the environmentalist position, is the 20 pages of highly empirical research studies cited in its bibliography.

In case you yet have a doubt that biology has an effect on our social and emotional lives, consider the following examples of some clear biological influences on behavior.

1. *Menstruation* affects some women more than others, but many have more mood swings during, and just before, menstruation. The reason is that women's hormones change drastically during this time, with dramatic up and down surges of estrogen and progesterone.

2. *Pregnancy* also affects hormones and therefore emotions. In many cases, a woman seems calmer than usual when pregnant, not reacting as she normally would to the stresses of work and life. Hormones in pregnancy have a lot of functions, including effects on mood.

   Can you think of any evolutionary reason why women should be calmer during pregnancy? I discuss evolution and natural selection in a later chapter to explain the mechanisms; but in most cases, for a trait to be kept through many generations, it must have some benefit (even if the benefit is rather obscure) and it must be genetically controlled.

The benefit of feeling calm during pregnancy is fairly obvious. We all know that stress is bad for us. If you are stressed, you are also more likely to become sick. Stress can be even more severe during pregnancy, not only because it may harm the mother, but also because it could have severe deleterious effects on the fetus. Therefore, hormones that protect against stress have major effects on behavior, which are beneficial to the fetus.

3. *Puberty* is another example with which everyone is familiar. During the transition from childhood into a sexual world, teenagers go through some profound emotional and behavioral changes usually suffered along with them by their parents, other relatives, and teachers. Eventually they mature and become adults; but in the years of puberty, the change in outlook and disturbance of behavior can be profound. But again, the environmental influences are crucial in how puberty, a biological change, is realized. As we all know, puberty occurs when a lot of other changes are occurring in children's lives. Adolescents have a growing awareness of adulthood and their role in a peer group, and they often think they have become adults and should be treated as such; whereas adults around them continue to treat them as children, or at least as "teenagers." Their hormone fluctuations result in mood swings and behavior changes and these cause very real, and often embarrassing, situations to occur. Eventually, at biological maturity, the hormones level off and the mood swings cease. Negotiating the new pitfalls of a social life that now includes sexuality, and managing the integration of the new sexual needs and awareness (biology) with peers and adults (society) is a major problem that confronts teens; most make the adjustment.

Can you think of any benefits of such early and biologically based behavior from an evolutionary point of view? Medically, the ideal age for childbirth is when women are young; and not very far back in the past, most women reproduced at a very young age. In addition, young boys became men early, fighting in wars, working, and marrying at an early age. The mean age of death was also lower by far than today. Thus, if people did not reproduce when they were young, they would not live long enough to raise and protect their children. So these biologically based behavior changes may stem from earlier days when people competed for mates and resources, and reproduced during their teenage years.

We can see more clearly then that biology is an important influence on behavior and that scientific research can help us find out what this influence is. Our thought experiments were designed to show that biology and society, the body and behavior, learning and genetics, phases in physical development and social mores, are interactive. We next need to explore more fully from where this resistance comes from.

In the past, some people erred strongly in the opposite direction and pronounced biology — and especially genetics — as the key to the understanding of all behavior, and the present resistance in the social sciences has a lot to do with this error. According to the older uses of biological models, social life did not count for much as an influence — the great "new" idea of the late 19th and early 20th centuries was to see biology as the inevitable and sole cause of criminal behavior. In the past, there were many efforts to explain crime simply and directly, through biology. However, as we will see, the "data" upon which this view was based (if they can be called that) were often wrong. They resulted from poorly designed experiments or experiments performed in deliberate attempts to support specific ideas. Many of those involved believed behavior could be explained entirely by biology, which as we have seen with the case of genetics, is simply not true. Today no right-minded scientist would try to tell you that any complex behavior could be entirely biological in origin. Some very simple behaviors are under total genetic control, but no complex behaviors could be. There is always going to be an environmental component — usually a large one.

In the early 19th century, inaccurate or pseudo-science was used to support many proposed theories, such as that of *phrenology*, a belief that the shape and characteristic bumps of the head could be used to determine personality. It was an extraordinary idea by today's standards, but in the 1800s it was an accepted practice (Ivry, 1997). The erroneous belief that crime was entirely biological has also led to many horrible political decisions, most notably in Nazi Germany.

I would like to point out, however, that although some people believed these theories and managed to convince people in power to act on them, most people — particularly scientists — did not believe them, and in fact derided the believers at the time. Unfortunately, they were ignored, as most of the general public did not understand science well enough to be able to dispute their claims. The author hopes this book will help people understand the true science of behavior, and also make them ready to dispute false or pseudo-science if it is ever misused again.

Since that time, much more unbiased research has been performed and that is what we look at throughout this book. It is not a good idea to ignore the good research that has been performed rigorously in more recent years simply because people in the past twisted the theories to support their bigotry. Honest research should not be dismissed or suppressed for fear that politicians or others will misuse it. A tool can be used in many ways. It is one of the ethical cornerstones of this text that if scientific research into criminal behavior is used properly, it can prevent social injustice.

## Further Cautions

We can now turn to the way in which we can use this *interactionist* biological explanation of behavior to approach crime. My hope here is to lay down a few of the conditions for our upcoming study. Let us begin with a fundamental question. If we are going to study the biology of crime, we will need to have a good working definition of crime. What then is crime? And a related question: What is anti-social behavior? These are actually difficult questions to answer; definitions are difficult because crime is a social construct. We cannot simply equate breaking the law with a biological cause such as disease or genetics. We might seem to do this when we refer to programs in prisons and counseling for juvenile offenders as "treatment," which indicates that we think crime is an illness — but these programs of "treatment" are clearly not based on biology. The disease metaphor for the definition of crime is highly limited. Some forms of civil disobedience, for example, are the result of fiercely believed moral values and are designed to change policy, the law, or the prevailing practice. In the 19th century in Canada, Louis Riel fought for the rights of his fellow Métis and, at the time, was judged a criminal and hung. Now we recognize him as a hero. Women broke the law during the early part of the past century to win the vote. In the 1960s, civil rights protesters such as Martin Luther King broke the law as they tried to eliminate racial segregation in the United States. These types of "crime" are not the result of the biological backgrounds of those who protested, any more than they are, in any determined way, the result of their environments. They arose from particular injustices and appeared at specific times — they were based on a rational moralism of choice. Legally, they broke the law, but today they are celebrated as heroes, and no one could possibly consider them as "criminals."

There are also many so-called "crimes," such as smoking marijuana, or the ancient peyote cults, that are accepted by the groups that practice them and often by society at large. Some behavior that is labeled crime, such as smoking and drinking, are only crimes when people below a certain age indulge in them, and this age limit varies depending on where you are in the world (Rutter, 1996). Ellis and Walsh (2000, p. 5) refer to this as the "moving target perspective." There are numerous examples of actions that are considered

criminal in one region or country but are perfectly acceptable in other countries, such as female circumcision or marriage of young girls to adult men,
which are widely practiced in some parts of the world and yet are considered
child abuse and rape in Western countries (Ellis and Walsh, 2000). As well,
behaviors and actions that were once considered criminal are no longer
considered a crime today, and vice versa. For example, in the past, homo-
sexuality was considered a crime punishable by castration and even death.
Conversely, in the late 1800s in the United States, the Bayer Drug Company,
now famous for producing aspirin, legally sold heroin over the counter as a
cough suppressant (Ellis and Walsh, 2000).

It must not be forgotten that crime in itself is a legal concept based on
political processes. As such, all crime in a country could be eliminated in one
sweep by simply eliminating all its criminal statutes. This would effectively
eliminate crime, but would have had no effect whatsoever on criminal behavior (Ellis and Walsh, 2000). Although this is a bit far-fetched, countries are
always changing and revamping their criminal statutes, thereby redefining
what is or is not legally considered a crime.

If we try to restrict the concept of antisocial behavior to that which is
socially disapproved of in practically all societies, such as killing someone
(Rutter, 1996), we find that in war even this most violent of acts is positively
approved. In war, killing in defense of your country is usually not thought
of as a crime, but as an act of survival and often as heroism for which medals
are awarded. The act is the same, the interpretation is radically different.
Tendencies that are bad in some situations may thus be useful in others.
Aggression may lead to violence, for instance, but in some professions, such
as the military, this is useful behavior; politicians or entrepreneurs who have
retiring personalities will rarely do well.

Ellis and Walsh (2000, p. 7) attempt to distinguish between acts that are
almost always criminalized, such as intentionally killing or harming someone
or stealing their property, versus those behaviors and actions that are sometimes criminalized and sometimes not. The usual practice in criminology is
to refer to them as *mala in se* and *mala prohibita*, respectively. *Mala in se*
refers to something that is "inherently bad" and *mala prohibita* refers to
something that is bad because it is prohibited. This is referred to as the
"Stationary Core Perspective" (Ellis and Walsh, 2000) in criminology and has
use for this introduction.

The distinction helps us understand that we are then not usually concerned with biological influences when we consider socially constructed labels
of criminality. When we think of crime in the context of biology, we almost
automatically think of *violent crime*; that is, we suppose that a violent nature
may be inherited or is caused by physiological determinants such as hormones. Violent crimes are defined as those that cause or threaten to cause

bodily harm to another person (Ellis and Walsh, 2000, p. 27). Although we concentrate in this text, as in most research into crime, on violent crime, we must remember that violent crime is actually quite rare. We think of it more often than common crimes such as shoplifting because the popular media too often emphasize and exploit violence. So, although the bulk of the research we discuss concentrates on violent crime, we must also consider nonviolent crime in our study. As we will find, some research also shows a predisposition to nonviolent crime.

As we found with our thought experiments on genetics and its value in explaining behavior in general, any criminal research, not just that dealing with biology, requires equal caution and an appreciation of interaction with environments. The following basic facts about crime and crime statistics must also be taken into account before beginning our study into biological influences. In "The Causes of Crime, New Biological Approaches," Trasler points out several cautions that should be considered in relationship to all studies of crime (Trasler, 1987, p. 7–12).

1. *Adolescence.* Adolescent crime is very common, almost the norm. Studies in many countries have repeatedly shown that a surprisingly large number of adolescents are involved from time to time in minor crimes such as theft and property damage. In the past, only a few were thought to take part in such crimes, but this is clearly not so. It appears to be so common that it could almost be considered a normal part of growing up in much of Western society (Trasler, 1987).

2. *Research sample.* People with criminal records are not necessarily representative of all the people who have committed offenses. Studies looking at the factors that affect whether a police officer will record or overlook an offense, or charge a person or just give a warning, indicate that such decisions can selectively exclude some people and include others (Trasler, 1987). As a result, the people convicted of particular crimes are just a small sample of the people who commit such crimes, and may be a biased sample. Other factors such as lack of skill or intelligence, impulsivity or lack of impulsivity, planning, and plain luck may affect whether a person is caught. "Caught" offenders may also not be representative of all who offend. A study in the late 1970s (Petersilia et al., 1978) showed that there was a distinction in arrest rates between intensive offenders who were continuously engaged in crime and committed to criminal lifestyles and who were careful to avoid arrest compared with those who committed crimes irregularly with less care and planning. This research estimated that the average intensive offender committed ten times as many crimes as the intermittent offender,

but was five times less likely to be arrested for any one crime. Once arrested, the intensive offender was also less likely to be convicted and incarcerated.

3. *Self-reporting.* Self-reporting of a crime may not be accurate. People may underestimate the serious crimes they have committed or over-estimate them in order to boast. Also, it is often difficult for respondents to give accurate information about breaking the law. Many people may not fully understand what being arrested entails and may feel that a simple street contact with a police officer was an arrest (Trasler, 1987). Also, many studies on self-reporting only relate to juvenile cohorts.

4. *Representative statistics.* Many crimes, whether trivial, quite serious (e.g., assaults, robbery, fraud), or even major (e.g., rape), are not reported to the police, even in law-abiding societies (Clinard, 1978). Many crimes such as shoplifting and vandalism are not reported unless the culprits are actually caught in the act. However, estimates of stock losses in retail stores show that such minor crimes take place on an enormous scale, so they must involve a large number of people (Trasler, 1987).

These matters are important when you look at studies of crime, not just those that have potential biological implications. There are a number of other limits to current facts about crime:

5. *Biased sampling.* In many cases, comparisons are made between groups of "criminals" and "non-criminals." The "criminals" are usually incarcerated offenders, in prisons, or young-offender facilities; and the "non-criminal" or "non-delinquent" controls are groups of students or people in the military. However, if you consider the points noted above, it is obvious that such distinctions can be misleading:

   • Offenders in custody may not be representative of criminals in general or even of chronic offenders; it is likely that they are a highly selected subset of that minority of offenders who have been caught, charged, and convicted.

   • Control groups almost certainly include some people who have committed crimes (Trasler, 1987).

In some studies, the workers have carefully checked the records of their control subjects, but, again, not all people who commit criminal acts have criminal records.

6. *Ephemeral crimes.* Another point to note is that delinquency is often a transient or passing phase; many people who commit criminal acts when they are juveniles cease to do so as they reach adulthood (Trasler, 1987). In the past, some believed that they stopped because they were

locked up and thereby "cured." However, self-report studies show the opposite. People who admit they committed crimes as juveniles are also a subset of the whole. Although the admission is voluntary and anonymous, we have to ask whether it is representative. Still, in such self-reporting studies, it appears that many young people just seem to stop committing crimes. Their behavior may be a natural part of maturation or adaptation to the different circumstances of adult life. For example, peer pressure is immensely important in the teenage years, and teenage crime is often a social activity and an adventure. As people grow up, they develop other interests and can gain satisfaction from jobs, girlfriends or boyfriends, and eventually spouses and children. They become less dependent on peers, and their new life patterns are inconsistent with delinquency, so they outgrow it (Trasler, 1987).

7. *Mistaken explanations.* Another cautionary instance is that when we look at heritable characteristics that result in a physical attribute, which, in turn, has social implications, it is often difficult to distinguish the biological from the social effect. For example, if possessing a particular genetic trait places a person at a social and educational disadvantage in a given society, such as gender or skin color, then social failure will be attributed to the genetic characteristic (Trasler, 1987). But in reality, the genetic makeup has nothing to do with the social failure. The genes produce a particular trait, say gender, and society decides that a person with that trait will have less opportunity than someone with the opposite trait. As a result, the person is disadvantaged, but the reason is not biological, but purely environmental. Not too many years ago, it was extremely rare for women to be taught to read. They were educated in music, running households, and sewing, but they were not expected to know about or engage in political or academic activities. The belief then developed that women were much less intelligent than men. This was due to a simple lack of education.

In such cases, it is difficult to determine what is genetic and what is purely environmental. In the past, much emphasis was placed on racial contribution to criminal behavior, and assumptions were frequently made about the intelligence of certain races. However, skin color and racial background has, particularly in the past, a tremendous effect on the level of education that a person would receive and the type of job and life in general that could be expected. In such cases, the only hereditary factor is the race or skin color, which then led to the person, environmentally, being treated very differently from those of other skin colors.

## The History of Biology and Crime

One of the biggest stumbling blocks facing researchers in this field is that many judge it by its past. Because the early attempts to understand the basis of crime were in most cases unscientific, biological explanations of crime and violence came to be viewed as deterministic and oppressive. There were also major errors in many other fields at the time, but *their* failed theories are not used to judge present work. Unfortunately, in this field, some of the old ideas resulted in horrible actions that have not been forgotten. It must be clearly understood that past atrocities were not based on true science, but occurred when people with very specific agendas used public ignorance of science to further their own causes.

Long before people understood almost anything about science, they were trying to understand why some people committed crimes and others did not. Because we can see and measure physical attributes, the search for the difference between those who kill and those who do not act violently began with attempts to correlate physical features with personality traits.

Franz Gall (1758–1828) was a physician and anatomist who believed that there is a relationship between a person's mental attributes and the shape and size of their head (Fiez, 1996; Ivry, 1997). He believed that he could determine which parts of the brain were responsible for different emotions and behaviors, and that the relative size and shape of bumps in the skull over each area could be used to predict a person's personality and subsequent behaviors. This theory was termed "phrenology."

Phrenology now seems absurd, and there were certainly many people who considered it absurd at the time. We tend to think it was generally accepted, but Gall's critics also pointed out the obvious holes in his theory when it was first put forward. They argued that his theories were not based on any scientific evidence or clinical data. He leapt to conclusions based on observations seen in just one patient. For example, he stated that "destructiveness" could be predicted based on the presence of a lump close to the ear, as he had observed such a lump in a student who tortured animals and in an executioner (Niehoff, 1999; Ivry, 1997). This was the sum total of his so-called evidence. His "research," such as it was, was no more accepted by intelligent people in his time than it would be now. Nevertheless, Gall attracted an international cult following.

Gall's ideas were brought to the United States by one of his supporters, an American doctor named John Bell. Bell founded the Central Phrenology Society in the United States in 1822 and lectured throughout the United States (Niehoff, 1999). One of the so-called "studies" he was fond of quoting was written by Spurzheim, one of Gall's students. Spurzheim had phrenelogically examined 30 women who had been convicted of killing their own children.

According to Spurzheim, 26 of these women had an underdeveloped brain center for "philoprogenitiveness" (love of children), and thus concluded that their crimes were the result of their physically defective brains (Niehoff, 1999; Ivry, 1997).

These claims resemble the much more recent XYY misunderstandings of the "super male" in the 1960s (Mednick, 1987). In both cases, researchers looked only at offenders, a closed population, so they came to their conclusions without seeing how common the trait was in the general population. A true control for Spurzheim's study group could easily have included 30 women who had not killed their children, which would probably have disproved the theory immediately.

Interest in phrenology began to die out and was finally destroyed when actual experiments and data failed to support it. Public interest collapsed when the scientific community finally managed to convince the public that there was absolutely no empirical evidence to support the theory. However, the belief that it was possible to determine a person's personality and behavioral patterns from assessing some aspect of their physical looks was still attractive and was taken up by the Italian criminal anthropologist Cesare Lombroso in the latter part of the 19th century (Niehoff, 1999). Lombroso is frequently considered the father of criminology.

Lombroso performed examinations of a range of people, including convicted criminals, people in mental institutions, and cadavers, and compared his results with those from non-incarcerated individuals (Neihoff, 1999). He reported that certain features, such as sloping foreheads and twisted lips, were more commonly seen in criminals than in law-abiding citizens (Papez, 1937; Broca, 1878, cited in Niehoff, 1999). He referred to these features as "atavisms" and declared that people possessing such atavisms had lesser or more primitive levels of development than non-criminal people (Niehoff, 1999) He was particularly interested in those who had committed violent offences as he considered them to be inferior "morally, mentally, and physically" and likened them to Neanderthals (Niehoff, 1999, p. 8). Incidentally, there is no evidence that early man was any more violent than modern man, but people still regularly accuse uncouth and violent people of "acting like Neanderthals." Lombroso thought such people were "born that way" and could not change (Niehoff, 1999). Lombroso felt that female crime rates were lower than male crime rates because women were caregivers, generally passive, and weak with low intelligence; so when women did offend, they had to override these obstacles to crime and thus were particularly evil (Lombroso and Ferrero, 1895, cited in Quinsey et al., 2004).

Of course, now it seems totally absurd to use the way a person looks to predict whether he or she is a violent criminal. However, people do make similar personal assessments all the time. The average person puts a lot of emphasis on what he or she sees every day. First impressions are very important, so when we look at someone, we automatically size them up. We make assessments of a person's personality and abilities by the way he or she looks. We reassess our opinions when we get to know the individuals, but those first impressions are based entirely on looks. Women can probably relate to this fact more than men. A woman walking alone at night probably watches and assesses anyone approaching more than a man would. Most people can remember embarrassing instances of rapid assessments based on appearance, clothing, hairstyle, etc., many of which turned out, on later assessment, to be entirely wrong. Of course, this is quite different than stating unequivocally that a certain "look" results in a dangerous person, but it does perhaps make it easier to understand why Lombroso's theories seemed, at first, acceptable to the nonscientific and often uneducated public of the time.

Due to the lack of scientific support for Gall and Lombroso's theories, they eventually fell out of favor. At around this time, however, Darwin's Theory of Evolution was first being discussed. Darwin revolutionized the way people looked at all aspects of science. His work was solid and based on years of studies. His theories had nothing to do with criminal behavior or any suggestions to attempt to control destiny, but other people began misreading his work and dangerous and entirely erroneous relationships between evolution and crime began to be considered (Niehoff, 1999).

Darwin's Theory of Evolution explained how traits such as beak size and shape in birds could be selected for over time, based on environmental conditions and changes (see Chapter 2). People already knew that offspring inherited some of their parents' features, as children resembled their parents, inheriting, for example, eye and hair color. Farmers had used such information to breed the best farm animals for centuries. Darwin's work was sound but evolution and natural selection can only work on heritable traits, those under genetic control (Chapter 2).

It was other people, most notably, Darwin's own cousin, Francis Galton, who began to suggest that just about everything was a heritable trait, including poverty and crime. Thus, not long after evolution was first understood, in some cases it was used as a framework for developing ideas to control such things as prostitution, petty crime, poverty, promiscuousness, destitution, and alcoholism. This was a complete misunderstanding and misuse of Darwin's work, as such characteristics are clearly not inherited. However, many people jumped on this bandwagon as a way to control the Victorian "lower classes."

It was then that reproductive control was first suggested. There was concern among the more powerful Victorian families that the large numbers of children born to the poor were contributing to the moral decay of society. Galton argued that the more "exemplary" members of society (meaning the rich) should have larger families, whereas the "lesser" members (meaning the poor) should be encouraged to have fewer children (Kupfermann, 1991; Niehoff, 1999).

Galton called his theory **eugenics,** after the Greek word *eugenes,* or "good in birth" (Niehoff, 1999). Galton's proposal was actually positive eugenics, wherein those considered most fit were to be encouraged to have more children. He did not suggest that those considered less fit should be prevented from reproducing. Needless to say, however, it was not long before some began to advocate negative eugenics, wherein people considered unfit for whatever reason were actively discouraged and even prevented from reproducing (Kupfermann, 1991).

This frightening misunderstanding and misquoting of science drew support from around the world. At the beginning of the 20th century, eugenic advocates in Britain, America, and Germany began collecting information on hundreds of thousands of people and, using this supposed "hereditary data," began initiating what they referred to as "genetic hygiene" measures, which ranged from segregating the supposedly "unfit" from the rest of society in "work colonies" to compulsory sterilization (Niehoff, 1999; Kupfermann, 1991).

The eugenics movement took off in the United States as Americans were afraid that the large numbers of immigrants arriving on their shores would take their jobs and produce so many children that they would overrun the existing population (entirely forgetting that they themselves had recently done the same to America's aboriginal peoples). Politicians pointed out that the immigrants came from countries where, traditionally, larger families were the norm, in comparison with the upper classes of New England. They declared that this would result in greatly increased rates of crime, poverty, and insanity. Some even blamed labor unrest and strikes on genetics (Niehoff, 1999). These few people managed to convince many citizens that immigration would mean the end of the average American.

Things got much worse when these so-called "superior" people began to claim that race was a major issue and swore that their intent to control both immigration and reproduction of non-whites and eastern Europeans was not prejudiced but was merely an attempt to "maintain purity" (Niehoff, 1999; Kupfermann, 1991). This sort of terrifying propaganda resulted in the passage of immigration laws that limited the number of immigrants allowed into the United States from so-called undesirable countries and in miscegenation statutes that outlawed interracial marriages (Niehoff, 1999). What these proponents of negative eugenics were doing was a form of genocide, with absolutely no basis in scientific fact.

In Europe, similar measures were being taken that escalated, with Hitler's regime, into genocide. Measures that had begun with public education escalated to forced abortion, sterilization, and finally death camps (Niehoff, 1999). At the end of World War II, when the enormity of the atrocities was uncovered, the general public declaimed eugenics and the movement thankfully collapsed. Evolutionary non-Mendelist genetics were, however, also used in arguments by the left against capitalism with, for example, T.D. Lysenko's "socialist biology" theory of genetics in the Stalinist Russia of the 1940s.

It is often forgotten, however, that some forms of eugenics still remained in both the United States and Canada well into the 1960s, with people, frequently children, being compulsory sterilized. There are many people alive today who were sterilized without their knowledge, mostly at the request of parents who found them unruly or promiscuous. Groups of such people are now taking legal action in British Columbia (Canada). Today we feel confident that eugenics is not being practiced in our country — but is it? One could describe lengthy prison sentences as a form of eugenics. Men and women who are incarcerated for long periods of time during their reproductive years are, in a sense, being prevented from reproducing. The right to have conjugal visits under some circumstances could be said to offset this, but still, reproduction remains heavily restricted and, in most cases, curtailed.

In all these historic cases of unarguable atrocities, both the theorists and average people were ignorant of the facts. They did not understand genetics and had no valid data on which to base their theories. The media promoted their ideas, so they were accepted by the public. Often, theories were supported by people who were already racially prejudiced. Facts that are not understood are often misused. This is why it is so important, in this subject and others, to prevent such public hysteria from breaking out again. There will always be people who believe this kind of propaganda, so it is essential that there also be informed people who can say with authority, "That is not true; it does not work that way."

At the height of the eugenics movement, people did not understand genetics, but certain people found the theory useful to support their causes. In the early 20th century, for example, most Americans believed intelligence was based entirely on genetics (not on a mix of genetic and environmental influences, as would be more accurate), and new immigrants were forced to take IQ (or intelligence quotient) tests. The original idea behind the IQ test was that it would provide a teaching aid for children under the age of 14. A child's answers to a set of questions were compared with the answers given by a large number of children of the same age. In other words, an IQ test gave an idea of where those tested stood in relation to others in their peer groups. American immigration officers used this test on adults, which made the results invalid. They misunderstood the very limited knowledge available about intelligence and used a test that had no validity in the situation, and was particularly inappropriate to use on those who did not even speak

English. Thousands of immigrants were sterilized before 1935 in certain states because they were not considered intelligent enough to be allowed to contribute their genes to the country. It was only with the rise of Hitler that people began to realize that what was going on in the United States was not so different and the practice stopped.

Meanwhile, people were still trying to use physical attributes to determine a person's behavior. William Sheldon (1898–1977) classified people into three different groups: (1) endomorphs, (2) mesomorphs, and (3) ectomorphs. Endomorphs were those with relatively soft, rounded bodies; mesomorphs were the more athletically built types; and ectomorphs were thin people (Sheldon et al., 1949). Sheldon thought certain behaviors correlated with each of the three body types. Although these terms acquired support and are still referred to today, this classification, again, was not valid. Some studies have shown that there may be some relationship between body type and behavior, but most such studies have used small samples and have not been repeatable.

We still judge people today by the way they look — "I would not want to meet him in a dark alley" — although we are now reluctant to admit it. It is important to remember that factors that clearly have genetic components result in major phenotypic "looks." A person's body build is inherited to a large extent and may affect his or her behavior — not in the direct manner Sheldon meant, but indirectly. For example, a large child may discover quite early that an effective way to end conflict is to use his or her build — in other words, to use violence — to win a conflict. A smaller person learns quickly that physical violence is not a good way to settle disputes, and develops other methods to resolve disagreements, such as skillful dialogue. Early success in violence and bullying to resolve social conflicts may encourage a person to use force in adulthood.

So, body build might indeed be linked to delinquency and crime in later life, but the link is most probably through social learning, not through genes. In other words, the genes give the child a large body and thus expose him to a different environment than he would experience were he smaller. This is yet another example of how no factor linked to crime should ever be viewed in the old terms of genetics versus the environment. Instead, we must look at both and try to understand how the two factors work together.

## Conclusion

We have been remiss in our study of criminology to the extent that we have not, until quite recently, included biology as one of its necessary sub-disciplines. The reasons are understandable; the atrocities of the past are powerful deterrents.

But these were, as we have seen, based on bad science, inhumane political agendas, and execrable ethics. We now have some very much better studies, and a humane ethic on which to base serious analysis of the biological dimension of behavior; and, as we will see, criminogenic behavior. The effects of biology on behavior are very clear. Inherited diseases, hormonal changes, and physical changes during pregnancy are some of the aspects of biology that impinge on our existence and influence our behavior in serious ways. We have also begun to see the ways in which science itself can go wrong in the study of behavior: small sample size and poor experimental design can vitiate results. They provide a good way to evaluate all the studies we will be surveying in the following pages.

## Questions for Further Study and Discussion

1. Even talking about the idea of a possible biological basis for crime has been considered taboo for years. What are the major reasons that people deny that biology could have an influence on behavior?
2. What political or social agendas other than fear of immigration do you think were involved in the eugenics movement?
3. Discuss Lombroso's theory of body types. Is there any truth to his atavistic categories?
4. What is meant by an "interactionist" approach to the biology of crime?

## References

Broca, P. (1878). Anatomie comparée des circonvolutions cérebrales: Le grand lobe limbique et la scissure limbique dans la serie des mammifères. *Revue d'Athropologie*, Ser. 2(1), 385–498. (Cited in Niehoff 1999.)

Clinard, M. (1978). *Cities with Little Crime*. Cambridge: Cambridge University Press.

Ellis, L. and Walsh, A. (2000). *Criminology: A Global Perspective*. Boston: Allyn & Bacon.

Fiez, J.A. (1996). Cerebellar contributions to cognition. *Neuron*, 16, 13–15.

Ivry, R. (1997). Cerebellar timing systems. *Int. Rev. Neurobiol.*, 41, 555–573.

Klein, M.W. (1987). Watch out for that last variable. In Mednick, S.A., Moffitt, T.E., and Stack, S.A. (Eds.), *The Causes Of Crime: New Biological Approaches* (p. 35). Cambridge: Cambridge University Press. Proceedings NATO Conference, Skiathos, Greece, Sept. 20–24, 1982.

Kupfermann, I. (1991). Hypothalamus and limbic systems: peptidergic neurons, homeostasis and emotional behavior. In Kandel, E.R., Schwarz, J.H., and Jessell, T.M. (Eds.), *Principles of Neural Science* (pp. 735–749). East Norwalk, CT: Appleton and Lange.

Lombroso, C. and Ferrero, G. (1895). *The Female Offender.* New York: Appleton.

Mednick, S.A. (1987). Biological factors in crime causation: the reactions of social scientists. In Mednick, S.A., Moffitt, T.E., and Stack, S.A. (Eds.*), The Causes of Crime: New Biological Approaches* (p. 7). Cambridge: Cambridge University Press.

Moss, R.B., Rodman, D., Spencer, T.L., Aitken, M.L., Zeitlin, P., Waltz, D., Milla, C., Brody, A.S., Clancy, J.P., Ramsey, B., Hamblett, N., and Heald, A.E. (2004). Repeated adeno-associated virus serotype 2 aerosol-mediated cystic fibrosis transmembrane regulator gene transfer to the lungs of patients with cystic fibrosis: a multicenter, double-blind, placebo-controlled trial. *Card. Crit. Care J.,* 125(2), 509–521.

Niehoff, D. (1999). Seeds of controversy. In *The Biology of Violence: How Understanding the Brain, Behavior and Environment Can Break the Vicious Circle of Aggression* (pp. 1–30). New York: Free Press.

Papez, J.W. (1937). A proposed mechanism of emotion. *Arch. Neurol. Psychol.,* 38, 725–743. (Cited in Neihoff, 1999.)

Petersilia, J., Greenwood, P.W., and Lavin, M. (1978). *Criminal Careers of Habitual Felons.* Washington, D.C.: National Institute of Law Enforcement and Criminal Justice.

Quinsey, V.L., Skilling, T.A., Lalumière, M.L., and Craig, W.M. (2004*). Juvenile Delinquency: Understanding the Origins of Individual Differences.* Washington, D.C.: American Psychological Association.

Rommens, J.M., Iannuzzi, M.C., Kerem, B., Drumm, M.L., Melmer, G., Dean, M., Rozmahel, R., Cole, J.L., Kennedy, D., and Hidaka, N. (1989). Identification of the cystic fibrosis gene: chromosome walking and jumping. *Science,* 245, 1059–1065.

Rutter, M. (1996). Introduction: concepts of antisocial behavior, of cause and of genetic influences. *Ciba Foundation Symposium,* 194, 1–15.

Sheldon, W.H., Hartl, E.M., and McDermott, E. (1949). *Varieties of Delinquent Youth.* New York: Harper.

Trasler, G. (1987). Some cautions for the biological approach to crime causation. In Mednick, S.A., Moffitt, T.E., and Stack, S.A. (Eds.), *The Causes of Crime: New Biological Approaches* (pp. 7–24). Cambridge: Cambridge University Press. Proceedings NATO Conference, Skiathos Greece, Sept. 20–24, 1982.

Wright, R.A. and Miller, J.M. (1998). Taboo until today? The coverage of biological arguments in criminology textbooks, 1961–1970 and 1987–1996. *J. Criminal Just.,* 26(1), 1–19.

# Basic Biological Concepts

$2$

## Introduction

This chapter provides an introduction to biological concepts that should first be understood in order to follow the approach to crime we will develop in the text. We introduce *natural selection* and then compare the behaviors of humans and other animals. More specifically, we look at the questions of how natural selection or evolution works, how organisms adapt to their environments, and how some traits are selected over others and passed to the next generation. These traits include structural, biochemical, and physiological aspects, but also, and more importantly for our study, *behavioral* traits, which are equally adaptive. We also look at the nature-versus-nurture argument and show that there is really not a dichotomy but an interaction between these influences; neither works in isolation. We discuss how natural selection occurs and how behavior can be either entirely genetic or a mixture of genetics and the environment, the contribution of each varying with the behavior. At the end of this chapter we introduce the relatively new approach to the biology of crime, the evolutionary behavioral views of researchers such as Ellis and Walsh and the idea that even crime may have been adaptive.

## Natural Selection

"Natural selection" is the proper term for what most people call evolution, and a brief explanation of it is given. You will soon see why a basic understanding of natural selection is important in this field.

All living organisms *adapt* to their environments, and these adaptations lead to increased survival and reproductive success for organisms that possess them. Adapting does not mean that a single organism can adapt — it cannot. Adaptation occurs over generations, usually a great many generations. So when we use the term "adapt," we do not mean it in the casual sense of, say, a person adapting to a new culture or a new climate when they immigrate. In that case, a person is getting accustomed or acclimated to something. For example, a population of rats in New York may adapt, over many generations, and become resistant to a poison designed to kill them. The individual rat does not adapt, but some of its offspring are slightly more resistant to the poison than others, so perhaps two out of a hundred offspring will survive and reproduce. Something in their genetic makeup makes them more likely to survive than the others; perhaps they have slightly more of a body chemical that protects them from the toxin, or maybe they are fatter and can store the toxin better, or possibly they are more shy and do not go near new potential food sources. Whatever it is, something makes these rats less likely to be poisoned. So out of that particular family of rats, only two survive and reproduce. A trait such as avoiding new foods, having extra fat, or being shy must be genetically controlled for evolution to act on it. So anything that is modified by evolution has a genetic component; otherwise, it would not work. Evolution selects individuals with genes that result in traits that help them survive and reproduce. They pass on this favorable trait. So, for example, if you are short, it might be genetic. Similarly, having brown hair is genetic. These are traits that you might pass on to your offspring. However, if you were to lose an arm in an accident, would your child be missing an arm? No, of course not.

A trait is selected because it is favorable, but it relates entirely to the environment and the time frame. Something may be very favorable at certain times but not at all favorable at other times. For instance, in the example of the rats, let us say that the favorable trait was avoiding new types of food. When a poison is put out, this trait is definitely a benefit because these rats will not go near it. However, the trait could cause problems if the normal food supply dwindles, and the rats have to find a new food supply. These unadventurous rats will die off.

Another example is the large cactus finch (*Geospisa carnvirostris*) in the Galapagos Islands (Campbell, 1996, pp. 408–409). In the natural population, this species has considerable variation in beak or bill size (Figure 2.1). Some of the birds have very long beaks and others have very wide beaks, but most have average beaks. In 1977, there was a prolonged drought that killed 70% of the finch population. It was found that finches with the extreme beaks, whether very long or very wide, had survived, whereas the intermediate birds had died out. So the extremes were favored by natural selection. Why? Under

**Figure 2.1** Finches with different-sized beaks adapt better to different environmental conditions. Source: SFU Publications.

normal conditions, there are many food sources available, such as insects (out in the open or under bark that can be peeled off), large seeds, small seeds, and everything in between, as well as cactus fruits. There is a great range of food available for birds with average beaks, so this beak size is normally favored by natural selection. That is, birds with average beaks were the most successful, so they survived longer and produced more offspring, passing on the trait of an average beak size to more offspring.

The drought brought a new selective pressure; many food sources, such as small seeds and insects, were rapidly depleted because all the population could eat them. The small seeds were not replaced, and the insect population was greatly reduced. There were only a few food sources left. Only the wide-beaked birds could crack the large, hard seeds and get at the insects under the bark of trees. The long-beaked birds could open up the cactus fruits to get at the seeds, so they also survived. Meanwhile, the birds with average bills starved.

So something that is a good trait may become unfavorable if circumstances change. Think about this in terms of a behavior that might have been advantageous once but is no longer advantageous because society has changed. Violence may be an example.

So, all living organisms, including humans, are adapted to their environment (Campbell, 1996, pp. 1071–1073).

This adaptation takes many forms:

1. *Structural modifications* that enhance survival and reproduction. Examples include the development of complex organs, such as eyes, ears, and wings. A more specific example is that of an orchid, in which

the flower has become modified so that it resembles a female wasp. Male wasps attempt to mate with the flower and will then attempt to mate with another orchid, thereby pollinating the flowers (Cain et al., 2000, p. 326). The wasp does eventually learn and will find a real wasp.

2. *Biochemical pathways,* such as the development of metabolism, photosynthesis (plants' ability to convert sunlight energy to food), respiration, etc.

3. *Behavioral adaptations* that increase survival and reproductive success, such as learning to avoid predators or developing courtship dances that enable individuals to find strong, suitable mates. Specific examples include a species of harmless fruit fly that has developed structural modification so that it looks like a jumping spider and behavioral adaptations so that it actually assumes the posture of a jumping spider (Mather and Roitberg, 1987).

The process that results in these adaptations is called *natural selection,* which is the differential survival and reproduction of individuals within a population. That is, some individuals have a better chance of living to reproductive age and having offspring that will carry the same traits that helped their parents survive and reproduce. Thus, adaptations are behavioral, structural, or biochemical pathway changes that enhance the survival and reproductive success of an organism.

There are three conditions necessary for natural selection to occur (Darwin, 1859, p. 859):

- *Variation.* There must be variation among individuals. Many variations of different traits are obvious in any population. The variations can be structural, behavioral, physiological, and/or adaptations in the biochemical pathways. One can see lots of physical variation in our own species.
- *Heritability.* The variation must be heritable; that is, it must be under genetic control so that it can be passed on to the next generation.
- The individual must *differ* in its ability to *survive* or *reproduce* depending on this trait. That is,, the trait must give the individual a better chance of surviving or help it produce more offspring.

If all three conditions are met, certain individuals will leave more offspring because they are better able to survive and reproduce, and the trait will become increasingly represented in subsequent populations. Eventually, a change in the population occurs that makes it better adapted to the environment.

One of the most famous examples of natural selection is the English peppered moth (Curtis and Barnes, 1989, pp. 962–963). There are two varieties of this moth. One is light colored, with splotches of dark pigment, and hence the name "peppered." The other variety is dark all over. So here we have variation in the population, and it is inherited. Peppered moths feed at night and rest during the day, and they like to rest on rocks and trees that are encrusted with light-colored lichens. In this situation, the light moths are well camouflaged, but the dark moths are easily spotted by their main predators, birds (Figure 2.2). Before the Industrial Revolution in England in the late 18th century, dark peppered moths were rare, presumably because they became bird food and rarely got a chance to pass on their genes to the next generation. So one can see that this trait for color, which varies and is heritable, also has fitness consequences; because of this trait, the individual has a better or worse chance of surviving and, therefore, of living long enough to reproduce. In this situation, being a light-colored moth was definitely an advantage. However, the Industrial Revolution brought heavy pollution, and in the late 1800s, most of the lichens died off, leaving the general background of tree bark, which is much darker. The environment had changed, and the dark moth was now at an advantage because it is well camouflaged against the dark tree bark and the light-colored moths were easier to see (Figure 2.3).

**Figure 2.2**  The dark English peppered moths are easier to spot on trees covered in light- colored lichens. Source: SFU Publications.

**Figure 2.3**  The dark moths are better camouflaged and therefore selected for when the tree bark is dark-colored. Source: SFU Publications.

After a while, there were many more dark moths around than light ones because the light ones were more often eaten before they could reproduce. This phenomenon also occurred in many other moth species.

The happy ending to this story is that now we have realized what pollution is doing to us, apart from affecting moth populations. England has made great efforts to reduce atmospheric pollution. The lichens have returned, and the moth population is once again primarily light-colored.

These examples demonstrate that for natural selection to act, these three characteristics must be present. There must be variation in the particular trait, the variation must be heritable, and it must affect the ability of the organism to survive and reproduce. However, there are also some constraints on the ability of natural selection to produce adaptation of organisms to their environment.

- *Adaptations are often compromises* (Freeman and Herron, 2004, p. 90). Any organism must do many things, and an organism that develops a new structure or behavior carries a cost because it requires energy to develop and carry out the change; and it may also reduce the ability of the organism to do something else. For example, male peacocks have very long tails to attract females. They can use their tails to give a very attractive display, as you have no doubt seen. There is a very heavy cost associated with this tail. It is "expensive" for the bird to construct and maintain, and dragging this heavy tail around greatly reduces its ability to get away from a predator. However, it also greatly increases the bird's reproductive success so the cost is more than made up for. Therefore, the beautiful tail is selected because peacocks with lovely tails produce more offspring.

Humans frequently enter into this process and produce *unnatural* selection or artificial selection. For example, we have made pets from animals that were originally wild (Starr and Taggart, 2004, pp. 270–271). Wolves were bred to make their descendants into dogs. If pet dogs go back to the wild, natural selection takes over after a few generations and produces a wolf/shepherd type dog, which is obviously the best type to survive in the wild. However, because we want pet dogs and can provide things that the wild environment does not, such as protection and food, a large variety of dog breeds survive in our society just fine, usually on someone's bed.

Another classic example of man's interference with natural selection is the racehorse (Raven and Johnson, 1995, pp. 290–291). A wild horse is strong, stocky, shortish with powerful legs. We have taken wild horses and bred the fastest individuals with the longest legs together to create today's thoroughbreds. They are very pretty and very fast, and now we race them and gamble on the outcome. However, they are only very fast as long as we provide flat, well-surfaced tracks for them to run on, in which case they go much faster than a wild horse ever could — over short distances. The Quarterhorse, which is much stockier than a thoroughbred, was bred especially to run races over a quarter mile, hence the name. These horses do not have the endurance of the wild horse; and if they are allowed to run on anything but a track, they will break their legs at the first molehill. Even on the track, they frequently break their legs. Such an animal would never arise by natural selection because the cost of speed is too high: light legs that break easily. If racehorses were to be put into the wild, the ones with the strongest legs would be naturally selected for, and those with very fine legs would become fodder for predators early on. The population would gradually revert to the design nature or natural selection intended.

- *Natural selection can only work on existing traits* (Freeman and Herron, 2004, p. 88). Evolution does not totally scrap the old biochemical pathways, structures, behaviors, and so forth and start anew. It modifies existing traits as the environment or conditions change; that is, it does not rebuild from scratch.

## Behavior in Humans and Other Animals

Everyone has heard the argument about nature versus nurture, which means does the biological background dominate or does the environment dominate? Although this argument has a long history, there has never been a real dichotomy. Anyone who works in biology knows that it is not a dichotomy but an *interaction,* nature and nurture. We are a product of what we are biologically as well as of the environment we have been exposed to over the course of our lives. Our society seems to have rejected the middle ground where biology and environment are seen as integrally linked, arguing that it has to be all one or the other. Nothing is ever likely to be all one thing or another; it is usually a mixture of many things. If everything were based on environment, we could say that someone who has had a terrible upbringing and was sexually and physically abused and grew up in poverty would definitely end up being a criminal, but this is certainly not the case. Many contributing members of society come from just such backgrounds; conversely, many criminals come from excellent homes. Assuming that it is all society or all biology is simply wrong, and no scientist accepts the argument. I do not think most social scientists do either.

As we understand more and more about the brain, we have learned that the environment begins to shape the nervous system before we are born. Nature and nurture (biology and environment) affect all parts of our lives, but because this text is looking at criminal behavior, we should define what behavior actually is. Behavior is simply what an animal does and how it does it; in this case, we are talking about the human animal. The study of behavior looks at both the *action* itself and its *motor components,* that is, the brain function and how the animal actually performs the behavior.

Behavior is adaptive in just the same way that a structure or a metabolic pathway can be adaptive. Studying behavior is probably the oldest form of biology. For early humans, knowledge of animal behavior was essential for survival. They had to learn about the habits of the animals around them to catch them for food and also to avoid predators. This still occurs today. Recently, a small village in Africa was suffering severe leopard predation, with several people killed in leopard attacks. One person in the village pointed out that people were only ever attacked from behind. The leopards never seemed to attack a person from the front. Therefore, the villagers made masks of human faces, which they wore on the back of their heads, so that, whichever way they were facing, it appeared that they were looking at you. It worked. No one was ever attacked while wearing his or her mask. By studying leopard behavior and learning from it, the villagers learned to protect themselves and survive, probably in the same way humans and other species have always done. The study of animal behavior increased fitness because it increased survival and thus the person's chance of reproduction. No doubt the leopards had also learned from observing, and from attempted attacks, that the easiest and safest way to attack a human was from behind.

Natural selection adapts an organism to its environment. It acts on every-thing we inherit from our parents. Mostly we see it acting on specific things such as the shape of a bird's beak, but it acts equally well to produce behaviors that increase an animal's fitness within an environment, and to produce structures and biochemical pathways that also increase it.

An animal must:

- Feed in a way that maximizes fitness.
- Reduce the risk of predation, that is, of being eaten.
- Increase its chance of mating.

Feeding behavior is likely to optimize efficiency and health, and the mate chosen tends to maximize the number of healthy offspring produced and so the contribution to the next generation. Natural selection will favor a behavior that increases fitness and reproductive success, but the behavior must have a heritable component. If there was no genetic basis, natural selection could not act on behaviors and they could not evolve. Behavior must have a genetic basis because behaviors do evolve. Even learned behaviors typically depend on genes that create a neural system receptive to learning.

There are many different types of behavior and some are discussed here — however, first an amusing example that illustrates how a behavior is governed by genes (Purves et al., 1995, p. 1036–1037). Two species of African parrot have different nesting behaviors. One is the Fischer's lovebird, which has a red head, and the other is the peach-faced lovebird with, predictably, a peach-colored face (Figure 2.4).

The females of both species make nests with strips of vegetation or, in captivity, with paper that they cut with their beaks. The female Fischer's lovebird cuts long strips and carries them back to the nest, one at a time, in her beak. The peach-faced lovebird has a different tactic. She cuts shorter strips and carries several at a time by tucking them into the feathers of the lower back. This maneuver is quite clever because it involves tucking the strips in firmly enough to stay and then smoothing the feathers over the strips. These two species are so closely related the birds can be interbred in experiments. The resultant hybrid females show an intermediate kind of nest material gathering. The strips themselves were intermediate in length, but the most interesting part is the way that they carried them. They usually tried to tuck them in the tail feathers, but they sometimes forgot to let go when they had the strips positioned so they kept ripping them out again; others stuffed them improperly and they fell out. These results show that

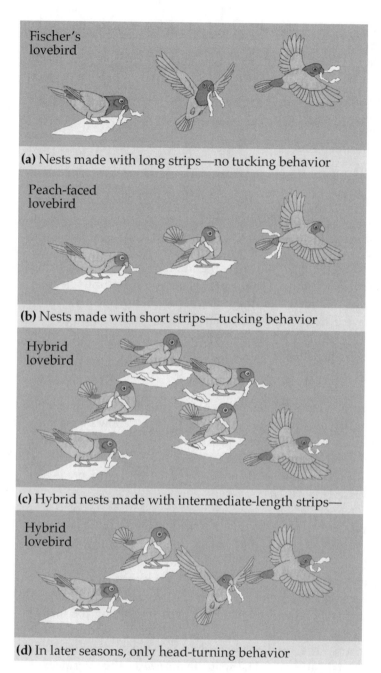

**(a)** Nests made with long strips—no tucking behavior

**(b)** Nests made with short strips—tucking behavior

**(c)** Hybrid nests made with intermediate-length strips—

**(d)** In later seasons, only head-turning behavior

**Figure 2.4**    Genetic and environmental components of behavior in lovebirds.
Source: N.A. Campbell and Reese, J.B. (2002) *Biology*, 6th Ed., Pearson Education.
Reprinted with permission.

there must be an inherited component. The babies did not learn to handle the strips in an intermediate manner; they had an inherited ability to do so, but it was confused by the mixture of genes from the parents. The result was that these birds totally failed to transport strips. In the end, the birds learned to transport the strips in their beaks. But even so, they still made token tucking attempts. After several years, these same birds still turned their heads to the rear before flying off with a strip. This experiment shows that the observed differences in behavior are based on different genetic background or genotypes and that they are a result of genes controlling these actions. However, these innate, inherited traits can be modified by experience or the environment, and so the hybrid birds eventually learned how to transport the strips. The observable end result is an interaction between the genes and the environment.

This is the point where the nature-versus-nurture debate is inevitably raised. The original argument about nature and nurture began a long time ago when scientists in Europe and America were both studying behavior but looking at different sides of the same coin (Campbell, 1996, p. 1180). In fact, genetics and the environment should be regarded as a continuum. All behaviors have some genetic contribution and some environmental contribution, and the division between the two groups of scientists was not as cut and dried as it seemed. Very few actually believed that behavior was either all genetically controlled or all environmentally controlled. The debate was really more about which input is most important. The amount of input from each varies with different behaviors, but nearly all have components of both as the small diagram shows. At the side of 1, the behavior is governed almost entirely by the genes; whereas at the side of 2, it is mostly the environment; and then there is a whole range in between. (Diagram source: SFU Publications)

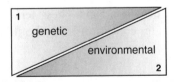

Behaviors can be divided into two main groups:

- Innate behaviors, which are governed entirely by the genes
- Learned behaviors, which require experience; they still have a genetic component but it is strongly affected by environment and experience (Starr and Taggart, 1995, pp. 914–915).

## Innate Behaviors

All animals, including humans, carry out many behaviors without ever having seen them performed. Because they could not have learned them, they did not come from the environment. Such behaviors are innate or genetically programmed. These behaviors tend to be constant and are performed in exactly the same way by every individual of that species. The usual term for these innate behaviors is "fixed action patterns" (FAPs). They can be performed in a complete, stereotypical fashion by an animal without prior experience and without the animal understanding the significance of the actions. When would you expect to see such innate behaviors, in what animals, and under what conditions?

1. In animals that have little opportunity for learning, for example:
   • Animals that have very short life spans, such as the Mayfly, which has just one day to mate, lay eggs, and die. If its survival and reproduction depended on learning something, it would have very low reproductive success.
   • Animals with low or no parental care that cannot learn from their parents.
2. In animals that do have an opportunity to learn, we still see innate behavior, usually when it is critical that the behavior is performed correctly the first time. For example:
   • A baby bird's first flight. Birds can fly with no previous practice.
   • A moth avoiding a bat. If it does not carry out the proper behavior the first time, it will not get a second chance.

These kinds of innate behavior are often related to predation, reproduction, or other very important activities. Innate behavior is often triggered by a stimulus of some sort, usually a sign. These tend to be very simple signs that will reliably occur under conditions that should lead to the appropriate response.

1. One of the best known is a visual sign. For example, a male stickleback builds a nest, herds in a female to lay her eggs, fertilizes the eggs, and then shoos her out. The male cares for the young. Males will fiercely guard their nests and show aggressive behavior toward other male sticklebacks. Niko Tinbergen, a scientist, showed several models to male sticklebacks (Figure 2.5). Some looked very much like a pencil drawing of a male fish, and others looked like line drawings of circles or squares, but the bottom half of these simple diagrams was painted bright red (Curtis and Barnes, 1989, p. 1055). The one that looks like

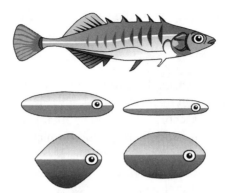

**Figure 2.5**   A male stickleback and several models. Source: SFU Publications.

a fish obviously looks the most like another male stickleback to us, but the fish ignored it. They did, however, react to the other models that look nothing like male sticklebacks to us. They appeared to be male sticklebacks to the fish because of the red underbelly; it is this red visual sign that is the stimulus for aggressive behavior, and not the shape of the fish. A researcher first reported this behavior when he realized that his tank of sticklebacks got extremely upset whenever a red truck drove by. So the fish does not have to recognize the shape and details of another fish, just the red underbelly. Because nothing else in the area has one, that is all they need to recognize an enemy.

2.  The stimulus may be auditory. Moths have excellent hearing to detect the ultrasonics that bats use in echolocation of prey. When the moths hear this sound, they immediately close their wings and go into a power dive — automatically.

3.  In turkeys, the sign for parents to be protective of their young is cheeping (Campbell, 1996, pp. 1,172–185). If a mother hears her babies cheeping, she will protect them; but a mother will ignore her offspring if it is placed under a glass dome. The parent can see the chick but cannot hear it, so she ignores it. A deaf mother will kill her offspring because she does not receive the "look after me" stimulus.

4.  The stimulus can be olfactory. Marine snails use olfaction to detect the presence of predatory sea stars and then can take immediate action.

5.  The stimulus may be temperature. Female mosquitoes detect their hosts by heat (as well as other stimuli).

6.  The stimulus can be a combination of simple signs, such as bird feeding. Adult birds feed young when they open their mouths and gape at the parent while cheeping loudly. The gaping mouth and

cheeping are the signs for the parent to feed the young. The chicks' stimulus to begin this behavior is the landing of the parent on the nest (Campbell, 1996).

Many animals behave in this automatic way. Humans respond much more to an entire situation than most other animals, integrating more information when making a choice. However, humans also have FAPs. Babies grasp strongly with their hands in response to touch and smile at a drawing of a face, even if it is just a circle with two black circles inside. Smiling helps make them attractive so that the parent will protect them.

In all these cases, natural selection has chosen the most obvious sign or stimulus to get the desired result. Experimenters often test animals with similar types of signs, like the unrealistic models for the sticklebacks, and sometimes the animal will respond to the wrong stimulus. However, in real life, the male stickleback would do just fine attacking anything with a red underbelly because it is almost invariably going to be a male stickleback in the real situation. If other objects that had this trait occurred naturally, natural selection would select a more discriminating mechanism. For example, Graylag geese assume that anything small near their nests is an egg that they have accidentally kicked out, as they are inclined to clumsiness (Campbell, 1996). Therefore, they roll anything small back into the nest, including golf balls and even toy dogs placed by experimenters. However, in real life, the only object likely to be just outside the nest is the egg, so the goose does not have to be more precise. On the other hand, other birds must be able to identify their own eggs. Cuckoos lay their eggs in other birds' nests; and if the host bird does not realize it, the baby cuckoo will destroy the other eggs or baby birds and will be raised by its new foster parent. It is obviously very important for reproductive success for the bird to be able to recognize intruder eggs.

## Learned Behaviors

*Learning* is defined as the modification of behavior by experience. Learning can act on a number of different components of behavior, including the stimulus response (usually it narrows the range of effective stimuli) so the animal can learn which is the most important and become more precise. It also acts on motor patterns; for example, a squirrel gnawing on a nut soon learns to gnaw with the grain because that makes the nut easier to open. Even learned behavior has a genetic basis. For example, rats are intelligent and can learn quickly that if they press a bar, they get food. You can teach them not to press the bar by giving their feet a tiny electric shock when they touch it. If they get the shock immediately after they touch the bar, they will learn not to touch it; but if you wait 30 minutes, they will not learn. Anyone who has toilet trained a puppy knows that if you catch it urinating on the carpet, your yelling *may* have an effect, but there is no point in yelling at the puppy when you come home to an accident; the puppy has entirely forgotten its mistake and now just thinks you are grumpy. However, the same rat that cannot learn not to touch something if it gets a shock 30 minutes later can learn about other things over a much longer time, for example, how to avoid poison. Rats live in colonies, and when a new food is introduced, they do not all eat it at once. They will send out a couple of food-tasters to try a little bit, and then they will observe them for 24 hours. If the testers get sick after eating the food, the rest of the colony will learn the smell of the food and avoid it. This is the reason that rats are so difficult to poison. The difference in learning about the reason for shock and the new food shows that there is an innate or built-in predisposition to learn about some things but not about others.

There are many different forms of learning and a few are discussed here, but first it is important to be able to define the difference between learning and maturation. Some behaviors that are clearly innate are performed better or faster as time goes on. This is often not the result of learning, but of the maturing process, the development of a more coordinated muscular system for flying, for example. A baby bird does it right the first time; it has to, but its flying improves as it matures and becomes physically stronger.

1. *Habituation* is a very simple type of learning that involves a loss of responsiveness to unimportant stimuli. There are many examples; grey squirrels react to alarm calls by members of their group, but they will stop reacting if these calls are not followed up by an actual attack — it is just like the old "cry-wolf" story (Campbell, 1996).

2. *Imprinting* can be illustrated by a famous old study. You have no doubt seen a group of ducklings or goslings waddling after their mother. Natural selection would select this behavior because the mother will help protect them, will lead them to food, etc. Konrad Lorenz took some Graylag goose eggs and raised some with the appropriate mother and the rest in an incubator. He was the first living thing that the goslings saw, and he spent their first few hours with them. After that, they assumed he was their mother and followed him everywhere. When they grew up, they preferred to associate with people, not geese, and even tried to mate with people. Apparently, they had no idea of "I am a goose, you are a goose" or of "mother." Instead, they *imprinted* on the first object they encountered. The most important imprinting stimulus was movement away from the goslings, preferably making a

noise at the same time. In fact, they would even imprint on a box with a clock in it. Another bird, a whooping crane called Tex, was hand-raised in a zoo on her own; and when she was an adult, she refused to mate with birds chosen for her. She was imprinted on humans so she was induced to lay eggs (which could be artificially fertilized) by "dancing" with humans (she preferred Caucasian men of average size with dark hair). Another example is salmon returning to their spawning ground. They manage to find exactly the same place because of olfactory imprinting when they were young. They can find the precise combination of smells that is "home." Imprinting, however, can only occur during a certain critical period; with the geese, it was the first 2 days of life (Campbell, 1996).

3. *Classical conditioning* was made famous by Pavlov's experiment with dogs in 1900. He sprayed powdered meat into their mouths, which made them salivate. Just before he sprayed them, he rang a bell. Finally, the dogs salivated whenever he rang the bell. They were conditioned to expect the meat spray (Campbell, 1996).

4. *Operant conditioning* is better called trial and error. Here an animal learns to associate one of its behaviors with a reward or a punishment (Campbell, 1996). Many well-known experiments have been done using animals in cages in which pushing a lever meant that they received a food treat. They learned to push the lever quickly. We train dogs in much the same way. Positive reinforcement (that is, a reward for an action) works much more effectively than negative reinforcement or punishment. A rat learns more rapidly to push a lever for food than it learns not to push it if it gets an electric shock. This is the reason the best dogs are taught by encouragement rather than by abuse. One of the most famous examples of conditioning involved certain birds in England, very much like chickadees' that learned to peck through the paper tops on milk bottles to get a free breakfast. In England, milk is still delivered to the door in glass bottles. By trial and error, these birds found that if you sat on the top of the milk bottle and pecked, you could get free milk.

5. *Observational learning* occurs when an animal learns from watching another animal doing something (Campbell, 1996). Watching birds quickly learned to open milk bottles too, and the habit spread throughout the country in one summer, much to the annoyance of people who objected to sharing their milk. People do the same thing all the time; we see someone do something in a new way and try it ourselves.

6. *Play* is common among young animals (Campbell, 1996). If you watch two kittens jump and wrestle and grab at each other, you will notice that no one gets hurt. Play is costly in terms of energy, and it is also

costly because it often makes young animals vulnerable to predators. However, it is thought to be beneficial because it provides practice for later attacks on rivals or prey, and most importantly, it is exercise that keeps the animal fit.

7. *Insight learning* occurs when an animal can perform an appropriate behavior the first time it is in a situation in which it has no previous experience (Campbell, 1996). This behavior is also called *reasoning*. For example, when a banana is hung high above a chimpanzee's head, and the chimp is provided with a pile of boxes, the chimp can reason that if she piles the boxes on top of one another, she can reach the banana. This behavior is most developed in mammals, with humans showing the most advanced levels of insight learning.

All this material demonstrates that behavior has both genetic and environmental components. Some of them are very simple and some are completely under genetic control. Remember that we are animals too; we have a slightly bigger brainpan but we are still animals. We reason things out more than most animals but we have many behaviors that are entirely genetic or automatic, such as the baby gripping a finger or smiling at a human face. But there are other entrenched human behaviors that are not learned. We can certainly improve them with learning but the original behavior is pure biology. One of the best examples is the sex drive; it is automatic and kicks in after puberty, once all the hormones are in place. It is definitely a behavior, and it is not learned; it is automatic and, therefore, genetic. People can have sex with no instruction. Just think of people of certain classes in the Victorian age who never mentioned sex, so most women did not know it existed until their wedding night. People who have been raised without any instruction still manage to have sex successfully, so it is obviously mostly controlled by the genes that control our hormones. Hormones are heavily involved in sexual attraction and sexual acts and therefore the sex drive. The sex drive comes from the limbic system of the brain and arises directly from the sex hormones. Learning certainly improves the timing and manner of expression of the sex drive but the drive itself is completely biological.

The effect the environment has on the behavior we observe varies dramatically. It has no effect on some behaviors, and a major effect on others. In fact, most behavior is genetically predetermined to be affected by the environment; it is designed that way, to be improved and changed by learning from experience.

Remember that almost everything has a component of both the environment and the genes — even things that we consider entirely genetic; for instance, eye color. But is it really? Yes, mostly, but the environment can still have an effect. A rescued dog was found to be very friendly but his eyes were the pale amber of a wolf, which made him look as if he was about to attack. We later discovered that this dog had been shut in a dark shed for the first 8 months of his life. He had not been exposed to daylight, so the color in his eyes had not developed properly. Such things also happen with people. Now the dog's eyes are darkening as he lives a normal life. Identical twins are genetically identical, so should look the same. However, the environment, again, can influence this. One member of a pair of twins may be considerably shorter that the other member, due to a childhood disease that stunted his or her growth, overriding their genetic destiny. In both cases, the environment affected the original genetic plan. DNA is not always destiny; the environment also has an impact. Sometimes the environment has little effect on the basic genetic information, such as with eye color, and sometimes it has a tremendous impact, as with behavior.

## Evolution and Behavior

We have shown that behavior is, at least partially, under genetic control. It is also influenced by the environment, and the contribution of the genes ranges from complete control as in innate behavior to a varying level of control, as in learned behavior. As behavior does have a genetic component, it can and will evolve. However, traits such as certain behaviors will only be selected for by natural selection if they contribute to the survival and reproductive fitness of the individual who exhibits such behavior. Reproductive success is measured by an individual's genetic contribution to future generations. It is clear how behaviors such as a baby smiling at a caregiver to increase affection and therefore care, or imprinting on a caregiver, is likely to increase survival and eventually increase the chance of that individual surviving to adulthood and reproducing. However, it is more difficult to relate this to a criminal behavior.

In general, crime is viewed with disfavor in our society and it is difficult to see how clearly anti-social behavior would be likely to result in increased survivability and reproduction. Even thinking that criminal behavior is not only potentially inherited but is being selected for and is, therefore, increasing in our society is very controversial and has meant that most criminologists have shied away from considering such ideas (Ellis and Walsh, 2000). Considering such evolutionary theories goes back to Lombroso (1911), who believed that criminals were evolutionary throwbacks in some way. However, this theory did not hold water and was eventually disproved. More recent theories have looked at the evolution of criminal behavior in a much different light (Ellis and Walsh, 2000).

Daly and Wilson, eloquent Canadian evolutionary psychologists, are leaders in the area of violent crime and evolution. They say that evolutionary psychologists frequently make the error of assuming that a behavioral trait will be selected for if it results in happiness, self-actualization, or homeostasis, whereas in actual fact, evolutionary biology states that behaviors will be selected to maximize Darwinian fitness, in other words, if it increases survival and reproduction (Daly and Wilson, 2001).

To consider criminal behavior in terms of reproductive success, we need to consider various reproductive strategies. In mammals, female animals contribute a tremendous amount of parental investment to their young, particularly during gestation, lactation, and early child-rearing, often at considerable risk to themselves. This helps the females ensure that their offspring, carrying their genes, will survive to reproduce themselves. This early investment in the offspring is almost entirely provided by the female, and Ellis and Walsh (2000) argue that this is one reason to explain the existence of gender differences in criminality.

In many species of mammals, the female will only mate with a male that first offers her food (Ellis, 1989) or with a male that has already secured and defended a desirable territory that offers resources (Bateson, 1983). These are evolved reproductive strategies that follow Bateman's Rule, which states that whichever gender makes the most parental investment will be the most careful in choosing a mate (Bateman, 1948). Ellis and Walsh (2000) consider that Bateman's Rule is fundamental to most of the theories of the evolution of criminal behavior. The rule indicates that females who are cautious about choosing a mate will probably rear more offspring than their less picky sisters. In so doing, these cautious females will not only contribute more of their genes to the next generation, but will also help males who are good providers to contribute their genes to future generations. This would suggest that both males and females who contribute more to their offspring, in terms of care and resources, will be selected for and, conversely, those males who do not provide support will be selected against. If so, this would result in a reduction in the number of males who do not support females and their offspring. Evolution is more interesting than this, however, as not only does it result in the development of such a reproductive strategy, but it also results in the development of counter-strategies that are evolved to circumvent the original strategy. Most of these counter-strategies involve a form of deception (Ellis and Walsh, 2000). An easily understood example of such strategy and counter-strategy is seen commonly in nature when looking at insects. Birds have evolved strategies to allow them to quickly identify and pounce on a potential food source. Therefore, many insects have evolved strategies to avoid such predation by developing structures that focus a predator's attack on a less significant body part. Many butterflies have bull's eye patterns on the tips of their wings, which simulate eyes. This not only suggests that the tiny delicate butterfly is more dangerous than it really is, but deceives the predator into striking this area, thinking it is the head. Instead, it merely strikes the outer edge of the wing, allowing the butterfly to escape. The damage to the wing is very minor in comparison with an attack to the head or body. Some caterpillars not only develop such patterns on their furthermost segments, but also show behavioral adaptations by making striking moves to reinforce the suggestion that this is the head end and it is dangerous. Animals also exhibit behavioral counter-strategies, such as female birds that pretend to be wounded and therefore easy fodder, to lure predators away from their nest (Ellis and Walsh, 2000).

If we go back to considering Bateman's Rule, if females develop a strategy of only choosing males that have demonstrated the ability to provide for offspring, then males can evolve strategies that accede to this, or can develop counter-strategies such as forcing a female to copulate against her will (rape) or pretending to provide resources for future offspring, then reneging on this after mating (Ellis and Walsh, 2000). Both such strategies are commonly found in animal studies (Lalumière et al., 2005; Ellis, 1998).

Ellis and Walsh (2000) review five major recent evolutionary theories that could relate to criminal behavior. Each considers an alternate reproductive strategy:

1. *Cheater theory.* The Cheater theory, also referred to as the Cad versus Dad theory, is often used to explain the evolution of psychopathic behavior. In this theory, the cheater exploits males that have developed traditional strategies to mate, such as providing food, resources, and territory. Females have a lower reproductive rate than males as they can only produce a limited number of offspring, during a limited period of their life, whereas males can sire offspring from puberty until death and could, hypothetically, sire many offspring in a single day. Women somewhat compensate for this by being more choosy in their mates, selecting mates that can provide for the offspring, whereas males will increase their reproductive success by mating with a large number of women. Males can either comply with choosy females (dad) or can trick or force a female to copulate (cad). Such behavior is seen in many species, and also in humans.

   Bluegill sunfish males come in two forms or morphs (Ellis and Walsh, 2000). One, the resident or parental male, devotes a great deal of energy and time to acquiring and protecting a territory to attract a female. Once a cozy nest is built, he attracts a female by displaying the proposed nursery. The choosy female selects such a male as he has clearly demonstrated the ability and desire to provide. The female enters the nest and is induced by the male to lay her eggs, whereby the male fertilizes them. This is the way it is supposed to happen. However, the other bluegill male morph is known as a sneaker. He waits until the resident male and female are courting; and as soon as the female lays her eggs, he dives in, fertilizes them with his sperm, and runs away (Ellis and Walsh, 2000). The sneaker is smaller, matures earlier, and lives a shorter life than resident males, but accounts for a larger number of offspring (Lalumière et al., 2005).

This is just one of many examples of such evolved behaviors. A population can only support a limited number of such cheaters. If the number of such cheaters grew above a certain threshold, then the population of conforming males would be outnumbered and there would not be enough conforming males to provide resources for the offspring of cheaters.

Evolutionary criminologists have suggested that such alternate reproductive strategies also exist in humans. As successful females will be choosy, males must either develop a reproductive strategy that supports this (that is, comply and provide resources such as the resident male sunfish) or develop an alternate reproductive strategy.

Mealey (1995) and Lykken (1995) suggest that there are two forms of this alternate reproductive strategy in human males: (1) those who are genetically predetermined to be cheaters and exhibit such symptoms from early in life and (2) those who learn the strategy and confine its use to youth, eventually growing out of it and conforming. Mealey and Lykken suggest that the first type are psychopaths and the latter are sociopaths.

Ellis and Walsh (2000) provide several trains of evidence that support this cheater theory. Cheater behavior is clearly genetically controlled antisocial behavior, and this theory states that it has evolved only in males. This would predict that criminal behavior is dominated by males and also most commonly seen in young males seeking mates. According to this theory, such antisocial behavior is most likely exhibited by males who cannot convince females of their ability to provide for offspring, suggesting that cheaters are more likely to be men of lower socioeconomic class. Cheater behavior is more likely to succeed in large impersonal communities rather than tight-knit communities, suggesting that such behavior is more likely seen in urban rather than rural communities. The theory also suggests that criminals and psychopaths are more likely to have numerous sexual partners and that such people will exhibit high levels of deception and lying. Although there are obviously many parameters that contribute to criminal behavior, the above characteristics of cheaters are supported by the literature. For example, there is a large body of literature that supports the contention that most crimes, particularly with regard to serious and recidivistic crime, are committed by young males during the early reproductive years (Boyd,

2000). Later chapters in this text indicate that a certain amount of criminal behavior is inherited, indicating a genetic basis. As well, although obviously not considering the myriad other causes of crime, criminal behavior is more frequently seen in poor, urban neighborhoods (Ellis and Walsh, 2000), and psychopaths are much more likely to move from relationship to relationship and to exhibit high levels of deception (Hare, 1981).

2. *r/K strategies*. These strategies were first described by MacArthur and Wilson (1967) to describe a reproductive continuum in organisms. The strategy describes two extremes: (1) organisms that produce a very large number of offspring with no parental care and little investment are termed r strategists and (2) organisms that produce a very few offspring with a great deal of parental investment and care are termed K strategists. As this is a continuum, some organisms may be closer to r or K. In general, it is thought that in environments or times with plenty of resources, r strategists are favored, whereas when there is competition for resources, K strategists will be favored.

   Clearly, animals such as insects are, in general, r strategists, whereas mammals, in particular humans, exhibit the extreme end of K strategy. Such differences between species are clear but individuals also vary within species as to whether they are closer to r or K strategists. A great example of this is seen in dandelions. One of the greatest mortality factors for a dandelion is a lawnmower. Lawnmowers kill instantly, regularly, and indiscriminately (Daly and Wilson, 1983). Frequent mowing will therefore select for an r strategy, with early, rapid, and intense reproduction. Researchers compared reproductive rates in two populations of dandelions, one that was frequently mowed and one that was not disturbed (Gadgil and Solbrig, 1972). The two groups of plants, despite being from the same species, exhibited very different reproductive strategies, even if they were transplanted to the laboratory and raised under identical conditions. In the same way, Ellis (1987) suggested that although humans are K strategists, some males are less extreme K strategists than others. Those who are less extreme will have more children, with lower birthweights, and earlier onset of reproduction as birthweight and age of onset of reproduction are considered to be major indicators of parental investment (Ellis and Walsh, 2000). Ellis believes that men who are less extreme in exhibiting K strategy will be more prone to criminal and antisocial behavior. This includes two major assumptions: (1) that humans vary in K strategy and that antisocial behavior reflects a more r strategy to reproduction (Ellis, 1987). Ellis and Walsh (2000) explain this by pointing out that property crimes result in the rapid acquisition of resources that might attract sexual partners, and violent sexual crimes are often motivated by maintaining or securing mating opportunities. They contend that antisocial behavior is related to an r approach to reproduction and, therefore, genes that support r-selected traits, such as low birthweight, large family size, and multiple births should be related to antisocial behavior. Again, although many other variables exist that influence these traits, as will be seen in subsequent chapters, these traits are more frequently associated with criminal behavior.

3. *Conditional adaptation theory.* This theory, first proposed by Belsky (1980), suggests that genes have an indirect rather than a direct impact on criminal behavior. It asserts that humans have an evolved, genetic ability to subconsciously monitor their environment when very young and subsequently adapt their behavior, depending on this formative environment. The most pertinent parts of the environment, in this theory, relate to availability of resources and the stability of interpersonal relationships (Ellis and Walsh, 2000). The theory indicates that if a young child is exposed to interpersonal instability, such as parental arguments, abuse or divorce, and lack of resources, such as poverty, they are more likely to become opportunistic with an increased risk for criminal behavior in later life. They are more likely to become sexually active early and reproduce when very young, as they are now programmed to believe that resources will be scarce and relationships will be unreliable and thus will "speed up" their lives (Ellis and Walsh, 2000). According to this theory, such people would then be more likely to procure resources by any means, including deception. Children from stable homes with sufficient resources are more likely to acquire resources in a more orderly manner. This theory is interesting and is supported by other evidence, much of which is discussed further in later chapters, such as the beneficial effects of a stable family home. However, as will become clear, there are many other negative aspects related to poverty and lack of parental care that also influence behavior.

4. *Alternate adaptation theory.* Rowe (1996) proposed the alternate adaptation theory, which states that people either emphasize mating effort, in other words, seeking mating partners, or parental effort, or caring for offspring. He believes that the strongest predictors of these are gender and a variety of behavioral traits such as sensation seeking, aggression, and sex drive (Ellis and Walsh, 2000). Persons low in these personality traits, particularly women, will put more effort into parenting, whereas those high in these traits, particularly men, will put more effort into mating (Ellis and Walsh, 2000). Ellis and Walsh

(2000) also point out that intelligence would be a third predictor as people with high intelligence would be more likely to be able to carry out long-term and complex resource accumulation and thus put more effort into parenting. Rowe's theory suggests that criminals would be biased toward mating effort rather than parenting effort, and therefore criminality would be biased toward males with a relatively strong sex drive. He states that criminal behavior is a very direct and immediate method of gaining resources. Rowe's theory is in contrast with the conditional adaptation theory as it suggests that the genetics of the parents are much more important than the rearing environment (Ellis and Walsh, 2000).

5. *Evolutionary expropriative theory.* This theory, first proposed by three sociologists, Cohen, Machalek, and Vila (Cohen and Machalek, 1988; Vila, 1994, 1997; Vila and Cohen, 1993), states that criminality is just a way of acquiring resources but is different from other ways of simply "making a living" in that it results in victims attempting to suppress it (Ellis and Walsh, 2000). All organisms require resources to survive and reproduce. This theory suggests that there are two ways in which to acquire resources: (1) generative resource acquisition, which involves traditional methods of growing and raising food, building homes, and educating others in similar vocations; and (2) expropriative methods of acquiring resources, which involves taking advantage of those who generated the resources, but also involves more risk (Ellis and Walsh, 2000). A great deal of crime actually fits into this theory as some people acquire wealth or resources by hard work and others cheat, trick, or steal those resources. Such a system works best in large societies that create more opportunity for expropriating resources. This leads society to the necessity of developing a system that will discourage such expropriation, that is, a criminal justice system (Ellis and Walsh, 2000). This would also explain why crime is more rife in cities than in rural areas. According to this theory, people with low intelligence and poor academic ability will be more likely to expropriate resources than those with higher education and intelligence who will be more likely to acquire resources with fewer risks and greater long-term rewards (Ellis and Walsh, 2000).

Daly and Wilson, in their groundbreaking text entitled *Homicide,* discuss how evolution applies to homicide, and how such behavior can be considered to maximize fitness and reproduction (Daly and Wilson, 1988). This text provides an excellent overview of evolutionary biology and is highly recommended for further reading in this area. The text covers many areas of homicide, such as infanticide, familial killing, and stranger killing. Daly and Wilson, using the evolutionary theories of inclusive fitness and kin recognition, present persuasive evidence to show that stranger killing is much more common than familial killing as there is a deep concern for the well-being of those who carry your genetic information. They also discuss infanticide in terms of survival. It would seem to go against evolutionary fitness to kill one's own biological offspring, but Daly and Wilson provide eloquent arguments to show that, in some situations, infanticide may be adaptive as it may allow the mother to raise a healthier offspring later, or to bring a child into the world at a better time, when resources are more plentiful, or a more stable relationship exists. Daly and Wilson also discuss violence and homicide between strangers. They point out that most such conflicts are between young unrelated men, who have a low chance of reproduction, through social position, genetic quality, lack of resources, etc., which make them less attractive to a potential mate This, they state, can make the "dangerous escalation of social competition attractive" (1988, p. 294).

In short, behavior does have a genetic component in humans and other animals; and although most behaviors are often heavily influenced by the environment, they do have a biological basis. It is not the purpose of this text to delve deeply into evolutionary psychology, but rather to discuss the more organic impacts of biology on criminal behavior.

## Conclusion

This chapter introduced some basic biological concepts to begin our discussion of the biological approach to crime we will be developing in subsequent chapters. We discussed *natural selection* and compared behaviors of humans and other animals. Natural selection works through the way organisms adapt to their environments; some traits are selected over others and passed to the next generation. These heritable traits include the structural, biochemical, and physiological makeup of the body, but also, and more importantly for our study, *behavioral* traits, which are equally adaptive. In addition, we discussed a short critical narrative of the *nature-versus-nurture* argument. In doing this we came easily to the idea that there is really no opposition between these two influences, but an interaction; neither works in isolation. Behavior can be either entirely genetic or a mixture of genetics and the environment, the contribution of each varying with the behavior. The final part of this chapter discussed the new area of evolutionary approaches to criminal behavior and looked at *cheater theory, r/K strategies*, in which amount of parental care is seen as a heritable trait; *conditional adaptation theory,* in which crime may be a deep structure adaptation to the amount and availability of resources in childhood; *alternate adaptation theory,* where mating effort, or parental effort, and caring for offspring are inherited traits and can be predictors for criminality; and *evolutionary expropriative theory,* in which two major strategies of survival are heritable — generative behavior and expropriative behavior. We next discuss genetics and the interesting question of the specific means by which adaptation, genetic inheritance and criminal behavior interact.

## Questions for Further Study and Discussion

1. As we have seen, even talking about the idea of a possible biological basis for crime has been considered taboo for years. After reading this chapter, what new elements can be brought into this argument? Are they convincing?
2. Discuss why nature versus nurture is wrong and nature *and* nurture is more correct.
3. What are the main features of the evolutionary approach to criminal behavior?
4. Discuss cheater theory and r/K theory in relation to dysfunctional families.

## References

Bateman, A. (1948). Intra-sexual selection in *Drosophila. Heredity,* 2, 349–368.

Bateson, P.P.G, Ed. (1983). *Mate Choice.* Cambridge: Cambridge University Press.

Belsky, J. (1980). Child maltreatment: an ecological integration. *Am. Psychol.,* 35, 320–335.

Boyd, N. (2000). The testosterone connection. *The Beast Within: Why Men are Violent* (pp. 115–138). Vancouver, BC, New York: Greystone Books.

Cain, M., Damman, H., Lue, R.A., and Yoon, C.K. (2000). *Discover Biology* (p. 326). Sunderland, MA: Sinauer Associates.

Campbell, N.A. (1996). *Biology* (4th ed., pp. 408–409, 1071–1073, 1172–1185). Menlo Park, CA: Benjamin/Cummings.

Cohen, L. and Machalek, R. (1988). A general theory of expropriative crime: an evolutionary ecological approach. *Am. J. Soc.,* 84, 465–501.

Curtis, H. and Barnes, N.S. (1989). *Biology* (5th ed., pp. 962–963, 1,055). New York: Worth.

Daly, M. and Wilson, E.O. (2001). Risk-taking, intrasexual competition and homicide. *Nebraska Symposium Motivation,* 47, 1–36.

Daly, M. and Wilson, E.O. (1988). *Homicide.* New York: Aldine De Gruyter.

Daly, M. and Wilson, E.O. (1983). *Life History Strategy; Sex, in Evolution and Behavior* (pp. 179–221). Boston, MA: Willard Grant Press.

Darwin, C. (1859). *On The Origin of Species by Means of Natural Selection; Or the Preservation of Favoured Races in the Struggle for Life.* (1st ed., p. 859). London: John Murray.

Ellis, L. (1998). Neodarwinism theories of violent criminality and antisocial behavior: photographic evidence from nonhuman animals and a review of the literature. *Aggression Violent Behav.*, 3(1), 61–110.

Ellis, L. (1989). *Theories of Rape: Inquiries into the Causes of Sexual Aggression.* New York: Hemisphere.

Ellis, L. (1987). Criminal behavior and r/K selection: an extension of gene-based evolutionary theory. *Dev. Behav.*, 8, 149–176.

Ellis, L. and Walsh, A. (2000). Evolutionary biosocial theories. In *Criminology, a Global Perspective* (pp. 432–468). Boston: Allyn & Bacon.

Freeman, S. and Herron, J.C. (2004). *Evolutionary Analysis* (3rd ed., pp. 88, 90). Upper Saddle River, NJ: Pearson Education.

Gadgil, M. and Solbrig, O.T. (1972). The concept of r- and K-selection: evidence from wild flowers and some theoretical considerations. *Am. Naturalist*, 104, 1–24.

Hare, R.D. (1981). *Psychopathy and Violence. Violence and the Violent Individual* (pp. 53–74). Hays, J.R., Roberts, T.K., and Solway, K.S. New York: SP Medical and Scientific Books: 53–74.

Lalumière, M.L., Harris, G.T., Quinsey, V.L., and Rice, M.E. (2005). Forced copulation in the animal kingdom. In *The Causes of Rape. Understanding Individual Differences in Male Propensity for Sexual Aggression.* Washington D.C.: American Psychological Association.

Lombroso, C. (1911). *Crime: Its Causes and Remedies.* London: Heinemann.

Lykken, D.T. (1995). *The Antisocial Personalities.* Hillsdale, NJ: Laurence Erlbaum.

MacArthur, R.H. and Wilson, E.O. (1967). *The Theory of Island Biogeography.* Princeton, NJ: Princeton University Press.

Mather, M.H. and Roitberg, B.D. (1987). A sheep in wolf's clothing: Tephritid flies mimic spider predators. *Science*, 236, 308–310.

Mealey, L. (1995). The sociobiology of sociopathy: an integrated evolutionary model. *Behav. Brain Sci.*, 18(3), 523–599.

Purves, W.K., Orians, G.H., and Heller, H.C. (1995). *Life, the Science of Biology* (pp. 1036–1037). Sunderland, MA: Sinauer Associates.

Raven, P.H. and Johnson, G.B. (1995). *Understanding Biology* (3rd ed., pp. 290–291). Dubuque, IA: Wm. C. Brown Publishers.

Rowe, D.C. (1996). An adaptive strategy theory of crime and delinquency. In *Delinquency and Crime: Current Theories* (pp. 268–314). J.D. Hawkins. Cambridge: Cambridge University Press.

Starr, C. (1995) and Taggart, R. (2004). *Biology: The Unity and Diversity of Life* (10th ed., pp. 270–271). Belmont, CA: Thomson Brooks/Cole.

Starr, C. and Taggart, R. (1995). *Biology: The Unity and Diversity of Life* (7th ed., pp. 914–915). Belmont, CA: Wadsworth.

Vila, B.J. (1997). Human nature and crime control: Improving the feasibility of nurturant strategies. *Politics Life Sci.,* 16, 3–21.

Vila, B.J. (1994). A general paradigm for understanding criminal behavior: Extending evolutionary ecology theory. *Criminology,* 32, 311–359.

Vila, B.J. and Cohen, L.E. (1993). Crime as strategy: Testing an evolutionary ecological theory of expropriative crime. *Am. J. Soc.,* 98, 873–912.

# Genetic Concepts

# 3

## Introduction

This chapter introduces some basic principles of genetics. Without this knowledge, it would be impossible for you to decide whether genetics can or cannot influence crime. This chapter provides a very basic overview of genetics and the patterns of inheritance. This will allow you to appreciate the complexity of genetics, meiosis, and patterns of inheritance and explain some of the terms used. By the end of this chapter, you should have an understanding of basic inheritance patterns and realize that although genetics influences our behavior, our genotype interacts with our environment and that DNA alone is not destiny.

## Introduction to Genetics

Most people who are not trained in biology tend to ignore genetics but they still draw conclusions about biological factors and experiments. Their conclusions are usually wrong because they do not understand the basic concepts of biology. This text will not look at complex genetic issues, only at basic biology; most of you will have touched on this in high school. It should however provide the background needed to understand genetics. It should show how the body works in relation to its environment and how natural selection actually works. Darwin did not know about genetics, although the man who is considered the father of genetics, Gregor Mendel, an Austrian monk, was alive at the same time as Darwin. It is one of the curiosities of the history of science that neither of them fully understood the importance of each other's work during their lifetimes; years later, someone else read both their works and figured out the relationship. Sadly, after his death,

Darwin was found to have a copy of Mendel's famous paper, with notations in the margins of the first few pages, but he obviously had not read further.

Just like every other plant and animal, humans carry their genetic material in their chromosomes, which are found in the nucleus of every cell in the body. Each chromosome consists of strings of genes. The human species has 46 chromosomes (other species have different numbers) in 23 pairs. Twenty-two of the pairs are somatic and one pair are the sex chromosomes. Everyone, therefore, has two chromosome 1s, two chromosome 2s, etc., and a pair of sex chromosomes. The sex chromosomes are noted as XX if you are female and XY if you are male. Each member of a pair of chromosomes has the same genes, in the same order, as the other member of the pair, so we call them matching or homologous pairs. Every one of these chromosome pairs is found in nearly every single cell in the body (exceptions include the red blood cells, which do not have a nucleus). Every chromosome consists of strings of genes made of DNA (deoxyribonucleic acid), and they code for life. They are our blueprint, and they affect just about everything about us. They are held together by "junk" DNA (this junk DNA is where we are most different from each other, so it is used to identify people by DNA fingerprinting and in the DNA databank).

What is a gene? It is a set of instructions that code for (or make the body produce) a particular protein (Griffiths et al., 2005, p. 2). This protein then does something in the body. It makes something or is involved in some mechanism. When something goes wrong with a gene, it means that the protein is not produced at all, or that it is produced in lesser quantities than normal, or that too much is produced. Any error can affect the end product.

Every gene has an address or a locus where it is found on the chromosome (Lamb, 2000, p. 7). For example, the gene for eye color may be on chromosome 3 (this is not a good example because eye color is actually governed by several genes, but let us pretend, for the sake of argument, that there is only one gene involved in eye color). Let us say that the gene for eye color is 20 genes up on chromosome 3. You will always find the gene for eye color there; that is its address or locus. The sequence of genes on each chromosome is the same in both members of the pair. This is what the human genome project is all about — mapping the address for all the human genes. So, in our example, the gene for eye color resides on chromosome 3, but this gene can have several different forms. It can be blue or gray or brown or green or violet or hazel. Each of these different versions of the gene is called an *allele* (Griffiths et al., 2005, p. 2). So an allele is a gene, but it is a more specific term. The gene is for eye color; the alleles would be a blue allele, a green allele, etc. Figure 3.1 is a simplified picture of a pair of chromosomes showing just one gene and two alleles. Remember that this is a great simplification because many genes often govern a single trait. Also, every chromosome has many genes. There also may be more than two alleles in the population, as there are in our eye color example, but each

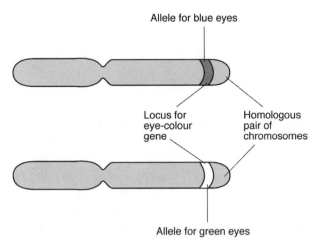

**Figure 3.1**  A simplified diagram of a pair of chromosomes showing just one gene and two alleles. Source: SFU Publications.

person gets only two because they only have two chromosomes in each pair. So although homologous chromosomes are very similar, they are not identical because they can contain different genetic information.

We inherited one chromosome of each pair from our mother and one from our father. Using the eye color example, remember that the father also has two copies of that gene, and so does the mother. Your father might have a blue allele and a green allele. He passed one of them to you. Your mother might have a blue one and a brown one. She can only give you one as well, so you might have ended up with two blue alleles, a blue one and a green one, a brown one and a green one, or a blue one and a brown one; that is, you could get any combination of the above alleles.

When we reproduce, we pass on our genes to our offspring. However, we cannot give a complete copy of all 46 chromosomes because our mate would do the same and the offspring would end up with 92 chromosomes. An egg and a sperm must fuse to produce a baby (Griffiths et al., 2005, p. 3). If the egg gave the baby 46 chromosomes and so did the sperm, the fetus would not be viable. It must have exactly the right number of chromosomes, with exactly the right number of genes on them to survive. Babies with extra sets of chromosomes do not survive. A single extra chromosome or even just an extra little part of a chromosome can result in death or produce an abnormality; for example,

- Down's syndrome (extra chromosome 21, physical and mental problems) (Lamb, 2000, p. 225)
- Patau's syndrome (extra chromosome 13, death usually after a few months)

- Edward's syndrome (extra chromosome 18, death in less than 6 months) (Lamb, 2000, p. 226)
- Certain forms of leukemia (loss of part of chromosome 22) (Griffiths et al., 2005, p. 561)
- Cystic fibrosis (loss of just one gene) (Griffiths et al., 2005, p. 44)

To produce a healthy baby, the parents must be able to halve their chromosome number precisely before they pass them on. So although each parent has 46 chromosomes, their gametes, or sex cells, which are the eggs and the sperm, must have only 23 chromosomes. When the egg and sperm fuse to make a single complete cell, or zygote, they each provide 23 chromosomes and the zygote now has the entire set. This zygote grows into a baby and then an adult by repeated cell divisions, like a photocopier making copies of that first original cell. As the organism grows, every cell contains the same genetic information. When something has only one set of the chromosomes, it is called haploid. The normal condition is diploid, which just means that there are two copies of each chromosome (Griffiths et al., 2005, p. 3).

For a baby to be viable, it cannot just get a random half of the genetic material from each parent. It must get one copy of every gene from each parent. This is the reason our chromosomes come in pairs. When the parent is producing sperm or eggs, one member of each pair goes to each new cell. This ensures that each gamete (egg or sperm) has a full set of genetic information from each parent. Natural selection had to develop a very precise mechanism to cut the chromosome number in half and to ensure that every egg or sperm has exactly the right number and type of chromosomes. This process is called *meiosis,* and it does two things. It carefully halves the chromosome number, but it also shuffles the chromosomes so that the offspring are completely different from their parents. This process occurs in the ovaries or testes, and it results in the chromosomes being first duplicated, then halved so that each cell eventually becomes, for example, four sperm. During meiosis, the chromosomes briefly stick together and homologous chromosomes actually swap bits of information exactly, gene for gene, before they split. At the end of the entire process, there are four cells, each with half the chromosome number and a unique set of chromosomes (Griffiths et al., 2005, pp. 74–75).

There are two major results of meiosis:

- The pairs of chromosomes have been separated so the number of chromosomes has been reduced from 46 to 23, with every chromosome still represented.
- The new cells are all different from each other and from the parent.

Thus, each sperm and egg is unique. This is the origin of all the genetic variation in our species. Why do we want that variation? Why, if you have a successful genotype, would you want to risk changing it? If it ain't broke, why fix it? The obvious answer seems to be that we would not want to take the risk. But although yours might be a successful genotype now in this environment, environments and situations do change. Your genotype might not be successful in the next generation. Remember the peppered moth! You want variety in your offspring so that if things change drastically, then at least some of them will survive. We need variation in the population to allow natural selection to act and enable our population to adapt to changing environments.

Every human being is unique. A human egg represents one of about 8 million possible chromosome combinations, and it is fertilized with one sperm, which also represents about 8 million possible chromosome combinations. Therefore, any two parents will produce a zygote with any of at least 64 trillion combinations; as a result, you might not look much like your siblings.

Genes code or instruct the body to produce a protein that does something; it may produce some metabolic action, it may determine that a person is blue-eyed, or it may affect a behavior.

## Genetics: The Study of Patterns of Inheritance

We have long known that offspring inherit qualities from their parents. Farmers, for example, have known for centuries that breeding a heavy animal with another heavy animal would likely produce heavy offspring and that the daughters of good milk-producing cows would be good producers as well. This is really just positive eugenics. If you had a particularly good sheep dog, you would breed it with another good worker, so that you always had good working dogs. You would not breed a dog that was not a good herder. So people have understood the basic concepts of genetics since time immemorial, but the way the genetics of inheritance actually works was not understood until relatively recently.

In the past, people believed that each offspring inherited a "blend" of its parents' features, a bit of both, because the offspring appeared to be a mixture of both parents. Even Darwin believed this premise. This idea seems logical when you think about things that are continuously graded (height, for example). You might be halfway between your parents' heights, for instance, but the theory does not account for most observations. If this blending theory was correct, variation would disappear. Think of different colors of paint. If you mix black and white, you get gray; then if you mix gray and gray, you get more gray. In the end, you lose the color distinction. This theory works for paint but not for organisms. If you bred or "mixed" a black horse with a white horse, the theory would suppose that you would always get a gray horse. But that is not true; the pair would actually produce black foals, white foals, and lots of intermediates. If inheritance worked by blending, it would eventually result in complete uniformity. Everyone would be the same height, weight, color, etc. People tended to ignore this obvious evidence that the blending theory is incorrect because they could not explain it. In fact, the theory does not work even for continuously graded characteristics such as height. If we were always an average of our parents, we would all be the same height in just a few generations.

Gregor Mendel carried out the first scientific investigation of inheritance in 1860. He did the exhaustive experiments and came up with the principles of genetics that are still valid today, yet he did not know that genes or chromosomes even existed because the science of microscopy was not yet at a level to make such features visible. So his work was truly remarkable. We still teach directly from his work, with some additions but no real corrections. There are not very many pieces of research in any field that you can say that about almost 150 years later. Some scientists still say that his was the best scientific paper ever written.

*Genetics* is the study of genes and how they are passed on to the next generation. Mendel worked on pea plants, and he did very careful experiments, breeding his plants for more than 2 years before even starting to use them in experiments. He wanted to be sure they bred true, and he used very large numbers so that he could perform statistics on his data, which although understood today, was a very unusual concept at the time.

One of his first experiments involved crossing pea plants that always produced only purple flowers with pea plants that always produced only white flowers (Mendel, 1901, pp. 8–11).

The original plants are referred to as *parentals* — we call them the **P** generation:

| Parents | **Purple** | X | **White** |
|---|---|---|---|
| | | ⇩ | |
| F1 generation | | All flowers **purple** | |

The first generation, which is called the F1 or the first filial generation, had only purple flowers (Mendel, 1901). So purple had completely obscured the white. Thus, there was no blending at all taking place; no pale purple or pink. This finding alone disproved the theory of blending. We call the trait that obscures the other one the dominant trait, and the concealed trait, the one that did not appear in this first cross, the recessive. So in this case, purple is dominant. These were Mendel's terms, and we still use these terms today. For example, brown eyes are dominant to blue eyes in people; blue eyes are recessive.

Mendel then let the first set of offspring self-pollinate. Many plants do that normally because they have male and female parts and can fertilize themselves. In the next generation, he obtained purple and white flowers in a ratio of 3:1, so the recessive trait, the white, had not totally disappeared (Mendel, 1901). It had just been "hidden" for one generation and reappeared in the second generation. It was unchanged, still white, not mixed with purple at all, so again, no blending.

It appeared then that the pea plants contained two hereditary factors for color. We now understand that these hereditary factors are genes. The pea plant has genes for flower color, and they come in two varieties (or alleles), purple or white. Each pea plant received one allele from the female parent and one from the male parent. Each gamete would contain only one of the two possible alleles, and it could be either purple or white. When two gametes get together, the offspring would have two alleles, one dominant to the other.

So this is the previous cross, giving letters to represent alleles:

| Purple | X | White |
|--------|---|-------|
| **PP** | | **Pp** |

Both plants are pure breeding, meaning that both alleles of the gene are the same in each parent. One has two dominant alleles, and one has two recessive alleles. We use an uppercase letter for the dominant allele, and a lowercase letter for the recessive. Now we do a simple cross. If one parent has two **P**s, it can only give a **P** to its offspring. The same for the white parent: it has only **p**s, so that is all it can give. Therefore, the offspring of the two must be **Pp**.

| Parents | **Purple (PP)** | | X | | **White (pp)** | |
|---------|-----------------|---|---|---|----------------|---|
| Gametes | P | P | ⇩ | | p | p |
| F1 generation | | | All **Pp** | | | |

Thus, one dominant allele is received from one parent, and one recessive from the other parent. All the offspring will have one dominant and one recessive allele. We call this outcome "heterozygous." Homozygous occurs when the offspring has two copies of the same allele for a gene, either dominant or recessive, and heterozygous occurs when the organism has two different alleles for that gene.

Then Mendel interbred this first generation, crossing **Pp** with **Pp**. Each parent donated one of two alleles to its gametes, either the dominant allele

**P** or the recessive allele **p.** The following table (known as a Punnett square) shows all the possible combinations:

|   | Pp × Pp | |
|---|---|---|
|   | ↙ P | ↘ p |
| P | PP | Pp |
| p | Pp | pp |

The dominant gene always produces the color purple; so if an uppercase P is present, the flowers will be purple. It can only be white if there is no uppercase P present. Three of the above (**PP, Pp,** and **Pp**) will be purple, and only one (**pp**) will be white (because it has no uppercase P). When you look at this table, you can see how the white, the recessive, reappears. It is useful to draw these tables when you are working out the possible outcomes of a cross.

You can notice here that there are two different genetic makeups (or genotypes) that produce purple. They can be **PP** or **Pp.** Although they look identical genetically, they are different, which affects the way they pass on their genes. One has two dominant alleles, two **P**s, so it can only pass on dominant alleles. The other has one dominant and one recessive allele, **Pp,** so it can pass on either. Dominant and recessive genes are very important when a doctor works out the risk of parents passing on a genetically controlled disease to an offspring. It may be hidden in the parents but could appear in an offspring. Genetic counselors determine the probability of a future offspring having the disease.

In this cross, the heterozygous **Pp** looks exactly the same as the homozygous **PP.** They are both purple. Now we can differentiate between the genotype and phenotype, which are not necessarily the same. The phenotype is the physical manifestation of traits or what the organism looks like or does. In this case, is it purple or is it white? The genotype is the genetic makeup of the individual, that is, which alleles it possesses. So **PP** and **Pp** have the same phenotype but different genotypes. **PP** has the same genotype and phenotype — purple — and **pp** has the same genotype and phenotype — white.

Mendel published his work in the 1860s but it was completely ignored. It was rediscovered in 1900 by three different people at about the same time, after the improvement in microscopes had resulted in the discovery of chromosomes. Then Mendel's work was discovered to contain a tremendous amount of data. By the time people began to recognize Mendel's work for what it was, sadly, he had been dead for 16 years. Later, his work was applied to natural selection, which had by then faded somewhat in popularity. However, when Mendel's work was put together with Darwin's work, natural selection soared to new heights because it was now possible to *understand* how natural selection worked. Darwin had been right all along; he simply did not know about genetics. If he had, both he and Mendel could have understood the process of natural selection *and* inheritance, and Darwin, for one, would have died a happier man.

Thus far we have been looking at a single gene, which guides one characteristic, flower color. Every living thing, however, has millions of genes, each guiding something. Sometimes, several genes act on one trait. In a real mating between two living things, the cross shown above would happen for *every* gene, so you can see how quickly it gets complicated.

There are quite a few genes that behave in this straightforward Mendelian, dominant/recessive form, but most genetic traits are not that simple. We will look at a few, slightly more complicated examples so that you realize how some of the traits discussed later *could* be affected by genes. Mendel provided the first understanding of genetics, but he was lucky in choosing a situation in which the genetics was straightforward. Otherwise, he would not have understood it. As discussed, most genetics is much more complex, and any genetic influence on behavior will *definitely* be very complex, not the simple one gene/one action described above. Here are a few of the different types of genetic inheritance patterns.

## Linked Genes

What happens if we look at two genes for two different things? If they are on different chromosomes, they will each act independently; but if they are on the same chromosome, they are said to be *linked*. This can make it more likely that they will be inherited together (Lamb, 2000, p. 12). For example, if you consider two genes, A and B, which are on two separate chromosomes and you crossed **AABB** with **aabb,** the first cross would result in offspring that are **AaBb.** If they were interbred, the next generation would look like this:

|      | AB   | Ab   | aB   | ab   |
|------|------|------|------|------|
| AB   | AABB | AABb | AaBB | AaBb |
| Ab   | AABb | AAbb | AaBb | Aabb |
| aB   | AaBB | AaBb | aaBB | aaBb |
| ab   | AaBb | Aabb | aaBb | aabb |

However, if genes A and B are on the same chromosome, they will not segregate independently; that is, they will stay together. The first cross will look like this:

| *Parents*       | **AB AB**     | X              |        | **ab ab** |
|-----------------|---------------|----------------|--------|-----------|
|                 |               | ⇩              |        |           |
| *F1 generation* |               | All **AB ab**  |        |           |

Everything seems the same at this stage but the gametes that are produced by the F1 generation are very different. Because they are linked, most of the gametes must be either AB or ab because the loci are physically tied together on the same chromosome. They are part of the same DNA molecule.

They might separate when the shuffling occurs in meiosis; but the closer they are together, the more likely they are to stick together. If the genes are very close together, it is unlikely that there will be a shuffle occurring between them, and they will almost always be inherited together. If they are at opposite ends of the chromosome, however, they could get separated when the chromosomes get stuck together and swap portions. So one might get a few Ab aB gametes if crossing over occurs between the two loci, but these will be rare; and the closer the two genes are on the chromosome, the more rare they will be. This is the reason people with dark hair usually have dark-colored eyes, and people with blond hair usually have light-colored eyes. Eye color and hair color are on the same chromosome. They may get separated at meiosis, so you may get a person with dark hair and light eyes but they are much rarer than people with dark hair and dark eyes because dark hair and dark eyes are genetically linked.

When things are linked in this way, a gene that is very advantageous to the organism will be selected for, and it might carry some other genes along with it that just happen to be closely linked. This is often the reason certain genes seem to stay in the population although they do not confer an advantage. They are closely linked to genes that do confer an advantage and so when those are selected for, they just sort of tag along. It also explains why some quite bad genes, such as those that cause certain diseases, remain. The desired gene outweighs the bad effects and is still selected.

## Sex- Linked Traits

Of the 46 chromosomes that a human being possesses, one pair (two chromosomes) are sex chromosomes. The female has two X chromosomes and the male has one X and one Y chromosome. When eggs are produced, one sex chromosome goes to each egg. A female can only provide an X for the eggs. The male, however, has both an X and a Y, so a sperm might carry either one (Griffiths et al., 2005, p. 48). The egg it meets up with will be carrying an X, so the sex of the offspring is determined entirely by the male and depends on whether the sperm that he contributes carries an X or a Y. Thus, although Henry VIII beheaded and divorced wives because they did not produce sons, the sex of the child depends on the male, not the female. Certain characteristics of the female reproductive system can favor a sperm that carries a Y or an X chromosome, meaning that the female may have some influence on the sex of the offspring but sex is primarily determined by the male.

The X and Y chromosomes not only determine sex, but also carry other genes. The X chromosome is quite large and carries many genes, but the Y chromosome is very small and carries only a few genes. If a gene is on a sex chromosome, it is said to be sex linked (Griffiths et al., 2005, p. 49). Usually, that means it is on the X chromosome, simply because it has more genes. We know about a few such sex-linked genes and the diseases they cause. We know the most about genes that cause diseases because they are of most interest to us. Genes that are involved in hair or eye color are not so vital and, therefore, they do not get the same research attention. Two classic examples of sex-linked conditions are color blindness and hemophilia (Griffiths et al., 2005, pp. 52–53). They are both usually found in men and only very rarely in women. It is quite common for men to be color blind, but not for women, and the same is true for hemophilia. The reason is that both diseases are caused by recessive genes. The dominant form is normal. If you think back to the earlier examples relating to dominant and recessive genes, you will see that people only express the recessive gene if they have two recessive alleles. If they had two dominant alleles or one of each, then the recessive gene would not be expressed, just as the purple flower "hid" the white flower. Also, these disease-causing recessive genes are usually fairly rare, so the allele ratio may be 98% normal and dominant and 2% disease-causing recessive allele.

Except for the sex chromosomes, a person always has two of each chromosome. With the sex chromosomes, females have two X chromosomes but males only have one. This means that the female can have one recessive gene that will not express itself because it will be protected or hidden by the dominant one. However, a male only has one X chromosome, so if he receives the recessive allele, there is not another allele to hide it and it will be expressed. As a result, the recessive allele is expressed in the male, while the female is normally only a carrier. The female will only actually have the disease if she gets a recessive gene from each parent, which is rare. There are lots of such traits, not just disorders, that are seen more commonly in males than females. Females who are carriers can pass recessive genes to their sons but their daughters will also only be carriers (Griffiths et al., 2005, p. 52).

There are some genes on the Y chromosome, but not many. One causes a disorder called Scaly Bark skin disease. Females are not carriers because it is only found on the Y chromosome.

## Incomplete Dominance

In the experiment with the pea flowers, the offspring always looked like one of the parents because of the complete dominance of one allele over another. But for some traits, dominance is not complete, and the offspring have an appearance somewhere between the phenotypes of the two parents (Griffiths et al., 2005, p. 194). For example, when a red snapdragon is crossed with a white snapdragon, all of the first generation has pink flowers. This is because the heterozygotes have less red pigment than the red homozygotes. However, it is important to realize that blending is still not occurring, as was the old belief, because if that was so, the original whites and reds could not be retrieved. However, if you breed the pink plants, you get red, white, and pink.

## Co-Dominance

In co-dominance, both alleles are expressed in the heterozygote. An example is the existence of three separate blood groups in humans — M, N, and MN (Lamb, 2000, pp. 10–11). These groupings are based on two specific molecules that people have on the surface of their blood cells. People of group M have one type of molecule, people of group N have the other type, and people of group MN have both types. M individuals are homozygous for one allele, N individuals are homozygous for the other allele, and MN individuals are heterozygous. The MN is not intermediate as both alleles are expressed.

## Pleiotropy

Thus far we have looked at genes that control just one phenotypic character. However, most genes actually have multiple phenotypic effects, which means that they control several things that affect the way we look. This situation is called *pleiotropy* (Griffiths et al., 2005, p. 197). For example, in tigers, the same allele causes both abnormal pigmentation and crossed eyes. You can see a similar effect in Siamese cats; the same allele that is responsible for their light body color and darker points (face, paws, and tail) are also responsible for crossed eyes. This is one of those unnatural selections that man has had a hand in. We liked the color combination, so we deliberately selected for it and, in so doing, we also selected for crossed eyes. These are clearly not a benefit and certainly would not help the animal survive in the wild. However, Siamese cat breeders highly value cross-eyed animals, and in their protected environment, they survive well.

## Epistasis

*Epistasis* occurs when one gene alters the way another gene is expressed (Griffiths et al., 2005, p. 203). An example is coat color in mice. Black coat color is dominant to brown. To be brown, a mouse must have two recessive alleles. Sounds simple, but there is another gene that determines whether the mouse will have color or no color, no matter which alleles it carries for black and brown. This gene controls the expression of the black and brown alleles. So, for a mouse to have any color at all, it must have a dominant color allele. If it does not have at least one allele for color, then it will be albino or white even though it has other alleles telling it that it should be either black or brown. So this color gene controls the black/brown gene.

## Polygenic Inheritance

Mendel studied characters that were either/or with the purple and white flowers, and the many other traits he investigated in these flowers, but many characters cannot be classified in this way because the characters vary in the population in gradations. These are called quantitative characters; examples in humans include skin color and height. Quantitative variation usually indicates polygenic inheritance, which is an additive effect of two or more genes on a single phenotypic character. This is the opposite of pleiotropy, where a single gene affects many phenotypic characters. Here we have lots of genes working on just one thing. Polygenes that affect a particular quantitative trait are commonly found on many different chromosomes. Genes are very simple and they code for simple things. Thus, complex things require the contribution of several genes. Even things that we might consider simple, such as hair color or eye color, are coded for by several genes. A good example is human skin color. Humans differ in the amount of melanin (dark pigment) found in their skin (Griffiths et al., 2005, pp. 8–9). There is a great variation in the amount of melanin that different people have, but much of this variation is a result of at least three separately inherited genes. There may be more, but for simplicity's sake, let us just look at three genes, with a dark skin allele for each, **A, B,** and **C,** each contributing one "unit" of darkness to the phenotype and being incompletely dominant over the other alleles **a, b,** and **c.** Someone who has **AABBCC** would be very dark, and someone with **aabbcc** would be very light. **AaBbCc** would be intermediate. If you make a calculation, you will see that there will be a wide range of graded values from very pale to very dark. You can also see how two people of intermediate skin color could still produce offspring with either very dark or very light skin. Also, skin color is not entirely determined by genotype; we can expose ourselves to the sun to produce more melanin.

The environment can have an effect on the translation of the genotype into the phenotype (Griffiths et al., 2005, pp. 18–19). Nutrition, exercise, experience, and other events all alter the phenotype. Nutrition affects size, exercise affects body shape, and experience can affect IQ. Even identical twins are not really identical although they are genetic equals; they still accumulate phenotypic differences as a result of their unique life experiences. In the example of the Siamese cat, I mentioned the coat color combination with a light body and dark ears, face, tail, and feet. Coat color is controlled genetically, but the environment has a strong effect on the phenotype. These darkened areas on the cat actually have a slightly lower temperature than the rest of the body. Experiments have shown that the Siamese cat has a genotype with dark fur, but it only appears at temperatures somewhat below the general body temperature. If some dark fur is shaved from the tail and the cat is then kept at a higher than normal temperature, the fur that grows back will be light. On the other hand, if the cat is shaved and made to wear an ice pack on a normally light area, the spot that is kept cool grows back with dark hair. So, genotype and environment interact to determine the phenotype of the organism.

The effect that the environment has on the phenotype varies dramatically. It has no or little effect on some things, like eye color, and a major effect on other things, such as behavior. There is certainly a genetic basis for behavior but the environment has a strong influence. In fact, most behavior is genetically predetermined to be affected by the environment. It is designed to be improved, modified, and changed by learning and experience.

## Recessive Alleles in the Population

Although recessive alleles are hidden by the dominant allele in a heterozygous individual, they are important in the population. In many cases, the dominant form is the normal form, and the recessive is the abnormal form. For example, in a disease, the dominant allele would be normal and the recessive allele would result in disease. However, when the dominant allele is present, the recessive allele is masked or blocked, so the person carries a gene for the disease but does not succumb to the disease. However, the person could pass on that allele to their offspring. It would only be a problem if the person who is a carrier had a partner who either had the disease or was also a carrier. In that case, they might produce a child with only recessive alleles who would thus have the disease.

Another point is that there are often unequal ratios of the different alleles. The population may include 95% dominant alleles and only 5% recessive alleles. In this case, the chance of two people with recessive genes coming together is low, so the chance of producing offspring with two recessive genes (and hence the disease) is also low.

Recessive alleles explain why there are taboos against marrying close family members. Cultures throughout history and prehistory have banned close family members from marrying. These early cultures did not understand genetics but did know from experience that incest frequently resulted in unhealthy offspring. When you understand genetics, it is obvious that there is a higher chance of finding someone else with the same recessive gene in your own family (Griffiths et al., 2005, p. 43). For example, say the gene that causes some horrible disease is the recessive form of the gene **A, a. A** is found in 98% of the population, and only 2% have **a**, so it is very rare. The mother is a carrier, so she is **Aa;** the father is normal (**AA**). They have eight children who will be **AA** or **Aa.** Therefore, none of the children have the disease. In fact, the family probably does not know that the mother is a carrier or that half of the children are carriers. If their partners are strangers, the chance of meeting another person also carrying a recessive **a** is small because the frequency of that gene in the population is small; therefore, it is entirely probable that the family is totally unaware of this potential time bomb in its midst. However, if siblings mate, then the chance is 50% that the mate also has that gene. So you could easily get a cross between two carriers. Like the purple and white flowers, the result would be a 3:1 ratio, that is, a 25% chance of producing a child with the disease and a 50% chance of producing more carriers.

A classic example is hemophilia, a clotting disorder; people with the disease bleed to death very easily (Griffiths et al., 2005, pp. 52–53). Queen Victoria was a carrier and one of her sons had the disease. He transmitted it to his daughter, who did not have the disease but was a carrier. Because royal families are very inclined to marry close relatives, the disease became common in virtually every royal family in Europe, except—conveniently—Britain. Victoria's granddaughter Alexandra was a carrier, carrying the gene on her X chromosome (hemophilia is a sex-linked disease). Alexandra did not have hemophilia as she had a normal X chromosome from her father. She married Czar Nicholas of Russia and passed the X chromosome carrying the gene for hemophilia to their only son, Alexei. Because of his illness, Alexandra fell under the sway of the monk and womanizer Rasputin, which was, in part, the reason for the fall of the Russian royal family and the massacre of all the members of the immediate family. Had Alexandra, by chance, passed on the normal X chromosome, her son would have been healthy, and the course of history may well have been different.

Another example is sickle cell anemia (Griffiths et al., 2005, p. 194). This disease of the blood is common in people of African descent and much rarer in others. The red blood cells of a person with sickle cell anemia cannot carry oxygen very well; so people suffering from sickle cell anemia develop a multitude of health problems, and the disease is usually fatal. It occurs in about 1 in every 400 African-Americans, which is a fairly high rate. Why would something like that be more common in one race rather than in another? Remember that there is a higher chance of producing one of these disorders if you marry close family members, and this concept can be expanded to show that this would also apply if you marry only within a particular group of people. Most people do marry within racial groups and sometimes even closer — within a village or regional area, for example. Therefore, there is a higher chance that they will meet someone else with the recessive gene also. The frequency of the alleles in different racial groups is different. It may be, for example, 20% in the African-American population, but only 2% in other races. Therefore, your chances of meeting someone with a recessive gene are higher if you marry within your own racial group. The same is true for Tay-Sachs disease, which is common in Jewish people, but only those whose ancestors come from Central Europe, a group called Ashkenazic Jews. There are many other such diseases; for example, porphoryia (the disease that is thought to have resulted in the belief in vampires) is more common among Caucasians.

An interesting point is that sometimes natural selection has selected for a disease because it confers some sort of advantage on the individual. In the case of sickle cell anemia, you only have the disease in its severe form if you have two recessive genes, or **ss.** However, if you are a heterozygote for this condition **(Ss),** you have some normal red blood cells and some abnormal ones. Normally, this condition would still not be good, but the majority of the people who have this disease are from Africa, where malaria is a common killer disease. Malaria is a parasite that lives in red blood cells. People who are **Ss** are much more resistant to malaria than people with normal blood **(SS).** Malaria kills millions of children every year in Africa, so a child in Africa who is heterozygous for sickle cell anemia has a much better chance of surviving malaria than one with normal blood. Therefore, that child is more likely to survive, grow up, have children, and hence pass on those anemia genes. Thus, the disease actually confers an advantage where malaria is prevalent. Descendents of these people who live in North America do not need to worry about malaria, so it is no longer a benefit. It is a detriment because people who are heterozygous have trouble breathing at high altitudes. Therefore, the frequency of the disease in the population in North America may eventually drop. However, it is still an example of how something that might appear to be bad can actually be selected for by natural selection.

## Aggression

Aggression should be discussed here only because it is always raised when we try to explain crime. Aggression is not the only cause of crime by any means, but it is certainly involved in many crimes that hit the headlines. We should then consider whether it could be inherited and why.

From an evolutionary perspective, aggression is an adaptive behavior; that is, it is a behavior that helps the organism survive. Remember that survival and reproduction are the two most important things in life for any organism. Aggression is a behavior in which physical or verbal force is used to counter a perceived threat. It has escalated into a maladaptive behavior, violence, which is aggression directed against the wrong target in the wrong place at the wrong time, with the wrong intensity.

Work on animals has frequently shown that we can genetically select for aggression. In a particularly nice series of experiments on mice, Gariépy and colleagues demonstrated not only that aggression could be selected for, but also showed how the environment would reverse the aggression (summarized in Gariépy et al., 1996). The fact that we can select for aggression means that it has a genetic component because selection only works on heritable traits. In these experiments, over a period of time, male mice that frequently attacked other mice were identified and mated with females whose siblings had also shown high levels of attack. The same procedures were duplicated each generation, with only the most aggressive being chosen for breeding. This line of mice was termed "aggressive" or NC900. At the same time, the least aggressive male mice were chosen and mated to females with siblings that were non-aggressive. This line was termed "low-aggression" or NC100. Non-selectively bred mice were used as controls (Gariépy et al., 1996). In each generation, the male mice were tested for aggression as adults by exposing them to a control animal and observing their reaction. The mouse lines were observed for aggression over 22 generations, and the researchers found that they could rapidly select for both aggression and non-aggression over just a few generations, with clear differences seen between the two groups within one generation and a significant statistical difference by the fourth generation (Gariépy et al., 1996). Interestingly, once aggression had been selected for, the level of aggression did not increase any further, although the reduction in natural aggression in the non-aggressive line continued to decrease to close to zero, and the animals were seen to frequently "freeze" in the presence of another male mouse. The very rapid selection for both aggression and non-aggression indicate that the aggression was highly heritable.

In a series of further experiments, the researchers looked at the effects of simple manipulations on this genetically selected aggression and found that the response was extremely plastic. That is, although the aggression was genetically determined, it was designed to be flexible so that it could adapt to changing conditions (Gariépy et al., 1996). For example, simple socialization with other mice completely reversed the genetic selection for aggression in the NC900 mice and for freezing in the NC100, indicating that, although the original trait is genetic, it can be completely reversed by an appropriate environment. Many other tests were performed to determine the many ways that this genetic effect could be neutralized.

Therefore, aggression, at least in the mice in this very robust set of experiments, was heritable. There were several replications of the experiments by people all over the world. The most interesting part was all the ways they could then use to change the aggression or prevent it entirely. These are called *protective factors*. This was one of the studies that actually tried to identify some of the protective factors. Simply socializing the animals was a major protective factor (Gariépy et al., 1996).

What about other animals, such as dogs? When humans first developed dog breeds, they bred deliberately for certain traits. These included physical looks, coat length and color, and temperament. Guard dogs were bred for aggression, sporting dogs for their retrieval abilities, and scent hounds for their nose. The most successful scent hounds would be bred to other successful scent hounds, to attempt to produce puppies that would grow up to be excellent hunting dogs. In the same way, aggression was also selected for. If the breeder wanted war dogs, then aggressive dogs were deliberately bred to aggressive dogs to increase the chance that the puppies would be aggressive. In more recent years, we have bred most dogs to be pets and companions, so we do not wish to develop aggressive dogs. However, temperament still differs greatly between dog breeds, in most cases based on what the dogs were originally bred for. Today, responsible dog breeders breed for good temperament. A responsible breeder would never breed an aggressive dog. A well-bred dog might still be aggressive and vice versa, but certainly the chances of aggression are reduced. The same is true with cats. Persians, for example, could not last in the wild. They have been bred to be house cats, gentle and affectionate, whereas many other breeds are still closer to the basic wild cat.

So we recognize that we can breed for selected traits in animals. If we can selectively breed for them, the traits are genetic and they include behavior. It is difficult to suggest what might be construed as criminal behavior in an animal but we can certainly define and see aggressive behavior. So most of us will accept that certain behavioral traits, including aggression, are affected by breeding, in other words, by genetics, in animals. Now the fact that the animal is genetically predisposed to be potentially aggressive does not mean that it will be so. For example, we have all met many dogs whose breed may once have been bred for aggression, but individual members of that breed, through good socialization and training, are extremely well tempered. Therefore, despite the fact that the animal may be predisposed to be aggressive, the environment in which it was raised has influenced its behavior. In the same way, a dog that is not predisposed to violence but that experiences abuse or a very harsh environment may become aggressive. So, again, the effect of the environment has a strong influence.

What about people? We are animals, just like dogs, and, in fact, we share more than 98% of our DNA with chimps. We do not selectively breed humans, although a certain amount of selection does occur. For example, most people have partners who live in the same area of the world as they do. This is simply because, as they both live in the same region, they are more likely to meet than two people from opposite ends of the world. Today, people travel all around the world and emigrate to new countries, and thus do meet and marry people from far away; but, in general, most people meet and marry people who often grew up in the same town. In the past, this was much more common, as even traveling to the next village could be a day's horseback ride. Therefore, in the past, most people married and raised children within their own small world. So although we do not selectively breed people, a certain amount of selection does occur.

Why would a trait such as aggression remain in the population? If natural selection has been shaping our species and all others forever, why are we not perfect? There are several reasons.

- The environment keeps changing, so we (and all species) are forever trying to keep up, adapting to new situations.
- Heterozygosity exists, which means that recessive alleles may be hidden.

We often ask why do not **recessive alleles** that sometimes cause problems like disease die out? Let us look first at a very harmless example. There are many more dark-haired people than blondes in the world. As people travel and emigrate they mix everywhere. Despite the fact that blonde hair is recessive to the dominant dark hair, it does not die out. There are always still blonde haired people. This is because there is *no down side* to being blonde; there is no selective advantage for either hair color. So if a dark-haired person mates with a blonde, they could have blonde or brunette kids. If two dark-haired people mate, the kids could still be either, depending on the genotype of the parents. If both are heterozygous, then the kids could be blonde. Blonde is not lost, just hidden for a generation. But what if it were a *disadvantage* to be blonde? Say a new disease appeared that only killed blondes. What then? Would blondes survive? Well, it would certainly have an influence on the frequency of the allele, just as we saw the populations of birds with different beak sizes shift. But blonde alleles would not die out. Why? There could be many reasons:

- The genes for blonde hair may be *linked,* that is, on the same chromosomes, as very advantageous characteristics that were inherited, so when the advantageous genes were selected by natural selection, the blonde genes would just get carried along.
- *Mutations* can occur. Even if the allele became low in frequency, it frequently pops back up as the result of mutation. The gene that causes the trait can mutate to bring the trait back.
- *Heterozygosity.* When someone is heterozygous for a gene, he or she usually does not show the recessive trait. It is masked by the dominant one. So, even if there was a selective disadvantage to having a trait,

natural selection can only act on it if it is expressed. That is, if there was a disadvantage to being blonde, natural selection would act on the blondes themselves, the double recessives, but it would *not* act on the heterozygous people, those who have an allele for dark hair and one for blonde because they are phenotypically dark-haired. In this way, the allele is hidden and protected from natural selection; and when two heterozygous people get together, some of the children will be blonde. So the trait is never lost. Also, being heterozygous, with one of the dominant and one of the recessive alleles, might actually be more advantageous evolution-wise, as in the case of sickle cell anemia. In that case, it is better to be heterozygous.

Thus, a trait that was perhaps very advantageous in the past, like being aggressive, but is maladaptive now, will stick around, for any of the reasons listed above, and it will still appear, although it is now no longer advantageous to possess it.

## Conclusion

We can now see why appalling policies such as negative eugenics could never have worked. Even ignoring the very obvious moral and ethical reasons why eugenics was wrong, scientifically it could never work. Megalomaniacs such as Hitler are not likely to be affected by ethical or moral reasoning. However, scientific reasoning can be much more persuasive, as it can show that the policies, however warped, *will not work*. Even if a trait chosen for eradication was purely genetic (and remember that the traits chosen by Hitler and other genocide perpetrators, such as poverty, were *not* genetic), killing people with that trait would *not* eliminate it. It would not work, for the reasons listed above (linked, mutations, heterozygosity). This is why it is so imperative that right-minded people understand basic science and genetics. Then when people attempt to put policies in place, such as the racist policies in the early and middle part of the past century in North America, moral, ethical, and scientific reasons can be given to counter them. By misquoting science and claiming a scientific background for theories that were not backed by any science, politically active people brought about the implementation of laws that violated the charter and civil rights of all peoples. As the general public did not understand science, they could not see that the rhetoric that was spouted was completely flawed. Had enough members of the general public understood genetics, perhaps some of the horrors of the past could have been avoided.

# Questions for Further Study and Discussion

1. Assuming that it is hereditary, why would something unpleasant, such as morning sickness when pregnant, actually be selected for by natural selection?

2. Assume that violence is hereditary. Why, when we do not approve of violence, would it still be around in our society today?

# References

Gariépy, J.-L., Lewis, M.H., and Cairns, R.B. (1996). Genes, neurobiology and aggression: time frames and functions of social behaviours in adaptation. In Stoff, D.M. and Cairns, R.B. (Eds.), *Aggression and Violence* (pp. 41–48). Mahwah, NJ: Lawrence Erlbaum.

Griffiths, A.J.F., Wessler, S.R., Lewontin, R.C., Gelbart, W.M., Suzuki, D.T., and Miller, J.H. (2005). *Introduction to Genetic Analysis* (8th ed., pp. 2–3, 8–9, 18–19, 43–44, 48–49, 52–53, 74–75, 194, 197, 203, 561). New York: W.H. Freeman and Company.

Lamb, B.C. (2000). *The Applied Genetics of Plants, Animals, Humans and Fungi* (pp. 7, 10–12, 44, 225–226). Covent Garden, London: Imperial College Press.

Mendel, J.G. (1866). Versuche über Plflanzenhybriden. *Verhandlungen des naturforschenden Vereines in Brünn, Bd. IV für das Jahr,* 1865, Abhandlungen, 3–47 (Translated into English by C.T. Druery and William Bateson in 1901, *Experiments in plant hybridization, J. R. Hortic. Soc.,* 26, 1–32).

# Introduction to Genetic Predispositions for Behavior

# 4

## Introduction

When most criminologists consider the words "biology" and "crime" together, they assume that they refer only to genetic issues. As most of this book demonstrates, this is clearly not true. Nevertheless, much work has been done in the area of genetics that is relevant to criminology. As this is a fairly large topic, it will be covered over the next two chapters.

The first object of this introduction is to explain the important misconceptions concerning genetics, behavior, and crime (the greatest of which surrounds the so-called "XYY Man"). With the brief study of genetics in the preceding chapter, we can now begin to undo some of these misconceptions. There are many myths that surround the relationship between biology and behavior, and most have no basis in fact or, at best, relate more to the effects of the environment than genetics. To understand the experimental research next discussed, it is also important to understand how to design a good experiment to test a hypothesis. Some purported genetic studies are weak both in conception and in experimental design. As we study some examples, it will become apparent how difficult it is to conduct such studies on humans. Aside from the moral and ethical issues in behavioral research, no two humans are exactly alike and this makes generalizations about genetics and behavior, even from simple observational research, extremely difficult. In the final part of the chapter we explore the implications of this stubborn fact for comparing the behaviors of identical and fraternal twins. Twins, as we will see, provide us with a natural way to separate the effects of genetics and the environment on behavior.

## Misconceptions about Genetics

### Misconceptions about Animal Cloning

The idea that there is a genetic basis for crime is perhaps the most controversial topic in the field of biological influences on crime, but the controversy arises primarily from misconceptions about genetics. Dolly, the cloned sheep, is a classic example of such a misconception. Dolly was an English Finn Dorset, and she was cloned in England in 1996; she died in 2003. Dolly was not conceived naturally between a male and a female sheep, but was instead cloned from a single mammary cell from her mother. This cell was then treated as a "test tube lamb" and implanted in the mother's womb. The experiment was a major medical breakthrough, not because the researchers were able to create a new individual from another one without benefit of egg and sperm (because we have been able to do that for a long time), but rather because they used a cell that was already differentiated: it had already become a mammary cell, dedicated to mammary functions and nothing else. All the other functions of the body were turned off.

When an egg and sperm of any species fuse, they create a single cell and, at that stage and for the first few divisions, each cell is capable of performing every function in the body. Each cell must be originally capable of performing all functions because, even when an adult, every cell is genetically identical in a single person. But as the zygote grows into a fetus, the cells become specialized to do special jobs, such as being a nerve cell or a cell that secretes digestive enzymes. They then are said to have become *determined* and only perform as a specialized cell. However, as all cells are genetically identical in the body, containing the same DNA, each cell still has the blueprints for all functions. Functions other than those for which the cell has become specialized are turned off. The Dolly project proved that although cells turn off the capacity to do other things, they could still be provoked to do them again if necessary. This is a big breakthrough medically because it may mean that cells could be persuaded to take over the function of a damaged organ, such as a kidney or even the spinal column. That is, the research was related to medicine and the possibility that in the future a person could regenerate his or her own cells, perhaps regenerating a part of the spinal cord or a damaged liver. However, the public and the media did not understand the research and the amazing opportunities it may one day lead to for so many people. They also believed that this was the first time an animal had been cloned; however, the first animals to be artificially cloned lived over 50 years ago. A furor arose about the horror-movie idea of cloning people, such as an army of white supremacists. Of course, the big question brought up regularly in the tabloids was: what if someone tried to clone Hitler?

## Misconceptions about Human Cloning

Hypothetically speaking, could we clone Hitler? We will gamely ignore the basic fact that cloning requires some tissue and that Hitler was burned beyond recognition in a bunker in 1945. Even if some loyal supporter had managed to find some tissue, the preservation methods of the time were poor, so this is all a moot point. However, while we have the technical potential to genetically clone a person, we are not there yet. As well, what would be the point? The aim of cloning research is to work medically with individual cells in attempts to heal people with damaged organs or nerves. However, just for the sake of argument, let us just consider whether, if we were to hypothetically clone Hitler today, or any other evil person, would we have to be concerned? Think about this idea before reading further.

It is fiction that Hitler could be recreated by cloning, but the belief clearly implies that his criminal behaviors were genetic, and almost entirely genetic. This is patently not true. The truth is that if Hitler were cloned, there would be little to worry about. There is a general belief, perpetuated by television and film, that when a person is cloned, the result will inevitably be a carbon copy. We expect another identical adult, fully formed with brain, mind, and behaviors intact. This cannot happen. Dolly was created in a test tube and was implanted in her mother, who later gave birth to Dolly in the normal manner. But she could not have exactly the same Dolly sheep behaviors as the original.

To see why this is, consider another example. Imagine that a family lost an 18-year-old daughter in a car crash and wished to clone her. Despite today's headlines, they would not end up with a brand-new identical 18-year-old daughter. The reasons are strongly environmental:

1.  Someone would have to carry that fetus for 9 months, give birth to her, and then raise her until the age of 18. She would thus have either a much older original mother, or a completely new surrogate mother. With her older (or brand-new) mother, this girl could not be identical to the original; for one thing, if it were the original mother, she would probably try not to make any of the mistakes of the past.
2.  Her immediate family will also influence her in different ways. Let us assume that, in life, she had a sister who was one year older than herself and that they grew up together during the 1960s and 1970s. The new cloned baby would, in contrast, grow up over the next two

decades; and although the two may spend a lot of time together, she will be a child growing up with an adult sister, someone who is now at least 20 years old (assuming the dead sister was cloned immediately and allowing for 9 months *in utero*). This would be a very different sisterly relationship. The sibling rivalries would differ and, at maturity, the relationship, would also differ — she would, for example, always be the "baby sister."

3. The more general social environment will also have clearly changed. The cloned child will be raised amid different political and social values from the original. The 1960s had a pronounced effect on teenagers and young adults. For the Woodstock generation, social protest was high, anti-authoritarian and alternative roles were stressed, and the heroes and heroines of both political and popular culture were attractive role models. The original daughter would have known the Kennedys, the Beatles, the Marlboro Man, Vietnam, the new McDonald's chain, Pink Floyd, Sonny Bono and Cher, Peter, Paul, and Mary, marijuana as the illicit drug of choice, and relatively cheap college tuition. These and many other cultural influences helped form her wider social values and expectations. The generation X of the 1980s and 1990s had different priorities: first president Bush, terrorism, the first Gulf War, Rwanda, Sting, Madonna, getting any kind of job beyond the low end, Starbucks, Ecstasy as the probable new illicit drug of choice, health gyms, women's cancer rates, second-wave feminism, women and agency, tattoos, body piercing, narratives of sex abuse, and much higher college tuition were probably important to this generation. Would it even be stylish to smoke?

4. The neighborhood in which the clone daughter grows up will also have a major effect on her life; will it be a quiet town in northern British Columbia, downtown Toronto, the urban sprawl of California, or uptown New York? If it were the original neighborhood, this will also have changed.

5. The income level of her family will also affect her. The clone may grow up with a wealthy family, but the original's environment may have been relatively poor, especially when her parents were younger.

With just these five social influences, the chances that she will she end up exactly the same as the original sister are very low.

Genetically, she has the identical genes and is probably pretty much identical in looks to the original. But as a person, will she be the same? No, her life experiences will have been very different. Some general personality characteristics may be similar; she may still have the same type of passive personality or she may still be moody, but the *environment* and *social situation* she grew up in will have a major effect on all these traits. She will be an entirely unique human being, even more different from the original girl than identical twins would be. Identical twins, even if raised apart, are raised in the same decades; whereas this young girl will have completely different life experiences, making her absolutely unique.

So what about Hitler, or any other genocidal dictator? A cloned dictator would not be the same as the original. The person who was Hitler was created not only through his genes, but also (as are we all) through upbringing, experiences, and environment. Strict German schools, a certain family situation, and World War I had a major effect on the formation of the original personality, as did a bankrupt German economy and the Versailles Treaty. A cloned Hitler might strike fear into the hearts of everyone (even those who swear there are no biological explanations for crime), but it would be an unfounded fear — a cloned Hitler would not be the same man.

## Does All Crime Have the Same Single Cause?

Another misconception about genetics deals with overly reductive under-standings of genetics. Some people assume that by studying the relation between genetics and crime we are trying to find a single cause for all criminal behavior. As we have seen, there is a clear interaction between the environ-ment and genetic inheritance, and such an easy explanation is highly unlikely. At a minimum, we know from motivational studies that anomic stress is common in our competitive culture, and that mental illness or somatic dys-function is often involved in crime; we also know that the highly dysfunc-tional family environments can create anti-social personality types. Person A might kill his mother "because I always hated her getting on my case;" person B might kill her mother "because I want my inheritance;" person C might do it because "she ran off with my boyfriend;" and person D might do it because he or she was mentally ill and thought the mother was a demon. It is the same crime, matricide, but the reasons for committing it are widely different. In the same way, we all might have the same reason for committing a multitude of different crimes. The interactionist and dynamic nature of gene expression tells us that we need to look for multiple causes of multiple crimes.

When we look at genetic studies, it is easy to assume that something is a genetic trait when it is really an environmentally influenced trait, although it might be triggered by an underlying genetic trait. For example, a father, reunited with his son after many years, may be surprised to discover that his son has many of the same mannerisms as he does. Traits such as posture may be similar in both men. This could not have been learned as the two have only just met, so they assume it to be genetic. As with most things, such behavior has both genetic and environmental features. The actual posture they use is not inherited. However, their body shape is inherited, and most of us develop stances that are comfortable for our bodies. Because they both have the same body shape, the posture comes naturally to both of them. The posture is not a result of genetics; the body shape is.

## XYY Man: Truth and Fallacy

The relationship between genetics and aggression is often misconceived. The XYY chromosome episode may have been the most publicized event in criminology in the past century. Let us look at the history, the facts and the fallacies. People all have 46 chromosomes, 44 of which are somatic and two of which are the sex chromosomes. Women have two X chromosomes, and men have one X and one Y chromosome, so women are denoted as XX and men as XY; this is the normal configuration. The Y chromosome is considered the "male" chromosome because only men have it, but they have an X as well. You could say that they have one male and one female chromosome, but this would not be accurate. The "Y" chromosome does not mean "male;" XY together indicates a male (there are no people who are YY).

In 1961, a man was found with an extra Y chromosome — an XYY man. This interesting genetic anomaly was published quietly in a respected medical journal (Sandberg et al., 1961). This genetic event occurs once in about every 700 to 1000 male births (Hoffman, 1977). It is important to realize that this man was not, in any way, aggressive or a criminal, and the original researchers did not suggest that he was likely to be. Later readers of the article, however, assumed that an extra Y chromosome would lead to more "maleness," which was defined as aggressive and violent. Other researchers jumped on this bandwagon and began to take surveys of chromosome number, but they were not based on a wide sample taken from the general public. Instead, they made a simple statistical mistake; they used men in institutions for the criminally insane. These studies did show that XYY men seemed to be exceptionally violent. Then the media learned of this and greatly exaggerated the horror of the crimes committed by these few men. This, then, suggested to the public that XYY men were "huge hulks of 'supermaleness' spurred on to aggressive acts by the extra Y chromosome" (Mednick, 1987).

Officially, there were two groups that responded to this work and the resulting media and public hysteria. Kessler and Moos (1970) reviewed the literature and reasonably pointed out that the mental hospital findings were quite inconsistent. They were based on extremely small and carefully selected samples. A review of the same work today would result in the same response. This review prompted more scientific study of this arguably interesting genetic phenomenon, but this time using much more powerful and scientific studies. These researchers did not preselect by choosing people already incarcerated in criminal institutions, but instead examined large, non-criminal populations. One study examined 4139 men (the tallest in a birth cohort because XYY does usually produce tall men). In this group, only 12 were found to be XYY. They were found to be mildly criminal, but none were, in any way, violent (Mednick, 1987).

Sarbin and Miller (1970) performed a second review of the original work at the same time as the Kessler and Moos review. However, instead of the reasoned response of Kesler and Moos, this review was highly emotional, with a strong political agenda. Sarbin and Miller referred to all genetic studies of this type as "Demonism Revisited" and wanted all such studies banned, demanding that criminological research should be limited to social, economic, and political variables. Biology should never be considered (Mednick, 1987).

Any change in the chromosome number has major effects on a person, so having an extra Y chromosome is not good. Scientific, unbiased research on large samples of men found that XYY men are, in general, very tall; may have a certain level of mental retardation (Horgan, 1993; Hoffman, 1977); and also develop very bad acne (Witken et al., 1976). As well, a disproportionate number of men with XYY are criminal, but mildly criminal and not violent. Possession of an XYY genotype was attempted as a criminal defense in several cases in the 1970s, but it was not successful. The primary reason for its lack of success is that the courts stated that XYY evidence failed to meet reasonable standards of certainty because a causal link between the defendant's mental capacity and the genetic syndrome was not proven (Denno, 1988).

What then is the truth about this anomaly? The genetic part of XYY results in men who tend to be very tall and have bad acne, and are often, although not always, slightly mentally retarded. This is fact. But does it cause crime? Or, at least, are XYY men more likely to commit a violent crime than XY men? Here, we are back to the original argument about whether genetic inheritance causes something directly or indirectly. We need to ask how these genetic traits are going to affect the child's environment.

Imagine this boy's school days. Here is a boy of about 12 years old, an awkward age at best for boys. He is very tall for his age, maybe as much as a foot taller than the others. How will he be treated? His height alone might make him a bit of a hero, girls may be attracted to him, and the sports coaches will want him on their teams; so he might develop a lot of self-esteem, which boys of that age often lack, and he may do very well in later life. Now we need to add the mental retardation; it is not much, not enough to prevent him from going to a regular school or getting a job in later life, but it may be definitely noticeable. He is also prone to exceptionally bad acne, which alone often has a major effect during the teenage years. This boy, therefore, is not doing well in school and is probably going to get a low-paying, boring job as an adult. It is very likely that, in school, this boy will be teased and even bullied simply because he is different. Therefore, what began as a purely genetic phenotype — including abnormal height, low levels of mental retardation, and acne — is now being influenced by the environment created by the phenotype. Bullied children often turn to crime, in compensation or in retaliation. For example, if this boy is physically bullied, he might realize quickly that he cannot fight with his mind, but that he can fight with his size. In many cases, children with lower IQs, and low social skills, are predisposed to anti-social and even criminal behaviors. These will not necessarily be violent crimes, but crime all the same. So this XYY boy could end up committing criminal acts, but is it the result of his genetic make-up or because he has grown up in a bullied, nonnurturing environment? How much different would it be had he grown up in a different environment: if his teachers and sports coaches had praised his height and supported him in other activities to the best of his abilities? The answer is quite clear in the fact that many men in our society are XYY and are not even aware of it. Most live productive and satisfying lives. The basic genetic blueprint results in a phenotype but none of these genetic traits lead to crime. It is only when they are integrated with the environment that such predispositions could lead to crime.

And one final clarification about XYY — misconceptions about this trait have been used as an argument both for and against a biological explanation for crime. XYY is caused by a random mutation at meiosis, when the chromosomes are originally replicated, so XY becomes XXYY briefly. They should then separate once, and then again until each sperm has just one of the four. In an XYY male, for some unknown reason, one of the sperm cells ends up with two Y chromosomes instead of just one. So when it meets an egg with an X, an XYY child is produced. This is a random mutation and it is not heritable; that is, it is not passed on to the next generation. The most important fact for this study is often not mentioned at all: XYY is simply not a genetic issue in the traditional meaning of the word.

## Problems with Experimental Design

In performing a scientific experiment, the researcher must eliminate all variables between research subjects except the one trait being studied. This is done so that the researcher can see what effect varying that one variable has on the outcome of the experiment. For example, a researcher wishes to test a new diet for chickens to see if the chickens grow larger on the new diet. The researcher divides a group of chickens into two groups. One group, the experimental group, is fed the new diet and the other group, the control group, is fed the old diet. The results show that the chickens fed the new, experimental diet grew to be twice as large as the controls. Does this mean conclusively that the diet increased their weight? The answer is no; there is not enough information in the above example to come to that conclusion. However, people often do leap to such conclusions. It is important to look at all experiments very carefully to see whether they were conducted correctly before we can determine whether their conclusions are valid. With just the above information, it is not possible to determine whether it was the diet that caused the change in growth. To ensure that the results were valid, the researcher would have to eliminate all other differences between the experimental and control groups. For example, what if the experimental group was kept in nice, well-lit conditions with solid floors and lots of space in which to peck around, and the controls were kept in battery-hen conditions with a mesh floor, which chickens, and most animals, dislike? Do you still think that we could conclude that the diet made the difference? Perhaps it did, but maybe not; maybe the experimental chickens were much happier and healthier than the controls and thus just naturally put on more weight. The differing conditions could be the cause of the weight gain, and it might have nothing to do with the diet. So it is clear that we need to eliminate all the other variables to clearly see the effect of just one variable.

If we wish to study the effect of, for example, zinc on a plant, we would conduct an experiment with a large number of plants, divided into two identical cohorts. The plants should be genetically identical in all ways (plants are easy to propagate from a piece of plant and thus are very simple to clone). They should also be raised exactly the same way: the same lighting, food, soil, water, etc. The only thing changed would be the zinc level. Because zinc is the only difference between these two groups of plants, we can conclude that any differences are caused by the zinc, and we could look at thousands of plants quite easily — simple.

But it is not so simple in animals. If we wish to look at the effects of Vitamin B6 in rats, we could do the same sort of thing. We could test many rats (not so many as plants, of course, because it would be expensive and difficult). Rats do breed fast, but still they do not have that many babies, and we cannot get them all genetically identical like the plants because cloning is still very experimental and expensive. It is also ethically questionable as well as being very difficult. So, using the rats we have, we can go the next step as above and divide them into two groups and give them the same food and treatment in everything except for the vitamin difference. We should, therefore, be able to find that any differences would be related to the vitamin difference, right? Not necessarily. The observed differences might be the result of other differences in the animals, for example, genetic backgrounds. Even if the rats all had the same parents, they are not clones. They are still different; like brothers and sisters. They share some genes but are still unique. What else might make a difference? The environment is a likely suspect. Perhaps it is the way they were raised, the foods they had as babies, the exercise they got, etc. In a rat colony we can control for a lot of those things; but even with a simple lab animal, it is difficult to eliminate all the other variables.

Then we need to see what happens if there are other factors involved, such as how the plant reacts to getting both zinc and magnesium. There might be some interaction between these two metals that prevents the uptake of one or the other. A doctor will often tell a patient that a medicine will affect the uptake of certain vitamins, so they should take supplements. Therefore, the next step would be to start adding another variable, and then another and so on to see what might happen in real life. If a soil high in magnesium will either prevent the uptake of zinc or, worse, cause a fatal overload of the system, there is no point in advising farmers that zinc will help their crops grow. We need to know how the factor we have isolated reacts to other parts of its environment. But to do so, we must be able to separate each factor first, see the individual results, and then start looking at all the possible combinations.

Another confounding effect in any experiment is *sample size.* In the above chicken diet example, a researcher has two groups of chickens kept under identical conditions, with the same-sized cages, same lighting and everything else the same. The only difference between the experimental and control groups is the diet. The chickens in the experimental group grow twice as large as the control chickens. Think about the reliability of the conclusion if the experiment is performed on:

- 2000 chickens? Conclusive.
- 200 chickens? Still a good sample size.
- 20 chickens? May be significant; certainly interesting, and a diet company might like to take it further. This is not a very conclusive sample size as ten chickens in each group is not many. Perhaps the results would suggest that a larger experiment is warranted.
- 2 chickens? Clearly not conclusive.

In a sample size of two chickens, one chicken was fed one diet and one another, and there certainly was an effect. Unfortunately, we see people accepting this as evidence every day: "My friend tried this diet and lost 20 pounds." But does the person check to see how many people did not lose any weight on this diet, or even gained weight? How many people make assumptions about a country based on their experience of meeting two people from that country? We should not do it, but we do.

In science, a sample size of one is not an experiment. Why not? In the two chicken sample, one chicken is definitely larger. Why would that not be acceptable evidence? Because it could easily be the result of chance. It is similar to tossing a coin twice and coming up heads each time. If you tried that now, I am sure that many people would get this result. But what if you tossed the coin 200 times and it came up heads every time, or even 75% of the time? You would be suspicious and not want to make any bets with the owner of that coin. Therefore, random chance must be taken into account. Chance could easily explain why one chicken gained weight and the other did not. It might even explain the difference in ten chickens. However, when the sample size increases to 100 or 1000, then chance will only play a very small role. Therefore, to eliminate the risk of chance entering into the experiment, an experiment must have a large sample size.

An experiment can also be strengthened by conducting a crossover study. This involves swapping the treatment and control groups halfway through the experiment. In this way, half the chickens get the new diet and half get the old diet. The researchers record weights and then feed the diets to the opposite group and weigh them. If all the variables are balanced, then the weight increase should follow the diet type. This proves that the effect is not just in "those chickens."

To consider an experiment valid, it must also be *repeatable*. If a single experiment shows an effect in 2000 chickens, it sounds valid. But what if no other researcher can duplicate the result? Often we see an experiment that has been repeated many times. This is good; it validates the results. However, it is also interesting to note whether the experiment is being replicated by the same researchers or by a different group. Often researchers will continue the same line of thought over several years of research, so experiments get repeated in the same lab by the same people. There is nothing wrong with this practice, as it would be foolish to research one area and then suddenly change research field. People frequently continue in the same research area and their results are perfectly valid. However, it is always nice to see that other researchers in other labs have been able to repeat the experiment with different animals or plants and get the same general result. This does not always happen because few want to be part of a second group to prove something new. But when you look at studies, consider whether it is a series of studies by the same group or different research groups. If it is a similar study performed by many different labs and researchers, then it is considered much more robust. The case gets even stronger, or more robust, if the experiments are repeated in different countries and researchers still get the same result. For example, the breeds of chickens may be quite different, but the diet still works. Or, more to the point with our interests, the entire human culture may be quite different in different countries. So a strong or robust experiment will have a large sample size, and is repeated many times, by different researchers, in different labs and different countries, and gets the same results.

What happens when we want to look at a factor in humans? It is much more difficult than with plants or animals. Clearly, we cannot ethically deal with them like lab animals. Actually, we can and do in some respects. For example, when we test a new drug, we frequently take 500 people with a particular disease who are desperate for a cure and treat half with the new drug and half with a placebo (or a fake drug). These are generally *double-blind studies*, so the experimenters and the patients are both unaware of what they are taking to eliminate the risk of either the patients "wanting a cure" so badly that they will think they are getting better when they are not; or the researchers expecting those getting the drug to improve and thus ranking them as improved, when they are not. For example, 100 people were monitored after having heart surgery, and it was found that those who (insert phrase of interest at this point — e.g., ate real butter, drank red wine, etc.) had a higher survival rate. What is the problem with such an experiment? People are different in just about every way. Thus, they would have been of different ages, different exercise levels, etc., and definitely of different genetic backgrounds. We all know that many things have a genetic predisposition for certain problems, such as heart disease or diabetes. A family doctor always asks new patients for their medical history and that of their parents, as people with parents who have had heart problems or diabetes are predisposed, or more likely, to develop these problems. When we do experiments with people, therefore, it is almost impossible to control for all other variables. It is difficult to know which variable is causing an effect. Is it something different in their environment? Is it one particular part of the environment? Or is it their genetics?

Clearly we cannot clone people either ethically or even possibly, but clones do exist in nature — identical twins. Twin studies are a remarkably helpful way of studying many factors, both genetic and environmental, in humans.

## Introduction to Twin Studies

There are two types of twins: (1) monozygotic twins (MZ) and (2) dizygotic twins (DZ). The terms relate to the number of zygotes taken to create these two people. Mono (one) zygotic means just one zygote was involved, and dizygotic means that there were two zygotes.

When an egg meets with a sperm, they each carry half the genetic complement needed to create a person. As well, the egg carries everything else needed for life. When the two meet, they create one complete zygote; that is, a single diploid cell (diploid = organism with its chromosomes in pairs). This single cell contains everything it needs to eventually become a complete person. This single cell then divides into two, then those two divide into four, those four into eight, etc., and this division keeps on going and the entire fetus is produced. Indeed, it keeps on going until the person dies because cells must be replaced all the time; for example, blood cells only live about 28 days.

Normally, one zygote equals one person. And also, normally, although a man releases millions of sperm, a woman usually only releases one egg at a time, once per month.

## Dizygotic Twins

Dizygotic twins are a result of two zygotes creating two people. Instead of releasing one egg, the female releases two. There are thus two eggs floating around and millions of sperm, so both eggs are fertilized, and the result is two babies. The only unusual thing here is that the woman released two eggs. This is relatively unusual but it is an inherited feature. Women who release two eggs at a time tend to have daughters who also release two eggs at a time. Each individual is still absolutely unique, just like siblings, only they result from two eggs and two sperm that happened to fuse at the same time, within hours or up to 3 days of each other, rather than some years apart.

We traditionally say that siblings share 50% of their genes with each other, although this is a little misleading, as the entire human race shares 99% of their genes with each other. This is really quite obvious if you think about it. If you were to take two random people and look at the similarities between them, you would see that we are all almost identical. We all have two arms, two legs, and two eyes; we digest the same way, using the same enzymes, which are produced by the same metabolic processes; etc. It is only the little things that make us different, such as facial shape, height, hair color, etc. We focus on these differences but there really is not that much difference between us. Look at people around you and observe their features. Everyone is designed on the same plan. Our eyes are all close to being in the same place, and our mouths are very much the same shape. There are only small differences.

So, as all humans share 99% of the same genes, when we say that siblings share 50% of their genes, we really mean 50% of that 1% that makes us different (Raine, 1993). And actually, this 50% is a bit of an error too because 50% is an average. By random chance, some twins will share more than 50% and some will share less.

Full siblings inherit their genes from their parents but they are not the same as their parents. Every gene has several possible versions (or alleles), and the parents each have two copies of that gene; they might both be the same allele or different ones, and they each give one to each offspring. So, siblings share the same genetic pool; they both obtained their genes from the same place, but each child can have a different version of the gene, which is why we are all unique. Thus, dizygotic twins are as similar to each other genetically as regular siblings; the only difference is that they are the same age.

## Monozygotic Twins

Monozygotic twins are two people that come from one zygote, a zygote that was supposed to produce only one person. During the early stages of development, each cell still has the ability to do everything. After a few more cell divisions, the cells will become *determined;* that is, it is as if they decide what they are going to do with the rest of their lives, and for a cell, the choices are skin cell, nerve cell, kidney cell, blood cell, etc. They are not changed yet; they are just becoming determined; that is, they have become committed to a particular developmental pathway. After a few more divisions, they become *differentiated;* that is, they actually change into the particular type of cell to which they were committed. They then change into a skin cell and turn off all the functions that they would have needed if they were a kidney cell or a blood cell and concentrate solely on being a skin cell. Remember that this was the important thing about Dolly the cloned sheep — not that she was cloned (that had been done) but that a mammary cell, which was committed to being a mammary cell and had been functioning as such for years and had turned off all other functions, could be convinced to turn back on all the functions it had turned off and that one cell could do everything again and produce another entire sheep.

However, before the cells are determined and differentiated, when the zygote consists of just a very few cells, each cell can still produce an entire person. If something happens at this point (and in nature we are not sure exactly what it is that happens), something cleaves or splits this little zygote, so that instead of being, for example, a four-celled zygote, it becomes two separate and complete two-celled zygotes, which both go on to become separate people.

Therefore, one zygote, which came from only one sperm and one egg, becomes two zygotes and, therefore, two people. The difference between a monozygotic twin and a dizygotic twin is that monozygotic twins are genetically identical; they have the same genetic makeup exactly, so they are natural clones. They will grow into two identical people with exactly the same versions (or alleles) of every gene. They still share 50% of that 1% of their genes with each parent, but share 100% between each other. These are monozygotic twins. Unlike dizygotic twins, which share 50% of that 1% of their genes with each other, they share everything.

Can dizygotic twins be a boy and a girl? Yes, the mother contributed an X to each but the father could have contributed a Y to one and an X to the other. Can monozygotic twins be a boy and a girl? No, they are identical, so they share the same sex chromosomes; they can be boys or girls, but not one of each.

## Explanations for Twin Coincidences

We have all heard of twin coincidences in the popular tabloid press, such as the famous story of two identical (monozygotic) twins who were separated at birth and then "discover each other" as adults. It is somewhat unusual for identical twins to be separated, but people who want to adopt a child, particularly a baby, often do not want two babies at once. Authorities try not to separate twins, but it is not always possible to keep them together. In this story, these two identical twins are separated at birth, and they accidentally meet each other 40 years later. They look identical. We would expect that, because they are identical twins. The environment can affect the way we look but looks are strongly influenced by our genes. And then we hear all this other information that seems so amazing, such as the fact that they are both firefighters, they both wear glasses and have moustaches, they both married nurses named Linda, and they both own terrier dogs called Spot! Coincidence or biology?

This seems amazing. If you accept the story, then it would appear that genes not only control the way we look, but also our careers and the names and careers of our spouses. This is the sort of tabloid material that gives twin studies a bad name. Let us look at it and see if we can explain all these similarities. Which of these are inherited traits?

- *They both married women named Linda.* Is there a gene for that? No. It is probably just a coincidence... or maybe not; what else might affect that? Think of the names given to children today in North America. Although some names go back 2000 years, many names had never been heard of 50 years ago or even 20 years ago. The popularity of certain names rises and falls over time. Thus, the name may just have been common in the age group of people they associated with (they are the same age, remember). Also, names are often very specific to different countries. For example, extremely common names in America are not the same as common names in Japan or Germany. The twins we are discussing were probably both adopted in North America so it is not particularly far-fetched to find that they both married women named Linda.
- *They both have a dog named Spot, and it is a terrier.* Is this an inherited trait, to buy a terrier and to name him Spot? I do not think so, but maybe they both grew up at a time when there was a cartoon that they both watched in which there was a dog named Spot. I wonder

how many people have Jack Russell terriers named Eddie after the one on the show *Frasier?* So the fact that they both married someone named Linda and had a dog named Spot is probably related to their mutual environment — not that they grew up together, but that they were both adopted in the same country at the same time. It has nothing whatsoever to do with their genes. There are often sensible explanations for what seems like something that is just too much of a coincidence.

- *They both have moustaches.* Is this inherited? Men's facial hair arrangements go in and out of fashion. Recently, goatees were popular, whereas very few men wore them a few years ago. Both these men probably succumbed to fashion, so there was a very good chance that both would have moustaches. This would be an entirely environmental reason. However, there might also be a genetic component. The ability to grow a moustache is inherited to a certain extent. Some men have much thicker facial hair than others, and the ability to grow a thick moustache may well relate to their shared genes. Did their genes make them grow a moustache? No; well, actually, yes and no. Why do we do anything like cut our hair or curl our hair or grow a beard? Usually we do it because it suits us. So why would both men grow a moustache? Presumably it suited their facial shape, and that was inherited. So there is a genetic component in there, but only a very indirect one. There is no gene that says, "Grow a moustache, young man," but there are factors, both genetic and environmental, that might predispose a person to wear a moustache. Facial hair is also often grown to hide a defect, such as a hare lip or receding chin. The problems that are being hidden were genetic, so the facial hair growth could be said to have its roots in the genes, but only very indirectly. There is no direct genetic link that makes a person grow a moustache, but there *might* be an underlying genetic predisposition, a very indirect link.
- *They both wear glasses.* This could be related to a genetic predisposition for bad eyesight.
- *They both became firemen.* Could this be related to genetics? Not very likely. However, careers go through popularity surges. Some years ago, a popular television show about a country veterinarian in Yorkshire inspired many children to become veterinarians. Forensic shows and movies have dramatically increased public interest in becoming a forensic scientist. Therefore, the fact that these two men both became firemen could easily have been the result of fashion or of a big drive to recruit firemen when both men were young. What else might affect their choice? Genes could have had an effect, albeit indirect once again. Certain people crave excitement more that others or are more

fearless than others. As well, a part of a person's physical build is genetic, although it is obviously influenced by diet and exercise. They would need to be strong and physically fit to be firemen.

- *Both men married nurses.* It again sounds like an amazing coincidence, but this was an obvious career choice for women at a certain time. Both men were the same age, and they probably married women of similar ages, so the women had the same cultural influences. What else might influence their choice of spouse? People with professions in similar fields often meet; for example, both would work shift work, they may come into contact professionally, and both are in caring professions, and thus might have similar outlooks.

Therefore, it is clear that although it may have sounded amazing when the story was first presented, most of the coincidences can be easily explained. The explanations are based in the repeatability or standardization of roles and styles in culture — not in genetics.

In all the cases addressed in this book, any genetic links to behavior, and therefore potentially criminogenic behavior, will be indirect links to a predisposition for a behavior. None will be direct links. Genetics does not work that way. It is never going to be possible to be able to say that the biological makeup of a person caused them to commit a crime, simply because it could not. All that genetics can do is give someone a predisposition to behave in a certain way. A predisposition. This does not mean that they will behave in that way, only that they are perhaps more likely to behave in that way than the average person. Also, the predisposition is toward a behavior, not to a crime. The behavior may lead to a person committing a crime, but may equally lead to something totally noncriminal. For example, the predisposition may be for a person to be somewhat impulsive. This may lead them to shoplift or steal a car. It may equally well lead them to shop impulsively at garage sales. The predisposition and the behavior it may lead to — impulsivity — are the same, and may have a basis in biology; the results are quite different. Whether the behavior is criminal or not will be greatly affected by upbringing, environment, and choice.

One of the reasons that people often seem fearful of considering a biological basis for behavior and, subsequently, crime is that people believe that scientists will discover something that shows that "this causes that." Behavior is not that straightforward. An example of very straightforward genetics is: "this gene causes the flower to be colored red or white" depending on the version or allele of the gene the plant inherits. Even this kind of genetics often gets more complicated than one gene. Simple things such as hair and eye color are determined by several genes, so something as complex as behavior can only be influenced by many genes, and even then they can only offer a slight predisposition for a type of behavior. Whatever the genes produce will be strongly affected by the environment and can be totally changed by it.

When we look at the following twin studies, we need to look at the significance of the results just as we would look at any other data. We must not get caught up in the excitement of facts such as both men married a woman named Linda and named their dogs Spot. We need to look at the more important aspects of their similarities and also at their differences; then we can see what is significant and what is just a case of random chance. We need to compare the similarities between these two men and the general population in order to work out whether something is significant. For example, if you were to consider a random group of 1000 people in the world, is it significant that, of this group, 90% are under 30 years old, 100% speak and write the English language extremely well, and 80% are wearing jeans. This would not be at all significant if your group of people were undergraduate university students in North America. It might be much more significant in a different culture or country. Therefore, before you determine whether something is significant, you must first compare the trait with the norm for that population. A behavior that might seem very significant may not be at all significant in that particular situation or population.

## Using Twins to Study Genetic and Environmental Influences on Behavior

Twins provide a totally natural, nonexperimental situation, so they are a wonderful tool with which to study factors that are environmentally or genetically determined. Certain traits are often studied using *concordance rates*. For example, if the concordance rate for a certain trait in monozygotic twins is determined as 70%, then this means that the chance of the other twin developing the trait is 70%. If we compare the concordance rates for a specific trait between monozygotic (MZ) and dizygotic (DZ) twins — for example, if the trait is 70% in the MZ twins but only 5% in the DZ twins — then it would appear to have a heritable component. The twins who are genetically identical are more much more likely to share the same trait than twins who are not genetically identical. Therefore, the trait relates to genetics. If the concordance rates were 70% in both MZ twins and DZ twins, then it would obviously be an environmental effect, as the fact that the MZ twins are genetically identical does not appear to make any difference. If the researcher went further and compared the trait with unrelated people, and found that the concordance rate was 70% in both MZ and DZ twins but only 10% in unrelated people, then it would indicate something either environmentally specific only to twins or something that is both genetic and environmental.

In summary, MZ twins raised together share 100% of their genes and 100% of their environment. DZ twins raised together share 50% of their genes (remember in both cases that it is just 50% of 1%) and 100% of their environment. Thus, because they share the same environment, any differences in a trait between MZ twins and DZ twins is caused by their genetics, and not the environment. If the two, MZ and DZ twins have the same concordance rates for a trait, then the trait is more related to the environment, and not to the genes. So twins offer a perfect real-life method to study both the effect of genetics and the effect of the environment on a behavior. The next chapter considers some actual studies and their results.

## Conclusion

We have now worked through some of the important misconceptions concerning genetics, behavior, and crime, the greatest of which surrounds the so-called "XYY Man." The many myths that surround the relationship between biology and behavior either have no factual basis or relate more to the effects of the environment than genetics. We have also seen how a good experiment can be designed to test a hypothesis. We have found that some purported genetic studies are weak both in conception and in experimental design. The study of twins, as we shall see, provides us with a natural way to separate the effects of genetics and the environment on behavior.

## Questions for Further Study and Discussion

1. Explain why we need to remove all but one of the variables in an experiment to examine that variable. If we eliminate all the other variables, how then do we work out how the variable is influenced in the real world?
2. Why is it unlikely that we will ever find a gene for crime?
3. Why are twin studies so useful in criminological research?
4. Explain the concept of cloning. What prevents human "carbon copies"?

## References

Denno, D.H. (1988). Human biology and criminal responsibility: free will or free ride? *Univ. Pennsylvania Law Rev.*, 137, 615–671.

Hoffman, B.F. (1977). Two new cases of XYY chromosome complement. *Can. Psych. Assoc. J.*, 22, 447–455.

Horgan, J. 1993. Eugenics Revisited. *Sci. Am.,* 254 (June), 122–131.

Kessler, S. and Moos, R.H. (1970). The XYY karyotype and criminality: A review. *J. Psych. R.,* 7, 153–170.

Mednick, S.A. (1987). Biological factors in crime causation: the reactions of social scientists. In Mednick, S.A., Moffitt, T.E., and Stack, S.A. (Eds.), *The Causes of Crime: New Biological Approaches* (pp. 1–2). New York: Cambridge University Press.

Raine, A. (1993). Genetics and Crime. *The Psychopathology of Crime: Criminal Behavior as a Clinical Disorder* (pp. 47–80). San Diego: Academic Press.

Sandberg, A.A., Koeph, G.F., Ishihara, T., and Hauschka, T.S. (1961). An XYY human male. *Lancet,* 1, 488–489.

Sarbin, T.R. and Miller, J.E. (1970). Demonism revisited: the XYY chromosomal anomaly. *Iss. Crim.,* 5, 195–207.

Witkin, H.A., Mednick, S.A., Schulsinger, F., Bakkestrom, E., Christiansen, K.O., Goodenough, D.R., Hirschhorn, K., Lundsteen, C., Owen, D.R., Philip, J., Rubin, D.B., and Stocking, M. (1976). XYY and XXY men: criminality and aggression. *Science,* 193, 547–555.

# Evidence for Genetic Predispositions for Criminogenic Behavior

# 5

## Introduction

This chapter introduces the value of twin studies and the problems inherent in them. This will lead, in turn, to adoption studies, which more clearly separate genetics and the environment. Numerous researchers from many countries have amassed convincing data that demonstrate the relationship between genotype and behavior. Some of these studies have limitations, which will be discussed, but overall the evidence for a relationship seems overwhelming. These genetic studies also provide some of the most important data about the role of the environment in criminogenic behavior. It is clear from these studies that biological influences on behavior such as hormonal imbalances can be therapeutically altered or changed. Most of us have heard of hormone replacement therapy for menopause. Often, it is thought that if a behavioral problem has a genetic basis, then there can be no cure and DNA becomes destiny. This chapter begins to explore the reasons this is not so.

It is the genes that control such things as hormone levels; so if the genetic problem results in a hormone imbalance, it can probably be treated. Genes do not cause crime, they simply influence all aspects of our body, including all the chemical messengers in the body, such as hormones and neurotransmitters; these, in turn, influence behavior. Most of the studies examined simply indicate whether a particular type of criminal or criminogenic behavior has a genetic basis, and how much the genes influence that behavior. They do not go deeper into determining which genes are implicated and what they actually do in the body. In later chapters we consider other biological influences on criminal behavior, some of which have a genetic basis that has been linked to a specific gene variant, and to the problems caused by an anomaly in that gene.

## Twin Studies

As Chapter 4 indicated, twins provide a natural way to study the effects of the environment and genetics on behavior. Raine (1993) summarized some of the early twin studies, which vary widely in terms of the country of origin, age and sex composition, sample size, determination of zygosity (i.e., how they determined whether they were monozygotic [MZ] twins or dizygotic [DZ] twins), and definitions of crime (Table 5.1). However, all of the studies show greater concordance rates for criminality in MZ as opposed to DZ twins. That is, every study shows a heritable or genetic component to the behavior that results in crime. However, as Raine (1993) points out, there are many issues to consider here. In the earlier experiments, the sample size was quite small in some cases, although some of the studies did have reasonably large sample sizes. The more robust studies are those of Christiansen (1977a) and Dalgaard and Kringlen (1976). Christiansen's study also separated males and females, which few studies have done.

If you look at the list of studies in Table 5.1 and notice the years in which they were conducted, it is clear that two studies took place in Germany during the Nazi era (Stumpfl, 1936; Kranze, 1935). Therefore, it could be anticipated that these studies might have been politically biased, as the Nazi belief was that all crime, as well as poverty, mental disability, and other factors, were entirely genetically controlled. Therefore, one might expect these two studies to show the highest concordance rates for MZ twins as opposed to DZ twins. However, the concordance rates in these studies are actually much lower than in other studies. A later reanalysis of Kranze's work showed that it was one of the best of the early studies (Raine, 1993). In *all* cases one can see that there is higher concordance for crime in MZ twins than in DZ twins, indicating a genetic component.

Raine (1993), who compiled Table 5.1, averaged concordance rates across all studies and weighted them for sample sizes, giving greater weight to those studies with adequate samples. On average, he found that these 13 studies resulted in concordances of 51.5% for MZ twins and 20.6% for DZ twins.

Raine (1993) went further and reanalyzed all the raw data, eliminating or weighting other potentially confounding factors. He first removed the German studies from the Nazi era because of possible bias. He then removed those with small sample sizes. He then adjusted for zygosity determination. Twins

**Table 5.1   Concordance Rates from Twin Studies of Criminal Behavior**

| Ref. | Location | Sex | MZ Twins % Concordance | $(N)^a$ | DZ Twins % Concordance | $(N)^a$ | Zygosity |
|---|---|---|---|---|---|---|---|
| Lange (1929) | Bavaria | M | 77 | (13) | 12 | (17) | Resemblance |
| Legras (1932) | Holland | M | 100 | (4) | 0 | (5) | Blood |
| Rosanoff et al. (1934) | U.S.A. | M | 76 | (38) | 22 | (23) | Resemblance |
| | U.S.A. | F | 26 | (7) | 25 | (4) | Resemblance |
| Stumpfl (1936) | Germany | M | 65 | (18) | 37 | (19) | Resemblance |
| | Germany | F | 67 | (3) | 0 | (2) | Resemblance |
| Kranze (1935) | Prussia | M | 66 | (32) | 54 | (43) | Blood |
| Borgstrom (1939) | Finland | M | 75 | (4) | 40 | (5) | Blood |
| Slater (1953) | England | M | 50 | (2) | 30 | (10) | Not given |
| Yoshimashu (1961) | Japan | M | 61 | (28) | 11 | (18) | Blood |
| Dalgaard and Kringlen (1976) | Norway | M | 26 | (31) | 15 | (54) | Blood |
| Christiansen (1977b) | Denmark | M | 35 | (71) | 13 | (120) | Questionnaire |
| | Denmark | F | 21 | (14) | 8 | (27) | Questionnaire |
| **Total** | | | **51.5%** | **(262)** | **20.6%** | **(345)** | |

[a]   N = number of pairs of twins. Summary figures are weighted for sample sizes.

[b]   A reanalysis of these data with additional subjects by Cloninger and Gottesman (1987) resulted in correlations of .74 for MZ twins and .47 for DZ twins, indicating a heritability of .54.

*Source:* Raine, A. (1993). Genetics and crime. In *The Psychopathology of Crime: Criminal Behavior as a Clinical Disorder* (p. 57). London: Academic Press. With permission of Elsevier Press.

are often said to be MZ because they look very similar. However, siblings often look alike and would look even more so if they were the same age. Therefore, the only true way to determine zygosity (whether the twins come from one zygote or two) is by DNA analysis. DNA analysis was not available then, but blood type can be a useful indicator. Therefore, Raine separately analyzed the studies that used zygosity determined by blood. He also looked at data from males and females separately. In all cases, concordance rates were much higher in MZ twins than in DZ twins, ranging from 53.5:28 to 48.1:14.5 (Raine, 1993). As Raine points out, the two most recent and robust studies that he considered (Dalgaard and Kringlen, 1976; Christiansen, 1977b) showed concordance rates two to three times higher in MZ twins as compared with DZ twins, which clearly shows a significant heritability for crime.

Some people have suggested that all twin studies should be ignored due to possible political bias, small sample sizes, and lack of true determination of zygosity in some of the early studies, but Raine's reanalysis clearly shows that this is erroneous. Even when Raine eliminated the studies with potential political bias, small sample sizes, and those that did not determine zygosity by blood, the results still hold true. In almost all cases, MZ twins are at least twice as likely to be concordant for crime as DZ twins (Raine, 1993), which demonstrates a very powerful genetic component.

A few studies separated males and females and showed that, overall, the concordance rates were lower in females than in males, but this may just be an artifact of the small sample sizes involved, as fewer women are involved in crime (Raine, 1993). Although the small number of female twins studies should suggest caution in interpreting the results, the concordance rates in female MZ twins were extremely high, supporting a genetic component as well (Raine, 1993). Further studies in this area would be valuable.

These experiments are robust, as they have been repeated by different researchers, using different samples of twins, in different countries, and even in different decades. More recent studies of various groups of twins have confirmed a genetic basis (Carey, 1996).

One issue that is always of interest in criminology is whether juvenile and adult crime have similar or different etiologies. Cloninger and Gottesman reanalyzed many of the older classic twin studies and divided them into adult and juvenile crime (1987). They looked at studies from around the world, ranging from 1931 to 1977, and compared concordance rates between MZ twins and DZ twins for juveniles and adults (Christiansen et al., 1977, 1974; Shields, 1977; Dalgaard and Kringlen, 1976; Hayashi, 1967; Yoshimashu, 1961; Rosanoff et al., 1941; Kranze, 1937; Stumpfl, 1936; Lange, 1931). Although a strong concordance for adult crime was seen in MZ twins as compared with DZ twins, there was little or no concordance seen for juvenile delinquency. This finding may relate to the fact that juvenile crime is very common and that it is often a passing phase. In many cases, the same researchers have done research on both adult and juvenile crime, so the results are not related to researcher bias.

One of the most famous sets of twin studies was conducted in Denmark. Denmark is a remarkable country in the sense that it keeps official registries of many factors, including criminal activity, alcoholism, and mental illness. Denmark also permits researchers to obtain these data, including the names and addresses of the persons recorded. Although obtaining such information in many countries would not be considered acceptable due to privacy and human rights concerns, the Danish databases are extremely valuable in such research as they provide comprehensive data on a very large sample of people. These Danish data, first looked at by Christiansen (1977b, 1974), comprise one of the most famous and also one of the largest twin studies. Christiansen looked at a total twin population of 3586 twin pairs from one area in Denmark. As with all the previous studies, a much higher concordance was observed in the MZ twins for criminal behavior (male-male) than in male-male DZ twins. This finding again supports the premise that identical twins inherit some biological characteristic(s) that increases their risk of being registered for criminal activity.

Lyons (1996) performed a more recent study that relates to North America. This is an ongoing study that is still generating results. Subjects were drawn from the Vietnam Era Veteran Twin registry. The subjects were all male, and the registry was compiled from military records of men who served in the U.S. military during the Vietnam War. Utilizing such a database does remove certain variables, such as age, as all the men must have been within a specific age range, and political and social issues must have been relatively similar for all. However, all were soldiers who served in a specific war, which might have an influence on the results.

Zygosity was self-determined, and blood type and photos were also used (which was considered 95% accurate from previous tests). The study was very large, consisting of 3226 pairs of twins; 55% were monozygotic twins. The proportion of dizygotic twins was lower because there were no opposite sex twins involved — which reduces another variable.

Questionnaires were sent to the subjects, and thus all data were self-reported rather than from actual criminal records. Racial breakdown of the respondents was 90.4% white, 4.9% non-Hispanic, 2.7% African-American, 2.7% Hispanic, 1.3% First Nations, and 0.7% other (Lyons, 1996). Therefore, the data were heavily biased toward whites — their numbers were slightly higher than in the war itself, but whites also had a higher response rate to questionnaires (Lyons, 1996).

Lyons asked the respondents the following questions:

*Early arrest:* Were you ever arrested as a juvenile or sent to juvenile court? (score 1 or 0)

*Later arrest:* Were you ever arrested after age 15? (score 1 or 0)

*Multiple arrests:* Were you arrested more than once since age 15? (score 1 or 0)

*Felony conviction:* Were you ever convicted of a felony? (score 1 or 0)

*Early criminal behavior:* Before the age of 15, did you commit any criminal acts (i.e., steal from stores, parents or friends, damage property, start a fire)? (score 0 or 3, depending on number of offence groups)

*Later criminal behavior:* After the age of 15, did you commit any criminal acts (i.e., theft, threats, start fires, destroy property, paid for sex, made money from prostitutes, by selling drugs, illegal gambling)? (score 0 or 5, depending on number of offense groups)

Lyons did not ask directly about any truly violent behavior but rather concentrated on petty crime and self-reporting of arrests and behavior (Lyons, 1996). Several different levels of criminality were considered, including criminal behavior, arrests, and convictions. This is important because in many studies it is difficult to understand the researcher definition of crime. Many researchers put all convictions together, without weighing the level of severity. Some researchers consider that very minor acts categorize someone as a criminal, whereas others only count convictions. The data were analyzed by considering concordance rates between two or more traits. Lyons first looked at the prevalence rates of each of the categories, which showed that crime was rare among the sample, with the majority of respondents indicating no criminal behaviors, arrests, or convictions. Some 8.2% of respondents reported a single early arrest, 16.2% reported a single later arrest, 6.6% reported multiple later arrests, and 6.6% reported a felony conviction. Almost 28% of respondents reported a single instance of early or juvenile criminal behavior, with 5.1% reporting two instances of early criminal behavior and less than 1% reporting three instances. More than 10% reported a single instance of adult criminal behavior, with 3.9%, 1%, and 0.7% reporting two, three, and four instances of adult criminal behavior, respectively (Lyons, 1996).

Lyons (1996) then looked at correlations between and within the MZ and DZ twins. He found that there were significant influences from both genetic factors and the common environment on early arrests. Therefore, the environment, rather than genetics, significantly influenced early criminal behavior.

Conversely, genetic factors, but not the environment, significantly influenced adult crime. Genetics were seen to play a role in whether respondents were arrested after the age of 15, whether they were arrested more than once after age 15, and whether they were involved in later criminal behavior (Lyons, 1996).

Twins were found to resemble one another most in early arrest statistics, with almost three-quarters of the variance being explained by the genes, but there was also a significant and strong correlation with the shared environment. There was a significant influence of genetics, but not the environment, on later arrests and multiple arrests as well as on later criminal behavior, whereas the environment had a very significant effect on early criminal behavior. This finding seems somewhat anomalous: Lyons found a significant effect of genetics and the environment on early *arrest* but only a significant effect of the environment on early criminal *behavior*. This difference suggests that many of these twins got away with many criminal acts as juveniles, or that the crimes were too minor to be reported, such as stealing candy from a store. The difference appears to represent committing the crimes, which are strongly environmentally linked, and getting caught, which is both genetically and environmentally linked. It may be that genetic factors linked to getting caught, such as intelligence and impulsivity, play a greater role than the actual genetic determination of crime itself (Lyons, 1996). However, that possibility needs much more study because it could also be a factor of the experiment and the way the researcher worded what was to be considered a criminal offense.

This study confirmed that there is a higher genetic influence on adult rather than juvenile crime and that the environment has a greater effect on juvenile delinquency than genetics. The same results have been found in many other studies. It is important to realize that although this study claims support for a genetic role in criminal behavior, it also studied the environmental role. That is the beauty of twin studies; you cannot study one without the other. The researcher is always comparing the two; and in many cases, the results show as strong an influence of the environment as they do of the genes.

The benefit of Lyons' research is that the sample does not come from an institutionalized population or a treated sample but rather from the general population. However, it does not include women, so there is no way of knowing whether the data are applicable to women. It also only includes military personnel, which means some individuals may have been eliminated because of prior criminal activity. In addition, the individuals had been screened for health. The twins studied here had been raised together; at least, the study did not discuss adoption as opposed to being raised together; it was just assumed that MZ twins and DZ twins had the same environment. We discuss this topic later, but some people have suggested that MZ twins may share a more common environment than DZ twins because they are treated more similarly by parents and peers. Another problem is that these data depend totally on self-reporting; that is, on whether the men admit their crimes. Social desirability may reduce reporting, but this is just as likely with MZ as DZ twins so it probably does not affect the outcome. Also, some of the criteria used to define crime seemed very mild (e.g., stealing candy). Not every twin in the registry responded, and thus the question arises as to whether the ones who did not respond were more antisocial, criminal, or perhaps alcoholic than the ones who did respond (Lyons, 1996). This study remains ongoing, so much more in-depth analysis is expected.

Twin studies yield copious amounts of data, and they have been very useful. They are one of the few tools that allow us to separate the environmental and the genetic background in humans. However, there are some important questions about them.

# Problems with Twin Studies

## Similar Environments

One of the criticisms always aimed at studies that look at both MZ and DZ twins is that although it would appear that the environment for each set of twins is the same, in fact, that may not be the case. Dizygotic twins look different and may be of different sexes, whereas monozygotic twins look identical and are of the same sex. It is, therefore, possible that the environments in which monozygotic twins are raised may be more similar than those in which dizygotic twins are raised. We often see monozygotic twins dressed the same way, but it seems less common in dizygotic twins. Also, dizygotic twins who are of opposite sex are more likely to be treated differently than dizygotic twins who are of the same sex. This is the reason most twin studies only include same-sex twins. If monozygotic twins are treated more similarly than dizygotic twins, it would artificially raise the concordance rates.

However, there is also evidence that some twins make a great effort to be "different," and some twins may develop opposite (i.e., submissive/dominant) roles (Raine, 1993). These effects are likely to be higher in monozygotic twins because they look alike and would want to be more different than dizygotic twins, who do not look the same and thus have more of their own identity to start with. Therefore, this factor could artificially lower heritability estimates. However, the concern about parents raising monozygotic twins in a more similar environment than dizygotic twins is eliminated when adoption studies are used.

But is it really? There may be other intervening factors in an environment. Who, for example, legally adopts children? The types of adoptions used in such studies are legal adoptions; otherwise they would not be officially recorded and thus would not be available for research. People who are approved for adoption are invariably couples of a certain age with no criminal record and specific kinds of home life. So even adopted children may be raised in generally similar environments. Twins adopted by two different families are still likely to grow up in a "typical" middle-class environment and in the same era. This could mean that differences thought to be genetic (because they occurred in monozygotic twins with different environments) may actually be the result of the environment.

## Zygosity

One true methodological problem in twin studies is that of zygosity: are the twins really monozygotic? (Raine, 1993). A DNA test is the only certain way to prove zygosity, but it has never been used in twin studies thus far. It is quite possible that dizygotic twins have accidentally been classified as monozygotic twins by their parents. Many siblings look alike, and often age is the only clear difference. Therefore, if you eliminate the age difference, as you do with twins, then two siblings, or dizygotic twins, may be mistaken for monozygotic twins. If monozygotic twins were mistaken for dizygotic twins in any of these studies, then that would tend to underestimate the level of heritability of a trait. Future studies should obviously involve DNA tests to confirm zygosity.

## Differences in Monozygotic Twins

Just because monozygotic twins have identical genotypes does not mean that they have no differences. For example, dizygotic twins each have a separate placenta, but monozygotic twins usually share one placenta. This fact can lead to biological differences that are not caused by genetics: for example, birth weights of monozygotic twins are often less similar than those of dizygotic twins (Raine, 1993). Birth complications are also more likely, and they could result in an exaggeration of behavioral differences in monozygotic twins and thus a reduction in heritability estimates.

## Sample Size

Although some early studies had low sample numbers, later studies involved thousands of twin pairs, making them scientifically robust. However, the majority of crimes are committed by a small number of people (that is, there is not a large number of people who each commit one crime; rather, the majority of crimes are committed by repeat or chronic offenders). As a result, the number of people in the twin sets who have committed a crime is low — not too low to make a conclusion, but still low. The problem is even worse when we look at violent crime because it is rare in our society, no matter what the media might suggest. Thus, violent crime is rarely represented in high enough numbers in the studies for researchers to come to any conclusions.

It must also be noted that women are rarely represented in these studies because fewer women than men commit crimes, and violent crime rates in women are very low, making it difficult to reach any universal conclusions.

## Different Countries

Many of the studies come from European countries such as Denmark and Sweden, where the population is significantly more homogeneous than it is in North America. In many European countries, extensive social systems allow most people to have a relatively similar standard of living, and most European countries have much less racial diversity. The lack of diversity in the countries where much of these data originate is very valuable because it eliminates several variables. However, it could be suggested that these data may not apply to more diverse regions such as North America. As studies in North America have been conducted and the results support the conclusions of the European researchers, however, it would appear that the data are applicable.

## Political Bias

Some of the earlier studies were carried out and published in an era when political bias was extreme (i.e., the Nazi era). It is possible, therefore, that they should be dismissed. However, their results show the lowest concordance rates, and thus do not seem to have been biased. Even when they are eliminated, there is still ample evidence in which a genetic predisposition for nonviolent crime is apparent.

## Summary of Twin Studies

1.  Overall, almost all studies agree that there is some genetic predisposition for crime.
2.  Evidence for such a predisposition has been found by several different and independent research groups. Replication of any experiment by the same research group could repeat the same mistake, so replication by several independent research groups is more powerful.
3.  Heritability for crime has been found in several different countries, which suggests initial cross-cultural generalizations. However, all the studies have been done in Western countries, and it would be helpful to look at non-Western countries as well.
4.  There are only a few studies that have a large enough sample size to include violent crime as a separate parameter; however, those studies do seem to suggest that that there is a heritable component to petty property crime, such as stealing low-value items, but not to violent crime. However, because numbers involved are low, we may be missing this link.

## Identical Twins Reared Apart

One of the main criticisms of twin studies is that monozygotic twins may be raised more similarly than dizygotic twins. This problem is eliminated in studies that look at identical twins raised apart. There are lots of tabloid-type stories about their amazing similarities, but there also have been some scientific studies done. These are rare but they are very powerful experiments.

In Christiansen's (1977b) Danish twin studies, there were eight cases in which monozygotic twins were raised separately and in which one twin was registered for criminal activity. Of these eight pairs, four were concordant for crime. A small study from Mexico described a pair of monozygotic twins who were separated at 9 months of age and brought up by parents who were reported to have very different personalities. One twin was brought up in a town after age 9 years, while the other twin remained in the desert. The twins had no contact with each other, and both started to commit juvenile crimes after puberty and both were institutionalized for their crimes (Schwesinger, 1952). However, this is a good example of the problem that arises with tiny sample sizes; they are suggestive but require more research to be substantiated.

A strong study was conducted by Grove and colleagues in 1990. They looked at 32 sets of monozygotic twins who were separated shortly after birth and reared apart. Zygosity was assessed using several techniques, including blood groups, which they stated resulted in less than a 0.1% chance of mis-identification. A score for antisocial behavior in both childhood and adult-hood was derived by interviewing each subject with a standardized interview schedule. Statistically significant heritabilities were obtained for antisocial behavior in both childhood (0.41) and in adulthood (0.28) (Grove et al., 1990).

## Adoption Studies

A much more powerful way to look at the effect of genetics on behavior is to look at adoption cohorts. This eliminates any risk of a greater or lesser shared environment (family or extended family contexts) by one set of twins. In such studies, we look at the life and behavior of children who were adopted by non-family members and, in particular, at their criminal behavior in relation to the criminality of their adoptive or biological parents. Adoption better separates environmental and genetic effects. If convicted adoptees have a significantly higher number of convicted biological fathers (assuming appropriate controls), it would suggest the influence of a genetic factor in criminal behavior. This theory is supported by the fact that almost none of the adoptees knew their biological parents and that adoptees often do not even know they are adopted.

Adoption studies have indicated a genetic influence on criminal, although not violent, behavior. In one study of 37 American adoptees from Iowa, an increased rate of criminality was seen in those who had criminal biological mothers (Crowe, 1974). In another Iowa study, 246 Iowans adopted at birth were found to have a higher level of antisocial behavior when they had biological parents with antisocial behavior (Cadoret, 1995). In Sweden, crim-inal behavior in the biological parents was significantly related to criminal behavior in the adoptees. In all cases, this relationship between crime and genetics was only valid for property crimes and not for violent crimes (Bohman et al., 1982).

## Mednick's Danish Adoption Studies

One of the largest and strongest adoption studies was performed in Denmark by Mednick and colleagues (Mednick et al., 1987, 1984). This study examined 14,427 nonfamilial (i.e., no genetic relationship) adoptions in Denmark from 1924 to 1947. The data were based on a register of nonfamilial adoptions maintained in Denmark, which includes information on the adoptees and their biological and adoptive parents (Mednick et al., 1984, 1987). Court convictions were used as an index of criminal involvement (Mednick et al., 1987). In many studies, it is often unclear how the researcher defined criminality. For instance, was it a serious offense or a very petty offense? In this study, the researchers were very thorough. The court records included details of the law violated, the date, and the sanction. Court records were obtained for all the individuals who had a known place of birth (such records are filed by place of birth and maintained in that region) — 65,516 records in all (Mednick et al., 1987). In Denmark, minors (below age 15) cannot receive court convictions. If an individual dies or reaches the age of 80, the record is sometimes removed. The only way to check whether this had occurred was to check the death register, which is the only place the record was maintained, and thus the researchers checked the death records for every individual.

All details of every individual, whether they were the biological parent, the adoptive parent, or the adoptee, were recorded (Mednick et al., 1987). These included sex, date of birth, address, occupation, place of birth, and size of the community into which the child was adopted. These data give an indication of socioeconomic status and whether the child lived in a rural or urban community. The majority of the data pertained to males, simply because significantly more males had criminal records.

Overall, the study showed that if neither the biological nor adoptive parents had criminal records, only 13.5% of the adopted sons were convicted of a crime. If the adoptive parents were convicted but the biological parents were not convicted, this figure increased nominally to 14.7%. However, if biological parents alone were convicted, then 20% of the sons had criminal records. If both sets of parents, biological and adoptive, had criminal records, then the level of conviction in the sons increased to 24.5% (Mednick et al., 1987). Altogether, the findings show a genetic basis, although this is clearly influenced by the environment.

In some cases, the adoptive parents did have criminal records, although their overall levels of conviction were below that of the national average, and most were one-time offenders with no criminal record for 5 years before the adoption (Mednick et al., 1987). However, one could say that adoptees in these homes were exposed to a criminogenic environment, and the level is difficult to judge. One should note that the genetic influence of the biological father is completed at birth so is easier to quantify. Although the overall data clearly indicated that risk of adoptee conviction was greatly increased if they had a convicted biological father rather than a convicted adoptive father, the researchers were concerned that even such low levels of criminality in the adoptive environment could skew the results. Therefore, the researchers further analyzed the data, eliminating adoptive families with criminal records, and found that whether the adoptive parent had a conviction or not had little effect on the rate of adoptees' rates of conviction. The rate of conviction in the biological fathers still had a major effect (Mednick et al., 1987).

Although violent crime is rare, the sample size in this study was large enough to allow researchers to separate violent and property offenses (Brennan et al., 1996). A later reanalysis of these data showed that the genetic relationship is highly significant for property crimes but not statistically significant for violent crimes, indicating a genetic predisposition for property crime, but not for violent crimes (Brennan et al., 1996). This is important because when most people think of genetics and crime, they immediately leap to the conclusion that the crime is violent. This and other twin studies indicate the opposite: property crime appears to have a heritable component but there is no scientific evidence yet for a genetic basis for violent crime.

The researchers also looked at recidivism levels to consider whether parental recidivism resulted in higher conviction rates in the sons. In the Mednick et al. (1987) study, convictions rather than arrests were looked at, and chronic criminality was counted as more than three convictions. Just under 5% of the male adoptees were chronic offenders but they accounted for more than two-thirds of the convictions in male adoptees. This is comparable with other studies that show that although chronic offenders are rare in the population, they commit a disproportionately large number of offenses (Wolfgang et al., 1972).

The data showed that as the number of offenses in the biological parents increased, so did the number of convictions in the chronic adoptees. The biological parents with zero, one, two, or three or more convictions had male adoptees (i.e., male children who were adopted by someone else), averaging 0.30, 0.41, 0.48, and 0.70 convictions, respectively (Mednick et al., 1987).

In some cases, a biological parent gave up more than one child for adoption, which allowed the researchers to perform a sibling analysis. The overall research suggests that a heritable component for property crime exists, so it would be expected that there would be stronger concordance for crime between separately adopted full siblings than between separately adopted half-siblings, and that both would show more concordance than nonrelated adoptees (Mednick et al., 1987). The data set showed that the chance of two randomly selected adoptees both having a criminal record was 8.5%, so the researchers considered that as their baseline (Mednick et al., 1987). The data showed that the concordance rate between two half-siblings was 12.9%, and between full siblings was 20%. The sample size for this subset of the data is very small as there were only 131 male-male half-siblings and 40 full siblings, but the results are in the predicted direction. As the degree of genetic relation increases, the level of concordance increases. The level of concordance shot up even further when considering whether the siblings had a criminal father (Mednick et al., 1987).

Very few convicted women were included in the data set; however, the researchers did repeat the analyses using only female data and found that, although the numbers were small, the relationship held true (Mednick et al., 1987). In fact, it was found that the relationship between the adoptee being convicted and having a biological parent convicted was actually stronger if the convicted parent was the mother. There was also a stronger relationship between biological mother convictions and female adoptee convictions than that between biological father convictions and male adoptee convictions. (Mednick et al., 1987). Although interesting and statistically significant, the authors felt that the numbers were too low to draw strong conclusions.

The influence of socioeconomic status was also considered; using occupation as a guideline Mednick and colleagues separated "genetic" social class and "rearing" social class. Biological parents' social status was found to have a greater effect on risk of conviction in the sons than adoptive parents' socioeconomic status. Highest levels of convictions were seen in sons whose adoptive and biological social status were ranked as low, and lowest levels were seen when both genetic and environmental socioeconomic status were ranked as high. In both cases, as socioeconomic status improved, the risk of conviction decreased (Mednick et al., 1987). This was one of the first studies to prove that environment does have an influence on criminogenic behavior and to show the beneficial and protective effects of improved socioeconomic status (Mednick et al., 1984).

## Some Caveats to Mednick's Adoption Studies

This is a large and exhaustive study and there are many factors that one might question, such as the effect of outside circumstances not included in the research. But this study was extremely thorough, and the researchers themselves recognized and tried to address any possible caveats (Mednick et al., 1987):

1.  *Historical period.* The period during which these adoptions took place (1924–1967) covers times of major upheavals and changes in the

world, including Denmark. These years cover the Great Depression, major industrialization, and a world war. So, it is possible that the influence of genetic factors might be affected by these social upheavals. It is also possible that changes in level or type of crime during these years might influence the relations observed. The researchers were cognizant of this and so, in order to check this possibility, they repeated all the analyses for every 5-year period. The results were virtually identical for all of the periods and virtually identical to the analyses of the total, so the time period was not an issue.

2.  *Time of Adoption.* How soon after birth the adoption took place might be an issue. If the child spent any time in the biological home, one could argue that this might have influenced subsequent behavior. However, it was shown that none of the adopted children spent time in the biological home because the newborn babies were either immediately placed in the adoptive home or placed in a group foster home for later adoption. Therefore, the children studied did not spend any time in the biological home, eliminating any environmental effect of the biological home on the child (Mednick et al., 1987). Realizing that the children might have spent some time in an institutional setting, the researchers were concerned that this early institutionalization might have an effect on behavior. They determined that of those who were not immediately adopted, over half were placed with an adoptive family within the first year, 12.8% were placed with an adoptive family in the second year, and 11.3% were placed after the age of 2 (Mednick et al., 1987). The researchers re-analyzed all the data, separating these groups, and found that the relationships held for all groups; so there was no effect of age of transfer to new homes (Mednick et al., 1987).

3.  *Conviction vs. arrest.* This study looked at conviction rather than arrest. However, the authors were aware that some or even many of the controls (in this case, the adoptive parents) might also be criminals but had not been convicted. In studies where self-reported data on crime are compared with official criminal records, however, criminal records seem to be representative of criminal behavior. Even when only a few of a person's many crimes may have actually resulted in a conviction, it has been shown that people who self-report frequent criminal activity also have larger criminal records than those who self-report minor or few crimes (Christie et al., 1965). So, proportionally at least, the conviction data appear to be valid. Also, from a criminological point of view, conviction is much more certain than arrest, as many people are arrested but not charged or convicted.

4. *Labeling the adoptee.* One of the big advantages of studying adoption data over twin data is that the genetic and environmental contributions to the child's development are separated (Mednick et al., 1987). However, if the adoptive parents were told of the criminogenic background of the parents of their newly adopted baby, this might result in "labeling" the child. The adoptive parents might subconsciously raise the child differently, based on a knowledge of their biological background, which, in turn, might affect the likelihood that the adoptee would commit a criminal act. The researchers considered this and reanalyzed the data set based on whether the adoptive parents were aware or not aware of the criminal history of the biological parent. If the biological parent was convicted of a crime prior to the adoption, the adoption agency would inform the adoptive parents; however, if the biological parent's conviction occurred after the adoption, they were not informed.

One third of the convicted biological parents were convicted before the adoption took place, and two thirds were convicted after the adoption. When the groups were considered separately, the probability of conviction in either male or female adoptees was almost exactly the same, whether the adoptive parents knew of the biological parents' criminal record or not. In a similar study, the same result was found when researchers looked at arrests rather than convictions (Hutchings and Mednick, 1977). Therefore, whether the adoptive parents knew of the criminal convictions of their adopted child's parents did not influence whether the child would themselves be convicted of a crime.

In summary, this study was extremely well conducted, and every caveat was thought through and reanalyzed. It was a large enough study so that, in most cases, valid statistics could be derived.

## Bohman's Stockholm Adoption Studies, 1996

Sweden is another country that has generated a lot of adoption research. These studies have looked not just at criminality, but also at its relationship to alcoholism and antisocial personality disorder (ASP). The studies began in the 1960s and continue today, using 862 men and 913 women who were born between 1930 and 1950 (Bohman, 1996).

This study found a high correlation between alcohol abuse in biological fathers and adopted sons, as well as a high correlation between crime and alcohol abuse in biological fathers and adopted sons. When alcohol abuse was studied alone, there was again a high correlation, which indicates a genetic predisposition for alcohol abuse (Bohman, 1996). This relationship is now well established for some types of alcoholism (Cloninger, 1973).

Therefore, it was possible that the correlation between crime and genetics might relate to alcoholism, which is a predisposer for crime, rather than directly link to crime. A later analysis removed the alcohol parameter but still found a strong link between criminality in the biological fathers and criminality in the adopted sons. It might be that there are two factors at work here — (1) genetic determinants for alcohol abuse and (2) other determinants for criminality — although these could also interact. In many of these cases, the criminality did relate to alcohol abuse.

In looking at individual cases, it was seen that alcoholic criminals often committed repeated violent offences, whereas nonalcoholic criminals tended to commit a small number of petty property offenses (Bohman, 1996). These nonalcoholic petty criminals more commonly had biological parents with histories of petty crime, but rarely alcoholism. In contrast, the risk of criminality in alcohol abusers was correlated with the severity of their own alcohol abuse but not with the criminality of their biological or adoptive parents. Therefore, it appeared that criminality without alcohol abuse is characterized by petty property offenses, whereas alcohol-related criminality was more violent and usually repeated (Bohman, 1996).

When alcohol was removed from the equation, the correlation between both environment and genetics showed a very marked increase in petty criminality in the adoptees but not in violent crime. When both the genetic and environmental risk were low, the rate of criminality in male adoptees was 2.9%. When the genetic risk was low (biological parents noncriminal) but the environmental risk was high (adoptive parents criminal), the rate was 6.7%. When the genetic risk was high but the environmental risk low, the rate was 12.1%. When both risks were high, the rate shot up to 40% (Bohman 1996).

The most interesting facet in this study is the interaction between the environment and the genetic background. When only the environment is taken into account, with a low genetic risk, the male adoptees had more than twice the risk of criminality than adoptees with low genetic and low environmental factors. When the genetic risks, but not the environmental ones, are taken into account, the risk was nearly fourfold; but when you add the two, the risk jumps to 40%. These experiments indicate a genetic and an environmental predisposition for both alcoholism and criminality, and suggest that there are separate mechanisms at work with each.

Bohman also considered the issue of serious mental illness. There was a threefold increase in the rate of schizophrenia for both male and female offspring of biological fathers convicted of violent offenses (Bohman, 1996). Previous studies have also indicated a genetic link with schizophrenia A study in Oregon had looked at the adopted offspring of schizophrenic mothers. A significant increase in schizophrenia was noticed in these children when they grew up, but there was also a significant increase in other antisocial behavior, including violence (Heston, 1966).

Bohman also looked at sex differences. Daughters with a criminal biological parent had a threefold increase in criminal behavior over daughters without a criminal biological parent (4.9% vs. 1.4%, 102 vs. 811) (Bohman, 1996). Female crime mostly involved nonviolent property offenses and was usually not associated with alcohol abuse. A lack of violence is common in female crime. The effect of the environment was different for males and females. For example, prolonged institutional care increased the risks of criminality in women but not in men. In contrast, many short-term homes of very low socioeconomic status increased the risk in men but not women. Significantly more of the women had fathers with repeated convictions than did the males (Bohman, 1996).

In all cases in this study, low social status alone was not enough to lead to petty crime, but it did increase the risk in combination with specific types of predisposition. An unstable home, repeated institutionalizations, or repeated foster homes did contribute to the risks of both petty criminality and alcoholism (Bohman, 1996). This study is still ongoing, with lengthy interviews of adoptive parents and adoptees now taking place.

In many of these cases, we see that a stable family home is a protective factor against crime. If a child has a predisposition for crime, based on biological family, the child can do just fine with a stable home. If some of this information were better known and understood by a larger group of criminologists and sociologists, it could go a long way toward helping some of these children. Saying that a child must have a supportive stable home is naïve, and not so simple in practice. Stable homes do not just appear, nor should we ever consider taking children from the natural home and putting them into an adoptive or foster home unless the natural home is dangerous. But it is possible to add structure to the life of a child even if the home situation is not stable. A stable long-term relationship with a teacher or teacher's aide can help; special assistants in schools and behavior assistants for CD (conduct disorder) children are now proving their worth. Teaching children themselves to respect diversity and changing the caring atmospheres in schools can help. Also, organizations such as *Big Brothers Big Sisters* can sometimes provide ongoing stable relationships exterior to the family — although these will not work with deeply antisocial children. But to work, these relationships and new structures must themselves be stable, they must be ongoing, and the CD child, for example, must be reachable. It is equally naïve to think that the children who have become deeply antisocial would automatically engage a new guidance structure; but long-term structural change and consistent guidance can help. If change is to come, it will come in this direction.

## Further Genetic Studies

Twin and adoption studies are still the design of choice for many genetic studies that focus on a myriad of genetic disorders, both behavioral and medical.

There have been many studies on alcoholism because, in addition to being a serious health problem, a large percentage of crimes are committed under the influence of alcohol. Researchers have found that there are two types of alcoholism (Yamauchi, 1998; Sigvardsson et al., 1996; Begleiter, 1995; Heath, 1995; Cloninger et al., 1981):

- Type I, which is found in both sexes, begins later in life and is under both environmental and genetic influence
- Type II, which is found primarily in men, begins in adolescence or early adulthood and is almost entirely under genetic control

### Type II Alcoholism

There is no single gene for Type II alcoholism but researchers have identified several genes that may be involved, particularly those involved with neurotransmitter function such as dopamine, serotonin, norepinephrine, and others (Virkkunen et al., 1996; Blum et al., 1995; Doria, 1995; Tiihonen et al., 1995; Linnoila et al., 1994; Virkkunen and Linnoila, 1990). These neurotransmitters are involved in brain function and have been linked to aggression and antisocial behavior. Serotonin has been very strongly linked to many aspects of antisocial behavior; and dopamine is related to the reward syndrome in people, whereby a person receives pleasurable feelings with everyday events. People with disruption of the dopamine system have a reward deficiency, meaning that they do not receive the cascade of pleasure that normal people feel, but instead feel anxious and angry and require a much greater amount of a drug or alcohol to feel pleasure (Blum et al., 1995, 2000). Chapter 8 discusses neurotransmitters in much greater detail.

Many young males commit delinquent acts in youth but only a very small fraction of these young males continue to exhibit antisocial behavior when they mature. Recent evidence has suggested that there may be a genetic difference between young males who commit delinquent acts in youth and then mature into nondelinquent adults, and those who continue to exhibit antisocial behavior all their lives (Taylor et al., 2000). Young males who continue to exhibit chronic antisocial behavior throughout their lives invariably began exhibiting such behavior early in life, before puberty, whereas transient delinquency usually begins after puberty. In this study, researchers evaluated 147 male pairs of twins throughout adolescence, breaking them into groups of those who exhibited early-onset antisocial behavior, those who exhibited late-onset antisocial behavior, and those who did not exhibit anti-social behavior at all. Antisocial behavior was assessed by teachers, parents, and the children themselves, as well as from documented contact with police. Concordance rates for early-onset antisocial behavior in MZ twins was found to be 55% as compared with 29% in DZ twins, indicating a substantial heritability to early-onset antisocial behavior (Taylor et al., 2000). Also, early starters had many more close relatives with adult antisocial behavior than later starters or controls. Researchers also found that early starters had a higher incidence of attention deficit hyperactivity disorder (ADHD), oppo-sitional defiant disorder, as well as lower verbal intelligence than controls or late starters (Taylor et al., 2000). It is possible, therefore, that the genetic link to delinquency relates to ADHD or other reductions in cognitive skills, rather than directly influencing delinquency.

## Conduct Disorder

Conduct disorder (CD) in children is characterized by many antisocial behav-iors, such as stealing, lying, bullying, cruelty to animals, aggression, violence, arson, and property destruction. The disorder is considered a strong risk factor for later criminality. A retrospective study of 2682 adult twin pairs from the community-based Australian Twin Registry showed that there was a substantial genetic influence on predisposition for developing CD (Slutske et al., 1997). The researchers found a concordance rate of 71% for CD but found little evidence for environmental influences. Although boys are much more frequently diagnosed with CD than girls, the researchers found that the level of genetic and environmental influences for developing CD did not vary between the sexes. A later study of 70 MZ and 42 DZ twins between the ages of 4 and 15 years found very similar results for CD with a heritability of 68% (Coolidge et al., 2001). Borderline personality disorder, which is also associ-ated with antisocial behavior, was found to have a heritability estimate of 63%; and overall, the mean heritability estimate for personality disorders in general was 58% (Coolidge et al., 2001).

## Attention Deficit Hyperactivity Disorder

Attention deficit hyperactivity disorder (ADHD) is one of the most com-monly diagnosed childhood behavioral disorders worldwide (Biederman, 2005). Children with ADHD display persistently disruptive behavior, a poor ability to sustain attention, are hyperactive and impulsive with a low frustra-tion tolerance, and have drastic, rapid mood swings (Ward, 2000). There have been several studies that have linked ADHD with increased alcohol and drug use (Johann et al., 2003; Molina and Pelham, 2003), and juvenile delin-quency as well as adult crime (Satterfield and Schell, 1997; Eyestone and Howell, 1994; Moffitt, 1990; Zagar et al., 1989).

Family, twin, and adoption studies have all been used to illustrate that ADHD has a genetic basis (Ward, 2000). One such family study showed that the risk of ADHD among relatives of children with ADHD was much higher than that of relatives of children without ADHD (Biederman et al., 1991). In a later study, Biederman and colleagues (1995) studied the children of adults diagnosed with ADHD, and found that 57% met the clinical diagnosis for ADHD. As we know, twin studies offer more conclusive evidence into a genetic predisposition for ADHD than family studies because a certain amount of the environmental component can be removed. Research conducted in 1992 looked at 84 MZ twin pairs and 62 DZ twin pairs as part of the "Colorado Reading Project." In each case, at least one of the twins was diagnosed with ADHD. Gender, IQ, and reading ability were all taken into account. The researchers found concordance rates for ADHD at 79% for MZ twins and 32% for DZ twins; this is highly significant statistically (Ward, 2000; Gillis et al., 1992). Further studies have supported this finding, with concordance rates of 68% in MZ twins compared with 29% in DZ twins in one study (Ward, 2000; Edelbrock et al., 1994) and 62% for MZ twins and 26% for DZ twins in another (Ward, 2000; Goodman et al., 1995).

In a recent twin study, Arsenault et al. (2003) analyzed the behavior of 1116 pairs of 5-year-old twins. What makes this study particularly robust is that antisocial behavior was determined using four different types of observers: (1) mothers, (2) teachers, (3) research examiners, and (4) the children themselves. This meant that the children's behaviors were not only assessed by those who knew them very well and those who did not know them, but also in a variety of settings, including home and school and with people who were familiar to them and those who were strangers. The researchers found that antisocial behavior that was agreed upon by all four sets of observers was very highly heritable, with a heritability estimate of 82%. The heritability of antisocial behavior that was reported by only one of the four observers varied from 33% (self-report) to 71% (teachers) (Arsenault et al., 2003). The researchers felt that this latter finding was important because it indicated that unequivocal antisocial behavior that was observed in all settings and by all observers was highly heritable, but that milder, situational antisocial behavior was less genetically influenced. In a meta-analysis of twin studies to date, Biederman (2005) found a mean heritability for ADHD of 77%.

In an adoption study, adoptive parents of children with ADHD were compared with biological parents of children with ADHD and to controls with no ADHD in the family (Sprich et al., 2000). Only 6% of the adoptive parents and 3% of the control parents exhibited symptoms of ADHD, whereas 18% of the biological parents exhibited symptoms. Also, high rates of mood and anxiety disorders were found among the biological family but not the adoptive family of ADHD children (Sprich et al., 2000). The study therefore suggests a strong heritable component for ADHD.

Almost a quarter of children with ADHD also suffer from reading disabilities, which further hamper their ability to benefit from education, and is likely to increase their propensity to "act out" in school. Recently, a genetic link has been suggested between reading disability and ADHD. Loo et al. (2004) conducted a genome-wide scan of reading ability in sibling pairs with ADHD. A linkage study was used to search for molecular markers. The researchers detected evidence of shared genetic factors for ADHD as well as reading disability in three chromosomes (10, 16, 17) and evidence for reading disability, but not ADHD at three other locations (on chromosomes 2, 8, and 15) (Loo et al., 2003). ADHD has also been linked to a variant of the dopamine transporter gene (DAT1) (Cook et al., 1995). Medications that are often beneficial for ADHD children, such as methylphenidate (Ritalin), amphetamines, pemoline, and bupropion, all work by inhibiting the dopamine transporter system, which returns dopamine back to the nerves that release it, in a negative feedback mechanism (Cook et al., 1995). As more and more research identifies not just a genetic basis, but a very specific allele or variant of a gene that increases susceptibility to a disorder such as ADHD, the chances of treating the disorder increase. If we can understand the subtle genetic mutation and its resultant chemical change, medications could be targeted to that very specific area, rather than using a more broad-spectrum approach likely to result in more side effects.

There are clearly many studies that indicate that there is a genetic predisposition for ADHD and CD as well as other antisocial behavioral disorders. However, these are just predispositions and there are many other nongenetic causes that have been cited, such as fetal alcohol spectrum disorder, birth and pregnancy complications, maternal smoking during pregnancy, and environmental variables (Biederman, 2005). Psychosocial adversity also has an effect on the development of ADHD, but also seems to be a predictor for a child's general emotional health as well as universal behavior issues. It has therefore been suggested that psychosocial adversities are not specific predictors of ADHD, but rather are nonspecific triggers of the underlying genetic or biological predisposers (Biederman, 2005).

## Aggression

Despite the earlier twin and adoption studies, which showed a genetic link only with petty crime, several studies have indicated a genetic predisposition for aggression. In a recent animal study, it was noted that female rhesus macaque monkeys exhibited levels of aggressive behavior that were very similar to those of their mothers. Such monkeys live in female communal groups, so the researcher was interested in whether this aggressive behavior was inherited from the mother, or merely an imitation of her behavior (Maestripieri, 2003). Maestripieri switched ten female babies immediately after birth with babies from unrelated mothers and observed their behaviors as they grew up, raised by unrelated mothers. The two groups of monkeys had no physical or visual contact with each other after the switch. Over the following 3 years, Maestripieri found that the adopted babies exhibited very similar aggression to that of their biological mothers and appeared unaffected by the behavior of the mother who raised them. This even extended to the types of aggression, such as slapping or threatening. The similarity between biological mothers and daughters appeared to grow stronger as the infants grew up. In contrast, other behaviors such as grooming and submission appeared to be much less influenced by genetics and more related to social environment (Maestripieri, 2003).

Human studies have also found a connection between aggressive and antisocial behavior. A rather unique adoption research design was used to study aggressive and delinquent behavior in adolescents. Usually, adopted children are compared with children who were raised by their own biological parents. In this international study, 221 pairs of biologically unrelated siblings in adoptive families were compared with 111 pairs of biologically related siblings who had been adopted together, and 94 singleton children (Van den Oord et al., 1994). The researchers found that genetics accounted for 70% of the variance for aggressive behavior and 39% of the variance for delinquency (Van den Oord et al., 1994). In a twin study, 183 adult twin pairs were compared with 64 DZ same-sex twin pairs (Vernon et al., 1999). The study was unusual in that the majority of twin pairs were female. The researchers tested the participants on many measures of aggression, including physical and verbal aggression, hostility, and impatience; they found that multiple measures of different types of aggressive behavior had moderate to high heritabilities (Vernon et al., 1999). In another twin study, involving 492 pairs of MZ and DZ twins, genetic influences were found to be high for attention problems, aggression, and anxious or depressed behaviors in both sexes (Hudziak et al., 2000). Another twin study of 142 MZ and 70 DZ twin pairs compared two facets of psychopathic behavior: (1) impulsive, antisocial behavior and (2) callous, unemotional personality. Both traits were found to be significantly influenced by genes (Taylor et al., 2003).

Eley et al. (1999) studied more than 1500 pairs of MZ and DZ twins from Sweden and Britain to compare two types of antisocial behavior: (1) aggressive behavior, such as bullying and fighting; and (2) nonaggressive antisocial behavior, such as truancy and petty theft. They found that genes played a powerful role in determining whether a child was aggressive, and this held true for both sexes. Nonaggressive antisocial behavior was strongly influenced by genetics in girls, but was much more influenced by environmental factors in boys (Eley et al., 1999). The results were similar for both countries studied. The researchers speculated that the genetic predispositions may be specifically related to variations in neurotransmitter regulation systems such as dopamine, serotonin, and monoamine oxidase A (see Chapter 8).

Not only have studies shown that certain antisocial behaviors have a genetic component, but other studies have also shown that a child's genotype may actually protect him or her from the deleterious effects of an adverse childhood. Researchers studied 1116 women and their 5-year-old same-sex twins, and assessed the families' economic situation and the level of support and warmth of the mother toward the children (Kim-Cohen et al., 2004). In a comparison of MZ and DZ twins, 70% of the variability in the children's ability to overcome the detrimental effects of poverty and 46% of the variance in cognitive ability were under the influence of genetics (Kim-Cohen et al., 2004). Environment was also important because children with more stimulating environments had higher IQs. In an earlier study, Caspi, one of these researchers, found that children with a particular variant of a gene involved in neurotransmitter function were highly likely to commit antisocial acts only *if* they were severely abused as children. Children with the same genotype who had happy childhoods were no more likely to commit antisocial acts than controls (Caspi et al., 2002) (see Chapter 8 for details). Time and time again, the results show that a genetic predisposition for crime can be ameliorated by a stable, happy home life.

## Conclusion

When people think of crime and genetics, they frequently think of violent crimes. Although many of the earlier twin and adoption studies show a clear relationship between genetics and property crime, they did not show a relationship between genetics and violent crime. This may be because violence is much less common than property crime, so the sample sizes were small when considering violent crime alone.

More recent studies have indicated a genetic predisposition for many disorders and antisocial behaviors, including aggression and violence. However, it must be remembered that these are, again, predispositions. Although, in most cases, twin studies can indicate whether a trait does or does not have a genetic basis, they do not indicate what that genetic relationship actually is. All the chemical messengers in our body are influenced by genes, including our hormones and neurotransmitters. Studies that implicate a particular gene or series of genes in metabolizing a particular neurotransmitter are extremely valuable. For example, several studies have implicated dopamine in the etiology of ADHD (Young et al., 2002; Cook et al., 1995). These allow us to target that particular anomaly, both medically with drugs that can intervene in this system, and also emotionally and socially by understanding the behavioral challenges caused by the genetic deficit. More specific studies are needed to identify the gene(s) and their alleles or variants that are involved in different problems so that these can be directly targeted.

The following chapters consider the role of these natural body chemicals on our behavior. Some research has already indicated that a genetic predisposition for criminogenic behavior relates to a very specific gene influencing a very specific neurotransmitter or hormone, which then influences a behavior.

## Questions for Further Study and Discussion

1.  Twin studies clearly show a genetic predisposition for petty crime in adults. However, this is not shown in juveniles. Why would juvenile crime be different from adult crime?
2.  Twin and adoption studies clearly show a genetic predisposition for petty crime in adults. Why, evolutionarily, might there be a genetic predisposition for petty crime but not violent crime?
3.  Twin and adoption studies have not only indicated risk factors for crime, but have also identified protective factors. Discuss these protective factors and how we might use them to reduce crime.

## References

Arsenault, L., Moffitt, T.E., Caspi, A., Taylor, A., Rijsdijk, F.V., Jaffee, S.R., Ablow, J.C., and Measelle, J.R. (2003). Strong genetic effects on cross-situational antisocial behavior among 5-year-old children according to mothers, teachers, examiner-observers, and twins' self-reports. *J. Child Psychol. Psychiatry,* 44(6), 832–848.

Begleiter, H. (1995). The collaborative study on the genetics of alcoholism. *Alcohol, Health and Research World,* 19(3), 228–236.

Biederman, J. (2005). Attention-deficit hyperactivity disorder: a selective overview. *Biol. Psychiatry,* 59(1), 829–835.

Biederman, J., Faraone, S., Keenan, K., Steingard, R., and Tsuang, M.T. (1991). Familial association between attention deficit disorder and anxiety disorders. *Am. J. Psychiatry,* 148(2), 251–256.

Biederman, J., Faraone, S.V., Mick, E., Spencer, T., Wilens, T., and Keily, K. (1995). High risk for attention deficit hyperactivity disorder among children of parents with childhood onset of the disorder: a pilot study. *Am. J. Psychiatry,* 152, 431–435.

Blum, K., Sheridan, P.J., Wood, R.C., Braverman, E.R., Chen, T.J., and Comings, D.E. (1995). Dopamine D2 receptor gene variants: association and linkage studies in impulsive-addictive-compulsive behaviour. *Pharmocogenetics,* 5(3), 121–141.

Bohman, M. (1996). Predisposition to criminality: Swedish adoption studies in retrospect. *Ciba Foundation Symposium,* 194, 99–109.

Bohman, M., Cloninger, C.R., and von Knorring, A.-L. (1982). Predisposition to petty criminality in Swedish adoptees I. Genetic and environmental heterogeneity. *Arch. Gen. Psychiatry*, 39, 1233–1241.

Borgstrom, C.A. (1939). Eine Serie Von Kriminellen Zwillingen. *Archiv fur Rassenbiologie*, 511–516. (Cited by Raine, 1993).

Brennan, P.A., Mednick, S.A., and Jacobsen, B. (1996). Assessing the role of genetics in crime using adoption cohorts. *Ciba Foundation Symposium*, 194, 115–123.

Cadoret, R. (1995). Adoption studies. *Alcohol Health and Research World*, 19(3), 195–200.

Carey, G. (1996). Family and genetic epidemiology of aggressive and antisocial behavior. In D.M. Stoff and R.B. Cairns (Eds.), *Aggression and Violence* (pp. 3–21). Mahwah, NJ: Lawrence Erlbaum Associates.

Caspi, A., McClay, J., Moffitt, T.E., Mill, J., Martin, I., Craig, W., Taylor, A., and Poulton, R. (2002). Role of genotype in the cycle of violence in maltreated children. *Science*, 297(5582), 851–854.

Christiansen, K.O. (1977a). A preliminary study of criminality among twins. In Mednick, S.A. and Christiansen, K.O. (Eds.), *Biosocial Bases of Criminal Behavior* (pp. 89–108). New York: Gardner Press.

Christiansen, K.O. (1977b). A review of studies of criminality among twins. In Mednick, S.A. and Christiansen, K.O. (Eds.), *Biosocial Bases of Criminal Behavior* (pp. 45–88). New York: Gardner Press.

Christiansen, K.O. (1974). Seriousness of criminality and concordance among Danish twins. In Hood, R. (Ed.), *Crime, Criminology and Public Policy*. London: Heinemann.

Christie, N., Andenaes, J., and Skerbaekk, S. (1965). A study of self-reported crime. *Scand. Studies Criminol.*, 1, 86–116.

Cloninger, C.R. and Gottesman, I.I. (1987). Genetic and environmental factors in antisocial behaviour disorders. In Mednick, S.A., Moffitt, T.E., and Stack, S.A. (Eds.), *The Causes of Crime: New Biological Approaches* (p. 98). Cambridge: Cambridge University Press.

Cloninger, C.R., Bohman, M., and Sigvardsson, S. (1981). Inheritance of alcohol abuse: cross-fostering analysis of adopted men. *Arch. Gen. Psychiatry*, 38, 861–868.

Cook, E.H., Stein, M.A., Krasowski, M.D., Cox, N.J., Olkon, D.M., Kieffer, J.E., and Leventhal, B.L. (1995). Association of attention-deficit disorder and the dopamine transporter gene. *Am. J. Human Genetics*, 56(4), 993–998.

Coolidge, F.L., Thede, L.L., and Jang, K.L. (2001). Heritability of personality disorders in childhood. *J. Personality Disorder*, 15, 33–40.

Crowe, R.R. (1974). An adoption study of antisocial personality. *Arch. Gen. Psychiatry*, 31, 785–791.

Dalgaard, O.S. and Kringlen, E. (1976). A Norwegian twin study of criminality. *Br. J. Crim. Psychol.*, 16, 213–232.

Doria, J.J. (1995). Gene variability and vulnerability to alcoholism. *Alcohol Health and Research World,* 19(3), 245–248.

Edelbrock, C., Rende, R., Plomin, R., and Thompson, L.A. (1994). A twin study of competence and problem behavior in childhood and early adolescence. *J. Child Psychol. Psych.,* 36(5), 775–785.

Eley, T.C., Lichtenstein, P., and Stevenson, J. (1999). Sex differences in the etiology of aggressive and nonaggressive antisocial behavior: results from two twin studies. *Child Development,* 70(1), 155–168.

Eyestone, L. and Howell, R. (1994). An epidemiological study of attention-deficit hyperactivity disorder and major depression in a male prison population. *Bull. Am. Acad. Psychiatr. Law,* 22(2), 181–193.

Gillis, J.J., Gilger, J.W., Pennington, B.F., and DeFries, J.C. (1992). Attention deficit disorder in reading-disabled twins: evidence for a genetic etiology. *J. Abnormal Child Psychol.,* 20(3), 303–315.

Goodman, R., Simonoff, E., and Stevenson, J. (1995). The impact of child IQ, parent IQ and sibling IQ on child behavioral deviance scores. *J. Child Psychol. Psychiatr.,* 36(3), 409–425.

Grove, W.M., Eckert, E.D., Heston, L., Bouchard, T.J., Segal, N., and Lykken, D.T. (1990). Heritability of substance abuse and antisocial behavior: a study of monozygotic twins reared apart. *Biol. Psychiatr.,* 27, 1293–1304.

Hayashi, S. (1967). A study of juvenile delinquency in twins. *Bull. Osaka Medical School,* 12, 373–378.

Heath, A.C. (1995). Genetic influences on alcoholism risk. A review of adoption and twin studies. *Alcohol, Health Research World,* 19(3), 166–170.

Heston, L.L. (1966). Psychiatric disorders in foster home-reared children of schizophrenic mothers. *Br. J. Psychiatr.,* 112, 819–825.

Hudziak, J.J., Rudiger, L.P., Neale, M.C., Heath, A.C. and Todd, R.D. (2000). A twin study of inattentive, aggressive, and anxious/depressed behaviors. *J. Am. Acad. Child Adolescent Psychiatr.,* 39, 469–476.

Hutchings, B. and Mednick, S.A. (1977). Registered criminality in the adoptive and biological parents of registered male criminal adoptees. In Mednick, S.A. and Christiansen, K.O. (Eds.), *Biosocial Bases of Criminal Behavior* (127–142). New York: Gardner Press. 127–142.

Johann, M., Bobbe, G., Putzhammer, A., and Wordaz, N. (2003). Comorbidity of alcohol dependence with attention-deficit hyperactivity disorder: differences in phenotype with increased severity of the substance disorder but not in genotype (serotonin-transporter and 5-hydroxytryptamine-2c receptor). *Alcoholism: Clin. Exp. Res.,* 27(10), 1527–1534.

Julkowski-Cherkes, M. (1998). Learning disability, attention-deficit disorder and language impairment as outcomes of prematurity: a longitudinal descriptive study. *J. Learning Disabilities,* 31(3), 294–306.

Kim-Cohen, J., Moffitt, T.E., Caspi, A., and Taylor, A. (2004). Genetic and environmental processes in young children's resilience and vulnerability to socioeconomic deprivation. *Child Development,* 75(3), 651–668.

Kranze, H. (1937). Untersuchungen und Zwillingen in Fursorgeerziehunganstalten. *Zeitschrift Induktive Abstammungs-Vererbungslehre,* 73, 508–512. (Cited by Raine, 1993).

Kranze, H. (1935). Discordant Soziales Verhalten eineuger Zwillinge. *Monatschrift fur Kriminalpsychologie und Strafrechtsreform,* 26, 511–516. (Cited by Raine, 1993).

Lange, J. (1931). *Crime as Destiny.* London: Allen and Unwin. (Cited by Raine, 1993.)

Lange, J. (1929). Verbrechen als Schiskal. In Thieme, G. (Ed.), *Monatschrift fur Kriminalpsychologie und Strafrechtsreform* (pp. 511–516, Vol. 26, English edition 1931). Leipzig and London: Unwin Brothers, Kranze. (Cited by Raine, 1993.)

Legras, A.M. (1932). *Psychese en Criminaliteit bij Twellingen* (pp. 511–516). Utrecht: Kemink en Zoon. (Cited by Raine, 1993.)

Linnoila, M., Virkkunen, M., George, T., Eckardt, M., Higley, J.D., Nielsen, D., and Goldman, D. (1994). Serotonin, violent behavior and alcohol. *EXS,* 71, 155–163.

Loo S.K., Fisher, S.E., Francks, C., Ogdie, M.N., MacPhie, I.L., Yang, M., McGracken, J.T., McYough, J.J., Nelson, S.F., Monaco, A.P., Smalley, S.L. (2004). Yenomewìdé scan of reading ability in affected sibling pains with attention deficit/hyperactivity disorder: Unique and shared effects. *Molecular Psychology,* 9(5), 483–493.

Lyons, M.J. (1996). A twin study of self-reported criminal behavior. *Ciba Foundation Symposium,* 194, 61–70.

Maestripieri, D. (2003). Similarities in affiliation and aggression between cross-fostered rhesus macaque females and their biological mothers. *Develop. Psychobiol.,* 43(4), 321–327.

Mednick, S.A., Gabrielli, W.F.J., and Hutchings, B. (1987). Genetic factors in the etiology of criminal behavior. In Mednick, S.A., Moffitt, T.E., and Stack, S.A., *The Causes of Crime: New Biological Approaches* (pp. 74–91). Cambridge: Cambridge University Press.

Mednick, S.A., Gabrielli, W.F.J., and Hutchings, B. (1984). Genetic influences in criminal convictions: evidence from an adoption cohort. *Science,* 224, 891–894.

Moffitt, T. (1990). Juvenile delinquency and attention deficit disorder: boys' developmental trajectories from age 3 to age 15 child development. *Child Develop.,* 61, 893–910.

Molina, B.S. and Pelham, W.E.J. (2003). Childhood predictors of adolescent substance use in a longitudinal study of children with ADHD. *J. Abnorm. Psychol.,* 112(3), 497–507.

Raine, A. (1993). Genetics and crime. *The Psychopathology of Crime: Criminal Behavior as a Clinical Disorder* (pp. 47–80). San Diego: Academic Press.

Rosanoff, A.J., Handy, L., and Plesset, I.R. (1941). The etiology of child behavior difficulties, juvenile delinquency, and adult criminals with special reference to their occurrence in twins. *Psychiatric Monograph, 1.* Sacramento: Dept. Institutions.

Rosanoff, A.J., Handy, L.M., and Rosanoff, F.A. (1934). Criminality and delinquency in twins. *J. Criminal Law Criminol.,* 24, 923–934.

Satterfield, J.H. and Schell, A. (1997). A prospective study of hyperactive boys with conduct problems and normal boys: adolescent and adult criminality. *J. Am. Acad. Child Adolescent Psychiatr.,* 36(12), 1726–1735.

Schwesinger, G. (1952). The effect of differential parent-child relations on identical twin resemblance in personality. *Acta Gene. Med. Gemell.* (Cited by Raine, 1993.)

Shields, J. (1977). Polygenic influences. In Rutter, M. and Hersov, L. (Eds.), *Child Psychiatry: Modern Approaches* (pp. 22–46). Oxford: Blackwell.

Sigvardsson, S., Bohman, M. and Cloninger, C.R. (1996). Replication of the Stockholm Adoption Study of alcoholism. Confirmatory cross-fostering analysis. *Arch. Gen. Psychiatr.,* 53(8), 681–687.

Slater, E. (1953). The incidence of mental disorder. *Ann. Eugenics,* 6, 172.

Slutske, W.S., Heath, A.C., Dinwiddie, S.H., Madden, P.A., Bucholz, K.K., Dunne, M.P., Statham, D.J., and Martin, N.G. (1997). Modeling genetic and environmental influences in the etiology of conduct disorder: a study of 2,682 adult twin pairs. *J. Abnorm. Psychol.,* 106(2), 266–279.

Sprich, S., Biederman, J., Crawford, M.M., Mundy, E., and Faraone, S.V. (2000). Adoptive and biological families of children and adolescents with ADHD. *J. Am. Acad. Child. Adolesc. Psych.,* 39(11),1432–1437.

Stumpfl, F. (1936). Erbanalage und Verbrechen. Charakterologische und Psychiatrishe Sippen-Untersuchungen. *Julius Springer,* 117–141. (Cited in Raine, 1993.)

Taylor, J., Loney, B.R., Bobadilla, L., Iacono, W.G., and McGue, M. (2003). Genetic and environmental influences on psychopathy trait dimensions in a community sample of male twins. *J. Abnorm. Child Psychol.,* 31(6), 633–645.

Taylor, J., Iacono, W.G., and McGue, M. (2000). Evidence for a genetic etiology of early-onset delinquency. *J. Abnorm. Psychol.,* 109(4), 634–643.

Tiihonen, J., Kuikka, J., Bergstrom, K., Hakola, P., Karhu, J., Ryynanen, O.P., and Fohr, J. (1995). Altered striatal dopamine re-uptake site densities in habitually violent and non-violent alcoholics. *Nat. Med.,* 1(7), 654–657.

Van den Oord, E.J., Boomsma, D.I., and Verhulst, F.C. (1994). A study of problem behaviors in 10- to 15-year-old biologically related and unrelated international adoptees. *Behav. Genet.,* 24(3), 193–205.

Vernon, P.A., McCarthy, J.M., Johnson, A.M., Jang, K.L., and Harris, J.A. (1999). Individual differences in multiple dimensions of aggression: a univariate and multivariate genetic analysis. *Twin Res.*, 2, 16–21.

Virkkunen, M. and Linnoila, M. (1990). Serotonin in early onset, male alcoholics with violent behaviour. *Ann. Med.*, 22(5), 327–331.

Virkkunen, M., Goldman, D., and Linnoila, M. (1996). Serotonin in alcoholic violent offenders. Genetics of criminal and antisocial behavior. *Ciba Foundation Symposium.* New York: John Wiley & Sons.

Ward, A.C. (2000). Evidentiary Use of Biological Disorder: Ethics and Justice. Thesis, School of Criminology, Simon Fraser University, Burnaby, B.C.

Wolfgang, M.E., Figlio, R.M., and Sellin, T. (1972). *Delinquency in a Birth Cohort.* Chicago: University of Chicago Press.

Yamauchi, M. (1998). Association of polymorphism in the alcohol dehydrogenase 2 gene with alcohol-related organ injuries, especially liver cirrhosis. *Addiction Biol.*, 3(2), 151–158.

Yoshimashu, S. (1961). The criminological significance of the family in the light of the studies of criminal twins. *Acta Criminol. Med. Legal. Japan,* 27, 117–141.

Young, S.E., Smolen, A., Corley, R.P., Krauter, K.S., DeFries, J.C., Crowley, T.J., and Hewitt, J.K. (2002). Dopamine transporter polymorphism associated with externalizing behavior problems in children. *Am. J. Med. Genet.*, 114(2), 144–149.

Zagar, R., Arbit, J., Hughes, J., Buscell, R., and Busch, K. (1989). Developmental and disruptive behavior disorders among delinquents. *J. Am. Acad. Child. Adolesc. Psych.*, 28(3), 437–440.

# Hormonal Effects on Behavior

# 6

## Introduction

This chapter is one of several that considers areas of biology that do not directly deal with genetics, although hormones and neurotransmitters are controlled by genes. It first provides a brief overview of the normal function of hormones and how they influence behavior. There is a very fine control kept on hormone levels through negative feedback mechanisms, and this system in turn is one of the controls of behavior. One of the most hotly contested areas in biological criminology relates to the "so-called male and female hormones" as well as their relationships with other hormones. Hormone imbalances are treated medically every day, and, as we will see, there is no reason why hormone imbalances that can cause antisocial behavior could not also be favorably treated.

## The Functions of Hormones

Hormones (from the Greek word *hormon*, meaning to excite or to set in motion) are chemical signals. They are released into the blood by *endocrine cells* (the building blocks of the endocrine system, which include the hypothalamus, pituitary, and thyroid glands) and *neurosecretory cells*, which are specialized nerve cells that also make hormones (Campbell, 1996). These cells sometimes release the hormones directly, but they also often store them in a gland for later release (e.g., the digestive glands or the pancreas). Once something gets into the bloodstream, it will reach every cell in the body because that is what the blood is designed to do; to take oxygen and nutrients to every

single cell and take away waste products such as carbon dioxide and nitrog-
enous waste. However, although the hormones will get to every cell, only
certain types of cells, the *target cells* for that particular hormone, will respond.
The other cells will ignore it. Changes in hormone response could therefore
be caused by the hormone itself, by the cells that produce it, or by the target
cells' ability to respond.

Hormones regulate our metabolism, growth, development, and behavior.
They are active in tiny amounts, and a slight change in concentration can
have a dramatic effect on the body. Endocrine cells are usually clustered
together in organs or glands such as the pancreas, testes, and ovaries, and
they secrete a variety of hormones (e.g., insulin, testosterone, progesterone,
and estrogen). There are more than 50 known hormones in the human body.
In many cases, a hormone is countered by an antagonistic or opposing hormone. For example, insulin is produced by the pancreas in response to high
sugar. High blood sugar prevents the cells from absorbing nutrients; so, if
the sugar in the blood gets beyond a certain point, receptors in the pancreas
release insulin to bring it back down; but if the blood sugar gets too low, an
antagonistic hormone (i.e., glucagen) is released to send the blood sugar level
back up (Campbell, 1996). This is a simple feedback mechanism that keeps
the blood sugar at a concentration very close to a set point, whatever your
diet. When this system fails, diabetes occurs. The body has many systems
similar to this one that maintain the status quo. Some hormones fluctuate
naturally in the body (e.g., during a woman's menstrual cycle).

If hormonal balances or levels are abnormal, the effects can be severe.
We can experience behavioral changes and mood swings, or we can at the
extreme end of the range become ill and even die. Hormones are vital to our
normal body function, and experiments have proven that they do many things:
*affecting our behavior is one of their functions.* When levels of hormones change
because there is a change in the amount of the hormone or the antagonist or
a change in the target cells, things can go wrong. Remember that hormones
are designed to influence behavior and that levels vary in different people for
a variety of reasons, and several major hormones have been linked with criminal behavior.

## Testosterone

Even people who are strongly opposed to the idea that any aspect of a person's
biology can influence their behavior still seem to accept that testosterone
equals aggression, and the more testosterone, the more violent the man. The
idea that a violent person has too much testosterone is "common knowledge."
But is there any truth behind this belief? Is there a link between testosterone

and aggression? And, if so, is it *causal*? That is, even if there is a link, does the testosterone cause the aggression, does the aggression result in higher testosterone levels, or are the two mediated by something else entirely?

Testosterone is a steroidal hormone, one of several androgens or "male hormones" that are important in developing and maintaining male primary and secondary sexual characteristics. These characteristics include increased muscle mass and strength, increased bone density and strength, stimulation of growth in height, growth of penis and testes, deepening of the voice, and growth of facial and body hair.

Animal research suggests that testosterone plays an important role in some forms of aggressive behavior in rodents, and early exposure to testosterone has been found to increase aggression in a wide range of animal species (Brain, 1993). These findings lead to the question: does testosterone have the same effect on humans?

More than 100 years ago, a highly respected French doctor, Charles Sequard, shocked the scientific community, and later the world, with his discovery that testicles contained an invigorating substance that could be extracted from animals and injected into humans (Boyd, 2000). The elderly doctor admitted trying the substance himself and reported increased mental concentration and physical endurance, and many other physical and mental benefits. Although, unfortunately, Sequard was ridiculed at the time, today he is recognized for the pioneering work he did with hormones and glands, discovering the effects of testosterone some 50 years before testosterone itself was actually discovered in 1935 (Boyd, 2000).

It has always been understood that the testicles related in some way to sexual ability in males. Farmers knew that a castrated animal could not reproduce; and in days past, the same relationship was seen also in humans. So the testicles and, consequently, testosterone are clearly linked to sperm production and sex drive, but are they related to aggression? It was also common knowledge that castrating or "neutering" an animal reduces its intra-species aggression and overall "spirit." A gelded or castrated male horse is much more malleable, and a neutered dog is far less aggressive toward other male dogs.

Animal studies show a clear link between aggression and testosterone, and also show that the link may relate not just to the presence of the hormone, but also to the timing of exposure in the developing body (Boyd, 2000). But do these findings relate to aggression in humans? There is indisputable evidence that testosterone is related to sex drive. Men with low sex drive as a result of age or lack of testicular function can often become sexually active as well as more mentally and physically able when they are treated with testosterone (Boyd, 2000). Many studies have noted improved sex drive and sexual performance. However, there is no evidence from these studies that the testosterone level also causes increased aggression (Albert et al., 1993).

In his book entitled *The Beast Within*, Boyd talks about the age curve of crime. This is a well-known graph that shows that violent crimes committed by young men suddenly increase sharply around the age of 15. It peaks at about age 20 and then falls dramatically by age 30. By age 40, violent crime is rare. The graph looks like a sharply rising mountain peak that drops off just as dramatically. Although the size of the peak varies because crime rates vary in different countries, the same pattern is found in every country studied. The graph for testosterone levels in males is very similar (Quinsey et al., 2004); it also peaks at about age 20 but the greatest increases are in the teen years, the same time that violent crime increases (Boyd, 2000). The parallel is certainly suggestive but is it not proof. It does indicate a possible relationship that should be investigated. In addition, before puberty, the rates of homicide and suicide are similar for boys and girls; but by age 13, male rates for both are double and by age 16 they are four times as high (Denno, 1990). Cultural differences are usually given as an explanation but the difference between the levels of violence in girls and boys is universal. It occurs in all cultures that have been looked at around the world and throughout time as well (Moffit et al., 2001). As Boyd points out, it seems most unlikely that all the different cultures and societies that exist and have existed would produce the same results; it would seem much more logical that the difference is a result of hormones, which are known to differ between girls and boys (Boyd, 2000).

Many studies on the possible relationship between aggression and testosterone show mixed results, perhaps partially because it used to be very difficult to measure testosterone levels. In many of the studies, only one blood test was taken. Testosterone is secreted episodically, so a single reading is not a reliable indicator. A good sample requires at least three blood samples taken at least 15 minutes apart and averaged (Goldzieher et al., 1976). In addition, blood is not a good sampling medium. Blood tests are invasive, and 98% of the testosterone in the blood is bound to sex hormone-binding globulin (SHBG), which means that this 98% is not free to enter target cells and bind with receptors. So, only 2% of the testosterone in blood is physiologically active (Raine, 1993). Testosterone levels are now usually measured in saliva, which is a much less invasive test (Landsman et al., 1976). In addition, the testosterone in saliva is unbound and therefore free to act, and it has been found to correlate highly with free serum testosterone (Tames and Swift, 1983).

People have been fascinated with the idea of increased "maleness," aggression, and testosterone for decades. Remember the "XYY man" media circus? Researchers have looked at levels of testosterone in violent and nonviolent men and, in some cases, women. They have looked at the effects of increasing testosterone levels artificially for medical reasons (Brain, 1993) and in illegal steroid use in sports as well as at the effects of decreasing testosterone levels by either chemical or physical castration.

## Natural Testosterone Levels in Aggressive Men

Researchers have wondered for years whether some men have naturally higher levels of testosterone than others and are more violent as a consequence (Boyd, 2000). Innumerable studies have been done in an effort to relate testosterone levels to various measures of aggression. Every type of measurement for aggression and testosterone level has been employed, and men from incarcerated violent offenders to volunteer students have been studied. The results have been mixed but none have shown that it is possible to use testosterone levels to predict whether a person will be aggressive (Boyd, 2000).

A famous prison study in the late 1960s looked at blood testosterone levels in relationship to aggression; and although they did not find a direct relationship between testosterone and aggression, it did appear that those prisoners with a history of violence during adolescence had higher testosterone levels than those who were not aggressive as adolescents (Kreuz and Rose, 1972). The researchers thought this finding meant that high testosterone levels play a role in the development of aggression during adolescence (Boyd, 2000). Researchers looking at 194 male adolescent offenders found that the violent offenders did have higher levels of testosterone than nonviolent or sexual offenders (Brooks and Reddon, 1996).

In a more recent prison study, a very large sample of 4462 inmates were examined for testosterone levels and antisocial behavior (Dabbs and Morris, 1990). High levels of testosterone were positively correlated with a variety of problems, including delinquency, substance abuse, conflicts with authority figures, and promiscuity (Dabbs and Morris, 1990), although many of these problems have myriad causes. In an earlier study on incarcerated young males, Dabbs et al. (1987) found that high testosterone levels were positively correlated with more violent crimes, rule violations in prison, and parole board decisions against release (Dabbs et al., 1987).

Although testosterone is always considered a male hormone, it is also found in women, produced by cells in the ovaries. In a prison study of incarcerated women, Dabbs et al. (1988) also found a correlation between high testosterone levels and violence in women. High testosterone was found to be specific to the type of violence. It was highest in female prisoners who had committed unprovoked assaults, and lowest in inmates who had only reacted violently when they were physically assaulted (Dabbs et al., 1988). In a later study of 87 female inmates in a maximum security prison, Dabbs et al. compared both the women's ages and testosterone levels with the level of violence of the crime for which they had been convicted, as well as their aggression and dominance while in prison (Dabbs and Hargrove, 1997). The workers found a direct link between testosterone, criminal behavior, and aggressively dominant behavior in prison, and also found that criminal violence and aggressive dominance decreased with age (Dabbs and Hargrove,

1997). This may have been due to reduced testosterone levels in older women, but could also be linked to many other factors linked to increased age, as well as length of time spent in prison and the total numbers of years spent incarcerated, which were not considered. As well, the level of violence of the crime committed before incarceration may well indicate the level of violence once imprisoned. Interestingly, the five women who had the lowest testosterone levels were reported by prison staff to be very treacherous and "sneaky." The researchers suggested that because there is a strong link between dominance and testosterone, those women at the bottom of the dominance scale, due to low testosterone levels, may have had to resort to less confrontational methods of dealing with others (Dabbs and Hargrove, 1997).

More recently, Dabbs et al. (1995) focused on specific types of crimes, such as those involving sexual assault or violence. They measured salivary testosterone levels in 692 adult incarcerated men and compared these with their criminal records and the prison records of behavior while incarcerated. Offenders convicted of crimes that involved interpersonal violence such as sexual assault and violence had higher levels of testosterone than offenders convicted of property crimes or drug offenses. During incarceration, offenders with higher levels of testosterone were more likely to break prison rules and be overly confrontational (Dabbs et al., 1995). They extended this study in 2001, examining data from a subset of 230 male prisoners from the previous sample in order to investigate not only the type of crime committed, but also the way in which the men had actually committed their crime(s), such as level of planning, whether the consequences had been intended, the level of violence of the crime, whether the action was especially callous, whether the victim was a stranger, and whether sexual assault occurred (Dabbs et al., 2001). The results varied, depending on the crime. In homicide cases, inmates with higher testosterone levels were significantly more likely to kill people they knew, and also more likely to plan the action ahead of time. They tended to be more callous than those with low testosterone levels, but not significantly so (Dabbs et al., 2001). Interestingly, testosterone level was not related to these parameters in inmates who committed crimes of robbery, assault, and sexual assault, without homicide. The authors interpret the results to mean that high-testosterone killers were more ruthless than low-testosterone killers. However, the sample size, although originally good, becomes much smaller when sub-sampled in this manner.

In a study of 54 culturally diverse nonincarcerated men from low socio-economic backgrounds, elevated testosterone levels correlated with committing domestic abuse, as well as the levels of verbal and physical domestic violence (Soler et al., 2000). However, alcohol consumption and demographic characteristics were also significant in predicting levels of abuse, so although the testosterone may play some role, it is unclear from this study whether it relates directly to the domestic violence, or more indirectly through other parameters such as alcoholism. Previous studies have suggested a link between high levels of testosterone and alcoholism. In a study of 61 men undergoing forensic psychiatric examinations, Stalenheim et al. (1998a) measured testosterone in three ways: (1) blood serum levels of free testosterone; (2) total testosterone; and (3) levels of sex hormone-binding globulin (SHBG), which is correlated with testosterone concentration. They found that high levels of total testosterone and SHBG were highly correlated with type II alcoholism (Stalenheim et al., 1998a). Type II alcoholism has a very strong genetic basis, an early onset (childhood or adolescence), and is frequently associated with criminal behavior (Cloninger et al., 1981). High levels of total testosterone and SHBG were also correlated with antisocial personality disorder (ASP) and to higher ratings of socially deviant behavior on the Psychopathy Checklist-Revised (PCL-R). Interestingly, free testosterone was more strongly associated with personality-related scores on the PCL-R (Stalenheim et al., 1998a). Again, it is difficult to see whether the link in this case is between psychopathy or ASP and testosterone, or between alcoholism and antisocial behavior.

As we have seen, sample size is crucial in reaching worthwhile conclusions. In a preliminary study of elderly men with dementia, for example, physical aggression was correlated with increased levels of testosterone, although nonaggressive agitation was not correlated (Orengo et al., 1997). This study, however, only involved 13 men, and dementia can involve many different disorders, including brain injury, so here is a case where it is clearly difficult to generalize without a larger sample size.

Testosterone is usually considered to exhibit effects after puberty but testosterone is an important hormone in development from conception onward. Researchers in Spain studied 28 male and 20 female preschoolers, evaluating their levels of aggression in free play with peers, during social and play interactions, and compared their behavior with salivary testosterone levels (Sanchez-Martin et al., 2000). They found a positive correlation between testosterone levels and serious aggression in boys in social situations but not in playful aggression. No correlation was seen in girls (Sanchez-Martin et al., 2000).

Some testosterone studies are interesting but remain suggestive. It is well known that testosterone levels are not static but fluctuate throughout the day and in response to a variety of stimuli, and some proponents of the testosterone and aggression theory have suggested that it is this fluctuation that correlates with aggression — rather than the levels themselves (Archer, 1991). Interesting research has considered competition rather than aggression and its relationship to testosterone fluctuations. A study of wrestlers found that winners of wrestling bouts had higher testosterone readings than the losers, but the results were only significant for about 10 minutes after the fight (Archer, 1991; Boyd, 2000). Research on young male judo competitors found that vigorous exercise increased testosterone levels more than the fighting (Salvador et al., 1985). However, a later study by the same authors, again looking at judo competitors, found a positive correlation between testosterone levels before and after a fight, with aggression during the fight (Salvador et al., 1999).

Even vicariously experiencing sporting events by watching favorite sports teams compete has been shown to influence testosterone levels. Bernhardt et al. (1998) measured salivary testosterone levels in fans before and after a sports match in two experiments. In the first experiment, eight male fans were assessed before and after attending a basketball game between two traditional university sports teams; and in the second study, 21 male fans were assessed before and after watching a televised World Cup Football (soccer) match between international rivals. In both studies, before and after comparisons showed that testosterone levels increased in the fans of winning teams and decreased in the fans of losing teams, and the results were quite dramatic (Bernhardt et al., 1998). The authors concluded that testosterone may be important in self-esteem, and that the findings could also reflect the interaction between competition and status. These findings point to an adaptive evolutionary response. The success in competition results in an increase in status and an increase in testosterone; this, in turn, offers greater chances of further success. On the other hand, failure in competition results in reduced status, reduced testosterone levels, and increased risk of failure in the future, thereby reducing future confrontations (Bernhardt et al., 1998). While a basketball game hardly seems to be important on an evolutionary scale, if viewed in light of our simian heritage, where competition most usually involved competition for resources or a mate, it does seem to suggest that those who win would have an evolutionary advantage and would be more likely to survive and reproduce. In addition, the fewer competitions necessary, the greater the chance that both parties will survive. An interesting question that follows this evidence of increased levels of testosterone in vicarious sports wins is what influence, if any, does this have on the sometimes vicious sports violence that often follows large sports events?

Competition does not have to involve aggression such as in contact sports, or even physical exertion. Even totally cerebral competitive activities such as chess games and simple coin tosses have been shown to cause increased or decreased testosterone levels, depending on whether the subject wins or loses (Mazur et al., 1992; McCaul et al., 1992).

In sum, although the studies on testosterone have been mixed in terms of showing a conclusive and direct relationship to aggression, many studies have shown a link between testosterone levels and competitive success. This is illustrated in the above studies that look at sports events and games, but has also been seen in other life events that involve an increase in status (such as graduation from medical school) (Mazur and Lamb, 1980). Mazur (1985) has proposed a biosocial model that suggests that testosterone is more related to status and dominance than to actual aggression. Interestingly, Mazur and Booth (1998) have shown that testosterone levels in men change with marriage and divorce. They reported that male testosterone levels decrease after marriage but increase again in the event of divorce. Quinsey et al. (2004) explain this as a shift from mating effort to commitment to a partner and offspring. Although siring offspring is obviously important in evolution, parental investment is required to ensure that those offspring survive to reproduce and pass on parental genes.

## Serotonin and Testosterone

Almost nothing in the body acts in isolation. Hormones, genes, and neurotransmitters (brain messengers) all interact and influence each other. It has been suggested that the purported relationship between testosterone and aggression may not be direct, and may instead be more closely related to other chemicals in the body that are modulated by testosterone. One of the most likely candidates is serotonin. Serotonin is a neurotransmitter in the brain that has been repeatedly linked to aggression and impulsivity (see Chapter 8 for a discussion of serotonin). High testosterone levels are often correlated with low levels of serotonin, which have in turn been strongly linked to aggression. In a study of rapists, Giotakos et al. (2003) found that plasma levels of testosterone, as well as other androgens, were significantly higher than in controls, but that levels of 5-HIAA (the major metabolite of serotonin) were significantly lower (Giotakos et al., 2003).

Bernhardt (1997) and Mazur (1985; Mazur and Booth, 1998) believe that testosterone is more directly related to dominance than to aggression *per se,* and this is supported by the several studies that indicate increased testosterone levels during sporting competitions and games. Such dominance could lead to aggression but is more related to improving status and is usually nonaggressive (Mazur and Booth, 1998). Bernhardt (1997) suggests that aggressive men may have a combination of high levels of testosterone and low levels of serotonin, and that aggression may ensue when such a man is frustrated in his attempts to achieve status or dominance. People with low serotonin levels are impulsive and inclined to over-respond to aversive stimuli. Bernhardt thus speculates that high testosterone levels would encourage dominance-seeking behavior, which, if it led to failure, could result in violence associated with low serotonin levels (Bernhardt, 1997).

Higley et al. (1996) suggest that testosterone relates to aggressive drive and serotonin relates to regulating the intensity, threshold, and frequency of the expression of aggression. Therefore, males with high testosterone levels but normal serotonin levels might exhibit aggression in certain situations and be dominant, but would be unlikely to be violent. Conversely, males with high testosterone levels but low serotonin levels would have greater impulsivity and a lower threshold for aggression, resulting in more frequent episodes of violence. As well, such males would be less able to prevent aggression from escalating into violence and injury (Higley et al., 1996). Higley et al. (1996) studied adolescent male rhesus monkeys and found that testosterone levels alone positively correlated with competitive aggression but not impulsivity; serotonin levels negatively correlated with impulsive behavior and severe unrestrained bouts of violence but not general aggression overall; and males with low serotonin and high testosterone levels exhibited an increased number of incidents and an increased intensity of the aggression. This animal study does support an interaction between serotonin and testosterone. Such an interaction is logical and supports the idea that high testosterone alone does not result in violence, but merely competitive aggression. This competitive aggression could relate to attaining resources or a mate. The findings also point to a certain definition of aggression in the animal kingdom: unrestrained, forceful, and highly violent behavior, including biting and beating, but a pattern that is goal directed. Does the same definition hold for humans? One could argue that most successful people are competitively aggressive to a certain extent or they would not be successful. This is not to suggest, however, that such people are aggressive *per se*, or violent, but merely that competition for status is fairly normal. However, if such a drive is combined with other behavioral conditions such as low neurotransmitter function, then behavioral disorders could result.

## Increasing Testosterone

Many researchers have shown higher testosterone levels in aggressive individuals but none have shown that the testosterone causes the violence, although it is frequently intimated. There can be, and no doubt are, many other factors at work to create aggressive behavior, and the link to testosterone levels may be very indirect. Clearly, not everyone with a high testosterone level is violent; in fact, the great majority are not and frequently live very successful lives. This would support the idea that the true relationship is between dominance and testosterone rather than aggression. However, a simple experiment to determine the effects of increased testosterone would be to increase testosterone artificially in normal men and observe the effects. Naturally, this is not easy to do ethically and thus most experiments in this arena have been problematic (for a review, see Boyd, 2000). Experiments can be divided into three groups:

(1) artificially increasing testosterone in an experimental situation, (2) observing the effects of medically prescribed testosterone on elderly men with sexual dysfunction, and finally, (3) observing the effects of the illegal use of anabolic steroids in athletes. Experiments to date on increasing testosterone artificially in an experimental situation have failed to prove consistent results, but due to ethical and medical reasons have traditionally involved only very low doses of testosterone, and thus are unlikely to show dramatic results.

Testosterone is frequently medically prescribed for men with sexual dysfunction or for elderly men; yet although the hormone frequently increases sexual desire, and, in elderly patients, results in greater mental acuity, there are no reports of concurrent increases in aggression in these patients. Performance athletes who use high doses of illegal anabolic steroids would be a more appropriate experimental group because they are young and healthy and are taking very high doses. However, one could also argue that due to the sports in which they are involved, they may already exhibit a predisposition for violence (Boyd, 2000). Thus far, studies of such athletes have had mixed results and also suffer from extremely low sample sizes.

The research on the effects of increased testosterone does not show whether or not increased testosterone results in increased aggression. Perhaps there is no direct relationship, or perhaps the experiments have not been well conducted. Medical and ethical concerns prevent good experimental design so there have been no large-scale, double-blind studies where neither the subjects nor the researcher knows who is in the control group and who is in the experimental group. Therefore, it is difficult to tell whether increased testosterone would result in behavioral changes.

## Chemical and Physical Castration

If we have not succeeded in examining the results of artificially increased testosterone levels, then perhaps information could be gleaned from observing the effects of removing testosterone. Removal of parts of the body that relate to the production of testosterone has been used to curb behavior for centuries. The most obvious method of removing testosterone is to remove the testes, and castration of men or animals has a long history. However, although the testes actually produce the testosterone, it is the brain that controls its production. The part of the brain that is responsible for controlling the production of testosterone is the amygdala, and past attempts to reduce aggression involved trying to remove or destroy that part of the brain. As discussed in a later chapter, brain damage of any sort is liable to influence behavior, and no part of the brain is responsible for only one action; thus, such surgery was highly speculative and carried high risks. Such amygdalectomy surgeries did achieve a certain popularity in the mid-1960s and 1970s with predictably inconsistent results (Boyd, 2000).

The critical question is always whether any relationship that may exist between violence and testosterone is *causal*. That is, does a high testosterone level cause the violence? Although studies have shown that there are some correlations, with higher testosterone levels in violent individuals, they do not prove that there is a causal relationship (Boyd, 2000). The best experiment would be to look at someone's level of violence or aggression, remove the testosterone, and measure the level of violence once the level of testosterone has dropped dramatically. We could do such an experiment with animals but not with humans. However, real-life scenarios exist that can be studied, which leads us to castration.

Castration using surgery or chemicals is the most common way to reduce testosterone. Physical castration removes the testes, while chemical castration involves regular doses of anti-androgens, which lower testosterone production. Chemical castration is less permanent than physical castration but often results in unpleasant side effects, such as breast enlargement, loss of body hair, weight gain, and drowsiness, and, of course, is only effective when the drugs are taken consistently (Meyer and Cole, 1997). Anti-androgen, or anti-male hormone, therapy reduces sexual interest and therefore reduces the risk that an offender will commit future sexual crimes, but it does *not* reduce antisocial or violent behavior. Also, many people refuse to take the drugs, even when they are in prison. Once they get out and are no longer monitored, compliance is even worse. Once a man stops taking the drugs, normal libido will return in about 3 weeks (Meyer and Cole, 1997). As well, there are serious ethical issues to consider here. Is castration a treatment or a punishment? If a judge were to impose castration, even if only chemical, as part of the sanction for a crime, does that mean our judges are acting as unqualified doctors? (Miller, 1998). The anti-androgens used are medical treatments that do have side effects, and only a doctor is qualified to determine whether it is appropriate to use such treatment. Even if such treatment is not imposed as a sanction, and is only ever used at the request of the offender, we still return to the question of whether one can ever consider that someone who is incarcerated can truly give permission — especially if there is a perception that a certain choice might increase the chance of parole. In fact, such treatment is really just a form of negative eugenics as the man is being prevented from having sexual relations and, therefore, reproducing.

A commonly used anti-androgen in the United States is the synthetic progesterone, medroxyprogesterone acetate (MPA); (Meyer and Cole, 1997). Progesterone is a primarily female hormone but does occur naturally in low levels in men. At high doses, MPA therapy is equivalent to physical castration but low doses will still allow low levels of sexual activity to be maintained, although testosterone levels and consequent sex drive are reduced (Boyd, 2000). In a series of 11 studies on the efficacy of MPA reviewed by Meyer and Cole (1997), the recidivism rate was found to vary from 0 to 83%, depending on the study. Even when recidivism was dramatically reduced, this related only to sexual crimes, and no reduction was observed in nonsexual crimes.

MPA is also used medically for women, in contraceptives and in hormone replacement therapy, and side effects that have been reported include depression, mood swings, and loss of libido. In primate research, six female ovariectomized macaques were tested for 1 week each on estrogen alone, estrogen plus natural progesterone, estrogen plus MPA, and a placebo. Monkeys given MPA exhibited much greater levels of anxiety and aggression than on any other treatment (Pazol et al., 2004). This work, although non-human and only on a few subjects, does support reports of side effects caused by MPA; and although this study refers to women, it is of concern that a synthetic hormone that can increase aggression under some circumstances is recommended to reduce aggression in men. The effects of progesterone in women, however, who normally have high levels of the hormone, are likely to be quite different from those in men, who normally have only very low levels. Following from this study, two experiments in mice showed that eliminating progesterone in males greatly reduced their normal aggression toward their offspring, and even resulted in paternal nurturing (Schneider et al., 2003). In the first experiment, genetic manipulations resulted in a line of mice that was missing the gene that encodes for progesterone receptors, which means that the mice would not respond to progesterone. Male mice missing this gene behaved dramatically differently from normal male mice. Normal male mice showed severe aggression to conspecifics (members of the same species) and to their offspring, with 72% of control mice killing their own infants. However, mice without the ability to recognize progesterone were not only completely nonaggressive to their offspring, but were also actually caring and nurturing fathers (Schneider et al., 2003). In the second experiment, a drug was used to block progesterone receptors and again the male mice became very caring toward their offspring and showed no aggression. Both sets of male mice were unchanged in their aggression to conspecifics (Schneider et al., 2003). This again suggests an increased role (rather than a decreased role) of progesterone in males, which again suggests that MPA, although reducing sexual desire in men, may have undesirable behavioral side effects. These studies should be broadened to include humans to understand the effect in man.

Cyproterone acetate (CPA) is another anti-androgen more commonly used in Europe and Canada. The results of treatment with this drug seem somewhat better, with recidivism ranging from 0 to 33% (Meyer and Cole, 1997). Most of the re-offending was committed by offenders who were not complying with the treatment. Both types of anti-androgens are only considered effective when they are used in conjunction with psychotherapy (Meyer and

Cole, 1997). It is possible in the future that less drastic reductions in testosterone level might also be effective. In a study of eight normal men, suppressing gonadal function using a gonadotropin-releasing hormone antagonist but maintaining testosterone at low normal levels with injections resulted in definite reductions in externalizing anger in all subjects, with half also showing reductions in anxiety and sexual desire (Loosen et al., 1994). The authors suggested that outward-directed anger was sensitive to very small reductions in testosterone. However, the sample size was very small, so studies should be repeated on larger groups to determine efficacy, and on offenders to find out whether such treatment would reduce recidivism.

Contrary to common belief, castrated men can still engage in sex. Spontaneous erections do not occur after physical castration (Boyd, 2000) but erections are possible after intensive stimulation and even ejaculation is possible in almost one third of cases (Wille and Beier, 1989), which proves that the brain really is the major sex organ.

Physical castration is rare but it has been practiced in Switzerland, Germany, and Czechoslovakia (Boyd, 2000). Castration is only performed if the patient requests it and, even then, only after lengthy medical and legal examinations. A study from Germany compared behavior in men before and after voluntary castration (Wille and Beier, 1989). Testosterone levels were reduced by medically castrating volunteer sex offenders, and then following up with these subjects after release from prison to assess whether recidivism was reduced. In this study, 99 castrated sex offenders and 35 noncastrated sex offenders were followed for, on average, 11 years after release. They accounted for about 25% of all castrations in the period from 1970 to 1980, so they are reasonably representative of this population. Obviously, you cannot randomly assign the men to the experimental or control groups, yet the controls were sound as all 35 had originally requested castration and then changed their minds, so they were about as close a control group as could be achieved ethically in such a situation. The control group was matched for previous criminal record, age, intelligence, social background, and marital status. The recidivism rate over an average of 11 years post-release was 3% in castrated offenders, compared with 46% in noncastrated offenders (Wille and Beier, 1989). This result is fairly consistent with previous studies on sex offenders. It is often supposed that once a man is castrated, he cannot commit a sexually violent offense. However, a sexual assault is more an act of violence and dominance than of sex. An impotent man can sexually assault a person. Penetration could occur with a stick, a knife, or a gun barrel. Many people are raped in such ways, so the lack of testes would not prevent attack.

These studies are interesting but they still do not prove conclusively that high testosterone levels are causally related to criminal violence; and, in particular, we cannot conclude much about nonsexual violence. For nonsexual crimes, there was no difference in the recidivism rates for castrated and non-castrated offenders whether physical or chemical castration was used. The nonsexual crimes of the castrated men are still socially destructive; and although sexual drive is reduced, the inappropriate targets of sexual desire do not change (e.g., a desire for sex with young children) (Meyer and Cole, 1997).

So all in all, there is some evidence that testosterone has some relationship with violence and aggression, but the relationship is not direct and seems to be quite complex. Testosterone levels are partly inherited, which might suggest that a genetic predisposition to crime may relate less directly to the genes and more directly to the testosterone levels. It is most likely that testosterone is only one of many hormones that influence aggressive behavior, and it is likely that these hormones interact with each other and that they are also influenced by many environmental factors (Raine, 1993). Testosterone levels are directly related to other biological chemicals in the body, such as serotonin, and it is possible that the link to aggression is through serotonin rather than directly through testosterone.

To summarize, testosterone is the most controversial hormone, and there are arguments both for and against a relationship between testosterone levels and aggression. There are certainly a plethora of studies that indicate some sort of link, although no one has been able to show a causal link. As well, the removal of testosterone chemically or physically does have a significant effect on crimes of sexual violence (Meyer and Cole, 1997; Wille and Beier, 1989). Sexual crimes are crimes of violence, related to power and dominance. However, the reduction in sex crimes via a reduction in testosterone indicates that sexual violence relates both to sex and to power and dominance (Boyd, 2000).

Boyd claims that sex is the connection to aggression rather than testosterone directly, as testosterone influences the sex drive and this in turn affects aggression (Boyd 2000). Bernhardt (1997) and Booth (1998) feel, instead, that testosterone relates more to dominance. The two theories are not mutually exclusive because sex, especially in evolutionary terms, does relate to dominance over potential rivals. This would explain why, although it is difficult to show a direct causal relationship between testosterone and aggression, peak ages for violence and homicide in men are so similar to age-related testosterone peaks. The age at which a young man reaches sexual maturity, and consequently peak testosterone levels, is also a period of confusing social signals and competition for status, as well as being an intensely sexual period when youths first begin to develop relationships and compete with peers (Boyd, 2000). This, it could also be argued, is also a time when status and dominance over peers are extremely important, both sexually and for self-esteem. Combined in some cases with low serotonin levels, and its consequent links to impulsivity and aggression, it is not surprising that testosterone still appears to have an intriguing link to male aggression. What is clear is that there is no identifiable causal link, and at no time could one measure a man's testosterone level and predict that he is likely to become a criminal, any more than you could predict that he is likely to become a successful lawyer or doctor.

## Other Androgen Activity

Androgen is a generic term used for a large group of steroidal hormones that primarily affect male sexual and behavioral characteristics but are also present and active in women. Testosterone is the most common androgen but there are several others.

Testosterone and other androgens, although always associated with men and even considered as the "male hormones," are also found in women. In a study on the relationship between externalizing behavior and testosterone and 5-alpha-dihydrotestosterone (DHT), another androgen, researchers compared 36 male and 51 female 14-year-old children (Maras et al., 2003). The children had been assessed for externalizing behavior at age 8, 11, and 14 years as part of a larger study. Blood plasma levels of the primary metabolites of testosterone and DHT were highly correlated with aggression and externalizing behavior in boys but not in girls. The most persistent and aggressive boys had the highest plasma levels of both metabolites (Maras et al., 2003).

In a study of 15 aggressive, antisocial boys diagnosed with conduct disorder (CD) and 25 control boys, the CD boys were found to have significantly higher levels of the androgen dehydroepiandrosterone (DHEAS) than normal boys, but did not have higher levels of testosterone. DHEAS is secreted by the adrenal glands. The boys were between 8 and 12 years old when tested, a time when androgen levels are beginning to substantially increase. Boys with the highest levels of DHEAS were those with the greatest levels of aggression and other antisocial behavior as rated by both teachers and parents (Van Goozen et al., 1998).

All hormones are controlled by genes, and a gene termed the AR gene has been identified as an androgen receptor and has several alleles or variants. One of the alleles is referred to as the "short" allele or version of the gene, and it has been associated with increased androgen activity, as well as ADHD, CD, and oppositional defiant disorder (Comings et al., 2002). Early menarche (or puberty) in girls was correlated with paternal abandonment. Psychologists have assumed that this relates to increased stress caused by the abandonment, which in turn results in depression, insecurity, and weight gain; and it is this weight gain that initiates hormonal changes that result in early menarche. Early menarche has both psychological and medical implications as such girls are sometimes found to be more promiscuous and more likely to have babies earlier than girls who are not abandoned and have a normal menarche. As well, early menarche is linked to higher rates of breast and cervical cancers as well as other health problems. The relationship between the father leaving and the girl's early menarche and consequent behavioral problems were thought to be primarily psychosocial, but recent experiments have suggested that the link may be a very simple genetic relationship between father and daughter (Comings et al., 2002; for a well-known alternative theory, see Belsky et al., 1992).

Comings et al. (2002) evaluated 121 men and 164 unrelated women for the presence of the short allele of the AR gene. This gene is sex-linked, so is found on the X chromosome. This means that, similar to hemophilia and color-blindness, women are carriers unless they receive the allele from both parents, and men express the effects of the gene as they only have a single X chromosome. If the father carries the allele, he will pass it to a daughter but not a son. If a woman carries the allele, she can pass it to either a son or a daughter. The researchers found that men who possessed the short version of the allele were more violent and impulsive than men without this allele, and also more sexually compulsive, with an increased number of sexual partners. Women who had two copies of the allele, and thus would express the gene, were found to have significantly higher rates of divorced parents, fathers who abandoned them in childhood, and early menarche or puberty (Comings et al., 2002). The authors claim that their research indicates a biological link between the fathers' behaviors, such as marital disharmony and abandonment of family, and the daughters' early puberty and sexual activity, resulting in early childbearing. The link is the shared genotype passed from father to daughter on the X chromosome. Because the gene is on the X chromosome, the father does not pass it to his sons, which, the authors say, could explain why girls seem to be much more influenced by the fathers' abandonment than boys. They also point out that girls whose fathers die rather than leave do not experience these biological and behavioral changes, as there is no reason to assume that fathers who die early are any more likely to carry this allele than the general population (Comings et al., 2002). This study is highly intriguing and does give a neat and simple genetic explanation for both biological (early puberty) and psychological behavior changes. However, it is certainly preliminary and further research is required before drawing additional conclusions.

## Premenstrual Syndrome and Crime

Most studies looking at hormones consider testosterone as the main hormone that could be involved in antisocial behavior. However, there are many other hormones in a person's body that affect, among other things, behavior. Hormone levels in women in general are well studied, not for criminogenic reasons but simply because they fluctuate so greatly during an adult woman's life. Many hormones in a woman's body fluctuate dramatically over a monthly cycle from puberty to menopause as a woman's body prepares every month to be ready to accept a fertilized egg (zygote). If the female is not impregnated, then the body goes through all those hormonal fluctuations again a month later. If she is impregnated, different fluctuations occur.

During ovulation, when a woman releases an egg, which occurs roughly midway between menstrual periods, estrogen and progesterone levels are high. Progesterone levels drop prior to menstruation and the other hormones increase. In some women, these changes result in the clinical syndrome of premenstrual syndrome (PMS; or more properly called late luteal phase dysphoric disorder). It can result in increased irritability, concentration problems, and emotional changes, including depression and aggression. Some people believe that PMS can also escalate into an increased propensity for violent and antisocial behavior (Raine, 1993).

In the past, anti-feminist reports dating from the 1800s have tried to relate menstruation to many criminal acts, suggesting that women are "unstable" at such times (Harry and Balcer, 1987). More recent and serious studies have attempted to determine whether hormonal fluctuations in a woman could actually predispose her to criminal behavior, although none are conclusive.

One of the first and best-known scientific studies looked at over 150 newly convicted women in prison (Dalton, 1961). The researcher found that almost half of the crimes for which the women were convicted had occurred either 4 days before or 4 days after menstruation (sheer chance would have been 29%) (Raine, 1993). As the crimes were almost all nonviolent, these data merely relate to nonviolent crime. PMS, however, is usually reported to occur a week or two prior to menstruation, with clinical signs improving after menstruation begins. In this case, only crimes that occurred the week prior to menstruation would occur during the risk period. In a later study, Dalton also suggested that menstruation might relate to timing of maternal child abuse (Dalton, 1966).

More recent studies do suggest that a small group of women may be more susceptible to cyclical fluctuations in hormone levels that make them more prone to anger during menstruation (Fishbein, 1992). Although most women show few or no effects of PMS during menstruation, some do seem to suffer much more severely. Whether those women who suffer more are more likely to be involved in crime is a different matter entirely. There is another problem with any study that looks at incarcerated women — women who spend time together frequently cycle together. No intimate contact is needed, just simply being around other women. Also, if a male is present only at certain times, then a group of women will cycle so that they are fertile when the male is present, again with no intimacy suggested, merely presence. This cycling may be a hangover from prehistoric days when men went out and hunted and were only present rarely. All the women being fertile at the same time would have increased reproductive success and, therefore, survival.

Critics of the idea that PMS can result in aggression point out that stress can also affect the menstrual cycle (Raine, 1993). They suggest that the stress caused by committing the crime and the following arrest and police interrogation could potentially trigger menstruation, which would mean that stress brought on menstruation rather than vice versa (Horney, 1978). As well, there are many other changes in body chemistry taking place during menstruation, including a reduction in both norepinephrine and blood glucose levels (Fishbein, 1992). Both of these factors have separately been linked to violence (discussed in later chapters), so any of these factors, or an interaction between them, could be responsible for any possible link between PMS and violence (Raine, 1993).

A study on serotonin levels in premenstrual women suggested that lowered serotonin could result in increased aggression. Twenty-four premenstrual women were given amino acid drinks prior to commencing a reaction time test. Half the women were given a drink containing tryptophan, the dietary precursor for serotonin, and half received a placebo. When the women performed the tests without stress, both groups performed equally well. When placed under stress (exposed to loud, unpleasant noise), the women who had reduced levels of serotonin were significantly more aggressive than those with normal levels of serotonin (Bond et al., 2001). Although none of the women were classified as hostile in initial tests, those who scored the highest on the initial hostility tests were most aggressive when they had lowered serotonin in combination with stress (Bond et al., 2001). However, the authors did not test women at other times of the menstrual cycle to determine whether the effect was related to a combination of premenstrual timing and serotonin, or was just related to depleted serotonin, which has been repeatedly linked to aggression (see Chapter 8).

The fact that we do not have any concrete evidence for or against a link does not mean that a link does not exist. One thing that does suggest some sort of link is that progesterone therapy given for medical reasons has been reported to reduce aggressive behavior in women (Raine, 1993). In most cases, the idea that PMS is linked to crime has been blown out of proportion by tabloid newspapers. More research is necessary to determine whether any such link actually exists.

There are obvious legal and ethical implications. PMS distress has been used as a defense, in some cases successfully, and there are many articles that argue the validity of such a defense (Pahl-Smith, 1985; Holtzman, 1984; Press, 1983; Taylor and Dalton, 1983). If further work in this field does suggest a link, we have to consider how it might affect women's rights. Some authors warn of the political, moral, and ethical concerns related to using such a defense in court (Kendall, 1991).

## Growth Hormones

One of the earliest criminological theories put forward in the latter part of the 19th century was that of Lombroso, who suggested a link between facial features and size and criminal activity. As with so many theories of the time, the idea was later found to be no more scientific than phrenology. However, the way people look is an easy thing to measure; and whether we admit to it or not, most people do make judgments based on the way a person looks.

Early research efforts somewhat supported Lombroso's theories suggesting that both juvenile delinquents and adult criminals differed from controls in body shape. They said that the offenders were, in general, bigger (meso-morphic and mesomorphic–endomorphic) than controls, who were more inclined to be slight and thin (ectomorphic) (Sheldon et al., 1949). Raine (1993) reviewed several such studies, which do suggest that both male and female offenders tend to be more muscular and heavier than non-offenders, although all suffer from several methodological flaws, such as extremely poor sample sizes, low numbers of women studied, and rarely matched control groups.

Naturally, there has always been concern about such research because of the fear that people will be unjustly labeled as criminals. As a result, the area has been ignored in recent years (Raine, 1993). If there is a link between body shape and crime, is it genetic? Body build is largely controlled by the genes. Is the link hormonal? We do have a growth hormone, and the chemical that controls it also controls serotonin, the neurotransmitter or chemical messenger in the brain. Serotonin does have an influence on impulsivity and criminal activity, as discussed in a later chapter. Perhaps there is no link at all and the effect simply comes from having a large body in our society. That is, the genes and hormones create the body shape, but perhaps the environment creates the effect. As mentioned previously, a big young person might easily decide to use his size to resolve conflict instead of using his mind and social skills.

## Cortisol

Many studies have linked cortisol to antisocial behavior (Pajer et al., 2001; McBurnett et al., 2000; Van Praag, 1996; McBurnett et al., 1996; King et al.,

1990; Virkkunen, 1985). Cortisol is regulated by the hypothalamic-pituitary-adrenal axis, so disruption of this system, via neurotransmitters, hormones, or brain pathology, can result in abnormally low cortisol levels. This hormone is also involved in autonomic arousal, which means that those who are low in cortisol do not fear punishment unless it is immediate. We might therefore expect to see reduced levels of cortisol in antisocial people, and quite a number of studies have demonstrated such a link. For example, one study found that low cortisol levels were associated with both early onset of aggression and persistent aggression. Boys whose levels were low both times they were measured (2 years apart) had triple the number of aggressive symptoms as boys who were low at only one reading (McBurnett et al., 2000). In another study, adult substance abusers were found to have lower cortisol levels than controls (King et al., 1990).

A study looking at violence in boys with attention deficit hyperactivity disorder (ADHD) did not find any correlation (Schulz et al., 1997), although a study of adolescent girls with conduct disorder (CD) found significantly lower levels of cortisol in girls with CD than in controls (Pajer et al., 2001). The girls were tested on three separate occasions, and the researchers controlled for age, ethnicity, use of oral contraceptives (which are hormones), and socioeconomic status. In all cases, the CD girls had substantially lower levels of salivary cortisol. CD is prevalent, occurring in 10% of girls between the ages of 15 and 17, and these girls grow into women with 40 times greater rates of criminal behavior than non-CD women (Pajer et al., 2001). These women also have much higher levels of substance abuse, poor health, and a higher mortality rate than non-CD women. Therefore, understanding the underlying cause of this problem is crucial.

Low cortisol levels have also been reported in many different groups of people (Raine, 1993), including habitually violent incarcerated offenders (Virkkunen, 1985), aggressive school children (Tennes and Krey, 1985), adolescents with conduct disorder (Susman et al., 1991), and disinhibited children (Kagan et al., 1988). However, before we make any major conclusions, we need to look at cortisol levels and the levels of other hormones, and put them in context with all the other social and biological factors. Van Praag (1996) suggested that low cortisol and low serotonin levels relate to depression in the presence of stress.

A large, long-term, study has suggested that clinical anxiety might be the catalyst between conduct disorder and cortisol levels (Raine, 1993; McBurnett et al., 1991; Walker et al., 1991; Lahey et al., 1990). Other studies have linked alcohol and testosterone with cortisol levels (Raine, 1993). Cortisol has also been shown to moderate the relationship between testosterone and violence, which indicates that there is some type of interaction between the two (Dabbs et al., 1991).

So, like all hormones, cortisol appears to play a role in behavior, but it is also affected by and affects other hormones and functions, so they all must be studied together along with the environment before long-term conclusions can be drawn.

## Other Hormones

### Thyroid Hormones

The thyroid is a gland in the throat that produces two hormones: thyroxin (T4 or tetra-iodothymine) and tri-iodothyronine (T3). These, in turn, are regulated by thyroid stimulating hormone (TSH), which is produced by the pituitary gland.

Thyroid levels in dogs are very important in regulating aggression. In fact, when people buy purebred dogs, they usually ask whether the parents' thyroid levels are normal. Because thyroid levels are known to be genetic, dogs with abnormal levels (too low or too high) should not be bred. Any dog with a high thyroid level may be aggressive, but many aggressive dogs are put down because their owners do not understand that diet and medication can lower the thyroid level. It is possible that the same sort of relationship exists in people. In humans, the thyroid plays a role in mood regulation, body weight, physical activity, and attention. Many studies have linked thyroid dysfunction with aggression, psychiatric illness, and learning disabilities, although others have also failed to find such a link. Again, this is not particularly surprising because aggression no doubt has myriad causes. Thyroid insufficiency may be implicated in some.

Alm et al. (1996) examined levels of T3 and TSH in adults between the ages of 38 and 42. They divided the men into three groups: (1) those who had been considered juvenile delinquents at age 15 but no longer exhibited anti-social behavior, (2) those who were delinquent at age 15 and this delinquency had continued into adulthood, (3) and controls. The researchers found that the men who had been juvenile delinquents and had continued this antisocial behavior into adulthood had much higher levels of T3 than either men who were juvenile delinquents but had desisted from this behavior in adulthood and controls (Alm et al., 1996). In another study of 61 nonpsychotic men undergoing psychiatric evaluations and 66 controls, elevated T3 levels were found to be highly correlated with type II alcoholism (which is highly genetically correlated), psychopathy, criminality, and several personality disorders, including borderline personality disorder, although free thyroxine in the blood was found to be negatively correlated (Stalenheim et al., 1998b).

Researchers have also found links between abnormal thyroid hormone levels and various disorders, including attention deficit hyperactivity disorder (ADHD) (Wenar and Kerig, 2000; Stein et al., 1995), panic disorder, depression, and bipolar affective disorder (Bauer, 1990), although these are simply links and have not been shown to be causal. Other studies have failed to find such a link although most behavioral disorders can have many etiologies.

One case study of a merchant seaman is suggestive. His thyroxin levels were linked to his later violent behavior (Tardiff, 1998). At age 31, this sailor developed hyperthyroidism and so had most of his thyroid gland removed. Once the thyroid is removed, thyroxin is no longer produced so must be supplemented to keep a normal level in the body. The man took the supplements for some time, but then, while at sea, was unable to obtain his medication. He became depressed, paranoid, and delusionary, convinced his shipmates planned to attack and rape him. During one such hallucination, he murdered one of his shipmates. Once he was put back on his medication, all the delusions ceased and he was found not guilty by reason of insanity (not guilty by reason of mental disorder) (Tardiff, 1998). Although only a single case history, the results are interesting and were certainly considered mitigating by the U.S. courts.

## Adrenalin

Adrenalin is involved in excitement, among other things. We have all had adrenalin rushes, and some people thrive on them — these are the risk takers. Again, adrenalin levels can be a genetic trait; however, they may or may not lead to a criminal act. A desire for excitement and a craving for the adrenalin rush could lead people into doing something illegal, but it could equally well lead them to participate in extreme sports, such as skydiving.

## Conclusion

Our hormone levels vary widely on a daily basis. Most people have, at some time, woken up in the middle of the night in a panic, worrying about something although there was nothing that could be done about it at 3 a.m. These experiences normally occur when a major stressful event is on the horizon. In the morning, the situation does not seem so bad and can be coped with again, partly because your hormone levels have changed. The expression "the darkest hour is before the dawn" is certainly true hormonally. For most people, the lowest point, mentally and physically, is in the early hours of the morning, about 4:00 to 5:00 a.m.

Do these fluctuations mean we can use "my hormones made me do it" as a legal defense? In some cases of violent assault, hormonal imbalances have been raised as a defense. And hormone therapy is sometimes used for some offenders but the treatment is controversial (Raine, 1993). The best-known legal cases involve infanticide, the killing of a child under the age of 1 year by the natural mother. These cases are considered legally different from the killing of an infant by anyone else or from the killing of an older child by the mother because it is accepted that postnatal depression, caused by the fluctuations in hormones after the birth of a child, can affect the mother's behavior. The Canadian legal system does accept that there can be a biological basis for crime in this case.

Hormones affect behavior; that is what they are designed to do. Do they cause crime? Not on their own, but it is possible that they could affect behaviors and place a person at greater risk for committing a crime in some situations. Further research is needed to understand the possible effects of hormonal levels on antisocial behavior. If fully understood, treatment could be as simple and straightforward as adjusting diet or hormonal levels.

## Questions for Further Study and Discussion

1. Discuss some of the ethical issues related to castrating a sexual offender. Can it truly be voluntary if a man is in prison? Should it be used in lieu of prison?
2. What are some of the ethical issues raised by the arguments about premenstrual tension and crime?
3. There is one crime in the Canadian Criminal Code that accepts that there is a biological basis for a crime. That crime is infanticide. Why do you think that this crime is treated differently from others and a biological basis is accepted for it and not others? What is the U.S. equivalent?

## References

Albert, D.J., Walsh, M.L., and Jonik, R.H. (1993). Aggression in humans: what is its biological foundation? *Neurosci. Biobehav. Rev.*, 17(4), 405–425.

Alm, B., af Klintenberg, B., Humble, K., Leppert, J., Sorenson, S., Tegelman, R., Thorell, L.H., and Lidberg, L. (1996). Criminality and psychopathy as related to thyroid activity in former juvenile delinquents. *Acta Psych. Scand.*, 94(2), 112–117.

Archer, J. (1991). The influence of testosterone on human aggression. *Br. J. Psychol.*, 82, 1–28.

Belsky, J., Moffitt T.E., Caspi A., and Silva P.A. (1992). Childhood experience and the onset of menarche: a test of a sociobiological model. *Child Develop.*, 63, 47–58.

Bernhardt, P.C. (1997). Influences of serotonin and testosterone aggression and dominance: convergence with social psychology. *Curr. Dir. Psychol. Sci.*, 6(2), 44–48.

Bernhardt, P.C., Dabbs, J.M., Fielden, J.A., and Lutter, C.D. (1998). Testosterone changes during vicarious experiences of winning and losing among fans at sporting events. *Physiol. Behav.*, 65(1), 59–62.

Bond, A.J., Wingrove, J., and Critchlow, D.G. (2001). Trytophan depletion increases aggression in women during the premenstrual phase. *Psychopharmacology*, 156(4), 477–480.

Boyd, N. (2000). The testosterone connection. *The Beast Within: Why Men Are Violent* (pp. 115–138). Vancouver, B.C., New York: Greystone Books.

Brain, P. (1993). Hormonal aspects of aggression and violence. In Reiss, A. and Roth, J. (Eds.), *Understanding and Preventing Violence* (pp. 173–244). Washington, D.C.: National Academy Press.

Brooks, J.H. and Reddon, J.R. (1996). Serum testosterone in violent and nonviolent young offenders. *J. Clin. Psychol.*, 52(4), 475–483.

Buydens, B.L. and Branchey, M.H. (1992). Cortisol in alcoholics with a disordered aggression control. *Psychoneuroendocrinology*, 17, 45–54.

Campbell, N.A. (1996). *Biology* (4th ed., pp. 913–915). Palo Alto, CA: Benjamin Cummings.

Cloninger, C.R., Bohman, M., and Sigvardsson, S. (1981). Inheritance of alcohol abuse: cross-fostering analysis of adopted men. *Arch. Gen. Psych.*, 38, 861–868.

Comings, D.E., Muhleman, D., Johnson, J.P., and MacMurray, J.P. (2002). Parent-daughter transmission of the androgen-receptor gene as an explanation of the effect of father absence on age of menarche. *Child Develop.*, 73(4), 1046–1051.

Dabbs, J.M. and Hargrove, M.F. (1997). Age, testosterone, and behavior among female prison inmates. *Psychosomatic Med.*, 59, 477–480.

Dabbs, J.M. and Morris, R. (1990). Testosterone, social class and antisocial behavior in a sample of 4,462 men. *Psychol. Sci.*, 1, 209–211.

Dabbs, J.M., Riad, J.K., and Chance, S.E. (2001). Testosterone and ruthless homicide. *Person. Individ. Diff.*, 31, 599–603.

Dabbs, J.M., Carr, T.S., Frady, R.L., and Riad, J.K. (1995). Testosterone, crime and misbehavior among 692 male prison inmates. *Person. Individ. Diff.*, 18(5), 627–633.

Dabbs, J.M., Jurkovic, G.J., and Frady, R.L. (1991). Salivary testosterone and cortisol among late adolescent male offenders. *J. Abn. Child Psychol.*, 19, 469–478.

Dabbs, J.M., Ruback, G.J., Frady, R.L., Hopper, C.H., and Sgoutas, D.S. (1988). Saliva testosterone and criminal violence among women. *Persona. Individ. Diff.,* 9, 269–275.

Dabbs, J.M., Frady, R.L., Carr, T.S., and Besch, N.F. (1987). Saliva testosterone and criminal violence in young adult prison inmates. *Psychosomatic Med.,* 49, 174–182.

Dalton, K. (1966). The influence of mother's menstruation on her child. *Proc. Royal Soc. Med.,* 59, 1014–1016.

Dalton, K. (1961). Menstruation and crime. *Br. Med. J.,* 2, 1752–1753.

Denno, D.W. (1990). *Biology and Violence: From Birth to Adulthood* (p. 218). Cambridge: Cambridge University Press.

Fishbein, D.H. (1992). The psychobiology of female aggression. *Crim. Just. Behav.,* 19, 99–126.

Giotakos, O., Markianos, M., Vaidakis, N., and Christodoulou, G.N. (2003). Aggression, impulsivity, plasma sex hormones and biogenic amine turnover in a forensic population of rapists. *J. Sex Marital Therapy,* 29, 215–225.

Goldzieher, J.W., Dozier, T.S., Smith, K.S., and Steinberger, E. (1976). Improving the diagnostic reliability of rapidly fluctuating plasma hormone levels by optimized multiple-sampling techniques. *J. Clin. Endocrin. Metab.,* 43, 824–830.

Harry, B. and Balcer, C.M. (1987). Menstruation and crime: a critical review of the literature from the clinical criminology perspective. *Behav. Sci. Law,* 5(3), 307–321.

Higley, J.D., Mehlman, P.T., Poland, R.E., Taub, D.M., Vickers, J., Suomi, S.J., and Linnoila, M. (1996). CSF testosterone and 5-HIAA correlate with different types of aggressive behaviors. *Biol. Psychiatr.,* 40, 1067–1082.

Holtzman, E. (1984). Premenstrual syndrome; The indefensible defense. *Harvard Women's Law J., 1* 7, 1–3.

Horney, J. (1978). Menstruation cycles and criminal responsibility. *Law Human Behav.,* 2, 139–150.

Kagan, J., Reznick, J.S., and Snidman, N. (1988). Biological issues of childhood shyness. *Science,* 240, 167–171.

Kendall, K. (1991). The politics of premenstrual syndrome: implications for feminist justice. *J. Human Justice,* 2(2), 77–98.

King, R.J., Jones, J., Scheuer, J.W., Curtis, D., and Zarcone, V.P. (1990). Plasma cortisol correlates of impulsivity and substance abuse. *Personality and Individual Differences,* 11, 287–291.

Kreuz, L.E. and Rose, R.M. (1972). Assessment of aggressive behaviour and plasma testosterone in a young criminal population. *Psychosomatic Med.,* 34, 321–332.

Lahey, B.B., Loeber, R., Stouthamer-Loeber, M., Christ, M.A.G., Green, S., Russo, M.F., Frick, P.J., and Duncan, M. (1990). Comparison of DSM-III and DSM-IIIR diagnoses for prepubertal children. Changes in prevalence and validity. *J. Am. Acad. Child Psychol. Psych.,* 29, 620–626.

Landsman, S.D., Sandford, L.M., Howland, B.E., and Dawes, C. (1976). Testosterone in human saliva. *Experimentia*, 32, 940–941.

Loosen, P.T., Purdon, S.E., and Pavlou, S.N. (1994). Effects on behavior of modulation of gonadal function in men with gonadotropin-releasing hormone antagonists. *Am. J. Psych.*, 151, 271–273.

Maras, A., Laucht, M., Gerdes, D., Wilhelm, C., Lewicka, S., Haack, D., Malisova, L., and Schmidt, M.H. (2003). Association of testosterone and dihydrotestosterone with externalizing behaviour in adolescent boys and girls. *Psychoneuroendocrinology*, 28(7), 932–940.

Mazur, A. (1985). A biosocial model of status in face-to-face primate groups. *Social Forces*, 64, 377–402.

Mazur, A. and Booth, A. (1998). Testosterone and dominance in men. *Behav. Brain Sci.*, 21(3), 353–363.

Mazur, A. and Lamb, T.A. (1980). Testosterone, status and mood in human males. *Horm. Behav.*, 14, 236–246.

Mazur, A., Booth, A., and Dabbs, J.M. (1992). Testosterone and chess competition. *Soc. Psychol. Q.*, 55, 70–77.

McBurnett, K., Lahey, B.B., Capasso, L., and Loeber, R. (1996). Aggressive symptoms and salivary cortisol in clinic-referred boys with conduct disorder. *Ann. NY Acad. Sci.*, 794, 169–178.

McBurnett, K., Lahey, B.B., Frick, P.J., Risch, C., Loeber, R., Hart, E.L., Christ, M.A.G., and Hanson, K.S. (1991). Anxiety, inhibition and conduct disorder in children in relation to salivary cortisol. *J. Am. Acad. Child Adolesc. Psych.*, 30, 192–196.

McBurnett, K., Lahey, B.B., Rathouz, P.J., and Loeber, R. (2000). Low salivary cortisol and persistent aggression in boys referred for disruptive behaviour. *Arch. Gen. Psychol.*, 57, 38–43.

McCaul, K.D., Gladue, B.A., and Joppa, M. (1992). Winning, losing, mood, and testosterone. *Horm. Behav.*, 26, 486–504.

Meyer, W.J.J.I. and Cole, C.M. (1997). Physical and chemical castration of sex offenders: a review. *J. Offender Rehab.*, 25(3/4), 1–18.

Miller, R.D. (1998). Forced administration of sex-drive reducing medications to sex offenders: treatment or punishment. *Psychol. Public Policy Law*, 4(1–2): 175–199.

Moffitt, T.E., Caspi, A., Rutter, M., and Silva, P.A. (2001). Sex Differences in Antisocial Behaviour: Conduct Disorder, Delinquency and Violence in the Dunedin Longitudinal Study. Cambridge: Cambridge University Press.

Orengo, C., Kunik, M., Ghusn, H., and Yudofsky, S. (1997). Correlation of testosterone with aggression in demented elderly men. *J. Nervous Mental Disord.*, 185(5), 349–351.

Pahl-Smith, C. (1985). Premenstrual syndrome as a criminal defense. The need for a medico-legal understanding. *North Carolina Central Law J.*, 15(2), 246–273.

Pajer, K., Gardner, W., Rubin, R.T., Perel, J., and Neal, S. (2001). Decreased cortisol levels in adolescent girls with conduct disorder. *Arch. Gen. Psychol.*, 58(3), 297–302.

Pazol, K., Wilson, M.E., and Wallen, K. (2004). Medroxyprogesterone acetate antagonizes the effects of estrogen treatment on social and sexual behavior in female macaques. *J. Clin. Endocrin. Metab.*, 89(6), 2998–3006.

Press, M.P. (1983). Premenstrual stress syndrome as a defense in criminal cases. *Duke Law J.*, 1, 176–195.

Quinsey, V.L., Skilling, T.A., LaLumiere, M.L., and Craig, W.M. (2004). *Juvenile Delinquency: Understanding the Origins of Individual Differences.* Washington, D.C., American Psychological Association.

Raine, A. (1993). The Psychopathology of Crime: Criminal Behavior as a Clinical Disorder (pp. 191–214). London: Academic Press.

Salvador, A., Simon, V.M., Suay, F., and Lorens, L. (1985). Testosterone and cortisol responses to competitive fighting in human males: a pilot study. *Aggressive Behav.*, 13, 9–13.

Salvador, A., Suay, F., Martinez-Sanchis, S., Simon, V.M., and Brain, P.F. (1999). Correlating testosterone and fighting in male participants in judo contests. *Physiol. Behav.*, 68(1–2), 205–209.

Sanchez-Martin, J.R., Fano, E., Ahedo, L., Cardas, A.J., Brain, P.F., and Azpiroz, A. (2000). Relating testosterone levels and free play social behaviour in male and female preschool children. *Psychoneuroendocrinology*, 25(8), 773–783.

Schnieder, J.S., Stone, M.K., Wynne-Edwards, K.E., Horton, T.H., Lydon, J., O'Malley, B., and Levine, J.E. (2003). Progesterone receptors mediate male aggression towards infants. *Proc. Nat. Acad. Sci.*, 100(5), 2951–2956.

Schulz, K.P., Halperin, J.M., Newcorn, J.H., Sharma, V., and Gabriel, S. (1997). Plasma cortisol and aggression in boys with ADHD. *J. Am. Acad. Child Adolesc. Psychol.*, 36(5), 605–609.

Sheldon, W.H., Hartl, E.M., and McDermott, E. (1949). *Varieties of Delinquent Youth.* New York: Harper. (Cited in Raine, 1993.)

Soler, H., Vinayak, P., and Quadagno, D. (2000). Biosocial aspects of domestic violence. *Psychoneuroendocrinology*, 25(7), 721–739.

Stalenheim, E.G., Eriksson, E., Von Knorring, L., and Wide, L. (1998a). Testosterone as a biological marker in psychopathy and alcoholism. *Psychol. Res.*, 77(2), 79–88.

Stalenheim, E.G., Von Knorring, L., and Wide, L. (1998b). Serum levels of thyroid hormones as biological markers in a Swedish forensic psychiatric population. *Biol. Psychol.*, 43(10), 755–761.

Stein, M.A., Weiss, R.E., and Refetoff, S. (1995). Neurocognitive characteristics of individuals with resistance to thyroid hormone: comparisons with individuals with attention deficit hyperactivity disorder. *J. Develop. Behav. Pediat.*, 16(6), 406–411.

Susman, E.J., Dorn, L.D., and Chrousos, G.P. (1991). Negative affect and hormone levels in young adolescents. Concurrent and predictive perspectives. *J. Youth Adolesc.*, 20, 167–190.

Tames, F.J. and Swift, A.D. (1983). The measurement of salivary testosterone. In Tames, F.J. (Ed.), *Immuno-assays for Clinical Chemistry*. London: Churchill-Livingstone.

Tardiff, K. (1998). Unusual diagnoses among violent patients. *Psych. Clinics N. Am.*, 21(3), 567–576.

Taylor, L. and Dalton, K. (1983). Premenstrual syndrome: a new criminal defense? *Calif. Western Law Rev.*, 19, 269–287.

Tennes, K. and Krey, M. (1985). Children's' adrenocortical response to classroom activities in elementary school. *Psychosomatic Med.*, 47, 451–460.

Van Goozen, S.H.M., Matthys, W., Cohen-Kettenis, P.T., Thijssen, J.H.H., and van Engeland, H. (1998). Adrenal androgens and aggression in conduct disorder prepubertal boys and normal controls. *Biol. Psychol.*, 43(2), 156–158.

Van Praag, H.M. (1996). Faulty cortisol/serotonin interplay. *Psychiatry Res.*, 65(3), 143–157.

Virkkunen, M. (1985). Urinary free cortisol secretion in habitually violent offenders. *Acta Pyschiatrica Scand.*, 72, 40–44.

Walker, J.L., Lahey, B.B., Russo, M.F., Frick, P.J., Christ, M.A.G., McBurnett, K., Loeber, R., Stouthamer-Loeber, M., and Green, S. (1991). Anxiety, inhibition and conduct disorder in children. I. Relations to social impairment. *J. Am. Acad. Child Adolesc. Psychol.*, 30(2), 187–191.

Wenar, C. and Kerig, P. (2000). Developmental Psychopathology: From Infancy through Adolescence. New York: MacGraw-Hill.

Wille, R. and Beier, K.M. (1989). Castration in Germany. *Ann. Sex Res.*, 2, 103–134.

# Pregnancy and the Effects of Birth

# 7

## Introduction

This chapter complements the examination of hormones engaged in the previous chapter. During fetal development, all of a baby's systems are formed. Any damage that occurs during the mother's pregnancy or at the time of birth can have critical implications in the later life of the child.

Many complications can occur during pregnancy or at birth, and they may damage the brain or other systems in the body. Damage in the early stages of development can be dramatically more serious than similar levels of damage in adulthood. In many cases, simple and nonintrusive intervention can reverse the potential risks associated with the damage or reduce it directly.

## Birth Complications

Complications at birth can cause myriad injuries, from physical defects to direct brain damage. Because the brain is the seat of all behaviors, brain damage can obviously affect behavior and learning. Therefore, it is probable that birth or perinatal complications (*peri* meaning at the time of, *natal* meaning birth) can cause problems in later life, including criminal and violent behavior.

One of the most common perinatal injuries is hypoxia, or lack of oxygen to the brain, which is known to cause brain damage. Delays or difficulties in birth can easily result in hypoxia if not corrected rapidly. Such damage can result in later problems, such as learning disabilities, impaired cognitive abilities, attention deficit hyperactivity disorder, and schizophrenia. Hypoxia can result in physical disabilities due to a lack of nervous control of muscles.

Since the 1950s many studies have shown a link between birth complications and behavioral problems in children, ranging from a likelihood of temper tantrums to incarceration (Raine, 1993; Cocchi et al., 1984; Lewis et al., 1979), although other studies have failed to find a link (Denno, 1989).

In Denmark, a study from a cohort of babies born in one hospital over a 2-year period found that although complications during pregnancy (such as infection, anemia, bleeding, chemotherapy, x-rays, and eclampsia) had no effect on any type of criminal offense, complications during birth (such as a ruptured uterus or breech birth) strongly correlated with violent offending (Kandel and Mednick, 1991). Although the numbers of violent offenders were small, 80% of them had suffered severe birth complications, compared with 46.9% of the non-criminals and 29.1% of the property offenders. Although this finding is significant, violent crime is not common, so the numbers are quite low. However, there are still enough cases for analysis (Raine, 1993).

A later study by the same group went into more detail and looked not just at the direct relationship between birth complications and adult violence, but also at the psychiatric status of a parent; that is, they also considered the environmental component (Brennan et al., 1993; Raine, 1993). They found that those with only one factor (high birth complications or a mentally ill parent) had a low risk of violence, but the combination of a parent with a mental illness and high birth complications interacted to give a very significant result. It is important to note that high birth complications alone had no effect in this study. This study had a small sample size, and each group becomes smaller and smaller when it is further divided, but it is still of interest. The researchers concluded that the interaction between parental psychiatric disorder and birth complications showed that the birth complications played a role in triggering what they speculated to be a genetic relationship between parental psychiatric disorder and violence in the offspring, and that without that trigger, the genetic predisposition was not realized (Brennan et al., 1993).

Continuing to sub-analyze this same group, these researchers also looked at clinically diagnosed hyperactivity when the children were 11 to 13 years old (Brennan et al., 1993). They looked at the presence or absence of hyperactivity and high or low birth complications and their effects on an outcome of adult violence. Statistical analysis of these data showed a very strong interaction between hyperactivity and birth complications. Either alone resulted in a slight, but probably not significant, increase in violent crime in later life; but when the two are added together, there is a very significant increase in violent crime (Brennan et al., 1993).

A significant question arises from these studies: do some types of birth complications (and there are many) predispose to hyperactivity? These workers saw hyperactivity as a result of brain damage sustained during birth, which, in turn, led to an increase in violent offending. However, Raine (1993) suggests an alternate hypothesis: that hyperactivity, although possibly related to birth trauma and delivery complications that resulted in slight brain damage, is an independent predisposing factor for adult violence. He suggests that if hyper-activity is added to birth problems, the result is unusually high rates of violence. This hypothesis seems reasonable because there is a good deal of evidence that shows that the more separate types of childhood behavior problems that a child possesses, the greater the chance of adult offense (Raine, 1993).

A vast number of studies have looked at this topic, and many have found links, often quite strong links, between antisocial behavior and birth compli-cations; however, there are others that have not seen this link. Such discrep-ancies are probably a result of the differences in research design and the categorization of the types of birth complications included (because these vary greatly). As well, some studies do not explain exactly what they mean by "delinquency." Another major factor that must be included is the envi-ronment in which the child grows up. Environment in child development obviously has a major influence. Early brain and central nervous system damage may have no effect on a child raised in a good and stable environ-ment. Longitudinal studies have shown that prenatal and perinatal compli-cations had negligible or no long-term effects in advantaged families; whereas, in disadvantaged families, they did predict problems (Mednick and Kandel, 1988). Alternatively, a child with behavioral problems associated with birth complications may be more difficult to parent. It has been demonstrated that children with neurological problems have an increased risk for parental child abuse and often receive more harsh disciplinary measures than normal children, so it is possible that the birth complications are only indirectly responsible for the delinquent behavior with the negative and unsupportive child rearing environment having a greater effect (Quinsey et al., 2004).

In a study in Copenhagen, 847 children were randomly drawn from a birth cohort of more than 9000 babies (Baker and Mednick, 1984). The children were assessed for aggression at age 18 by their teachers. A retrospec-tive analysis determined that the children with high levels of birth compli-cations were found to be more aggressive than those with low levels (Baker and Mednick, 1984). However, it was also found that a stable home life counteracted the effects of the birth complications, so the biological damage could be counteracted by the later environment.

Of course, all of this work looks only at the time of birth and the com-plications that occur over a matter of hours. There are many things that could affect a fetus much earlier. These include the mother's nutritional well-being during the pregnancy, for example. Obviously, an unhealthy mother is likely to have an unhealthy child; that is, the child is likely to have a lower birth weight and to have missed vital nutrients and vitamins during the formative months. These deficiencies could affect the child's mental and physical well-being after birth.

Recent work on 8-year-old children has suggested that children born prematurely showed a reduction in brain volume in comparison with those born at full term, or preterm girls (Reiss et al., 2004). Magnetic resonance imaging (see Chapter 10) was used to scan the brains of 65 eight-year old children who had been born prematurely, with a matched group of 70 children who had been born at full term. The preterm children showed an overall reduction in brain volume, although this seemed to have a greater influence on boys over girls. Girls showed normal volumes of white matter but reduced gray matter, whereas boys had significant reductions in both gray and white matter (Reiss et al., 2004). Most of the deficit in boys was seen in the temporal lobe and deep cerebral region of the brain, which are important in emotion, learning, reading, and attention, and are often impaired in children born prematurely (Reiss et al., 2004). In a study of 28 five-year-old children who had been born prematurely (less than 38 weeks gestation with a birth weight of less than 2.3 kg (5 lb.), and did not show any overt signs of impairment, three quarters were found to have learning disabilities, ADHD, language impairment, neurological impairment, or general school problems, in comparison with 35% in a control full-term group (Julkowski-Cherkes, 1998).

Another obvious risk occurs when the mother is subjected to trauma during pregnancy. The mother and the fetus could be injured in an accident; however, maternal and fetal damage might also result from abuse. In the latter case, the child has a double risk: the actual physical damage caused during gestation, and also the potential risks from physical, emotional, and psychological damage when born into a dysfunctional and abusive environment.

## Fetal Development and Diet

When a fetus is developing, it is entirely dependent on the mother's diet. The growth of the baby can be retarded simply by the mother not eating enough. One major role of hormones in fetal growth is to mediate the use of the available nutrients: that is, to handle the nutrients and determine what goes where. One of those hormones is called insulin-like growth factor 1 (IGF1), which is involved in the regulation of fetal growth; levels of IGF1 in blood correlate with birth weight. Some researchers have shown that polyunsaturated fatty acids (PUFAs) may be very important in brain development and birth weight, as well as to myelination (covering) of the nerve cells in the brain, which is vital for nerve function. These essential fatty acids are required for the formation of the myelin sheath. They are only available from the placenta or diet. So a maternal diet that is high in these fatty acids is a protective factor in nerve maturation. On the other hand, if the mother's diet is low in these fatty acids, then myelination can be delayed or damaged. The result is reduced connections between the two sides or hemispheres of the brain, and brain problems involving cognitive, perceptual, and sensori-motor functions may occur. For example, for a person to be able to perform coordination tasks, communication must occur between the two hemi-spheres of the brain. Such developmental problems could eventually result in behavior disorders, developmental dyslexia, and other learning disorders (Saugstad, 1997).

Thus, an optimum amount of fatty acids in the mother's diet is critical to brain and neural development, but studies have also shown that if the amount is too high, the result may be poor development and aggression, at least in animals. In one study, pregnant mice were divided into two groups and fed either a normal or a very high fat diet. The offspring of the high-fat mothers were more active and more aggressive than those of normal mothers (Raygada et al., 1998). This finding is important because people in Western countries consume an excess of polyunsaturated fatty acids. Other dietary restrictions during pregnancy can also affect fetal brain development; for example, protein restriction has been shown to reduce brain development in animals.

Maternal diet during pregnancy and also during lactation, if the mother breast feeds, has been linked to IQ and early childhood behavioral problems. Low IQ and early behavioral problems can be important factors in determining whether a child will do well in school and in peer relationships, both of which are known to influence the child's later success in life.

Omega-3 and omega-6 fatty acids are important in normal health and development. Research today shows that most people living in modern society receive adequate amounts of omega-6 fatty acids from their normal diet, and may even receive an excess, but that many of us are lacking in omega-3 fatty acids. Omega-3 fatty acids are important in the healthy development of the brain and eyes (Helland et al., 2003). Children of mothers who received omega-3 fatty acid supplementation during pregnancy and lactation, in the form of cod liver oil capsules, were compared with children of mothers who received omega-6 fatty acid supplementation during pregnancy and lactation, in the form of corn oil supplements (Helland et al., 2003). The women received the supplementation from the 18th week of pregnancy until 3 months after birth, and the children of these women were assessed using an IQ test at age 4 years. After controlling for other variables, the researchers found that the children of the mothers who took omega-3 fatty acid supplementation scored higher on the IQ tests than did those whose mothers received supplemental omega-6 fatty acids.

In a similar study looking at Vitamin B6 in mothers' breast milk, mothers with higher dietary B6 had higher levels of pyridoxal, a form of B6, in their milk than those who did not have a high dietary intake, despite the fact that 24 of the 25 women studied were considered to have adequate B6 intake (Boylan et al., 2002). These infants were scaled using the Brazelton Neonatal Behavioral Assessment Scale. The NBAS scale, developed by Dr. T. Berry Brazelton in 1977, examines 28 behavioral and 18 reflex items of infants up to 2 months old and measures behaviors, strengths, and adaptation, as well as possible vulnerabilities. Those 2-week old infants whose mothers had low levels of pyridoxal in their breast milk scored badly in certain areas of the tests. These areas were related to regulation of arousal response to sensory stimulation, which in reality meant that these babies were less easily comforted, and were more likely to cry and react to aversive stimuli (Boylan et al., 2002). Vitamin B6 is very important in the biochemical pathways related to production of neurotransmitters such as serotonin, dopamine, and norepinephrine and thus has the potential to influence many behaviors. Therefore, although the mothers were all receiving what is considered adequate levels of vitamins, the authors recommended increasing the supplementation of B6 (Boylan et al., 2002). In another study, breast feeding in general was found to result in offspring with a generally higher IQ than offspring who did not receive breast milk and the effect seemed most pronounced in people who had received breast milk for most of their first year of life (Mortensen et al., 2002).

Not only is the fetus at risk if the mother misses vital nutrients, but also the risks increase if the mother has consumed damaging or undesirable substances during pregnancy, in particular, drugs, alcohol, and/or cigarettes. All of these can affect the health of the fetus; in the case of drugs, the child may be born addicted. Again, the child suffers the double burden of potential fetal damage as well as an addicted mother with the consequent dysfunctional environment.

## Fetal Alcohol Spectrum Disorder

Alcohol consumption during pregnancy may lead to fetal alcohol spectrum disorder (FASD), which causes a number of mental problems. These may or may not predispose the child to crime, but often cause mental retardation. When it is slight, the child will go to a regular school and receive little or no extra help. The subsequent environmental situation, such as being bullied, failing in schoolwork, and having low self-esteem, can result in antisocial behavior.

FASD has been known for centuries but was first officially described in 1968. The syndrome refers to a constellation of physical abnormalities particularly noticeable in the face and in reduced size at birth; it also leads to problems in behavior and cognition later in life (Mattson and Riley, 1998). These children are usually mentally retarded and hyperactive, and they have attention and perceptual deficits and motor abnormalities. In sum, there are physical problems, behavioral problems, and slower reaction times. The financial and emotional costs of such children are high. It has been estimated that one or two in every thousand children are born with FASD every year (Chen and West, 1999; Kaemingk and Paquette, 1999), making it the highest preventable form of mental retardation in the United States (Capron, 1992).

FASD is caused by prenatal exposure to high alcohol levels. This does not mean that the baby is born addicted to alcohol, as is seen in drug-addicted babies born to drug users. Instead, prenatal alcohol results in classic teratogenic effects. A teratogen is something that causes birth defects. German measles (rubella) is a well-known example of a teratogen, and pregnant women are now tested for the antibodies to rubella. The disease of rubella itself is not generally severe, so it does not normally have much effect on a person. However, if a women contracts it when she is pregnant, the fetus is deformed physically and mentally. This has been recognized for decades, and in the past, if a child contracted the disease, all their friends would be invited to a German measles party in an effort to expose all the children to the mild virus and therefore give them immunity for life. In this way, the chances of a young woman developing the disease during pregnancy were greatly reduced as she would be protected by the antibodies she had developed when she harmlessly contracted it as a child. Boys were also deliberately exposed so they could not infect their sisters and lovers. Now, most of us are vaccinated against rubella as children and the days of German Measles parties are long gone. However, protection against other, more insidious teratogens is not so simple.

One of the most serious and well-understood teratogens is alcohol. Although the manifestations of FASD can change with age, the syndrome never disappears and there is no cure; yet there can be some amelioration in some individuals, and the effect in each person varies (Mattson and Riley, 1998). Any conclusion that alcohol consumption is a minor environmental factor, and not a biological one, can no longer be taken seriously because the effects occur prenatally and affect the biological development of the fetus. FASD is a biological effect. The fetus develops everything it will need in life during a very short period of time, so any damage done during this time is not trivial.

There are several factors at work with an FASD child. The child is prenatally exposed, so that is biological. However, he or she is probably also born into a dysfunctional family. Although we, as a society, are well aware of the risks of drinking when pregnant, some pregnant women still drink, so it is probable that the child's family may be unstable. As well, a child who looks different and has low intelligence is more likely to have a difficult childhood, which results in additional environmental and social pressures.

In addition to the biological effect of maternal exposure, there is some evidence from twin studies for a genetic effect. In all cases, if one twin had FASD, so did the other, but in some there appeared to be variance in severity (Streissguth and Dehaene, 1993). Some dizygotic twins were affected differently by the mother's drinking, which suggests that there might be some genetic protective factors. However, the differences might equally well be explained by the different positions of the twins in the womb, the different blood supply, and the actual age of the twins; twins might be chronologically the same age but one might develop faster, so they would be exposed to alcohol at different stages of development. Because the stages would be so close, this last explanation seems unlikely. Another study looked at monozygotic twins; again, the effects were slightly different, although severe in both — indicating that other factors as well as genetics may be involved.

However, one aspect that does appear to be genetically controlled is the mother's metabolic reaction to alcohol. One of the critical factors thought to be involved in whether or not a child develops FASD is the acetaldehyde level in the mother's blood. People metabolize alcohol differently (Agarwal and Goedde, 1992). Some women who drink very lightly can have extremely high levels of acetaldehyde, and others who drink much more may have lower levels. Thus, because of some genetically determined or acquired liver function problem, acetaldehyde levels could rise to abnormally high levels in some women (Agarwal and Goedde, 1992).

The solution to FASD seems obvious: women who drink excessively should stop drinking when they are pregnant, and those who cannot stop drinking should not get pregnant. But of course, it is not that easy. If it were, FASD would not exist. FASD remains one of the major reasons for mental retardation today (Capron, 1992). In some cases, a woman may not even be aware that she is pregnant and thus does not realize that she should not consume alcohol, until the damage has been done. Resources need to focus not only on the pregnant mother, but also on the already-affected, developing child. FASD children are not always recognized, especially in cases where the symptoms are mild. Such children can easily slip through the cracks, receiving no help. Of course, it is a double-edged sword because children identified as FASD and allocated extra resources and assistance are then labeled as such, potentially creating further problems. A fine line must be drawn that allows a child the help he or she needs without stigmatization.

FASD is a constellation of myriad symptoms that deeply affect the child and the eventual adult's life. It has also been shown to be a predisposer to crime (Fast et al., 1999). However, like many such predisposers, the real problem is not FASD but the results of FASD, such as low self-esteem, poor learning and cognitive skills, poor peer relationships, low-skill job expectancy, etc. These are likely the actual predisposers. People with FASD are very easily led (Capron, 1992), possibly by someone who could lead them into crime, or, equally, by someone who could lead them away from it. This suggests that appropriate peer mentoring could dramatically reduce the risk of criminal involvement.

As well as the damage that alcohol does to the developing brain (Roebuck et al., 1999), FASD has specific effects on other biological systems that have been shown to be predisposers for crime. Prenatal exposure to alcohol affects the development of the neurotransmitter systems. It seriously impairs the development of the system that produces and regulates serotonin, a very important neurotransmitter. Serotonin is a major factor in criminogenic acts, as further discussed in a subsequent chapter. Low serotonin has been consistently associated with aggression and impulsivity, and alcohol exposure before birth results in low serotonin levels, so this mechanism alone could be related to criminal acts. Prenatal exposure to alcohol also affects the other neurotransmitter systems; it impairs the dopamine producing system, the norepinephrine producing system, and the acetylcholine producing system, all of which are vital in life. There is evidence that impairment of any of these systems may result in antisocial behavior. Alcohol also affects the hormone systems as they develop, and it can also affect the immune system and such other functions as hearing. The brain damage caused by FASD varies in severity from child to child; it can be as severe as anencephaly — wherein a child is born with no brain and no cranium and lives only a few hours — or it can be very minor.

FASD can also affect the maternal bond at birth. Because the child looks different, the mother may not bond with the child properly. As well, she may fail to bond because she feels guilty or because alcohol affects lactation or the production of the milk (Mannella, 1999). People who drink when they are pregnant may also use other drugs, which could have an interactive effect (Young, 1997).

How should FASD be taken into account when we are dealing with a criminal with this problem? Should FASD be considered a defense? In the United States, Robert Harris was sentenced to death for a horrific and brutal murder (Capron, 1992). He suffered from severe FASD and was born before FASD was officially described, so it could not have been taken into account at the trial. Harris was sentenced to death. Before he was executed many years later, the governor of the state said that he was sorry for Robert Harris the child, but had no pity for Harris the man (Capron, 1992). Should he have been executed? How should we handle such people in our criminal justice system? To date, FASD is not yet a "stand-alone" defense in any jurisdiction. If proven severe, it can sometimes lead to a finding of unfitness to stand trial although this depends on the jurisdiction. Very occasionally, it might be so profound that an accused person may be found "insane." In Canada, the defense is called "NCRMD," or "Not Criminally Responsible on account of Mental Disorder," and the term "insanity defense" has gone out of practice.

## Maternal Smoking

Although it is very well recognized by most people today that pregnant women should not drink, the risks associated with smoking are less well understood. We know that smoking is bad for us and causes many health risks, but these health risks also extend to the unborn child, and can not only cause health problems in the child, but also have been associated with a predisposition for aggression and even crime.

In the Netherlands, 1377 pairs of twins were examined using the Child Behavior Checklist at age 3 years (Orlebeke et al., 1997). The results showed that there was a significant effect of maternal smoking on aggressive, over-active, and oppositional behavior problems, but no observable effect on depression, anxiety, or withdrawal behavior problems. The researchers controlled for such variables as socioeconomic factors, birth weight, maternal age, and breast or formula fed. The major behavioral problem noted was aggression (Orlebeke et al., 1997).

Maternal smoking during pregnancy has also been linked to conduct disorder in children between 16 and 18 years old. More than 1000 children were assessed from birth to age 18 in a New Zealand study. Children of mothers who had smoked one or more packs of cigarettes a day during their pregnancy were more than twice as likely to develop conduct disorder than children of non-smokers, with a greater link seen in males (Fergusson et al., 1998). In a Canadian study, a link was found between IQ and prenatal exposure to tobacco in 9- to 12-year-old children. The relationship was dose dependent, meaning that the more the mothers smoked during pregnancy, the greater the drop in the child's IQ (Fried et al., 1998). In the same study, prenatal exposure to marijuana did not reduce IQ but did appear to impair executive function skills, such as impulse control and decision making (Fried et al., 1998). Maternal smoking during pregnancy has also been implicated as a risk factor for developing ADHD (Biederman, 2005). This is not surprising as ADHD has been linked to disruptions in the dopaminergic system and nicotinic receptors modulate dopaminergic activity (Biederman, 2005).

A study in Denmark compared maternal smoking with criminal records in adulthood. A single birth cohort of more than 4000 men who were born in Copenhagen between 1959 and 1961 were studied to assess the level of maternal smoking during pregnancy in comparison with the criminal arrest record at age 34 (Brennan et al., 1999). The researchers found that maternal smoking during the last 3 months of pregnancy was a significant predictor for adult criminal activity, including both violent and nonviolent crime. It was not, however, a predictor for juvenile crime alone. Birth complications were found to be a compounding factor. More than a quarter of the men who suffered from birth complications, as well as having a mother who smoked during pregnancy, were arrested for a violent crime (Brennan et al., 1999).

In Brennan et al.'s first study, only men were studied due to the low criminal arrest rates found in women, but a follow-up study in 2002 increased the numbers of individuals to more than 8000 and included both men and women (Brennan et al., 2002). A dose-dependent relationship between maternal smoking during pregnancy and subsequent criminal arrest was again seen. This relationship occurred with both men and women. A similar relationship was also observed between maternal smoking during pregnancy and subsequent psychiatric hospitalization for substance abuse (Brennan et al., 2002). The relationship held when other variables were taken into account, such as socioeconomic factors, perinatal risk factors, and maternal age. In females, the main criminal arrests related to the hospitalization for substance abuse; however, in males, maternal smoking during pregnancy was still related to criminal arrest for other crimes, even when the researchers controlled for hospitalization for substance abuse (Brennan et al., 2002). In animal studies, prenatal nicotine exposure can result in an increase in testosterone in males and changes in the serotonin receptor sites, both of which have been linked to aggression and substance abuse (Brennan et al., 2002).

The results of these studies do not show that smoking during pregnancy will cause children to become criminals or substance abusers, but they do show an interesting trend. We know that nicotine is harmful to our bodies and poses many health risks, and it is logical to assume that these risks would be compounded in a delicate, developing fetus. The researchers who have linked prenatal maternal smoking to crime suggest that the link relates to general neural damage in the developing fetus caused by nicotine.

## Maternal Age

Maternal age correlates surprisingly well with "externalizing behavior" in the offspring, exhibiting a very robust linear relationship. Younger mothers have children who exhibit much more externalizing behavior than do children of older mothers, and the levels of externalizing behavior drop consistently as maternal age increases (Orlebeke, 2001). Children who exhibit externalizing behavior are prone to developing later delinquent and eventual criminal behavior. In the United States, juvenile delinquency rates rose from 1987 to 1991 and have since exhibited a steady decline. Orlebeke suggests that this is related, in part, to an increase in maternal age at childbirth in recent years. In studying national statistics, Orlebeke found that drops in maternal child-birth age resulted in increased juvenile delinquency 17 years later; and conversely, increases in maternal childbirth age resulted in decreased juvenile delinquency 17 years later (Orlebeke, 2001). It could be argued that this stems from different and perhaps more mature and consistent parenting techniques in older mothers, but Orlebeke suggests that the reason may be, at least in part, related to testosterone levels. Younger mothers have higher levels of testosterone, with serum testosterone levels halving between age 20 and age 40 in women. This means that prenatal exposure to testosterone in the fetus is twice as high in a young mother as in an older mother. Prenatal exposure to testosterone affects the development of the nervous system, and rodent studies have shown that male offspring of older rat mothers have lower testosterone levels (Orlebeke, 2001). Orlebeke suggests that reductions in juvenile crime may relate not only to changing social conditions, but also to biological factors such as maternal age at childbirth (Orlebeke, 2001).

## Fetal Maldevelopment and Minor Physical Anomalies

Some children are born with what are termed "minor physical anomalies." These are very small defects that can occur during pregnancy, and several studies have shown that they can relate to later criminal behavior (Arsenault et al., 2000; Mednick and Kandel, 1988; Waldrop et al., 1978). Minor physical anomalies are thought to result from some form of fetal maldevelopment that occurs in about the third month of pregnancy, a period when the brain and many neurological details are being formed. Minor physical anomalies are minor physical defects such as low-seated ears, ear lobes that attach to the skull, a slightly curved fifth finger, a single crease in the palm instead of the two that most people have (incidentally, that is also seen in Down's syndrome children), gaps between the first and second toes, etc. (Raine, 1993).

These defects result from some disturbance in the development of the fetus. For example, when the ears develop, they begin low down on the neck and slowly drift into the usual position. If they stop moving and remain low seated, it is suggestive of some disturbance in fetal development during this time (Mednick and Kandel, 1988). Some minor physical anomalies have been linked to genetic factors but can also be caused by a range of environmental or teratogenic effects such as infection or low oxygen (Raine, 1993; Guy et al., 1983).

Minor physical anomalies certainly do not cause crime but do show that there has been some trauma or damage during the pregnancy; therefore, they may be indicative of other damage that is not visible but is perhaps more serious. Something that can change the development of the ears could certainly also damage such vital things as the central nervous system. Higher numbers of minor physical anomalies have been recorded in people with schizophrenia (Green et al., 1994), autism, hyperactivity (Fogel et al., 1985), as well as general aggressive behavior (Arsenault et al., 2000).

Minor physical anomalies are strongly correlated with hyperactivity (Mednick and Kandel, 1988). Studies in the 1970s showed that minor physical anomalies accounted for almost 50% of the variance in hyperactivity by age 3 (Waldrop and Halverson, 1971), which in turn has been associated with serious delinquency in adolescent boys (Satterfield et al., 1987). Mednick and Kandel (1988) examined the relationship between minor physical anomalies and police records of crime. They assessed 129 boys for the presence or absence of minor physical anomalies at age 12, and then followed up at the age of 21 to assess criminal activity. The results showed that there was no relationship between minor physical anomalies and property offenses, but there was a strong correlation between minor physical anomalies and violent offending (Mednick and Kandel, 1988).

In a follow-up study, Kandel et al. (1989) looked at minor physical anomalies in a large Danish birth cohort. The number of minor physical anomalies was measured when the children were 11 to 13 years of age and then their criminal records were assessed at age 20 to 22 years. The researchers found a significant positive correlation between number of minor physical anomalies and violent criminal recidivism, as compared with subjects having a history of only one or no violent offenses.

Later studies (Brennan and Mednick, 1993) showed that when birth complications are added to the presence of minor physical anomalies, the risk of violence increases. However, what is particularly interesting about these data is that minor physical anomalies only predicted for violent offending when they were coupled with an unstable home life. If a child with minor physical anomalies had a strong, supportive, stable home, then the effects of the minor physical anomalies were negated and the child grew up noncriminal. We find this result again and again when we study the biology of crime, not so much the causes of crime, but, more importantly, the protective factors.

In a longitudinal Canadian study, 170 adolescent males from a lower-income, inner-city region were examined for the presence or absence of minor physical anomalies, family adversity, and rates of delinquency (Arsenault et al., 2000). Delinquency was measured by self-reports, teachers' reports, and official crime records. Family adversity included parents' occupational socioeconomic level, parents' age at birth of first child, parents' educational levels, and whether the child lived with both parents. The researchers found that the total number of minor physical anomalies showed a significant positive correlation with violent delinquency in adolescence. In particular, minor physical anomalies in the mouth showed the highest correlation with violence. When minor physical anomalies of the mouth were removed from the analysis, minor physical anomalies in other regions of the body no longer predicted for violence, although family adversity still did (Arsenault et al., 2000). There was no correlation between minor physical anomalies and nonviolent delinquency.

The authors suggested two reasons for the high correlation between number of minor physical anomalies in the mouth and violence. First, as has been frequently suggested before, minor physical anomalies are probably a marker that indicates when deeper and more profound damage occurred *in utero*. A fetus develops from a single-celled zygote to a fully functional baby in just 9 short months. The central nervous system and organs in the fetus develop in a very preset, hierarchical way. Therefore, any insult that interrupts this process will have the greatest effect on the system that is at its critical period of development at that time. The critical period for the development of minor physical anomalies in the palate of the mouth starts at the ninth week of gestation (Arsenault et al., 2000). So the authors suggest that any trauma, whether physical or chemical, that occurs at this time results in neurological damage that could predispose to violence and also causes minor physical anomalies in the mouth region. Second, the authors suggest that even small irregularities can affect the child in other ways, such as it might affect the sucking reflex required to feed as a young baby. This, in turn, may have not only a nutritional effect, but also may affect the mother–child bond. Infants who have feeding problems have been reported to have other behavioral problems (Arsenault et al., 2000).

If there are few of them, minor physical anomalies are slight and do not necessarily make the child unattractive in any way. In fact, children with minor physical anomalies are just as attractive as other children. Even so, it could be suggested that other children's reactions to them could result in environmental or social factors that lead to an increased crime rate. The findings in preschool children tend to rule this out (Raine, 1993). The evidence therefore supports the premise of Mednick and Kandel (1988): that the minor physical anomalies represent more deep-seated and fundamental central nervous system damage that, in turn, leads to less visible problems such as learning deficiencies, disabilities, cognitive deficits, and hyperactivity (Mednick and Kandel, 1988; Raine, 1993).

These research studies are interesting, but what do they tell us? Understanding any of these issues means that we may be able to find ways to intervene. Biological problems are often easier to change than social ones. We do not have much chance of eliminating abuse or poverty from the world, but we can change many biological risk factors. Several of the examples just discussed showed that the biological problem that resulted in the child being at higher risk for crime could be almost entirely reversed with a good and stable home life. If we identified at-risk babies by the presence of minor physical anomalies or the fact that they experienced high birth complications or identified expectant mothers who were at risk, we could make sure that the mother and child receive extra health care and support, greater financial support, more home visits, greater education on the risks of smoking and drinking during pregnancy, and earlier hospitalization before the baby is born (Raine, 1993), all of which might completely counteract the risks.

## Other Birth-Related Difficulties

### Twins

It is now clear that birth trauma can result in some damage to infants. Whether that damage results in adult violence or other dysfunction remains somewhat questionable. Because the head is the largest part of the baby, once it is out, the rest of the baby comes quite easily; therefore, trauma to the head is most likely. Because babies' skulls are also soft, birth complications are more likely to cause brain damage rather than damage to, say, the left foot.

What effect might this fact have on some of the broader studies in this field? Remember that most of the studies that look at the genetics of crime look at twins, where the likelihood of birth trauma is greater because the birth process is much more complex. Twins are invariably smaller than singletons, so there is obviously also a gestational effect. Moreover, twins often spend time in incubators so that in the first few days or weeks after birth, they have much less human contact than a normally birthed baby. They also have less contact with their mother at a time when the main bonding takes place. There are twin studies that include birth complications as a factor, but can we measure the effect? Could they have affected one twin more than the other?

Are birth complications more likely in monozygotic twins than dizygotic twins? Studies have shown a significant difference between twin behavior and non-twin behavior problems. One study showed that twins showed small but consistently higher levels of problem behaviors than non-twins and suggested that these results may be the result of perinatal injury, which has a higher incidence in the twin population (Gau et al., 1992). It could also be the result of the environment in which twins grow up, and the researchers have admitted that they did not take regional differences or method of study into account.

Another point to consider in multiple births is position in the womb in relationship to the co-twin and hormone exposure. In animals that have litters, it is known that hormones in the uterus and position with respect to male and female littermates influence sexually related adult behavior. There may be a similar effect in twins. Sensation-seeking was studied in 422 twin pairs, including 51 opposite-sex twins. Previous work has shown that sensation-seeking is higher in males. This study found that girls who had a male twin had higher levels of sensation-seeking, although the opposite was not true of male twins, which does suggest some sort of *in utero* hormonal influence on later behavioral development (Resnick et al., 1993).

## Maternal Rejection

Early maternal rejection and separation has been shown in animal studies to cause morphological changes in brain structure that are often not identifiable until adulthood (Andersen and Teicher, 2004). To determine whether the normal development and changes that occur in the brain of a young animal as it matures are affected by maternal separation, Andersen and Teicher separated baby rats from their mothers for 4 hours a day between the ages of 2 and 20 days (2004). In comparison with baby rats that were not separated from their mothers, the separated baby rats showed delayed development of the hippocampus, a region of the temporal lobe and limbic system that is involved in learning, memory, and emotion (Andersen and Teicher, 2004).

Birth defects themselves may be implicated in early maternal rejection, as is the way the child is subsequently raised. For example, are birth complications likely to increase maternal rejection, especially when the child may not have been with the mother from birth because of medical needs? Research has shown that birth complications interact with early maternal rejection in predisposing individuals to violence at age 18 (Raine et al., 1994). The study considered more than 4000 male births in Denmark and assessed birth complications and maternal rejection before the age of 1 year. Criminal status was determined at age 17 to 19 years. A significant interaction was seen between birth complications and maternal rejection (Raine et al., 1994). As observed in previous studies, it is the interaction between both birth complications and early maternal rejection that was the predisposing factor, rather than either one on its own. However, this does not tell us whether the predisposition for violence relates to the fact that the mother rejected the child as an infant, or whether she rejected the child because of her own trauma or because the baby was not in her arms for the first days after birth.

A follow-up study looked at people up to age 34 and thus involved a greatly increased sample size, which meant the researchers could do more detailed analyses on onset and type of violence, the form of maternal rejection, and the effect of maternal mental illness (Raine et al., 1997). The sample consisted of 4269 males in Denmark who had complications in their births and were rejected by their mothers before age 1 year. Their history of criminal offenses was assessed at age 34. When they extended the age, the number of subjects with violent offenses increased threefold. In the original study, 145 were classified as violent, 540 as nonviolent, and 3584 as noncriminals. In the new study, 466 were violent, 844 were nonviolent, and 2959 were noncriminals. Thus, the second study was more significant. It showed a significant interaction between birth complications and early rejection in predicting violence at 34 years. The components of maternal rejection that seemed most important were attempts to abort the fetus and institutionalization of the infant; not wanting the pregnancy did not appear to be an issue. Maternal psychiatric illness had no effect on the interaction.

The authors suggested, as before, that if we were to identify women at risk and intervene to help them during their pregnancy and afterward, it might reduce later problems (Raine et al., 1997). The mother might be allowed to get closer to the baby, even if the baby is in an incubator. They could hold and feed them rather than having a nurse do that. Not so long ago, babies were swept away from their mother, and both were kept in the hospital for up to 2 weeks, with the baby brought out only for feedings. Now we recognize that those first days are vital for bonding, and babies stay with their mothers from the beginning. Fathers are allowed in the delivery room. It is all important to the bonding process on all sides. The baby needs to bond; but for the baby's sake, the parents must also bond. However, when babies are sick, premature (as twins often are), or have birth trauma, they are kept under special care, and their mothers may be squeezed out of the bonding process. Perhaps changes that would allow them to be closer to their babies more often would help with both problems caused by maternal rejection and those caused by birth trauma.

## Conclusion

Understanding good pre- and postnatal care is vital for the protection of both the mother and child. This holds not only for their physical health at birth, but also for the mental well-being of the developing child. Liu et al. have suggested prevention strategies to reduce aggression and violence related to birth complications (Liu and Wuerker, 2005; Liu and Raine, 2000). They suggest that care during the prenatal and perinatal periods should be clearly targeted for improvement. Nurses could instruct pregnant women on caring for themselves during pregnancy and in postnatal care after the baby is born. This is an area that is often neglected as a new young mother frequently finds herself suddenly alone with a baby, with very little training on how to care for the infant. It often appears to be thought that once a woman becomes a mother, she just "naturally knows;" however, this is not necessarily true, especially if the mother herself was a victim of poor parenting skills. Instruction on maternal health during and after the birth is very important for the health of the child, and also the continuing health of the mother. This could include advice on appropriate diet and supplements such as folic acid, and discussions on the risks of smoking and drinking alcohol. It could also extend to advice on how to protect a baby or young child's head from head injury, such as the selection of appropriate car seats, toys, and safety helmets. Nursing programs in hospitals and in the community could greatly increase parental knowledge about pregnancy and child care (Liu and Wuerker, 2005; Liu and Raine, 2000). Unfortunately, many young women do not seek medical advice when pregnant and only come to the attention of medical services at childbirth. Others give birth without medical assistance. In such cases, hospital nursing plans are unlikely to be of any assistance. Community services and outreach programs may be able to assist in getting the information to those who need it most.

## Questions for Further Study and Discussion

1. Discuss some of the ethical issues related to women's rights with regard to fetal alcohol syndrome.
2. Should birth complications or fetal alcohol syndrome affect a court's decision? Why or why not? If yes, how?
3. How do birth complications and having a mentally ill parent affect a child? Explain why this might be and how it could be ameliorated.
4. What can be done to help FASD children in schools? What FASD training or special education is available? Can this ameliorate FASD effects?

# References

Agarwal, D. and Goedde, H.W. (1992). Pharmacogenetics of alcohol metabolism and alcoholism. *Pharmacogenetics,* 2(2), 48–62.

Andersen, S.L. and Teicher, M.H. (2004). Delayed effects of early childhood stress on hippocampal development. *Neuropsychopharmocology,* 29(11), 1988–1993.

Arsenault, L., Tremblay, R.E., Billerica, B., Sequin, J.R., and Saucier, J.-F. (2000). Minor physical anomalies and family adversity as risk factors for violent delinquency in adolescence. *Am. J. Psychiatr.,* 157, 917–923.

Baker, R.L. and Mednick, S.A. (1984). *Influences on Human Development: A Longitudinal Perspective.* Boston: Kluwer Nijhof Press.

Biederman, J. (2005). Attention-deficit hyperactivity disorder: a selective overview. *Biol. Psychiatry,* 57(11), 1215–1220.

Boylan, L.M., Hart, S., Porter, K.B., and Driskell, J.A. (2002). Vitamin B6 content of breast milk and neonatal behavioral functioning. *J. Am. Dietetic Assoc.,* 102(10), 1433–1438.

Brennan, P.A. and Mednick, S.A. (1993). Genetic perspectives on crime. *Acta Psych. Scand. Suppl.,* 370, 19–26.

Brennan, P.A., Grecian, E.R., and Mednick, S.A. (1999). Maternal smoking during pregnancy and adult male criminal outcomes. *Arch. Gen. Psychiatry,* 56, 215–219.

Brennan, P.A., Grecian, E.L., Mortensen, E.L., and Mednick, S.A. (2002). Relationship of maternal smoking during pregnancy with criminal arrest and hospitalization for substance abuse in male and female adult offspring. *Am. J. Psychiatry,* 159(1), 48–54.

Brennan, P., Mednick, S.A., and Kandel, E. (1993). Congenital determinants of violent property offending. In Pepler, D.J. and Rubin, K.H. (Eds.), *The Development and Treatment of Childhood Aggression* (pp. 81–92). Hillsdale, NJ: Erlbaum.

Capron, A.M. (1992). Fetal alcohol and felony. *Hastings Centre Report,* 22, 28–29.

Chen, W.J.A. and West, J.R. (1999). Alcohol-induced brain damage during development: potential risk factors. In Hannigan, J.H., Spear, L.P., Spear, N.E., and Goodlett, C.R. (Eds.), *Alcohol and Alcoholism. Effects on Brain and Development* (pp. 17–37). Mahwah, NJ: Erlbaum.

Cocchi, R., Felici, M., Tonni, L., and Venanza, G. (1984). Behaviour troubles in nursery school children and their possible relationship to pregnancy or delivery complications. *Acta Psychatrica Belgica,* 84, 173–179.

Denno, D.J. (1989). *Biology, Crime and Violence: New Evidence.* Cambridge: Cambridge University Press.

Fast, D.K., Conry, J., and Loock, C.A. (1999). Identifying fetal alcohol syndrome among youth in the criminal justice system. *J. Develop. Behav. Pediatrics,* 20(5), 370–372.

Fergusson, D., Woodward, L., and Horwood, L.J. (1998). Maternal smoking during pregnancy and psychiatric adjustment in late adolescence. *Arch. Gen. Psychiatry,* 55, 721–727.

Fogel, C.A., Mednick, S.A., and Michelson, N. (1985). Hyperactive behaviour and minor physical anomalies. *Acta Psychatr. Scand.,* 72, 551–556.

Fried, P., Watkinson, B., Gray, R. (1998). Differential effects on cognitive functioning 9- to 12-year olds prenatally exposed to cigarettes and marijuana. *Neurotox. Terat.,* 20(3), 293–306.

Gau, J.S., Silberg, J.L., Erickson, M.T., and Hewitt, J.K. (1992). Childhood behavior problems: a comparison of twin and non-twin samples. *Acta Genet Med. Gemell.,* 41(1), 53–63.

Green, M.F., Satz, P., and Christenson, C. (1994). Minor physical anomalies in schizophrenia patients, bipolar patients and their siblings. *Schizophrenia Bull.,* 20, 433–440.

Guy, J.D., Majorski, L.V., Wallace, C.J., and Guy, M.P. (1983). The incidence of minor physical anomalies in adult male schizophrenics. *Schizophrenia Bull.,* 9, 571–582.

Helland, I.B., Smith, L., Saarem, K., Saugstad, O.D., and Drevon, C.A. (2003). Maternal supplementation with very-long-chain omega 3 fatty acids during pregnancy and lactation augments children's IQ's and 4 years of age. *Pediatrics,* 111(1), 39–44.

Jacobsen, B., Eklund, G., Hamberger, L., Linnarson, G., and Valverius, M. (1987). Perinatal origin of adult self-destructive behaviour. *Acta Psychatr. Scand.,* 76, 364–371.

Julkowski-Cherkes, M. (1998). Learning disability, attention-deficit disorder, and language impairment as outcomes of prematurity: a longitudinal descriptive study. *J. Learning Disabilities,* 31(3), 294–306.

Kaemingk, K. and Paquette, A. (1999). Effects of prenatal alcohol exposure on neuropsychological functioning. *Developmental Neuropsychol.,* 15(1), 111–140.

Kandel, E. and Mednick, S.A. (1991). Perinatal complications predict violent offending. *Criminology,* 29, 519–529.

Kandel, E., Brennan, P.A., Mednick, S.A., and Michelson, N.M. (1989). Minor physical anomalies and recidivistic adult violent criminal behaviour. *Acta Psychatr. Scand.,* 79(1), 103–107.

Lewis, D.O., Shanok, S.A., and Balla, D.A. (1979). Perinatal difficulties, head and face trauma and child abuse in the medical histories of seriously delinquent children. *Am. J. Psychiatry,* 136, 419–423.

Liu, J. and Raine, A. (2000). Prevention. In Gottesman, R. and Mazon, M. (Eds.), *Encyclopedia of Violence in the United States.* New York: Charles Scribner.

Liu, J. and Wuerker, A. (2005). Biosocial bases of aggressive and violent behavior — implications for nursing studies. *Int. J. Nursing Studies*, 42, 229–241.

Mannella, J.A. (1999). The transfer of alcohol to human milk: sensory implications and effects on mother-infant interaction. In Hannigan, J.H., Spear, L.P., Spear, N.E., and Goodlett, C.R. (Eds.), *Alcohol and Alcoholism. Effects on Brain and Development* (pp. 177–197). Mahwah, NJ: Erlbaum.

Mattson, S.N. and Riley, E.P. (1998). A review of the neurobehavioral deficits in children with fetal alcohol syndrome or prenatal exposure to alcohol. *Alcoholism, Clinical and Experimental Research*, 22(2), 279–294.

Mednick, S.A. and Kandel, E. (1988). Genetic and perinatal factors in violence. In Mednick, S.A. and Moffitt, T. (Eds.), *Biological Contributions to Crime Causation*. Dordrecht, Holland: Martinus Nijhoff.

Mortensen, E.L., Michaelson, K.F., Sanders, S.A., and Reinisch, J.M. (2002). The association between duration of breastfeeding and adult intelligence. *J. Am. Med. Assoc.*, 287(18), 2365–2371.

Orlebeke, J.F., Knol, D.L., and Verhulst, F.C. (1997). Increase in child behavior problems resulting from maternal smoking during pregnancy. *Arch. Environ. Health*, 52(4), 317–321.

Orlebeke, J.F. (2001). Recent decreasing trend in U.S. juvenile delinquency attribute to changes in maternal age. *Psychological Reports*, 88, 399–402.

Quinsey, V.L., Skilling, T.A., LaLumiere, M.L., and Craig, W.M. (2004). *Juvenile Delinquency: Understanding the Origins of Individual Differences*. Washington, D.C.: American Psychological Association.

Raine, A. (1993). The Psychopathology of Crime: Criminal Behaviour as a Clinical Disorder (pp. 191–214). London: Academic Press.

Raine, A., Brennan, P., and Mednick, S.A. (1997). Interaction between birth complications and early maternal rejection in predisposing individuals to adult violence: specificity to serious, early-onset violence. *Am. J. Psychiatry*, 154(9), 1265–1271.

Raine, A., Brennan, P., and Mednick, S.A. (1994). Birth complications combined with early maternal rejection at age 1 year predispose to violent crime at age 18 years. *Arch. Gen. Psychiatry*, 51(12), 984–988.

Raygada, M., Cho, E., and Hilakivi-Clarke, L. (1998). High maternal intake of polyunsaturated fatty acids during pregnancy in mice alters offspring's' aggressive behavior, immobility in the swim test, locomotor activity and brain protein kinase C activity. *J. Nutrition*, 128(12), 2505–2511.

Reiss, A., Kesler, S., Vohr, B., Duncan, C., Katz, K., Pajot, S., Schneider, K., Makuch, R., and Ment, L. (2004). Sex differences in cerebral volumes of 8-year-olds born preterm. *J. Pediatrics*, 145(2), 242–249.

Resnick, S.M., Gottesman, I.I., and McGue, M. (1993). Sensation seeking in opposite-sex twins: an effect of prenatal hormones?. *Behavioral Genetics*, 23(4), 323–329.

Roebuck, T.M., Mattson, S.N., and Riley, E.P. (1999). Prenatal exposure to alcohol: effects on brain structure and neuropsychological functioning. In Hannigan, J.H., Spear, L.P., Spear, N.E., and Goodlett, C.R. (Eds.), *Alcohol and Alcoholism. Effects on Brain and Development* (pp. 1–16). Mahwah, NJ: Erlbaum.

Satterfield, J.H., Satterfield, B.T., and Schell, A.M. (1987). Therapeutic interventions to prevent delinquency in hyperactive boys. *J. Am. Child Adolescent Psychiatry,* 26(1), 56–64.

Saugstad, L.F. (1997). Optimal foetal growth in the reduction of learning and behavior disorder and prevention of sudden infant death after the first month. *Int. J. Psychophysiology,* 27, 101–121.

Streissguth, A.P. and Dehaene, P. (1993). Fetal alcohol syndrome in twins of alcoholic mothers. *Am. J. Med. Genetics,* 47, 857–861.

Waldrop, M.F. and Halverson, C.F. (1971). Minor physical anomalies and hyperactive behavior in young children. *Exceptional Infant,* 2, 343–380.

Waldrop, M.F., Bell, R.A., McLaughlan, B., and Halverson, C.F. (1978). Newborn minor physical anomalies predict short attention span, peer aggression and impulsivity at age 3. *Science,* 199, 563–584.

Young, N.K. (1997). Effects of alcohol and other drugs on children. *J. Psychoactive Drugs,* 29(1), 23–42.

# Brain Chemistry

# 8

## Introduction

Brain chemistry is not often covered in criminology texts, probably because it requires a fairly deep understanding of neurology. However, a brief introduction to the brain and to neurotransmitters can help the reader navigate the general research in this area. The aim of this chapter is then to present a general overview of how neurotransmitters work and the roles that the major neurotransmitters — in particular, serotonin, dopamine and monoamine oxidase A — play in behavior. A fine balance exists between neurotransmitters and behavior, so slight changes can alter behavior in significant ways, most notably through affecting impulsivity and inhibition. As with so many biological issues, neurotransmitter imbalances that cause behavioral changes can sometimes be treated, in some cases with something as simple as a change in diet.

## Introduction to Neurotransmitters

The brain is the basis for all behavior, both innate and learned. Today we have a good understanding of how brain chemistry affects problems such as depression, which have for some time been accepted as medical disorders and not simply behavioral problems. We certainly do not understand everything yet, but current research reveals a good deal about how the brain works and which chemicals cause what reaction. This research has made it possible to help many people both medically and psychologically. However, there has been much less research on brain biochemistry and its possible relationship to criminal behavior.

Many criminology texts now include critical discussions of the link between genetics and crime, and most people immediately think of genetics when they think of biology and crime. However, very few texts mention neurotransmitters because neurochemistry is difficult and specialized. One does not need to be a scientist to understand basic genetics or to get a grasp of the basic genetic research in the field of biology and crime. Neurochemistry, on the other hand, uses many technical terms, and most people feel that they do not have the background to understand it. More collaboration is needed between criminologists and neurochemists. Still, there are quite a few studies on the effects of changes in brain biochemistry on criminal behavior.

Neurochemistry is an exciting area because innovations in technology are increasing rapidly, and many of the findings suggest that solutions to biochemical problems can be found. We have known that biochemistry affects behavior for many years. For example, it was shown long ago that increased dopamine might be implicated in schizophrenia, and that low levels of serotonin, norepinephrine, and/or dopamine relate to depression (Raine, 1993). It is not suggested that these chemicals are the cause of the disorder but they form a part of the total picture. More importantly, it has also been proven that certain chemical imbalances can be treated and provide patients with a hopeful prognosis. If and when any of these imbalances are conclusively linked to antisocial behavior, it is probable that they too can be treated.

## The Mechanism of Action

One can think of the body as having two communication systems: one system uses hormones and the other uses the neural system. The hormones are biological chemicals secreted into the bloodstream by endocrine organs or glands found throughout the body: for example, the testes, which produce testosterone, or the pancreas, which produces insulin. Most hormones communicate fairly slowly because they must travel through the bloodstream to get to where they are going and take effect (relatively speaking, that is, an exception may be adrenaline). Neural signals, on the other hand, are electric signals produced, received, and translated by nerve cells, and they act extremely quickly.

Neurons (or nerve cells) are specialized cells in the nervous system that transmit signals from one part of the body to another and instruct the body on how to act. For a greatly simplified example, imagine nerve cells sending signals through the neural systems to the hand to pick up a fork, use it to pick up a piece of chicken, and then move the hand holding the meat up to the mouth to deposit the food therein. Other signals tell the mouth to close the lips so the food will not fall out, and signals are sent to the mouth to chew, to the glands in the mouth to start spitting out digestive enzymes, etc.

This is greatly simplified but gives an idea of the messages going through your body in nanoseconds. There are many other kinds of nerve cells that we do not need to go into here, but it is essential to learn a little more about how nerve cells communicate. The communications take place between junctions called synapses. Figure 8.1 shows two nerve cells communicating. The cell sending the message uses the axon's synaptic terminals and the dendrites of the receiving cell receive the message. The transmitting cell is called the presynaptic cell (Figure 8.1), and the cell receiving the signal is called the postsynaptic cell (inset). There are two main types of synapses: (1) electrical synapses, which conduct electrical signals; and (2) chemical synapses, which conduct chemical signals. It is the chemical ones in which we are interested.

At a chemical synapse, there is a very narrow gap, called a synaptic cleft, that separates the transmitting or presynaptic cell from the receiving or postsynaptic cell. An electrical signal cannot span the gap, but a chemical signal can. So the electrical signal in the first cell is converted into a chemical messenger (or signal) so it can travel over the cleft. It is then converted back into an electrical signal in the receiving cell so the receiving cell knows what the message is. The chemical messengers used here are called *neurotransmitters*. Of course, this only describes communication between two cells.. For a

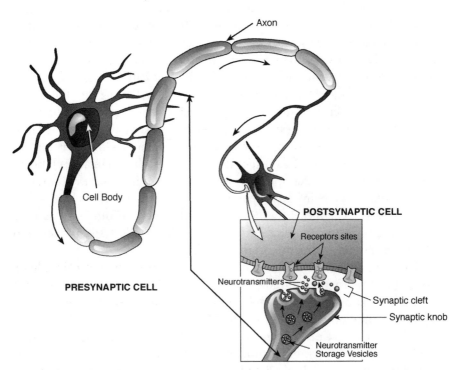

**Figure 8.1**    The presynaptic cell; the post- synaptic cell. Source: SFU Publications.

message to get from the brain, say to move one's hand, millions of cells must communicate (involving countless neurotransmitters) in a split second.

The chemicals that do the transmitting are called *neurotransmitters,* and they are stored in sacs called *synaptic vesicles.* Many neurotransmitters are known, including amino acids and biogenic amines. We are most interested in the amines, which include such basic neurotransmitters as dopamine, norepinephrine, and serotonin, because they are the basis for information processing and communication in the human brain. As a result, they are the basis of almost all behavior — from sensation (the ability to touch and feel), to perception, learning, memory, eating and drinking, and, more controversially, antisocial behavior. As they are produced and discharged into the cleft, these neurotransmitters transmit information throughout the brain. All three of these neurotransmitters are thought to be very important in the context of brain behavior.

Both medical diagnoses and research into criminogenic behavior need to measure the levels of these neurotransmitters in the central nervous system. There are several methods used. Neurotransmitters are made of precursors that are the basic proteins of life, amino acids. Each neurotransmitter has a particular amino acid precursor, which is synthesized to make the neurotransmitter. As well, there is a particular enzyme that catalyzes that reaction to convert the amino acid into a neurotransmitter. Once the neurotransmitter has done its job, it breaks down into its metabolites. There are sometimes other chemicals that fluctuate with the neurotransmitter, so they can tell us the levels of the neurotransmitters indirectly. You can measure any one of these elements in the chemical process (the precursor, the enzyme, the metabolites, or an indirect indicator) to get the levels of the neurotransmitter. The best method seems to be measuring the metabolites (Raine, 1993). It is rather like measuring the level of cocaine or heroin metabolites to determine the amount of drug a person has taken. In many cases, the original drug breaks down very rapidly; for example, heroin breaks down in a matter of minutes, so the heroin levels themselves are not measured, but rather, the levels of the metabolites, the chemicals that the body breaks heroin into, such as morphine. Because we know what levels of morphine reflect specific levels of heroin, we can determine the original level.

Three different body fluids can be tested for these chemicals in a living person: (1) cerebro-spinal fluid (CSF), (2) blood, and (3) urine. The studies we discuss next use one or more of these fluids. Neurotransmitters are synthesized in the brain and the metabolites go directly into the CSF (Raine, 1993). Thus, CSF is clearly the most accurate fluid to study. However, obtaining CSF involves performing a lumbar puncture, which is an extremely painful and fairly major medical procedure. It is an invasive method to measure neurotransmitters in a living person, and most people will not consent to it.

The procedure brings up an ethical issue; many studies do use CSF, and many of them use incarcerated offenders. Such studies balance on a thin line of the supposed voluntarism of an incarcerated population. Researchers in this area use such experimental designs with caution, and presumably with a greater value in mind.

From the CSF, the metabolites enter the bloodstream (Raine, 1993), so blood samples are the next most accurate measure of neurotransmitter levels. Blood sampling is much less problematic than CSF sampling, although still invasive. Finally, the eventual metabolites are excreted via the urine. By this time, they have been broken down significantly, they are contaminated with other breakdown products, and considerable time has passed since they were utilized, making urine sampling the least effective, but also the least invasive method of measuring neurotransmitter levels.

We know that neurotransmitters affect behavior. Research is thus guided by the goal that if it can be shown that neurotransmitters can be related to antisocial behavior, then altering the levels of the neurotransmitters, or their precursors, or the enzymes that synthesize them should reduce the undesirable behavior. There are many neurotransmitters that have been studied, the most common being serotonin, dopamine, norepinephrine, and monoamine oxidase A (MAOA).

## Serotonin

There is a great deal of information that suggests that serotonin (also known as 5-HT or 5-hydroxytryptamine) has a role in impulsive-aggressive behavior. Serotonin is thought to act as a behavioral inhibitor, and so it normally displays an inverse relationship with impulsive-aggressive behavior. That is, the lower the serotonin levels, the more impulsive-aggressive the person is; the higher the levels are, the calmer the person is (Coccaro and Kavoussi, 1996). Serotonin is produced from tryptophan, an essential amino acid obtained from our diets. This is converted to 5-hydroxytryptophan, which is converted to 5-hydroxytryptamine (5-HT) or serotonin (Bernet et al., 2006).

A link between low levels of serotonin and aggression was shown in a study in 1959, and the findings have been confirmed many times since then. Lower levels of serotonin (or its metabolites or precursors) have been associated with increased aggression, irritability, hostility, and impulsivity (Coccaro, 1989). The increase in aggression may occur because such behaviors are normally inhibited by a balance of neurotransmitters such as serotonin and dopamine. People with lower levels of these neurotransmitters lose that balance, so their behavior is no longer inhibited. Serotonin has many other functions, such as mood regulation, which could affect a person more indirectly and push him or her into aggression. However, it is rare for a biological system to be influenced by just one thing. Usually there are inhibitory and excitatory influences that interact and lead to some form of balance between the factors we can observe behaviorally (Coccaro and Kavoussi, 1996).

## Serotonin and Suicide Attempts

The original studies that linked serotonin to aggressive behavior compared the brains of people who had committed suicide with those of people who had died in accidents (Coccaro and Kavoussi, 1996). Suicide can be considered an act of violence although it is directed at oneself. Many of the studies found reduced levels of serotonin in the suicide victims compared with the accident victims. In living people, Asberg et al. (1976) found that depressed patients who had a history of suicide attempts had lower levels of the serotonin metabolite, 5-HIAA (5-hydroxyindolacetic acid), than patients who were clinically depressed but had never attempted suicide (Coccaro and Kavoussi, 1996; Asberg et al., 1976). This relationship was particularly clear in patients who had used violent methods in their suicide attempts (Asberg et al., 1976). In a more recent study comparing people who had attempted suicide, those with the lowest levels of the serotonin metabolite 5-hydroxyindolacetic acid (5-HIAA) were found to have used much more lethal methods to attempt suicide, than those with higher levels of the metabolite (Placido et al., 2001).

Obviously, not all suicides have low serotonin levels, but this study has been repeated so many times that it is clear that there is a link between low serotonin levels and suicide in many cases (Coccaro and Kavoussi, 1996). More recent work has now suggested a reason why low serotonin levels may be linked to suicide. Several studies have shown that there is a genetic link between low serotonin levels and the ability to handle stress. Everyone experiences stress and most people are able to survive such stress well. However, some people succumb to this stress, resulting in depression and suicide attempts. Evidence from animal and human studies suggest that some people are genetically less likely to be able to deal with chronic stress. Researchers found that mice that were genetically altered so that they lacked the serotonin transporter gene (5-HTT) behaved normally when their lives were stress-free, but became extremely upset, abnormally fearful, and anxious when placed in dark, unfamiliar mazes (Murphy et al., 2001). The 5-HTT gene is involved in the selective re-uptake or recycling of serotonin in the brain synapses, after it has been released into the synapses. The altered mice were also found to produce more stress-related hormones such as adrenocorticotropin than normal mice when exposed to stress (Murphy et al., 2001). A variant of the equivalent short allele in macaque monkeys was found to be regulated by adverse experience during rearing. Monkeys with this genotype that suffered from stress related to poor rearing conditions as infants were found to have decreased serotonergic function. Monkeys with the genotype that were not exposed to early stress developed normal serotonergic function, despite their genotype (Bennett et al., 2002). Therefore, the gene variant was found to be environmentally dependent and only expressed poor serotonin function in the presence of adverse rearing conditions (Bennett et al., 2002).

This relationship between stress, genes, and serotonin function has also been demonstrated in humans. Humans have been found to have two alleles or variants of the 5-HTT gene: (1) a short version, which appears to make a person more sensitive to stress; and (2) a long version, which makes them much more resistant to stress. A person can be either homozygous for the short version, meaning that both their alleles for this gene are the short version; or they can be homozygous for the long version; or they can be heterozygous, carrying both versions. In a prospective, long-term study in New Zealand, Caspi and colleagues (2003) examined 847 people and divided them into those who were homozygous for the short or stress-sensitive allele of the 5-HTT gene (17%), those who were homozygous for the long or stress-protective version (31%), and those who were heterozygous (51%). They then looked at individuals within each group who had suffered multiple stressful life events between the ages of 21 and 26 years. Among those who had suffered multiple stresses, 43% of those who were homozygous for the short version of the allele developed depression, in comparison with only 17% who were homozygous for the long version. Heterozygous individuals were intermediate. As well, 11% of those who were homozygous for the short version of the gene attempted suicide, in comparison with only 4% in those with the long versions (Caspi et al., 2003). This again indicates the major interaction that occurs between genes and the environment and how the environment modifies the effects of the genes. In many chapters we have seen that a good, stable upbringing and life can be a major protective factor against genetic predisposition for criminogenic behavior. Perhaps, in some of these cases, the mode of action is similar to the one described above, where a genotype is deleterious only under certain life circumstances.

## Serotonin and Aggression

Brown and colleagues (1979a, 1979b, 1982) were the first to report a clear relationship between levels of the serotonin metabolite 5-HIAA in CSF and aggression, rather than suicide, in humans. They started by looking at young male navy recruits who had personality disorders but were neither depressed nor substance abusers. They used medical and military records to assess aggression. They found an inverse relationship between aggression and the serotonin metabolite 5-HIAA levels; that is, the lower the serotonin metabolite, the higher the levels of aggression. However, although the subjects ranged in levels of aggression, the researchers did not look at any normal controls.

Similar studies followed but the most interesting observation was that subjects with histories of suicidal behavior had the lowest serotonin metabolite levels as well as the highest levels of aggression (Placido et al., 2001; Brown et al., 1982, 1979a, 1979b). This finding suggested that in some populations, at least, reduced levels of 5-HIAA predisposed people to aggression directed at themselves or toward others. This finding has been replicated by other researchers in humans as well as in monkeys. Some researchers have not found a link, although this is hardly surprising as no one suggests that all aggression has only one cause.

In a large-scale study, researchers studied the blood serotonin levels in 781 twenty-one-year-old men and women and compared the levels with criminal history, assessed by criminal convictions and self-reports (Moffitt et al., 1998). Low brain serotonin levels correlated with high blood serotonin levels due to the different origin and function of serotonin in the blood and brain. The researchers found that high levels of serotonin in the blood (indicating low brain serotonin levels) were highly correlated with violence in the men but not in the women (Moffitt et al., 1998). The results were specific to violent crime rather than crime in general. The results held true when all imaginable variables were controlled for including medications, diet, illegal drug use, alcohol or tobacco use, season, time of day, psychiatric diagnoses, body mass, IQ, socioeconomic status, among many others, and was significant based on either measurement of aggression — suicide or violence toward others (Moffitt et al., 1998). A study of 64 psychiatric patients suffering from a range of disorders indicated that CSF levels of 5-HIAA highly correlated with aggression. The aggressive patients had significantly lower CSF 5-HIAA than nonaggressive patients (Stanley et al., 2000). None of the patients had a history of suicide attempts.

Soderstrom et al. (2003) studied serotonin levels and also the levels of dopamine, another neurotransmitter, in 28 adult violent and sexual offenders (27 males and 1 female). They measured CSF levels of 5-HIAA and homovanillic acid, the major metabolites of serotonin and dopamine. The ratio between these two metabolites is considered very constant and thus an increase in the HVA:5-HIAA ratio is characteristic of a disruption in the serotonergic regulation of dopamine activity (Soderstrom et al., 2003). The researchers found that high HVA:5-HIAA ratios strongly correlated with psychopathy, in particular with traits such as impulsivity, aggression, and need for stimulation; and also correlated with childhood hyperactivity or conduct disorder (Soderstrom et al., 2003). The authors suggested that aggressive psychopathy may be related to both lowered serotonin levels and high levels of dopamine in the brain.

Mice that are genetically altered to lack a gene called Pet-1 do not develop most of the neurons that are critical to serotonin function, and those that do develop are abnormal. It was noted that as well as lacking in serotonin function, these mice were extraordinarily vicious and aggressive, as well as highly anxious (Hendricks et al., 2003).

## Serotonin and Impulsivity

Linnoila et al. (1983) were the first to suggest that there was also a relationship between serotonin and impulsivity. They studied violent offenders in a Finnish forensic facility, looking at the number of violent crimes committed and whether these were impulsive or premeditated crimes. CSF levels of the serotonin metabolite 5HIAA were found to be significantly lower in repeat violent offenders compared with those who had committed only one violent crime (Coccaro and Kavoussi, 1996; Linnoila et al., 1983).

However, perhaps more interestingly, the levels of the serotonin metabolite were also significantly lower in those who had committed impulsive violent offenses compared with those who had committed premeditated violent offences (Linnoila et al., 1983). In addition, violent offenders with histories of suicide attempts had lower levels than those who had never tried to commit suicide. This was the first evidence that related low serotonin levels to impulsivity. This was extremely important because it indicated that serotonin's link to criminal behavior is probably mediated by impulsivity. These findings may also explain why some researchers have not found a link with serotonin levels and aggression. If the link is serotonin and impulsivity, the impulsivity might result in violence, and serotonin would only show a relationship in violent offenders whose offenses related to impulsivity. Members of this research team later also found a link between low serotonin levels and impulsive firesetters (Virkkunen et al., 1996a).

Many researchers have now demonstrated a link between certain types of aggression and low serotonin levels. However, it is still not fully understood whether serotonin directly influences aggression or whether it regulates impulsivity, so that low levels mean that a person has less control. However, lack of control, or impulsivity, is frequently linked to crime, and serotonin normally acts as a behavioral inhibitor. Low serotonin would therefore be logically expected to result in less inhibition and increased impulsivity.

## Serotonin and Antisocial Personality Disorder

A study conducted on Finnish violent offenders with antisocial personality (ASP) or intermittent explosive disorders found a link between these disorders and serotonin levels (Virkkunen et al., 1995, 1996a). ASP is considered the most common personality disorder diagnosis among prisoners in Western countries; and the American Psychiatric Association estimated that, in 1994, more than 30% of new prisoners have ASP. In Finland, 80 to 85% of recidivist severe violent crimes are thought to be committed by people with ASP (Virkkunen et al., 1995, 1996a). In addition, people with intermittent explosive disorder are also impulsive violent offenders. Such people are fine when they do not drink or use drugs, but they react repeatedly and extremely violently when they do. These researchers found consistently and significantly low levels of CSF serotonin in people who had impaired impulse control, a history of suicide attempts, hypoglycemic tendencies, and hyperactivity (Virkkunen, et al., 1996b).

In a study of 193 newborn babies who were hospitalized and tested for fevers, researchers found that levels of 5-HIAA were significantly lower in babies who had families with a history of ASP than in those with no such family history (Constantino et al., 1997). A further study looked at the relationship between childhood aggression, parental anti-social behavior, and serotonin levels. Researchers studied ADHD boys and divided them into four groups — aggressive boys with and without aggressive parents and non-aggressive boys with and without aggressive parents — and measured overall serotonin function (Halperin et al., 1997). The researchers found that aggressive boys with aggressive parents had significantly lower serotonin function than aggressive boys with nonaggressive parents. Both groups of nonaggressive boys were intermediate. Other types of parental psychiatric illness had no effect (Halperin et al., 1997). The researchers suggest that ADHD boys who are aggressive and have a family history of aggression are neurochemically different from aggressive boys with no such family history. Aggressive boys with a family history were also more severely aggressive than aggressive boys without a family history. However, this study only looked at ADHD boys and thus may not be generalizable to a wider population (Halperin et al., 1997).

## Serotonin Binding Sites

Neurotransmitters such as serotonin need to bind to a site in the brain in order to act. If there is no binding site, there is no effect. Studies on the brains of suicide and accident victims showed that suicide victims had fewer binding sites than did accident victims (Coccaro and Astill, 1990). This finding means that normal levels of serotonin could be present, but unable to act. This theory is still controversial because the relationship between receptor sites and serotonin activity is not fully understood.

Platelet cells in the blood also have receptor sites for serotonin, and several studies have shown reduced numbers of sites in certain groups (Coccaro and Kavoussi, 1996). Marazziti et al. (1989) found reduced numbers of binding sites in people who had attempted suicide in comparison with volunteers.

In another study, aggressive hyperactive psychiatric patients with "mental deficiency" were found to have reduced numbers of binding sites compared with healthy volunteers (Marazziti and Conti, 1991); and in a third study, conduct-disordered children were found to have fewer binding sites than age-matched, non-affected children (Stoff et al., 1987). On the basis of this evidence, it has been suggested that people with low levels of serotonin may be less able to inhibit their responses to aversive stimuli and thus be more likely to resort to a more severe display of aggression than people with normal levels who can control their response. For example, someone with low levels may respond to a negative situation by striking out directly, while someone with normal levels may respond to the same situation by yelling (Coccaro and Kavoussi, 1996).

## Serotonin Precursors

Neurotransmitters are synthesized from basic amino acids. Each neurotransmitter has a precursor amino acid. The precursor for serotonin is tryptophan, which cannot be synthesized in the body, but rather must be ingested in the diet. If the diet is low in tryptophan, even people with normal serotonin activity will have low levels of serotonin because they are unable to synthesize appropriate amounts of serotonin.

Lithium carbonate is a controversial drug that is often used to treat aggression in many populations, including prison inmates, mentally retarded patients, schizophrenics, and conduct and attention deficit-disordered children (Raine, 1993). One of its functions is to increase the uptake of dietary tryptophan, which will consequently increase the levels of serotonin in the body and thus could explain the reduction in aggression.

Although many studies indicate that serotonin and aggression are related, many also show that low serotonin levels seem to relate more directly to impulsivity than to aggression. Thus, it may be that high impulsivity is the direct effect and aggression is a consequence. The reason that this work on lack of serotonin is exciting is that it is so easily affected by diet. In many people, increasing dietary levels of tryptophan can solve a problem caused by a lack of the precursor in the diet. High levels of dietary tryptophan can increase the levels of serotonin, thereby reducing impulsivity and often creating a general feeling of well-being. Traditional Christmas and Thanksgiving meals involve ingesting large quantities of roast turkey and frequently this is followed by guests relaxing, snoozing, and generally feeling mellow and peaceful. This is often thought to be related to simply eating too much but, actually, turkey is very high in tryptophan and the mellowing effects are most probably due to high levels of serotonin.

Of course, there may be many other reasons why serotonin levels are low and these may not be rectified by dietary correction. These reasons include an innate inability to convert tryptophan to serotonin, or a lack of receptor sites. Still, when something is the result of a chemical imbalance, it should be possible to eventually readjust that balance.

## Serotonin in the Courts

Low serotonin levels have been argued in court to suggest that a person did not have the required intent to commit a crime (*mens rea*), or to mitigate evidence during sentencing, although these, to date, have not been successful (Bernet et al., 2006). For example, in State *v.* Godsey (2001 WL 1543474, Tenn. Crim. App. 2002), the defense introduced expert testimony to show that the defendant suffered from intermittent explosive disorder and thus his second degree murder conviction was the result of an impulsive rather than intentional act. The jury rejected this and he was sentenced to 25 years in prison (Bernet et al., 2006). In Tennessee, a man was convicted of the first degree murder of his wife (Hall *v.* State, Tenn. Crim. App. 2005). During the post-conviction hearing, expert testimony was presented in an attempt to illustrate that the defendant was unable to achieve the necessary mental state due to his low serotonin levels. This was rejected and his death sentence was confirmed (Bernet et al., 2006). In State *v.* Payne (Tenn. Crim. App. 2003), expert testimony was presented to indicate that the defendant had such low serotonin levels that he was incapable of controlling his impulses. Specifically, low serotonin levels were introduced in an attempt to show that the defendant did not have the ability to form *mens rea*, to suggest the lack of impulse control provoked the defendant, and in an effort to mitigate the sentence. All claims were rejected by the jury as the prosecution could demonstrate premeditation, and provocation is only considered if perpetuated by the victim and not from some internal mechanism (Bernet et al., 2006). In Michigan, the defense attempted to introduce expert testimony that the defendant had biological issues that affected his ability to control his impulsivity and to reason (People *v.* Uncapher, 2004 WL 790329, Mich. App. 2004). Interestingly, the testimony was excluded because Michigan State law prevents the presentation of biological condition in order to rebut the defendant's capacity to form *mens rea* (Bernet et al., 2006). Finally, in South Carolina, David Hill was convicted of first degree murder and sentenced to death in 1995 (Hill *v.* Ozmint, 339 F. #d 187, 4th Cir. 2003) (on appeal from South Carolina). Expert testimony was allowed to be introduced during the sentencing phase to show that the defendant had a serotonin deficiency based on spinal fluid analysis and therefore his aggressive behavior was based on genetics and thus not under his control, and furthermore, that this condition was treatable and that he had been successfully treated. This was rejected and Hill was executed by lethal injection in 2004 (Bernet et al., 2006).

Genetic makeup has also been examined in some courts. In several U.S. cases, whether a person was genetically prone to depression and stress by being homozygous for the short version of the 5-HTT gene has been or is under consideration (Bernet et al., 2006).

## Norepinephrine

Norepinephrine is a common neurotransmitter but it is not as well studied as serotonin. Animal studies have shown that high levels of norepinephrine correlate with aggression, and some studies in humans have suggested a similar relationship (Coccaro and Kavoussi, 1996). Although there are fewer direct human studies, in many cases we can infer information from studies that had objectives other than behavioral, such as drug tests. Certain drugs are known to reduce norepinephrine levels, so we can observe whether they also have an effect on aggressive behavior. For example, reserpine reduces the levels of norepinephrine, and it has been shown to reduce aggressive behavior. On the other hand, drugs that are known to increase norepinephrine levels, for example, tricyclic antidepressants, usually increase aggressive behavior in agitated, depressed patients (Raine, 1993). So, in general, the studies show that increased levels of norepinephrine result in increased aggression, whereas a decrease in norepinephrine results in a decrease in aggression. However, there has still not been enough research in this area to draw strong conclusions.

## Dopamine

The dopamine system, another significant neurotransmitter system, is highly important to the body's reward system. Dopamine produces strong positive feelings that occur regularly in the course of everyday events. These pathways provide the pleasure drives for sex, love, food, and other such sought-after goals. The body thus produces its own natural rewards through a cascade of pleasurable feelings and these feelings depend on the release of dopamine (Comings and Blum, 2000). Unnatural or artificial substances such as illicit drugs, alcohol, nicotine, etc. can also target this region and bring on this cascade of pleasure, so the dopamine system is the major target of most abused drugs due to the pleasure that stimulation of this system produces (Volkow et al., 2003). Such drugs rapidly induce elevations of dopamine in the brain, which result in intense euphoria, the typical "highs" of illicit drugs. Although different drugs have different mechanisms of action, all elevate dopamine (Volkow et al., 2003). Both illegal and therapeutic drugs, such as amphetamines and cocaine, greatly increase dopamine production, and sometimes also increase human aggression (Coccaro and Kavoussi, 1996). Although many people smoke, drink alcohol, and perhaps even take drugs, only some of these people become addicted. It is believed that these people suffer from a "reward deficiency syndrome" (Comings and Blum, 2000; Blum et al., 2000). Such people have deficiencies in this normal reward cascade, and thus do not receive the normal pleasures from life and hence crave greater stimulation. They are at much greater risk for addiction than people with normal systems. Because dopamine is the main neurotransmitter in the reward pathway, variants of the genes involved in this pathway are most likely responsible and some have been identified. Type II alcoholism, which is very strongly influenced by genetics, has also been linked to disruption of several of the genes related to dopamine receptors (Blum et al., 1995; Tiihonen et al., 1995). Obesity, smoking, and pathological gambling have also been linked to variants in the dopamine receptors, in particular, DRD2 (Blum et al., 1995). However, serotonin, norepinephrine, and other neurotransmitters also regulate dopamine, so variant genes in any of these pathways might contribute to a predisposition for addiction.

High levels of dopamine have also been shown to increase aggression and fighting in patients, again mostly from medical studies looking at the effects of drugs that change dopamine levels in patients. Antipsychotic drugs that reduce the levels of dopamine tend to decrease fighting in patients, aggressive delinquents, and people with borderline personality disorder. One review found no results in patients on antipsychotic medications (Raine, 1993), but it is not very likely that all people who require them have the same problems. Drugs such as methylphenidate (Ritalin) are often effective in reducing behavioral problems seen in such disorders as conduct disorder (CD) and attention deficit hyperactivity disorder (ADHD) by altering the function of the dopamine transporter (DAT). The transporter stops dopamine activity by transporting it from the nerve synapses, back to the cells that released it (Young et al., 2002).

More recent research has suggested that some behavioral problems, in particular, externalizing behaviors such as chronic aggression, delinquency, and destructive and impulsive behaviors, which respond well to drugs such as Ritalin, may have a genetic basis (Young et al., 2002; Cook et al., 1995). Youngs et al. recruited 790 children from the Colorado Longitudinal Twin Study and the Colorado Adoption Project and evaluated their behavior, based on parents' ratings, at age 4, 7, and 9 years. The researchers found that a particular allele of the DAT1 gene involved in dopamine transport was a significant risk factor for behavioral problems at aged 4 and 7 years. This allele, the 9-repeat variant of the DAT1 gene, has also been suggested as a risk factor in alcoholism; and a different variant of the same gene, the 10-repeat variant, has been linked to ADHD (Young et al., 2002). Although the 9-repeat variant was not directly linked to externalizing behavior at age 9 years, the researchers did find a significant association across the three ages. This work supports the hypothesis that dopamine and changes in the dopamine system can result in undesirable behavior (Young et al., 2002).

As dopamine is very important in producing pleasure, it has been suggested that people with low dopamine levels have a biochemically reduced capacity for receiving pleasure from normal activities and thus may be more vulnerable to alcohol or drug abuse (Volkow et al., 2003). Experiments with rats that had been genetically altered to crave alcohol concluded that inserting a gene for the dopamine D2 receptor into the brain of such rats dramatically decreased their craving for alcohol (Thanos et al., 2004). The authors suggest that high levels of D2 receptors serve as a protective factor against alcoholism.

## Monoamine Oxidase (MAO)

### MAO and Aggression

As we continue looking at neurotransmitters, we find that the mechanism of its influence becomes more and more complex. Monoamine oxidase (MAO) is an enzyme in the mitochondria (the powerhouses found in large numbers in every cell that provide the cell with energy). MAO is the enzyme responsible for breaking down several neurotransmitters, including serotonin, dopamine, and norepinephrine (Beitchman et al., 2004). Therefore, it also has an effect on the levels of these neurotransmitters in the body. There are actually two MAO enzymes, MAOA and MAOB, and they are produced by two different genes that have loci (or "addresses") close to each other on the short end of the X chromosome (Brunner, 1996). This means that these genes are sex-linked.

It is well known medically that inhibiting the production of MAO, particularly MAOA, using drugs is a very effective way of treating depression. So, by inference, it would seem that altering MAO enzymic activity can affect the brain (Brunner, 1996). Brunner et al. (1993) identified a large Dutch family with an abnormality in MAO production. Although it is only one family, the implications are very interesting. Over four generations, there were many perfectly normal people in this family, but 14 males had a complex behavioral syndrome. These males were borderline mentally retarded and had numerous behavioral problems, including aggressive behavior, which was mostly verbal but could become violent. They had also committed many crimes, including rape, assault, and arson (Brunner, 1996). The problem was only ever seen in males, but it was transmitted through the females, who were normal. This showed that the condition was sex-linked and carried on the

X chromosome, in a similar manner to hemophilia and color blindness (discussed in Chapter 3).

The family had known about the problem for years, and one family member had even documented all the occurrences over the previous 35 years. All family members clearly knew who had the problem and who did not. When it was proven to be sex-linked, it was found to be a result of a very minor change in the gene that produced MAOA (Brunner, 1996). Affected males could not produce MAOA, which again highlights that even a minute change in a single gene can be devastating. Proper gene function can be likened to opening a safe; if you have the combination, you can open it; but if you get just one number wrong, it will not open. Whether you have just one wrong number in 6000 or in 6 million does not matter — one wrong number and the safe will not open. It is the same way with genes. Everything must be perfect; a minute mutation can prevent proper functioning.

In this case, the affected males could not produce MAOA, which affected their ability to break down serotonin and dopamine. They produced serotonin normally but it was not broken down and, as a result, their levels of serotonin were higher than normal. This finding seems to go against everything we have just discussed. Although a lot of the information we have is not so clear, the relationship between *lowered* serotonin levels and impulsiveness and, therefore, aggression is fairly obvious. These men are aggressive, and thus one would expect them to have lowered serotonin levels.

However, we also know that any sort of problem with the normal levels of any body chemical could cause problems. Brunner, who first discovered this family, speculated that if brain serotonin levels were high throughout life, from conception onward, as they would be when the MAOA gene is defective, it might have had an effect on the number and density of the receptor cells for serotonin. If so, it could mean that although there is too much serotonin, it has a lesser effect because there are not enough receptor cells: that is, the overall effect would be less serotonin activity. The evidence shows that MAOA inhibition does lead to significantly raised levels of serotonin in the brain, which causes changes in the brain (Brunner, 1996).

MAOA inhibitors are successfully used to treat depression. They may actually work to decrease the amount of serotonin produced by initially causing an increase (Brunner, 1996). This explanation would clarify this apparent paradox of high versus low serotonin levels and aggression. Drugs that inhibit MAO during fetal development in rats have been shown to change the development of the serotonergic system in the brain, so prenatal exposure may be very important (Whitaker-Azmitia et al., 1994). The males in this family were never able to produce MAOA, even in the womb, so they may have reacted similarly, as Brunner suggested. However, animals are not always good models for humans. For example, humans who do not have a functioning

HPRT (hypoxanthine phosphoriposyltranferase) gene have a disease called Lesch-Nyhan syndrome, which causes severe mental retardation and self-mutilation. However, mice that do not have a functioning version of this gene do not develop a similar disease (Brunner, 1996).

The fact that abnormal behavior can be directly linked to a genetic defect is not unusual. Lesch-Nyhan is caused by one gene defect and involves major behavioral abnormalities (Brunner, 1996). Attention deficit hyperactivity disorder (ADHD) has been linked to genetics, as have thyroid hormone resistance, anxiety disorder, and acute intermittent porphyria (which is caused by porphobilinogen deaminase deficiency). Porphyria is the disease that may have initiated the vampire legends; people with the disease are very pale, have blood in their urine, and are very sensitive to light, so they only go out at night. All these disorders include a change in the metabolism of the brain and behavior changes.

In a recent study, Beitchman et al. (2004) found that persistent and pervasively aggressive children were more likely to carry a particular MAOA allele that results in higher levels of MAOA transcription than that seen in normal adults. Although this is different from the above study, where reduced MAOA was linked to behavioral problems, Beitchman et al. speculated that the increased MAOA might affect persistent aggressive behavior by having a constant degradative effect on other neurotransmitters, such as serotonin, dopamine, and norepinephrine (Beitchman et al., 2004). Using a mouse model, genetically altered mice that have disturbed MAOA systems have been found to be extremely aggressive, frequently killing mates and conspecifics (Janssen et al., 2005; Kumar et al., 2004). Janssen et al. postulate that, due to our understanding of the mouse genome and our ability to manipulate it, we should be able to use a mouse model to assist in testing many genetic and environmental hypotheses related to violence (Janssen et al., 2005).

## MAOA and Child Abuse

Many people who were abused as children grow up to be criminals or abusers themselves, and this is often considered a result of their abusive background. However, many equally abused children grow up to be highly productive, nonabusive adults. Although it is unlikely that there is a single explanation for this discrepancy, exciting research into the gene that controls production of MAOA suggests that one of the differences between the two groups may be genetic (Caspi et al., 2002).

Caspi and co-workers analyzed data from 442 male adult New Zealanders and identified 154 who had been abused as children, including 33 who had been severely abused. Each participant was evaluated to determine whether he/she had a fully functioning variant of the MAOA gene or whether he/she had a "low-activity" variant. Some 85% of the severely abused participants with the low-activity variant of the gene developed some form of antisocial behavior. In contrast, participants who had the fully functioning variant of the gene rarely exhibited aggressive or criminal behavior as adults, even if they had been severely abused as children (Caspi et al., 2002). The authors contended that the combination of childhood abuse, together with the low-activity variant of the gene, could predict antisocial behavior in the same way that high cholesterol predicts heart disease. Simple possession of the low-activity variant of the gene did not predispose for aggression, nor did child abuse alone. Only those who had the low-activity variant of the gene and experienced abuse in childhood were predisposed to aggression. This indicates that the presence of a fully functioning MAOA gene provides protection against the effects of early childhood abuse, and could explain why only some victims of early abuse grow up to be abusers (Caspi et al., 2002). As the disease is sex-linked, the authors also suggest it could be one of the reasons that antisocial behavior is so much more prevalent among men.

More recent work also supports Caspi et al.'s findings that genetics can strongly influence a child's response to abuse. In Foley et al.'s (2004) study, 514 male twins between the ages of 8 and 17 years were assessed for childhood adversity as well as symptoms of conduct disorder. The researchers found that children with the low-activity variant of the MAOA gene who also experienced childhood adversity were significantly more likely to develop conduct disorder. However, children with the same gene variant who experienced happy childhoods in stable homes had a lower risk of conduct disorder.

These two studies are really quite groundbreaking. They illustrate beautifully the relationship between the environment and genetics. The genes provide the basic framework, but how the person will grow up depends on the environment working with the genes. We can see this clearly when we look at a physical phenotype, but it is much more difficult to envision when we talk of behavior. If a child is born to tall, large parents, it is likely that the child will also grow up to be large. However, if this child experiences extreme illness or malnutrition, he or she will not reach their full genetic potential. The genes were the blueprint for size but the environment influenced the final outcome and overrode the genetics. The above studies illustrate a similar situation with behavior. Children with the low-activity variant of the MAOA gene are genetically programmed to grow up normally, with no adverse consequences of a lower level of MAOA, unless the environment is harsh, in which case children with this genotype will be more prone to behavioral problems, including aggression. The genes create the framework but the environment will be what influences the final outcome. Again, the protective value of a stable, loving home clearly overcomes any genetic predisposition for antisocial behavior. The value of providing children with stability and care cannot be overstated. Funding for families, child-care support, mentoring programs, and school support would be repaid a thousand-fold.

## Body Build and Antisocial Behavior

One of the fallacies in the early history of criminology was the idea that there was a "body type." Sheldon believed that criminals had different body shapes from noncriminals and that it was possible to determine whether someone was a criminal just by looking at them. However, although Sheldon's theory was quite wrong in its original form, we discussed earlier why a larger person may be more prone to using violence: they may have found out in childhood that their size can be used to win arguments.

Lombroso's ideas had no basis in fact; but with the greater understanding of brain chemistry today, there is at least one suggestion why larger people may have a greater predisposition toward aggression than smaller ones. It is well established that low serotonin levels have an effect on behavior, primarily through greater impulsivity. There are many reasons why a person may have low serotonin levels. It may be genetic; it may be environmental; it may be a result of not eating enough of the precursor or of not having enough receptor cells, etc. However, a person may also have a low serotonin level as a result of decreased concentrations of somatostatin, a peptide in the body that stimulates the release of serotonin.

A person having low levels of somatostatin would, consequently, also have low levels of serotonin. Somatostatin not only controls serotonin function, but also controls the amount of growth hormone released (Raine, 1993). Growth hormone does exactly what its name suggests: it affects the growth of the child. Somatostatin inhibits or reduces the amount of growth hormone released. If the level of somatostatin is low, there will be a lack of inhibition of growth hormone, and thus more growth hormone will be produced and released, and there will be an increase in body size and muscle mass. At the same time, low levels of somatostatin will result in low levels of serotonin. So, in some cases, large people may have lower serotonin levels, which can lead to impulsivity and aggression. The larger body size is incidental but it might, in some cases, suggest lower serotonin levels.

Does having a big body result in more aggressive behavior as some used to believe? No, but as in the case of the XYY child discussed previously, we must consider what often happens to big children at school, especially if they have other antisocial problems that might be expected in someone with low serotonin. They are often challenged and get into fights, which may lead them to think that fighting is the way to handle conflict.

Thus, reduced serotonin levels might explain why the original theories were developed. However, there have not been many studies that looked directly at somatostatin levels. One study did find a significant reduction in the study group but another did not (Raine, 1993). There may be no relationship, or it may be that the level of somatostatin is just one of the many reasons why serotonin levels are lowered.

There have also been more recent studies that suggest that there may be some truth to the idea that larger body size is related to aggression. Raine and colleagues, in 1998, found a correlation between height and body bulk at age 3 with aggression at age 11 (Raine et al., 1998). To understand this better, Ishikawa et al. (2001) looked at three subgroups of antisocial adults: adolescent-limited, who only exhibit anti-social behavior as teenagers, life-course persistent anti-socials, whose anti-social behavior is severe and remains throughout life, and late-onset anti-social individuals who first exhibit antisocial behavior in late adolescence or young adulthood. The latter two groups were formerly diagnosed as having antisocial personality disorder (APD) or late-onset APD. The sample was recruited from the general population from temporary employment agencies. The complete sample of 87 men was divided into four groups: (1) life-course persistent antisocials, (2) late-onset antisocials, (3) adolescent-limited antisocials, and (4) controls. Several measures of antisocial behavior were used, including the Psychopathy Checklist-Revised (PCL-R) and DSM-IV diagnoses of APD or conduct disorder (CD). Height, weight, body mass index (BMI), a measure of obesity, and body bulk (an index of body stature) were recorded. Each participant was also scored for psychosocial adversity, such as whether parents had been on welfare, whether raised by someone other than a parent, number of schools attended, number of homes lived in as a child, parents' use of corporel punishment, and whether ever placed in a foster home, hospital, or institution as a child (Ishikawa et al., 2001). The researchers found no significant differences between the four groups based on weight and BMI, but did find a significant difference in height and bulk. In both cases, life-course persistent and late-onset antisocial individuals were taller and bulkier than adolescent-limited antisocial or control individuals. Psychosocial adversity did not account for the size differences (Ishikawa et al., 2001). Both groups that exhibited adolescent antisocial behavior (life-course persistent and adolescent-limited) reported higher levels of psychosocial adversity than either the late-onset individuals or the controls, suggesting that childhood adversity has a strong environmental effect on adolescent antisocial behavior, perhaps acting as a trigger, whereas the biological parameters that influence height and bulk predispose the person to continue such behavior throughout adulthood (Ishikawa et al., 2001). The authors suggest that there is a biological difference between adolescent-limited antisocial individuals and both life-course persistent and late-onset anti-social individuals. They felt that the larger body size related to APD.

Our earlier discussion relating to body size involved the idea that a larger child might be more inclined to use aggression than a smaller, weaker child. Although that may explain some of the above results, it does not explain why the late-onset antisocial individuals were not antisocial when adolescents. The authors suggest an alternative explanation. They suggest that the neuro-chemical processes that relate to height and bulk may be somehow linked to the biological processes related to antisocial behavior, suggesting that larger body size is a side effect of the biological processes predisposing for antisocial behavior (Ishikawa et al., 2001). For example, it may be that the larger size is related to somatostatin levels, which in turn resulted in lowered serotonin, which was the trigger for antisocial behavior. Bulk is also related to testoster-one levels but the evidence is still inconclusive regarding testosterone and aggression.

The results of this study are interesting but the sample size in each group (particularly the adolescent-limited and late-onset groups) was quite small, and larger experiments are required to verify the results. As well, body size was measured in adulthood; and although this may reflect childhood size, it may not be a direct reflection (Ishikawa et al., 2001).

## Other Factors

Sociological studies often show a relationship between crime and poverty or low socioeconomic status. However, the phrase "low socioeconomic status" simply means that many things could be influencing behavior. In particular, low socioeconomic status often involves a bad diet or poor nutrition (Raine, 1993). We will look at diet again but here we need to note that for the body to produce neurotransmitters, the diet must include the precursors, such as tryptophan in the case of serotonin and tyrosine in the case of norepineph-rine. Certain things in the diet can also block the body's ability to take up these substances. So, if the diet is low in these precursors or includes other elements that block the uptake of them, then the person will have low levels of the neurotransmitters. In some cases, even if the dietary problems are rectified, the brain levels never fully recover, which indicates permanent damage.

It stands to reason that those of low socioeconomic status will probably have poor diets, and the same is true of drug users and alcoholics. Therefore, poor nutrition in people of low socioeconomic status, including during preg-nancy, could very well affect neurotransmitter levels throughout life. This is just one more example of how biological factors do not act in a vacuum.

Social, environmental, and biological factors interact to influence behavior, which itself may alter the original factors. In this case, the environment — that is, the low socioeconomic status — could result in a poor diet that causes a biological problem.

Brain chemistry also has an effect on information processing, memory, understanding, and other cognitive factors. Hostile boys have been found to be more likely to misinterpret a situation and see hostile intent when it does not exist and to react aggressively and impulsively (Raine, 1993).

Somatostatin levels, which affect serotonin and growth hormone, may also affect memory and thus affect whether or not a person remembers the negative consequences of a past action (Raine, 1993). People with Alzheimer's disease have very low somatostatin levels, which is interesting but not conclusive; however, studies have also shown that memory in animals is affected by low somatostatin levels. People who have reduced serotonin, which is also a result of reduced somatostatin, may have reduced memory skills. They may not understand punishment or remember the cues that lead to it, so they do not learn how to avoid it; but it may also mean that they have a limited memory of the choices available in a hostile situation. For example, if they grew up with abuse, they may see aggression as the only response in a conflict situation.

It is well known that alcohol has major effects on criminal activity; in fact, the majority of crimes are committed by people under the influence of alcohol or drugs. Studies have shown that antisocial alcohol abusers have significantly reduced serotonin levels. There is also a lot of evidence that suggests low levels of serotonin are associated with impulsive violent behavior, and alcohol may provide further reduction in inhibition (Raine, 1993) because it inhibits the person's normal controls over behavior. As well, a low ratio of the concentrations of tryptophan and other large, neutral amino acids in plasma seems to correlate with early onset alcohol abuse and violent tendencies (Virkkunen and Linnoila, 1990). Some researchers have found that subjects with a history of paternal alcoholism had a significantly lower mean CSF 5-HIAA concentration (serotonin metabolite) (Linnoila and Virkkunen, 1992).

However, it has also been found that the effect of reduced serotonin is largest in antisocial groups with no alcohol abuse. Raine suggests that reduced serotonin levels in non-alcoholic antisocial people may lead to impulsive, violent antisocial behavior because alcohol also has a disinhibiting effect, which may be the final push toward antisocial behavior in people with normal or nearer-normal serotonin levels. So it is possible that there may be two groups, one of which is biochemically predisposed to crime by low serotonin levels but is not alcoholic and another that is influenced more by the disinhibiting effects of alcohol (Raine, 1993). These differences demonstrate again that there are many different motivations for crime.

## Conclusion

This exciting area needs much more research before stable conclusions about neurotransmitters and their effects on behavior and criminal behavior can be reached. Many different chemical actions occur in the brain, and a change in any one chemical affects many others. There are various models that suggest how changes begin to work together, with people showing variation in levels of excitatory and inhibitory chemicals (Coccaro and Kavoussi, 1996).

It has been suggested that given the proper environmental circumstances, the threshold to act aggressively is controlled by overall serotonin functions. The lower the functional status of the serotonin system, the more likely the individual is to respond with an aggressive outburst to circumstances perceived as threatening. Also, the lower the serotonin level, the more severe the aggression is likely to be. Verbal aggression, such as yelling and profanity, is less severe than hitting someone or self-mutilation. This finding is entirely consistent with the evidence that indicates that serotonin, in its normal function, is a behavioral inhibitor. The role of other neurotransmitters in modulating aggression is more difficult to understand, but Coccaro and Kavoussi suggest that it relates to the role they play in recognizing threat or frustration (norepinephrine) and in activating the mental and physical systems (dopamine) that are needed to actually mount an aggressive response. If the researchers are correct, there may be a way to intervene in this situation. Counseling could be used to decrease the level of arousal in individuals, change their circumstances to reduce perceived threat, and change their way of thinking to a less confrontational viewpoint (Coccaro and Kavoussi, 1996).

The body functions as a result of interactions between numerous systems and chemicals. Therefore, none of these systems works alone. They all affect each other, and one of the major links is between serotonin and glucose (sugar levels), a fascinating study that we discuss in the chapter on diet.

## Questions for Further Study and Discussion

1. Why might serotonin levels only be related to certain types of violence and not others?
2. Although it would be unethical in many cases to do direct studies on neurotransmitter levels in humans, there is an indirect method

of determining the effects of neurotransmitter levels on behavior. Explain how we do this and what the ethical implications may be.
3. What is the function of dopamine? Why might it be related to drug abuse?
4. What is the known brain chemistry for a predisposition to suicide?

# References

Asberg, M., Traskman, L., and Thoren, P. (1976). 5-HIAA in the cerebrospinal fluid: a biochemical suicide predictor?. *Arch. Gen. Psych.,* 33, 1193–1197.

Beitchman, J.H., Mik, H.M., Ehtesham, S., Douglas, L., and Kennedy, J.L. (2004). MAOA and persistent, pervasive childhood aggression. *Mol. Psychiatry,* 1–2(10), 401–492.

Bennett, A.J., Lesch, K.P., Heils, A., Long, J.C., Lorenz, J.C., Shoaf, S.E., Champoux, M., Suomi, S.J., Linnoila, M.V., and Higley, J.D. (2002). Early experience and serotonin transporter gene variation interact to influence primate CNS function. *Mol. Psychiatry,* 7(1), 118–122.

Bernet, W., Vnencak-Jones, C.L., Faraheny, N., and Montgomery, S.A. (2006). Bad nature, bad nurture, and testimony regarding MAOA and SLC6A4 genes at murder trials. *American Academy of Forensic Sciences Annual Meeting,* Seattle, WA.

Blum, K., Braverman, E.R., Holder, J.M., Lubar, J.F., Monastra, V.J., Miller, D., Lubar, J.O., Chen, T.J., and Comings, D.E. (2000). Reward deficiency syndrome: a biogenetic model for the diagnosis and treatment of impulsive, addictive and compulsive behaviors. *J. Psychoactive Drugs,* 32(i–iv), 1–112.

Blum, K., Sheridan, P.J., Wood, R.C., Braverman, E.R., Chen, T.J., and Comings, D.E. (1995). Dopamine D2 receptor gene variants: association and linkage studies in impulsive-addictive-compulsive behavior. *Pharmocogenetics,* 5(3), 121–141.

Brown, G.L., Ballanger, J.C., Minichiello, M.D., and Goodwin, F.K. (1979a). Human aggression and its relationship to cerebrospinal fluid 5-hydroxyindolacetic acid, 3-methoxy-4-hydroxyphenylglycol and homovanillic acid. In Sandler, M. (Ed.), *Psychopharmacology of Aggression* (pp. 131–148.) New York: Raven Press.

Brown, G.L., Ebert, M.H., Goyer, P.F., Jimerson, D.C., Klein, W.J., Bunney, W.E., and Goodwin, F.K. (1982). Aggression, suicide, and serotonin: relationships to CSF amine metabolites. *Am. J. Psych.,* 139(6), 741.

Brown, G.L., Goodwin, F.K., Ballenger, J.C., Goyer, P.F., and Major, L.F. (1979b). Aggression in humans correlates with cerebrospinal fluid amine metabolites. *Psychol. Res.,* 1, 131–139.

Brunner, H.G. (1996). MAOA deficiency and abnormal behavior: perspectives on an association. *Ciba Foundation Symposium,* 194, 155–164.

Brunner, H.G., Nelen, M., Breakefield, X.O., Ropers, H.H., and van Oost, B.A. (1993). Abnormal behavior associated with a point mutation in the structural gene for monoamine oxidase A. *Science,* 262(5133), 578–580.

Caspi, A., McClay, J., Moffitt, T.E., Mill, J., Martin, I., Craig, W., Taylor, A., and Poulton, R. (2002). Role of genotype in the cycle of violence in maltreated children. *Science,* 297(5582), 851–854.

Caspi, A., Sugden, K., Moffitt, T.E., Taylor, A., Craig, A.W., Harrington, H., McClay, J., Mill, J., Martin, J., Braithwaite, A., and Poulton, R. (2003). Influence of life stress on depression: moderation by a polymorphism in the 5-HTT gene. *Science,* 301(5631), 386–389.

Coccaro, E.F. (1989). Central serotonin and impulsive aggression. *Br. J. Psych.,* 155(8), 52–62.

Coccaro, E.F. and Astill, J.L. (1990). Central serotenergic system function in para-suicide. *Progressive Neuro-Psychopharm. Biol. Psych.,* 14, 663–674.

Coccaro, E.F. and Kavoussi, R.J. (1996). Neurotransmitter correlates of impulse aggres-sion. In Stoff, D.M. and Cairns, R.B. (Eds.), *Aggression and Violence: Genetic, Neurobiological and Biosocial Perspectives* (pp. 67–85). Mahwah, NJ: Erlbaum.

Comings, D.E. and Blum, K. (2000). Reward deficiency syndrome: genetic aspects of behavioral disorders. *Prog. Brain Res.,* 126, 325–341.

Constantino, J.N., Morris, J.A., and Murphy, D.L. (1997). CSF 5-HIAA and family history of antisocial personality disorder in newborns. *Am. J. Psychiatry,* 154(12), 1771–1773.

Cook, E.H., Stein, M.A., Krasowski, M.D., Cox, N.J., Olkon, D.M., Kieffer, J.E., and Leventhal, B.L. (1995). Association of attention-deficit disorder and the dopamine transporter gene. *Am. J. Human Genetics,* 56(4), 993–998.

Foley, D.L., Eaves, L.J., Wormley, B., Silberg, J.L., Maes, H.H., Kuhn, J., and Riley, B. (2004). Childhood adversity, monoamine oxidase A genotype, and risk for conduct disorder. *Arch. Gen. Psychiatry,* 61, 738–744.

Halperin, J.M., Newcorn, J.H., Kopstein, I., McKay, K.E., Schwartz, S.T., Siever, L.J., and Sharma, V. (1997). Serotonin, aggression, and parental psychopathology in children with attention deficit hyperactivity disorder. *J. Am. Acad. Child Adolesc. Psychiatry,* 36(10), 1391–1398.

Hendricks, T.J., Fyodorov, D.V., Wegman, L.J., Lelutiu, N.B., Pehek, A., Yamamoto, B., Silver, J., Weeber, E.J., Sweatt, J.D., and Deneris, E.S. (2003). Pet-1 ETS gene plays a critical role in 5-HT neuron development and is required for normal anxiety-like and aggressive behavior. *Neuron,* 37(2), 233–247.

Ishikawa, S.S., Raine A., Lencz, T., Bihrle, S., and LaCasse, L. (2001). Increased height and bulk in antisocial personality disorder and its subtypes. *Psych. Res.,* 105, 211–219.

Janssen, P.A., Nicholls, T.L., Kumar, R.A., Stefanakis, H., Spidel, A.L., and Simpson, E.M. (2005). Of mice and men: will the intersection of social science and genetics create new approaches for partner violence?. *J. Interpersonal Violence,* 20(1), 61–71.

Kumar, R.A., Chan, K.L., Wong, A.H., Little, K.Q., Rajcan-Separovic, E., Abrahams, B., and Simpson, E.M. (2004). Unexpected embryonic stem (ES) cell mutations represent a concern in gene targeting: lessons from "fierce" mice. *Genesis,* 38, 51–57.

Linnoila, M., Virkkunen, M., Scheinin, M., Nuutila, A., Rimon, R., and Goodwin, F.K. (1983). Low cerebrospinal fluid 5-hydroxyindolacetic acid concentration differentiates impulsive from non-impulsive violent behavior. *Life Science,* 33, 2609–2614.

Linnoila, V.M. and Virkkunen, M. (1992). Aggression, suicidality, and serotonin. *J. Clin. Psych..* 53, 46–51.

Marazziti, D. and Conti, L. (1991). Aggression, hyperactivity, and platelet imipramine binding. *Acta Psych. Scand.,* 84, 209–211.

Marazziti, D., DeLeo, D., and Conti, L. (1989). Further evidence supporting the role of the serotonin system in suicidal behavior: a preliminary study of suicide attempters. *Acta Psych. Scand.,* 80, 322–324.

Moffitt, T.E., Brammer, G.L., Caspi, A., Fawcett, J.P., Raleigh, M., Yuwiler, A., and Silva, P. (1998). Whole blood serotonin relates to violence in an epidemiological study. *Biol. Psych.,* 43(6), 446–457.

Murphy, D.L., Li, Q., Engel, S., Wichems, C., Andrews, A., Lesch, K.-L., and Uhl, G. (2001). Genetic perspectives on the serotonin transporter. *Brain Res. Bull.,* 56(5), 487–494.

Placido, G.P., Oquendo, M.A., Malone, K.M., Huang, Y.Y., Ellis, S.P., and Mann, J.J. (2001). Aggressivity, suicide attempts, and depression: relationship to cerebrospinal fluid monoamine metabolite levels. *Biol. Psych.,* 50(10), 783–791.

Raine, A. (1993). Neurochemistry. *The Psychopathology of Crime: Criminal Behavior as a Clinical Disorder* (pp. 81–102). San Diego: Academic Press.

Raine, A., Reynolds, C., Venables, P.H., Mednick, S.A., and Farrington, D.P. (1998). Stimulation-seeking, fearlessness, and large body size at age 3 years as early predispositions to aggression at age 11 years. *Arch. Gen. Psych.,* 55, 745–751.

Soderstrom, H., Blennow, K., Sjodin, A.K., and Forsman, A. (2003). New evidence for an association between the CSF HVA:5-HIAA ratio and psychopathic traits. *J. Neurology, Neurosurgery, Psych.,* 74, 918–921.

Stanley, B., Molcho, A., Stanley, M., Winchel, R., Gameroff, M.J., Parsons, B., and Mann, J.J. (2000). Association of aggressive behavior with altered serotonergic function in patients who are not suicidal. *Am J. Psych.,* 157, 609–614.

Stoff, J.M., Pollock, L., Vitiello, B., Behar, D., and Bridger, W.H. (1987). Reduction of 3-H-imipramine binding sites on platelets of conduct disordered children. *Neuropsychopharmacology,* 1, 55–62.

Thanos, P.K., Taintor, N.B., Rivera, S.N., Umegaki, H., Ikari, H., Roth, G., Ingram, D.K., Hitzemann, J.S., Fowler, J.S., Gatley, S.J., Wang, G.J., and Volkow, N.D. (2004). DRD2 gene transfer into the nucleus accumbens core of the alcohol preferring and nonpreferring rats attenuates alcohol drinking. *Alcoholism Clin. Exp. Res.,* 28(5), 720–728.

Tiihonen, J., Kuikka, J., Bergstrom, K., Hakola, P., Karhu, J., Ryynanen, O.P., and Fohr, J. (1995). Altered striatal dopamine re-uptake site densities in habitually violent and non-violent alcoholics. *Nat. Med.,* 1(7), 654–7.

Virkkunen, M. and Linnoila, M. (1990). Serotonin in early onset, male alcoholics with violent behavior. *Ann. Med.,* 22(5), 327–331.

Virkkunen, M., Eggert, M., Rawlings, R., and Linnoila, M. (1996a). A prospective follow-up study of alcoholic violent offenders and fire setters. *Arch. Gen. Psych.,* 53(6), 523–529.

Virkkunen, M., Goldman, D., and Linnoila, M., (Eds.). (1996b). Serotonin in alcoholic violent offenders. Genetics of criminal and antisocial behavior. *Ciba Foundation Symposium,* 194, 168–177.

Virkkunen, M., Goldman, D., Nielsen, D.A., and Linnoila, M. (1995). Low brain serotonin turnover rate (low CSF 5-HIAA) and impulsive violence. *J. Psych. Neurosci.,* 20(4), 271–275.

Volkow, N.D., Fowler, J.S., and Wang, G.-J. (2003). Positron emission tomography and single-photon emission computed tomography in substance abuse research. *Sem. Nuclear Med.,* 33(2), 114–128.

Whitaker-Azmitia, P.M., Zhang, X., and Clarke, C. (1994). Effects of gestational exposure to monoamine oxidase inhibitors in rats: preliminary behavioral and neurochemical studies. *Neuropsychopharmocology,* 11, 125–132.

Young, S.E., Smolen, A., Corley, R.P., Krauter, K.S., DeFries, J.C., Crowley, T.J., and Hewitt, J.K. (2002). Dopamine transporter polymorphism associated with externalizing behavior problems in children. *Am J. Med. Genet.,* 114(2), 144–149.

# Organic Brain Dysfunctions: Part I

*9*

## Introduction

This chapter examines brain damage and its many causes and implications for our study of biology and criminality. Because the brain is the seat of all behavior, it is logical that any damage to the brain is likely to affect our actions. This chapter first discusses the role the brain plays and the effects on human action of damage to various areas of the brain. Although brain damage can be severe at any age, damage to the developing brain is most severe. Brain damage is surprisingly common in society, and modern medical techniques have made it possible for us to understand much more about the brain and brain damage than in the past. In many cases, even minor injuries to brain function can have a major influence on future behavior. This chapter looks at a number of important studies focusing on the effect of this type of damage on antisocial and criminal activity. A correct understanding of the types of brain injury and their results can also help in finding ways to ameliorate their effects.

## Head Injury

We have just discussed how the chemical balance of the brain can affect behavior. If impeding or changing the tiny chemical messengers in the brain can impact behavior to such an extent, imagine the results of direct mechanical damage to the brain. It is important to remember when discussing the impact of biological factors on behavior, and potential criminogenic behavior in particular, that the great majority are not biological factors that a person was *born* with. Many are directly related to environmental factors that change a person's biology during their lifetime. Our biology changes depending on the way we live our lives. We are well aware that many things that we do or do not do will impact our health over time. For example, a nutritionally balanced diet and regular exercise is more likely to lead to general good health and longevity than a nutritionally poor or high fat and sugar diet, or the use of drugs, cigarettes, or alcohol. Ill health is a biological change, often caused by just such environmental factors. Such environmental factors can impact all aspects of life, including behavior. This is most obvious when we look at trauma or injuries. Social scientists often equate biological factors with genetics alone and do not realize that many biological factors that may predispose for crime are directly caused by environmental influences. They include such events as head injury, exposure to neurotoxins, diet, and birth complications, etc. Biology is not destiny; it is just life. It can be affected by many things that change it over a lifetime.

The brain is protected by the bony protective case of the skull. Inside the skull there are three layers of tissue called the meninges, which surround and cushion the brain. It is these membranes that are affected if a person develops meningitis or swelling of the meninges due to trauma or infection. This swelling puts pressure on the brain and can cause damage and even death. The brain is divided into two matching halves (or hemispheres), the right and the left, which are mirror images of each other. The two halves are separate but they are connected by a bundle of nerve fibers called the *corpus callosum*. The brain can also be divided into lobes or areas. The frontal lobe is the largest, taking up about one third of the brain (LoPiccolo, 1996). The frontal lobe begins around the middle of the top of the skull to the most anterior part of the brain (Kalat, 1995; Davidson and Neale, 1996), so it includes the part of the brain above the eyes and the forehead. The front part of the frontal lobe, the part above the eyes, receives all of the body's sensory information. The rear part of the frontal lobe controls fine voluntary movement, such as moving one finger at a time (Kalat, 1995). The part of the frontal lobe just behind the eyes is involved in inhibiting inappropriate behavior (Greene et al., 1997), so it is obviously very important from the point of view of antisocial behavior. Behind the frontal lobe lies the parietal lobe and beneath this is the occipital lobe. The temporal lobes are symmetrically placed on either side of the head.

The brain is the basis for all behavior. Whether learned or genetic, the knowledge required to remember, retain, retrieve, and perform behaviors are contained in the brain. The behavior may be simple (e.g., eating, lifting a hand, walking) or highly complex (e.g., thinking about and analyzing a situation and then reacting to it). Some are innate, or genetically controlled behaviors, and others are learned behaviors, such as language. Learning is a process that is both psychological and biological. As a person learns, the brain actually changes physically. It does not simply learn the information; rather, the acquisition of knowledge as environmental information is taken in, processed, and understood, causes changes to take place in the biochemistry and cell structure of the brain (Jeffery et al., 1985). Most people are inclined to assume that a baby is born with a complete brain which is a blank slate that only needs to be filled with information. This is not true; the brain grows and changes in response to the environment. Even genetically governed behavior is predisposed and designed to be changed by the environment. One of the brain's normal functions is to be changed physically by experience: that is, the brain does not fully develop without experience. The brain is, therefore, a complex mixture of genetics and the environment, just like behavior.

Our behaviors depend on the brain for storage, retrieval, and performance, so any damage to the brain can have a devastating effect. Brain development requires not just the genetics to develop the neural circuits, but also input from the psychological environment and the cognitive environment. It is a bit like a computer that comes with all the hardware to do important things but is useless until you add software programs to it. For example, biology provides the neural base for prefrontal lobe development, but learning and experience are also necessary for complete development to occur (Golden et al., 1996).

The brain is not fully developed at birth; it continues to develop and change biochemically for years. Some brain structures develop faster than others. For example, the prefrontal areas of the brain reach maturity in late adolescence (Golden et al., 1996). The developmental phase in which injury occurs will thus have an effect on the severity of damage to the brain. For example, the frontal lobe is involved in control so there is often a lesser impact from frontal lobe trauma on adults (who normally have already developed good internal control systems) than on children. Children will not yet have developed their full complement of internal control systems (Golden et al., 1996), nor learned the acceptable social mores (Anderson et al., 1999) to help them do so. Brain damage need not be the result of direct trauma but can result from disruption of the normal environment required for healthy brain development during the early years. For example, in a study on rats, early maternal separation was shown to affect the structural development of the hippocampus, part of the limbic system, in the temporal lobes of the brain (Andersen and Teicher, 2004).

Head injuries in early life have been linked with several types of disorders in later life. In a comparison between 413 male pedophiles and 793 non-pedophiles, researchers found that early serious childhood injuries were correlated with adult pedophilia and lower levels of intelligence and education

(Blanchard et al., 2002). The association was only significant if the injury had been severe enough to cause the child to lose consciousness and had occurred prior to the age of 6 years. This could indicate that the brain injury itself increased the risk of pedophilia, or that other factors in the child's early development contributed to both the risk of head injury and pedophilia (Blanchard et al., 2002). Those subjects who developed pedophilia also reported a higher incidence of maternal psychiatric treatment, which the authors interpreted to mean that pedophilia may have a genetic root that manifests itself in psychiatric illness in the mothers and pedophilia in their sons. However, it could equally well be the other way around, in that mental instability in a parent may have influenced the risk of head injury in the child, and either the childhood environment or the head injury could have influenced the later pedophilia.

Childhood head injuries have also been linked to the development of schizophrenia and also to later violent behavior. Many factors have been implicated in the etiology of schizophrenia, including genetics and birth complications (Green et al., 1994; Cannon et al., 1993; 1994; Guy et al., 1983) but more recent evidence suggests that mild childhood head injuries may influence the expression of schizophrenia in families with a genetic predisposition for the disorder (AbdelMalik et al., 2003). In a study of the children from 23 families with a family history of multiple cases of schizophrenia, children with schizophrenia were compared with their unaffected siblings. The schizophrenic subjects were much more likely to have suffered from childhood head injuries than their unaffected siblings (AbdelMalik et al., 2003). Also, when considering only the schizophrenic individuals, those who had suffered head injuries developed schizophrenia approximately 5 years earlier than those without head injuries. All the head injuries had been judged to be mild, but within this category, the severity of the head injury correlated with the age of onset of schizophrenia (AbdelMalik et al., 2003). In a retrospective comparison of childhood trauma and school performance between violent and nonviolent offenders, researchers found that, although both had done poorly in school, only the violent offenders had a history of untreated head injuries during childhood (León-Carrión and Ramos, 2003).

A head injury can damage the brain and/or the central nervous system (CNS), and the injury could influence behavior that later predisposes the person to violence and crime. There have been many studies that have linked violence and crime to head injuries. In one such study, 31 accused and convicted murderers were examined for neurological disorders. Of the 31, 30 had some sort of brain dysfunction; 20 of the 31 (64.5%) accused murderers had some frontal lobe damage and 29% specifically had temporal lobe defects (Blake et al., 1995). The incidence of head injuries in the general population is considered to be between 5% (Blake et al., 1995) and 6% (Teichner et al.,

2001). However, the subjects were not all convicted, and they were chosen for examination by defense counsel rather than at random. As well, brain "abnormalities" were not well defined, and there was no true control group. However, the results do support a connection between frontal lobe damage and aggression (Ward, 2000).

Several studies have looked at death row inmates and found extremely high levels of head injury. In one U.S. study of 15 death-row inmates, all had suffered serious head injuries prior to their offense (Lewis et al., 1986); and in another study of 14 juveniles on death row, all were found to have a history of past severe head injuries (Lewis et al., 1988). Of these 14, 9 had major brain impairment, 7 suffered from severe psychotic problems that began prior to incarceration, 7 had severe organic dysfunction, and only 2 had IQ scores above 90, which means that nearly all of them could be considered mentally challenged. Almost all had also suffered severe physical abuse. However, no controls were presented to determine the levels of such problems in a non-death-row population (Lewis et al., 1988). None of these issues were recognized or taken into account at time of trial (Ward, 2000). These are obviously extreme examples and the sample size is small, without controls, but the results are striking. Perhaps more disturbing yet is that these *children* were on death row.

In studies of nonincarcerated individuals, the majority of men with problems of aggression against their families had suffered severe head injury (Rosenbaum and Hodge, 1989). In a follow-up study, Rosenbaum et al. (1994) compared the incidence of head injuries among men who had beaten their spouses; nonviolent, happily married men; and nonviolent unhappily married men (n = 53, 45, and 32, respectively). Head injuries were medically assessed by a doctor who was unaware of their domestic and criminal history. More than half of the men who had been convicted of spousal abuse had suffered an earlier significant head injury, as compared with only a quarter of the unhappily married, nonviolent men and 16% of the happily married, non-violent men (Rosenbaum et al., 1994). Spousal abuse is often thought to stem from marital discord and general unhappiness with the relationship, but the dramatic difference between men who abuse and those who were unhappily married but nonviolent show that the abuse was more likely to be related to the head injury than to general marital unhappiness. Alcohol is also often presented as a predisposer for marital violence, but the researchers controlled for alcohol abuse and no differences were found between batterers and non-batterers (Rosenbaum et al., 1994).

In an assessment of the cognitive functioning of male batterers, 48% were found to exhibit evidence of significant neurological impairment in a variety of tests (Golden and Golden, 2001). The impairment resulted in specific functional deficits, including long- and short-term visual memory, cognitive flexibility, attention, and psychomotor speed, as well as increased impulsivity (as indicated by an inability to inhibit verbal responses) (Golden and Golden, 2001). Such a finding is important in treatment because male abusers who have neurological deficits will not respond in the same manner to treatment and therapy designed for unimpaired male abusers (Golden and Golden, 2001).

## Frontal Lobe Injury

Behavior is affected by various parts of the brain. However, much of it is controlled by the frontal lobe. The frontal lobe is the part of the brain that extends over the eyes into the forehead. Think about what its position means. As this area is at the front of the face, and sticks out, it is one of the most likely parts to be injured in an accident. In a car accident, it is the first part that often hits the windshield. Because it is also the area involved in inhibiting inappropriate aggression or violence, an injury here is most likely to have an influence on behavior (Greene et al., 1997).

Another part of the brain known to be involved in emotion and behavior is the limbic system. This interconnected area is found within several of the lobes. The limbic area is primarily associated with emotion and the expression of emotion, which includes a faster heart beat, faster respiration, trembling, sweating, and facial expressions (Ward, 2000). The limbic system is also responsible for basic primary drives, such as sex, hunger, thirst, flight (as in running away from a conflict), and also fight, such as defense and attack (Davidson and Neale, 1996). The amygdala is also part of the limbic system and is involved in emotional and fearful situations (Davidson et al., 2000); and another area, the temporal cortex, is known to be involved in producing and constraining violence. The hippocampus, involved in memory, learning, and emotion regulation, is also part of the limbic system.

Much evidence shows that damage to or malformation (such as a birth defect) of the frontal lobe can have significant implications for a person's day-to-day functioning, emotions, and inhibitions. Frontal lobe damage can occur in a number of different ways: mechanical damage (e.g., a blow to the head, a car accident) or a developmental malformation (e.g., premature suture closure, Korsakoff's syndrome) (Ward, 2000). The frontal lobe has been implicated in many functions, including cognitive understanding, paying attention to people and the environment, regulating behavior through self-evaluation, planning ahead, using good judgment, being able to develop and sustain motivations, patience, filtering irrelevant information, recalling the temporal order of events, abstract thought, determining right from wrong, and, most importantly, inhibiting, controlling, and regulating violent impulses (Davidson et al., 2000; Ward, 2000; Comings, 1996; Golden et al.,

1996; Martell, 1996; Blake et al., 1995; Kalat, 1995; Bechara et al., 1994; Volavka et al., 1992; Volkow and Tancredi, 1987).

The frontal lobe is very sensitive to problems because it has an extraordinarily high demand for oxygen and nutrients. The frontal lobe needs very high levels of arousal to function. Even in "normal" individuals, frontal lobe functioning can deteriorate when they are tired, and this effect is much worse for people with brain damage (Ward, 2000). Most of us have noticed that when we have been working hard all day doing things that involve the brain (e.g., thinking or writing a paper), as opposed to working physically (e.g., gardening), our brain begins to shut down and our cognitive ability to analyze the work gets increasingly more difficult until eventually we stop understanding what we are reading. The next day we come back to it fresh, and it is easy. For proper frontal lobe function, a person must be wide awake and fresh; even tiredness affects this functioning, so any brain damage makes mental work much more difficult.

People who have suffered frontal lobe trauma also lose their social graces, including self-control and patience, so they demand immediate gratification rather than understanding the need to work to obtain a long-term goal. They may be prone to temper outbursts, irritability, and violence (Ward, 2000; Greene et al., 1997; Comings, 1996; Golden et al., 1996; Heinrichs, 1989; Volkow and Tancredi, 1987). These potential outcomes derive from case histories, so obviously do not represent controlled experiments. Some symptoms might appear in only a few subjects, and others might occur in most subjects. The results of damage to the frontal lobe vary greatly from person to person. The extent of the damage itself varies, but so does the pre-trauma profile of the injured person, which will have an impact on how much damage is sustained and how he or she will respond both to the damage and to any subsequent treatment (Ward, 2000). As well, damage is often not limited to the frontal lobe, but also affects other brain areas. Some people with injuries to the frontal lobe may develop "environmental dependency syndrome," which means they respond too strongly to environmental stimulation. Environmentally dependent people are inclined to react to environmental stimuli in a manner that is much stronger than is normal or necessary (Ward, 2000; Blake et al., 1995; Stuss et al., 1992). Taken to an extreme, it might mean that in a situation of provocation in which a "normal" person might become angry and frustrated, a person who is environmentally dependent may react extremely violently and even kill (Blake et al., 1995).

Head trauma is one of the most obvious ways that the frontal lobe can be damaged. Head trauma can occur due to accidents, fights, sports, or falls. Difficult births can result in brain damage, as already discussed. Another, and unfortunately very common, method of head injury is child abuse. Remember that children's brains are still developing, so a brain injury in a young child may have a much worse prognosis than the same level of damage in an adult. Brain damage in childhood may also be the result of maternal use of alcohol during pregnancy (FASD), or drugs, lead poisoning, malnutrition, or many other things. In some cases, a blunt force injury to the back of the head can cause a contrecoup injury to occur at the opposite side of the brain.

There are a number of ways an individual's brain can be damaged. Even minimal trauma, such as a minor bump on the head, can have a significant effect on behavior — especially in a young child or infant. Both genetic defects and acquired factors affect the frontal lobe and have a role in producing attention deficit hyperactivity disorder (ADHD), conduct disorder (CD), Tourette's syndrome (TS), antisocial personality disorder (Comings, 1996), and impulsive explosive aggression (Best et al., 2002).

Children frequently receive mild head injuries during play, particularly in contact and extreme sports. Many of these injuries are not even seen by a doctor as they are considered too mild. However, studies have shown that even very mild head injuries can result in the development of significant behavioral problems. Andrews et al. (1998) compared 27 un-injured children with those who had received a range of head injuries. None had suffered penetrating injuries, or abuse. None had prior developmental, learning, or psychological disorders. The injuries were divided into mild, moderate, and severe. Children who had experienced head injuries had significantly lower self-esteem and exhibited higher levels of maladaptive, aggressive, and antisocial behavior (Andrews et al., 1998). In particular, there were no noticeable differences between the children who experienced mild head injury as compared with those who experienced severe trauma, confirming that even mild injury can cause long-term damage.

In a case study of two young people who suffered brain trauma as babies, one from a brain tumor and one from an accidental head injury, both recovered physically but developed serious antisocial behavioral problems as they grew up (Anderson et al., 1999). As young adults, both subjects were intelligent but exhibited both antisocial and amoral behaviors. The young woman, although academically intelligent, stole from family and friends, lied, was physically and verbally abusive, sexually promiscuous, and entirely lacking in empathy toward anyone, including her own baby. The young man was reckless, slovenly, and unmotivated, and committed both property theft and violent assaults. He had also sired a baby and showed no interest in the child. Neither person showed any remorse or guilt for their actions, and both resembled psychopaths in much of their behavior, although, in general, they were more impulsive than directed, and more childlike in their behavior (Anderson et al., 1999). Both subjects came from loving and stable family homes with well-adjusted siblings. Both young people exhibited the same sort of deficits seen in adults with pre-frontal cortex damage, such as a failure to consider the consequences of their actions, a desire for immediate gratification, and a lack of social graces. However, the two subjects who suffered their brain trauma as infants also exhibited defective social and moral reasoning (Anderson et al., 1999). The authors suggested that people who are injured as adults possess the knowledge of social and moral rules, although their injury may prevent them from following them; whereas those injured as infants or children may never have been able to acquire the normal understanding of social graces and moral reasoning due to their impairment. Therefore, such children would never be able to learn the basic social rules, which could result in much greater levels of antisocial and amoral behavior than that seen in similarly injured adults (Anderson et al., 1999). This may mean that such children would be much more difficult to treat than similarly injured adults, whose brain had developed normally prior to the injury.

In a U.S. military study of medical outcomes, men who had received mild traumatic head injuries were 1.8 times more likely to receive a behavioral discharge than those in the general discharged population (Ommaya et al., 1996). Also, those with mild head injuries were 2.6 times more likely to be discharged for drug and alcohol abuse, and 2.7 times more likely to be discharged for criminal convictions. Soldiers who received moderate head injuries were even more likely (5.4 times) to be discharged for alcoholism or drug abuse (Ommaya et al., 1996).

Diseases such as alcoholism, premature suture closure, syphilis, meningitis, tumors, stroke, schizophrenia, and various neurological disorders can also damage the frontal lobe (Ward, 2000; Tardiff, 1998; Kalat, 1995). *Herpes simplex* encephalitis can result in violent attacks of rage, language and memory deficits, and coprophagia (Tardiff, 1998).

Perhaps one of the most cited examples of a brain pathology in an extreme adverse personality change with resultant violence is that of Charles Whitman. Whitman climbed a bell tower at the University of Texas, and with no obvious motivation or previous criminal behavior, opened fire on the students, killing 15. At autopsy, a large tumor was found in his amygdala, part of the limbic system involved in emotion and aggression control.

In another case study, a middle-aged, married schoolteacher with no history of abnormal sexual impulses suddenly changed his normal behavior (Swerdlow and Burns 2002). Originally a happily married man with a normal sexual appetite, he suddenly developed an obsession for pornography, began purchasing sexual favors, and made sexual advances toward young children. This escalated into pedophilia and he was convicted of child molestation. He continued to display inappropriate sexual behavior and even propositioned the female instructor of a treatment program, resulting in his expulsion from the program. He later went into the hospital complaining of severe headaches and confided his fears that he was about to rape a woman. He was observed to have balance problems and showed no concern when he soiled himself. A magnetic resonance imaging (MRI) scan indicated that the man suffered from a large tumor in the frontal lobe, specifically the orbitofrontal region, or the area just above the eyes. This area is responsible for self-control, judgment, and correct performance of acceptable social behavior (Swerdlow and Burns, 2002). The tumor was successfully removed, and the man's behavior returned to normal. He was able to successfully complete the rehabilitation program and return home. Sometime later, his abnormal behavior returned and a second MRI scan revealed that the tumor had returned. Again, its removal reversed the condition (Swerdlow and Burns, 2002). The position of the tumor was critical as it affected an area vital in judgment and control. However, the impact on his behavior may also have been hormonal as tumors can result in hormonal changes, which can also impact behavior (Swerdlow and Burns, 2002).

In another case study, an adolescent boy developed severe personality changes and became violent, withdrawn, and very tense, and experienced temporal lobe seizures. Doctors believed that his antisocial behavior related to a disturbed home life and did not investigate further. However, by age 19, he slipped into a coma and later died. At autopsy, a tumor was found in his right hippocampus (Tardiff, 1998).

Although these case histories only discuss the effects of abnormal brain pathology on just one or two patients, the dramatic results are very interesting. The use of drugs such as PCP, LSD, cocaine, heroin, alcohol, and legal medications that are taken inappropriately can also cause neurological damage referred to as frontal lobe dementia (Ward, 2000) and can cause direct damage to the brain as well as impact neurotransmitter functions (Volkow et al., 2003).

Because the brain is entirely responsible for behavior, brain damage can cause a wide variety of problems and behavioral changes. These include developing a more argumentative persona and an inability to distinguish right from wrong or to understand the consequences of actions; people often lose self-control, foresight, creativity, and spontaneity. They may become shallow, restless, selfish, impulsive, egocentric, inattentive, easily distractible, hyperactive, and have poor organization and planning skills as well as impaired problem-solving skills (Ward, 2000; Greene et al., 1997; Comings, 1996; Golden et al., 1996; Heinrichs, 1989; Volkow and Tancredi, 1987). A classic example of poor planning skills is given in Lewis's book, *Guilty by Reason of Insanity* (1998). She cites the case of a death-row inmate who saved the pecan pie from his last meal so that he could have a midnight snack after his execution.

One of the most terrifying examples of frontal lobe injury is also the first to be documented and the most famous: the case of Phineas Gage. Because the frontal lobe of the brain is the main site of our personality, damage to this area can dramatically change a person's personality but leave their memory and intellect unchanged. This is a terrifying idea when you think about it. In 1848, Phineas Gage was a 25-year-old supervisor of a railroad construction crew. He was packing gunpowder into a rock with a tamping iron when it prematurely ignited. The tamping iron shot up through his left cheek and went right through the top of his skull. Amazingly, he survived but his frontal lobe was destroyed. He recovered from this terrible injury and eventually went back to work. His memory, intellect, and ability to work were not damaged, but according to his family and friends, he was simply "no longer Gage." His personality had dramatically altered. He had previously been a kind, soft-spoken, polite, and considerate young man. After the accident, he became profane, irritable, and violent — in short, a different person. Although he had retained the knowledge and technical skills to perform his job, he had lost his social graces and his ability to work with others, so he lost his job and became a "vagabond." This transformation was definitely linked to frontal lobe trauma (Mashour et al., 2005; Ward, 2000; Blake et al., 1995; Stuss et al., 1992; Myers, 1992). A study of his skull more than 140 years after the accident indicated that the metal rod passed through the ventromedial portion of his prefrontal cortex, and his described personality and behavioral changes correlated well with those seen in modern patients with similar trauma (Damasio et al., 1994). What is so terrifying in this case is that he was able to function without a large part of his brain but his personality changed so dramatically. We can accept that someone might be damaged after an accident, have a limp, a scar, etc.; but for the person to still look just like the person you knew and loved but be no longer there anymore — "no longer Gage"? This situation is difficult to accept or adjust to.

A more modern example concerns a self-employed 51-year-old man who, in 1994, was happily married with nine children. He was injured in a severe car accident and received a depressed bone fracture to his frontal lobe (a closed injury). Before the accident, he had no history of mental illness (personally or in his family) and was a hard-working, energetic, optimistic man with a successful and happy family life (Ward, 2000; Sebit et al., 1996). After the accident, his intelligence, cognition, and memory were unaffected; however, his personality changed dramatically, just as it did with Phineas Gage. He had sudden unprovoked outbursts of anger triggered by trivial things; his behavior became very uninhibited, and he would make obscene sexual remarks and would sexually touch any females around (not just his wife, but also his children, friends, and family) (Ward, 2000; Sebit et al., 1996). He became hypersexual and placed abnormal sexual demands on his wife, and also became suspicious, verbally and physically aggressive, indifferent to people's reaction to his behavior, irritable and anxious, and had poor concentration and judgment (Ward, 2000; Sebit et al., 1996). Of course, as before in case studies, the findings from one case cannot be generalized to all people with frontal lobe injuries, but this case is a classic example of the kinds of changes that can take place and is almost a modern repetition of the case of Phineas Gage.

## Frontal Lobe Injury and Crime

There is a definite link between frontal lobe damage and crime, particularly violent crime, although the actual mechanism is not completely understood. It is possible that the damage itself could trigger violence because the frontal lobe is the primary site of inhibition of violence. Removal or damage to this control can remove the inhibition. However, it is also probable that frontal lobe damage can cause many other changes that might lead a person to behave erratically, unpredictably, impulsively, or argumentatively, and thus indirectly lead them into confrontational or conflict situations that could lead to violence (Ward, 2000; Golden et al., 1996; Heinrichs, 1989). Frontal lobe damage alone does not usually cause violence, although it is often a facilitator (Ward, 2000). Usually, people who have aggressive tendencies prior to the injury are the ones who will become violent afterward. So perhaps the inclination was there but was inhibited until the injury. People who were not aggressive at all prior to the injury are not usually aggressive afterward, although there are exceptions (Ward, 2000; Greene et al., 1997; Mills and Raine, 1994). Also, there does not seem to be any consistent relationship between the time of trauma and the first act of violence. Thus, the damage increases the possibility or risk that a person will become violent, but it does not mean that they will do so immediately or, in fact, that it will happen at all (Ward, 2000; Greene et al., 1997; Mills and Raine, 1994). It is an increased risk factor; that is, it increases the predisposition for violence but that is all. Many people receive brain injuries and never become violent, although some reports suggest that aggression and irritability (although not necessarily violence) occur after severe brain injury in more than 70% of cases (McKinley et al., 1981). However, irritability is a far cry from violent offending.

It is often thought that people who are violent and also have sustained head injuries, received the injuries due to their violent nature. It is back to the classic old chicken-and-egg question: which came first? As well, are people who are violent simply more likely to sustain head injuries because they are violent, or perhaps because they participate in other risk-taking activity that might result in violence? Is there actually a causal relationship between head injury and violence? It is possible, for example, that a life of violence and crime may predispose a person to head injury — as a type of occupational risk? Or, do the same factors (biological, environmental, or societal) that predispose an individual to violence and crime also predispose them to head injuries? For example, criminal parents could cause head injuries in a child by abuse, but the eventual criminal behavior in the child may be a result of genetic or environmental factors related to the parents and the childhood environment.

However, the evidence strongly suggests that this is not the case, and that a head injury can result in violent and criminal behavior. It is a logical finding because the brain is the foundation of all human behavior. If the brain is damaged, behavior is probably going to be affected. In a study of partner-abusive men, 92% of the men had suffered from a head injury before they began abusing their partners. Most of the head injuries had occurred in childhood, generally from accidents, falls, and sports injuries, and had not arisen due to interpersonal violence (Rosenbaum et al., 1994). This finding clearly does not prove anything one way or the other but it tends to rule out the opposing theory that marital violence causes head injuries, or even that the head injuries that may later have predisposed the men to become violent were originally a result of their violent behavior.

Epidemiological data in Caucasians shows that the highest rates of head injury occur in children and adolescents between the ages of 10 and 20 years. This is just before the peak in violent offending, which occurs in the late teens and early 20s, as opposed to property crimes, which peak earlier (Milner, 1991). Again, this fact does not prove any sort of causal link but it is at least consistent with the fact that head injuries seem to precede violent crime.

In a study of the causes of many head injuries, 74% of all head injuries occurring in suburban regions and 89% of all head injuries occurring in rural areas were found to be unrelated to interpersonal violence, and instead resulted from accidents such as bicycle and motorcycle accidents, sports, falls, and recreational accidents (Milner, 1991). Even when one looks at people living in inner cities, which are normally considered more violent, 60% of severe head injuries did not result from interpersonal violence (Milner, 1991). In support of this finding, 12 of 14 children on death row in the United States had had severe head injuries prior to their crime, which resulted from falls or traffic accidents; there were only two cases in which the injuries were the result of interpersonal violence (Lewis et al., 1988).

The findings reported above are not consistent with the theory that most cases of head injury result from a life of violent crime. However, there are other theories, such as the possibility that neurological or neuropsychological deficits occurring early in life (e.g., a birth complication) may predispose the person to have an accident that results in a head injury. In that case, the injury is a combination of the original condition and the later head injury. For example, some early problems may result in motor deficiencies that make the average person more clumsy and thus more likely to fall, whereas some other deficits may result in a lack of perception, which leads to a predisposition to accidents owing to a lack of attention to uneven pavement, steps, or traffic.

If head injuries can predispose a person to violent crime, what is the mechanism for this? There are many ways that damage to the brain can influence criminogenic behavior. The most direct method is that head injuries that do not fracture the skull most frequently result in damage to the orbitofrontal region of the frontal lobe and the anterior region of the temporal lobes. Damage to the right orbitofrontal region tends to result in edginess and anxiety, while damage to the left orbitofrontal regions tends to result in anger and hostility. People with frontal lobe damage often show increased impulsivity and have no regard for the consequences of their actions. They demand immediate gratification and are not capable of weighing the disadvantages of delayed punishment (Bechara et al., 1994). Therefore, they are unlikely to learn from past behavior and will not fear punishment.

Alcohol is a recognized predisposer for crime. Impairment of frontal lobe activity has been found to be a risk factor for alcoholism and destructive drinking. Cognitive tests measuring frontal and temporal lobe functioning were found to predict the age at which subjects first began drinking and how often they drank to get very drunk. In both cases, decreased brain activity was associated with increased alcohol-related behaviors (Deckel et al., 1995). As well, frontal lobe function was found to be highly correlated with the drinkers' expectations of how alcohol would affect them — with heavy drinkers expecting much more positive effects than light drinkers (Deckel et al., 1995). The same researchers also found a correlation between impaired frontal lobe function, antisocial personality disorder, and childhood behavior problems, and suggested that reduced frontal lobe function might be a biological link between antisocial personality disorder and alcoholism (Deckel et al., 1996). Thus, frontal lobe dysfunction may be a predisposer for alcoholism and, in turn, a known predisposer for crime. In contrast, head injuries are known to increase sensitivity to the effects of alcohol, so the criminal act may be the result of the head injury just tipping the scale when the individual drinks (Golden et al., 1996; Blake et al., 1995). Alcohol depresses inhibitions, so when someone with frontal lobe dysfunction consumes alcohol, it may have a compounding effect. The inhibition for violence is significantly reduced by alcohol and compounded by brain dysfunction. The earlier finding that frontal lobe impairment may predict alcoholism suggests that alcohol could have a double effect: it can predispose an individual to alcoholism in the first place, followed by a heightened effect of the alcohol.

Head injuries can result in deficits in cognitive skills — the ability to think and reason, social skills, self-esteem, problem-solving, and academic and work-related problems — all of which in their own ways predispose to crime and violence. An injury can directly result in post-concussional syndrome, which includes headaches, irritability, and sensitivity to noise, and can predispose individuals to lose their tempers. Of course, head injuries do not result in violence and crime in all cases; in fact, in many cases, such damage does not result in violence. It is probable that head injuries precipitate violence in those people who are already predisposed to violence through other factors, whether they are biological or environmental or social. Head injuries usually reduce coping skills, judgment, and restraint, and thus they might result in violence in normally nonviolent (pre-injury) individuals who are already deficient in those skills.

Child abuse is a major cause of brain injury. It can occur from just one slap to the head because a child's head is very soft. Shaking a baby roughly can cause whiplash injuries that shear the fiber tracts. Even a single blow to the head can cause multiple lesions in the brain. Such injuries are probably very common; they leave no external mark, and thus they are not discovered and reported. The majority of serious head injuries in infants are the result of child abuse. The implication of these studies is clear: head injuries can play a bigger role than is presently thought in predisposing a person to crime. Because these crimes are mostly not reported, individuals may not even realize that they have sustained a head injury. Many studies showing high rates of head injury in violent offenders also report high rates of severe child abuse, which makes it likely that such people have had two doses of brain damage. Thus, child abuse can add to a person's risk of predisposition for criminal behavior: by first biologically damaging the brain and then by predetermining a criminogenic social environment.

## Damage to Other Regions of the Brain

The frontal lobe is certainly not the only part of the brain that can be damaged. Injury to the temporal lobes can result in unprovoked or exaggerated anger, memory and intellectual impairment, auditory or visual hallucinations, delusions, and receptive language impairment. A case study of a middle-aged graphic designer with no history of psychological or behavioral problems reported that, after suffering a mild concussion in a car accident, the man developed a range of behavioral problems (Moon, 2000). The subject developed severe cognitive problems, memory loss and had problems with attention. He lost his creative abilities and thus was unable to continue in his profession, and began to exhibit impulsive criminal behavior such as kleptomania. A brain scan, using positron emission tomography (PET), showed that the concussion had resulted in reduced mental activity in the temporal lobes and right visual cortex (Moon, 2000).

Some brain dysfunction is simply not specified in studies. In a study cited previously that examined 31 convicted and accused murderers, 97% had abnormalities that reflected brain dysfunction although a specific neurological diagnosis could only be made in 64.5%. In 29% there was evidence of temporal lobe abnormality (Blake et al., 1995). However, there were no controls, and there was, therefore, bias because there were no blind observers (and one researcher "knew" the individuals). In addition, the researchers never operationally defined the term "abnormal" and there were many other problems involved. For example, many of the subjects were abused as children, which could lead to head injury, but the abuse was not necessarily verified. On the other hand, there was a good mixture of evaluation techniques, including interviews, neuropsychological and IQ testing, collection of historical information about their family backgrounds, and MRI and EEG tests.

The two halves of the brain may be unbalanced, which is referred to as an *inbalance in cerebral lateralization.* Lombroso was the first to document evidence of an imbalance between the cerebral hemispheres and facial asymmetry among criminals. He also reported a disproportionate number of left-handers among criminal populations. There were serious methodological problems with many of the early studies of this type of cerebral lateralization in criminals. However, possible differences in the balance of the brain hemispheres has recently been reinvestigated. Many more recent researchers have reported that psychopathy and other personality and behavioral disorders are associated with dysfunction of the left cerebral hemisphere (Raine, 1993). Different emotions and skills are controlled by different hemispheres of the brain, and a person's handedness (as in left- or right-handedness) is sometimes an indication of which of their hemispheres is "dominant." Because nerve bundles cross over at the brain stem, it follows that a right-handed person has more left hemispheric function, and vice versa. So, handedness can be used to determine lateralization. This means that there is evidence that suggests that because left-handed people are governed by the right hemisphere, they are inclined to be more emotional and impulsive and have problems with tasks controlled by the left hemisphere, such as language and reading. Some have suggested this is a reason why they might have a greater involvement with delinquency and violence (Denno, 1990). An investigation of hand preferences in 420 incarcerated adult males indicated that psychopaths had increased left-hand dominance, unrelated to age, intelligence, or ethnicity (Mayer and Kosson, 2000).

An analysis of more than 8000 men, criminals in general and sex offenders in particular, revealed a significantly higher rate of left-handedness or ambidexterity in offenders than in non-offenders, although the effects were small (Bogaert, 2001). This may indicate higher levels of cerebral asymmetry in offenders but should certainly not be used to suggest that left-handed people are predisposed to criminality or mental dysfunction. Some researchers have suggested that there is a greater left hemisphere deficit in both delinquents and people who have problems reading, despite their handedness (Denno, 1990). Some research has also found a link between cerebral lateralization dysfunctions and violent behavior (Nachshon, 1991), although other researchers found disproportionately fewer left-handers among violent offenders (Denno, 1990).

In several studies, researchers found left hemisphere dysfunction in 87% of those who commit sexual assault, but there have been no tests on controls to see how common it is in the general population. In another study, 12 incest offenders, 34 sexually aggressive offenders who offended against adult females, and 12 nonviolent, nonsex offender controls were studied. The researchers measured brain width and length and found that the left hemisphere of sex offenders was relatively smaller than controls, but there was no difference in other factors such as optical density. There was no difference in brain length but sex offenders had smaller widths in both hemispheres (Wright et al., 1990).

There does seem to be evidence that suggests that left hemisphere dysfunction relates to violent crime (Raine, 1993; Nachshon, 1991), but there is also evidence that right hemisphere dysfunction may relate to nonviolent crime (Raine, 1993). In a Canadian study, 72% of violent criminals had left hemisphere dysfunction, and 79% of nonviolent offenders had right hemisphere dysfunction (Yeudall, 1977). In a follow-up study, the researchers found that although 84% of persistent delinquents had some neuropsychological deficit, these deficits were greater in the right hemisphere than in the left (Yeudall et al., 1982). There is also evidence to suggest that damage to the *corpus callosum*, which joins the two hemispheres together, may relate to criminal behavior. This area has an important role in inhibition (Raine, 1993).

In a study of cognitive deficits in adolescents, Golden and Golden (2001) compared 11 adolescents who had received right hemisphere brain injuries with 12 who had left brain hemisphere injuries, 15 who were diagnosed with conduct disorder (CD) but no brain injuries, and 15 who had neither brain injuries nor CD. The teenagers with left hemisphere damage performed much worse in a series of cognitive tests than those with right hemisphere damage. Interestingly, the teenagers with CD but no brain injuries performed just as badly as the adolescents with left hemisphere damage (Golden and Golden, 2001). The researchers suggested that this may mean that adolescents with CD have a more subtle and undetected form of brain injury (Golden and

Golden, 2001). This may not be a result of direct trauma, of course, but could be related to many factors that affect brain development in youth. This is an important finding for CD treatment as it suggests that treatments presently successful with persons suffering from traumatic brain injuries may be of benefit to people with CD, such as high levels of routine and structure at school, work, and home (Golden and Golden, 2001).

In general, damage to any area of the brain can cause behavioral changes, but the most studied and most commonly injured area is the frontal lobe, and it is the area most commonly related to crime.

## Treatment and Legal Issues

Biologically predisposed disorders are treatable — this is a very important point. However, it is also extremely important that treatment begin immediately, and that family members receive counselling about what to expect and training on how to cope with the new situation so they can create the best environment for the injured person (Ward, 2000; Comings, 1996; Sebit et al., 1996). Without treatment, the prognosis for recovery is poor. There are many things that can help a person, such as providing them with a daily routine and being aware of the environmental triggers that set them off. Obvious antagonists such as alcohol and stress should be avoided (Ward, 2000; Comings, 1996; Sebit et al., 1996).

Different brain traumas result in different cognitive and behavioral changes, and it is important to realize that treatment for one type of brain injury may not be effective for another type of injury. As well, it is clear that although many recognized disorders, such as CD and impulsive explosive aggression, may not be the result of diagnosed brain trauma, the resulting deficits are very similar to certain types of brain injury. This may indicate that they are the result of a brain pathology unlinked to direct trauma, but perhaps linked to birth complications, genetic deficits, environmental trauma, neurotoxins, or a myriad other causes. Despite the etiology, what is perhaps more important is that the deficit is identified, as this would mean that treatment options that are effective in people with brain trauma may be valid in people with other mental disorders that may mimic the symptoms of brain injury.

On the other side of the coin, it is equally important that offenders who are not necessarily considered to have brain trauma are assessed medically and neurologically, as mild brain injury may never have been reported, and many people do not consider that they have ever received such an injury. Nevertheless, a number of the above studies have indicated that many offenders exhibit the results of brain trauma, whether from direct injury or other causes. In such cases, not only should such information be made available to the courts, it should most certainly be taken into account during sentencing and subsequent treatment. Cognitive and insight-oriented therapy, often used in many treatment programs, are unlikely to be effective with people who have sustained frontal lobe damage.

The question of how the law should treat such cases obviously arises. Ward (2000) cites a case in which an understanding of the brain trauma actually worked against the accused. A man charged with sexual assault causing bodily harm, R. *v.* Scott [1993], had been injured in a car accident and received damage to the frontal lobe. His behavior changed after the accident, and he showed poor impulse control, vivid aggressive fantasies, and other behavioral problems. The court decided that he would not improve, especially as he grew from boy to adulthood, and it was considered "virtually inevitable" that he would reoffend. He was found not criminally responsible on account of mental disorder and sent to a mental health center for an undetermined time (Ward, 2000).

However, in another case cited by Ward, frontal lobe damage was considered positively in sentencing. In R. *v.* Delorey [1997], the fact that the accused had progressive frontal lobe dementia was considered an extreme mitigating factor in his behavior. The judge stated that there was a direct link between the criminal act and the accused's brain injury, and he considered the brain trauma, together with other environmental factors (such as his previous lack of criminal involvement and his gainful employment) as well as emotional issues (such as rejection by friends and family). He allowed Delorey to serve his sentence in the community (Ward, 2000). However, how much of the judge's decision rested with the brain trauma and how much with the many other mitigating factors is not known.

Therefore, whether positively or negatively, the courts are beginning to consider biological risk factors such as head injury, particularly in sentencing.

## Psychosurgery

This chapter would not be complete without a mention of brain surgery. Although this conjures up ideas of old black-and-white horror films, surgical attempts to control antisocial and aggressive behavior have a long and often rather checkered history. Since it was first understood that it was the brain rather than the heart where behavior and emotion were controlled, attempts have been made to change behavior by physically changing the brain. Early attempts at what one might euphemistically call "brain surgery" date back to 5100 BC when skulls were opened or trephined with a form of cylindrical saw (Mashour et al., 2005). Archaeological studies of trephination suggest that such surgeries have been used to treat neuropsychiatric disorders since 1500 BC (Mashour et al., 2005). Such methods gradually lost favor, but the idea of neural surgery experienced a revival in the 19th and early 20th century as people began to gain a more sophisticated understanding of the function of the brain. Much of this understanding came from observing the results of brain injuries on a person's personality and behavior, the most dramatic of which that has been recorded is probably that of Phineas Gage, whose frontal lobe was accidentally pulverized by a metal rod.

Aside from the obvious moral and ethical problems with such drastic and entirely irreversible surgery, perhaps the major problem resulted from the simplistic belief that any behavior was controlled by one, and only one, tiny part of the brain. If that were true, then perhaps it does make sense to attempt to alter that tiny part of the brain to impact one behavior. However, as we know, both the brain and behavior are far more complex, with many parts of the brain influencing a single behavior.

When discussing psychosurgery we are talking about localized brain surgery. Most classic neurosurgery is performed for medical reasons, for example, to remove a tumor or to repair traumatic injuries. This is quite different from psychosurgery, which is performed in a deliberate attempt to alter behavior. However, the term "psychosurgery" and the images it conjures up certainly instill a negative response. It was recently suggested that a term more appropriate to today's more specific surgeries should be "neurosurgery for mental disorder" (NMD) to avoid the historical connotations of the term "psychosurgery" (Rosenfeld, 1999).

Although it is the Portuguese neurologist Moniz who is usually credited with the birth of modern psychosurgery, it was a Swiss psychiatrist, Gottlieb Burckhardt, who performed the first modern psychosurgery in 1888 (Mashour et al., 2005). Burckhardt removed parts of the cerebrum at multiple sites in the frontal, parietal, and temporal cortices in a surgery referred to as a "topectomy." The outcome of the surgery was considered "successful" in three of the six cases, but definitely unsuccessful in a fourth, as the patient did not survive. Burckhardt's research was not well received, and he abandoned this work (Mashour et al., 2005).

Some years later, in 1935, Fulton and Jacobsen reported at a conference in London, England the results of their surgery on chimpanzees (Rosenfeld, 1999). They reported that performing frontal lobotomies on two aggressive and anxious chimpanzees had resulted in the animals becoming very placid and calm. Dr. Egaz Moniz, an eminent Portuguese neurologist, was not concerned that this experiment was performed on only two animals and resulted in placidity and apathy rather than the desired reversal of aggressive behavior, and further researched this area to develop the first frontal lobotomy in humans (Rosenfeld, 1999; Raine, 1993). This involved disconnecting the frontal lobe region from the thalamus and limbic system using a knife (or leukotome) inserted into small holes drilled in the skull (Raine, 1993). In his first experiment on 27 patients, all survived and 7 improved, with those with agitated depression responding the most favorably (Moniz, 1936a, 1936b, cited in Da Costa, 1997). Although improvement of any sort was only noted in 26% of the patients, with no change in the vast majority, this work was considered seminal for its time and began a period of intense "psycho-surgery," a term coined by Moniz. Moniz eventually won a Nobel Prize for his work in 1949 (Rosenfeld, 1999). Although success was reported, Moniz apparently kept few records of his patients after surgery, and several patients were returned to asylums (Mashour et al., 2005).

Psychosurgery became the treatment of choice in a large number of patients from 1942 onward. Dr. Walter Freeman, a neurologist and psychia-trist, together with Dr. James Watts, a neurosurgeon, brought Moniz's work to the United States and began to perform frontal lobotomies, or leukotomies. At the time, mental illness was considered a tremendous "burden to society," with over half the hospital beds in the United States used for psychiatric patients (Mashour et al., 2005). Freeman believed that this radical new tech-nique was the answer to the country's mentally ill, and felt that he could clear out the mental asylums in the United States by disconnecting the "diseased" frontal lobe from the rest of the brain (Da Costa, 1997). Freeman and col-leagues performed so many of these surgeries that it almost became a pro-duction line, with such procedures being performed in surgeons' offices (Rosenfeld, 1999); they were eventually even performed by non-physicians (Mashour et al., 2005).

A similar craze for psychosurgery occurred in the United Kingdom, and over 10,000 patients in Britain, and 40,000 patients in the United States, received lobotomies in the 1940s and 1950s (Rosenfeld, 1999). Freeman him-self was credited with over 3,500 lobotomies (Raine, 1993). Most surgeries were performed on schizophrenics to treat aggressive and psychotic behavior, although people with other mental disorders or even just antisocial behavioral problems also underwent such surgeries.

Eventually it was noted that too many patients suffered from severe adverse side effects, such as epilepsy, personality changes, disinhibition, infec-tion, and even death, so popular opinion began to change. The scientific and medical community began to question the actual efficacy of the procedure, and it was eventually concluded that the treatment was worse than the orig-inal problem (Mashour et al., 2005). This is not really surprising when you recall Phineas Gage, whose injuries were similar to a very crude lobotomy. His memory and abilities were retained but his personality dramatically changed. We also know that behaviors are controlled by many parts of the brain and that any given area can have an affect on many behaviors. As well, we are aware that the frontal lobe has a major role in impulse control, the regulation of emotion and aggression, so damage or disengagement of such an area is likely to result in personality changes and lack of control. Animal studies have shown that such surgeries can sometimes increase aggression but often result also in apathy (Singh, 1976; Miller, 1976). It has been speculated that this indifference or apathy may be the reason that lobotomies first became popular, as the surgery could result in a quiet and placid, rather than aggressive, patient (Raine, 1993). However, this does not mean that the surgery is acting on aggression, but rather that it is simply making the patient too apathetic to act aggressively or otherwise.

In 1999, a group of Canadian researchers assessed the efficacy of these early prefrontal lobotomies on chronic, institutionalized, elderly schizophrenics (Black et al., 2000). They compared the results of frontal brain function, behavior, psychopathology, and neurological examinations, and computed tomography (CT) scans between 19 chronically institutionalized schizophrenic patients who had undergone prefrontal lobotomies between 1948 and 1972, and 11 matched institutionalized schizophrenics who had not undergone surgical intervention (Black et al., 2000). Despite the wide range of physical and mental tests used to assess the two groups, no significant differences were found between the two groups, indicating that the prefrontal lobotomies had not resulted in any improvement in performance. In several tests, those patients who had received the surgery performed slightly worse, especially in tasks that related to frontal lobe function. Both groups closely resembled elderly schizophrenics in general in cognitive impairment and in performance tasks related to the frontal lobe (Black et al., 2000).

The number of patients receiving any form of psychosurgery dropped dramatically from the 1950s onward. Many of the early surgeries were used to treat schizophrenia, so the development of new pharmacological treatments for schizophrenia and other mental illnesses reduced the need for such drastic and permanent intervention. Also, public concern and conspiracy theories related to mind control by the state made the surgery much less popular.

Psychosurgery is still performed today, but on only a very small number of people and only after all other possible treatment options have been exhausted. In most cases, psychosurgery is performed on patients with medically diagnosed mental and psychiatric disorders such as obsessive compulsive disorder, rather than to directly control aggressive behavior. In a 1980s study of 1500 psychosurgeries, only 2.5% were performed to control aggressive behavior (O'Callaghan and Carroll, 1982). Of this 2.5%, the authors concluded that the surgery was not effective in controlling antisocial behavior (O'Callaghan and Carroll, 1987).

A National Committee on Psychosurgery in the United States in 1976 decided that there was a role, although a very limited one, for psychosurgery as a last resort in certain mental illnesses (Rosenfeld, 1999), although such surgeries have become increasingly rare. Not only has the scientific efficacy been questioned, but also the ethics of performing such irreversible surgery on people who are mentally ill and who cannot give informed consent. In a landmark legal ruling in a Detroit court (Kaminowitz v. Department of Mental Health, cited in Mashour et al., 2005), the courts turned down an application to experimentally perform psychosurgery on a violent, recidivistic offender, and ruled that involuntarily detained mental patients cannot give informed or adequate consent to experimental psychosurgery (Mashour et al., 2005).

The general, nonselective lobotomies gave way, in the 1970s, to more precise surgeries targeting very specific parts of the brain. A technique referred to as stereotactic surgery allowed a neurosurgeon to create a much smaller lesion at a more precise site, which allowed much more specific surgery and fewer side effects (Mashour et al., 2005).

As scientists developed a better understanding of brain function, the role of the limbic system in emotion and aggression was examined more closely. The amygdala has often been considered to be the "seat" of aggression, and removing it was thought to make aggressive patients more passive. We mentioned this idea when discussing testosterone. Amegdalectomies were first performed in Japan and then in the United States. In his summary of four studies, encompassing 185 cases, Raine (1993) notes that there was "marked improvement" in 39% of cases; "some improvement" in 35%; and "no improvement" in 21% — 5% were worse after surgery. Thus, there was partial success in 74% and failure in 26%.

Once again it is clear that there is no such thing as "one bit of the brain = one behavior." All parts of the brain have many functions, and many parts of the brain are involved in behavior modulation. Therefore, when pieces are removed, whether they are large areas such as the frontal lobe or small areas such as the amygdala, there are likely to be a variety of results, including both excitatory and inhibitory effects on aggression (Raine, 1993). For example, in cats, some parts of the amygdala suppress predatory attack while other areas of the amygdala facilitate it (Siegel and Mirsky, 1990). So even removing a small area such as the amygdala is not likely to simply reduce aggression; it will also influence other behavior.

More recently, new brain imaging techniques (discussed in Chapter 10) have allowed a much greater understanding of brain function. The drastic and very generalized cutting of the past is no longer used. Today, precise thermal lesions are created using stereotactic radiofrequency electrodes in very specific regions of the brain in an effort to reverse the undesirable consequences of a psychiatric disorder, and without over-correcting (Rosenfeld, 1999). Obsessive compulsive disorder (OCD) patients are obsessive about certain things, and the aim of surgery in such patients is to reduce the obsessiveness to normal levels of caution without resulting in the patient becoming careless. Such precision is difficult to obtain and varies from patient to patient, with over-correction resulting in a deterioration of personality and intelligence, while other patients remain obsessive compulsive (Rosenfeld, 1999). Such surgeries today are carried out using modern imaging techniques such as magnetic resonance imaging (MRI) and are performed on a conscious, locally anaesthetized patient. Even with such precise techniques available, the overall success rate of such surgeries is low. Success is usually seen in a little more than half of patients, with others showing no improvement or even worsening. Currently, it is not possible to determine beforehand which patients are most likely to benefit (Rosenfeld, 1999).

In the past, many behaviors that were considered antisocial at the time were thought to be "correctable" with psychosurgery, including hyperactivity in children, substance abuse, pedophilia, and violent sex offending. Today, legislation and psychosurgery review boards are in place in many countries to prevent such misuse and also to ensure that the rare psychosurgeries that are carried out are only performed on patients who are capable of giving informed consent, that the physicians are appropriately qualified, and that the surgery has proven scientific and medical value. Rosenfeld (1999), in his review of psychosurgery, details the role and responsibilities of such review boards around the world.

Schizophrenia was the most common mental illness to be treated in the early days, but such radical treatment became unnecessary with the advent of anti-psychotic drugs in the 1950s. However, some very severe cases of schizophrenia remain intractable despite anti-psychotic drug treatment regimes. In such cases, the person might be a danger to themselves or to society, and, in such cases, some research has reported success using psychosurgery. Several studies have indicated a role of the prefrontal cortex and the limbic system in schizophrenia (Liddle, 1990; Torrey and Peterson, 1974). Da Costa (1997) suggests that psychosurgery might be beneficial in severe and chronic refractory schizophrenic patients, with symptoms including self-mutilation, suicide attempts, and severe aggression, where conventional treatments have failed. Da Costa (1997) reports the use of bilateral leukotomy using precise stereotactic thermal radiofrequencies to produce specific and defined lesions in the post-medial hypothalamus of 12 patients together with anterior cingulotomy, which disrupts a region of the brain called the circuit of Papez, from the anterior thalamic nucleus to the frontal cingulated cortex (Papez, 1937, cited in Rosenfeld, 1999). In a further four patients, the *fundus stria terminalis* was targeted instead of the hypothalamus. This was also combined with anterior cingulotomy. These surgeries were performed over an 11-year period on non-institutionalized patients. In all 16 patients, the effects of the leukotomy were obvious immediately after the surgery: five patients no longer exhibited any aggressive behavior, despite severe aggression prior to surgery; nine were greatly improved; and two were slightly improved (Da Costa, 1997). Most importantly, none of the patients exhibited worsened symptoms overall, although some transient adverse side effects were noted, including confusion, mild neurovegetative symptoms, and hypersexuality (Da Costa, 1997). Follow-up of the patients in the years subsequent to surgery indicated that quality of life improved in all cases and, although all had been unemployed before the surgery, four gained employment afterward (Da Costa, 1997).

As in the above-described surgeries, psychosurgery is today reserved as a last resort for people with severe neurological disorders who have not responded to other forms of less-invasive treatment. It has shown some success in patients with severe schizophrenia (Da Costa, 1997), depression, obsessive compulsive disorder, and severe anxiety disorders (Malizia, 1997). A successful outcome has usually been observed in 30 to 60% of patients (Malhi and Sachdev, 2002). With the more specific techniques in use today, severe side effects such as seizures, or even death, are extremely rare, although less severe side effects such as lethargy, lack of sphincter control, and confusion are more common, although transient (Malhi and Sachdev, 2002). Success, however, is primarily based on reduction of symptoms, and questions about long-term effects on personality and behavior are still being raised (Malhi and Sachdev, 2002).

As neurosurgery in general continues to expand and develop, and as scientific understanding of brain function increases, it is possible that psychosurgical intervention may have some value in extreme refractory cases. However, the ethical concerns and risk of side effects still limit such a technique to the most severe cases. The abuses of the past are difficult to forget, and the impressive regulatory bodies in place to guide all such psychosurgery are designed to prevent the repeat of such abuses.

Mashour et al. (2005) suggest that a combination of surgical and electrical modulation techniques may be the way of the future for such interventions. Electroconvulsive therapy has its own dark past, but a much more modified version of electrical stimulation to very specific parts of the brain has shown success. Surgical implantation of an electrode that targets specific areas of the brain such as the vagus nerve has shown promising results in patients with epilepsy or Parkinson's disease, and Mashour et al. (2005) suggest that it may also be valuable in neuropsychiatric disorders. Such psychosurgery would be stimulatory rather than destructive.

## Conclusion

This chapter examined brain damage and its influence on criminality. We found that because the brain is the seat of all behavior, any damage to the brain is likely to affect behavior. Thus, accidental trauma, birth trauma, abuse as a child, fetal alcohol spectrum disorder, or biochemical imbalances can affect action and can, often in concert with environmental or other influences, result in criminal behavior. We found that brain damage can be severe at any age, but damage to the developing brain is most severe. Modern medical techniques, including MRI, PET, and CT scans, have made it possible for us to understand much more about the brain and brain damage than in the past and have allowed us to see the links to criminal behavior. In addition to mechanical damage, chemicals and other toxins can have permanent and traumatic effects on the brain. Lead poisoning and other neurotoxins can affect the brain adversely; LSD and other kinds of psychotropic drugs can lead to psychotic reactions. Large-scale brain trauma as shown in cases like that of Phineas Gage can result in major personality changes and disorders including increased violence, spousal abuse, and hypersexualtiy. Damage to different areas of the brain such as the temporal lobe, the corpus callosum, amygdala, and hippocampus cause different types of behaviorial changes. In many cases, even minor injuries to brain function can have a major influence on future behavior. In the past, the treatments devised for this trauma were often worse than the originating disturbance itself. Surgical interventions from trephining to Freeman and Watts's discovery of the pacifying effects of lobotomy were often highly detrimental and are now closely regulated; more careful and precise types of psychosurgery are now available. A correct understanding of the types of brain injury and their results can help us find ways to ameliorate the effects and to prevent the misuse of therapies that have no chance of improving behavior. Obtaining these data depends on the techniques and instruments we use, and Chapter 10 discusses some of the new methods available.

## Questions for Further Study and Discussion

1. Discuss the *ethical* issues related to convicting and incarcerating (or worse) a person who has suffered a major head injury.
2. Brain damage, particularly to the frontal lobe region, can cause major behavioral changes and lead to antisocial behavior and in some cases even criminal behavior. In the United States, the majority of people on death row have suffered head injuries, many in childhood. Discuss

the *legal* issues related to convicting and incarcerating (or worse) a person who has suffered a major head injury.

3. We consider that committing a crime is a matter of "free will." But can we use the free will argument when brain damage, particularly that of the frontal lobe region, has caused major behavioral changes (increased aggression and hypersexuality) that have led to criminal actions? In the United States, the majority of people on death row have suffered head injuries, many in childhood.

4. Discuss the legal and ethical issues of psychosurgery. Has the basic ethical dilemma changed with the recent advent of more precise methods than frontal lobotomy?

# References

AbdelMalik, P., Husted, J., Chow, E.W.C., and Bassett, A.S. (2003). Childhood head injuries and expression of schizophrenia in multiply affected families. *Arch. Gen. Psychiatry,* 60(3), 231–236.

Andersen, S.L. and Teicher, M.H. (2004). Delayed effects of early childhood stress on hippocampal development. *Neuropsychopharmocology,* 29(11), 1988–1993.

Anderson, S.W., Bechara, A., Damasio, H., Tranel, D., and Damasio, A.R. (1999). Impairment of social and moral behavior related to early damage in human prefrontal cortex. *Nature Neurosci.,* 2(11), 1032–1037.

Andrews, T.K., Rose, F.D., and Johnson, D.A. (1998). Social and behavioral effects of traumatic brain injury in children. *Brain Injury,* 12(2), 133–138.

Bechara, A., Damasio, A.R., Damasio, H., and Anderson, S.W. (1994). Insensitivity to future consequences following damage to human prefrontal cortex. *Cognition,* 50, 7.

Best, M., Williams, J.M., and Coccaro, E.F. (2002). Evidence for a dysfunctional prefrontal circuit in patients with an impulsive aggressive disorder. *Proc. Nat. Acad. Sci. U.S.A.,* 99(12), 8448–8453.

Black, D.N., Stip., E., Bedard, M.-A., Kabay, M., Paquette, I., and Bigras, M.-J. (2000). Leukotomy revisited, late cognitive and behavioral effects in chronic institutionalized schizophrenics. *Schizophrenia Res.,* 43, 57–64.

Blake, P.Y., Pincus, J.H., and Buckner, C. (1995). Neurologic abnormalities in murderers. *Neurology,* 45, 1641–1647.

Blanchard, R., Christensen, B.K., Strong, S.M., Cantor, J.M., Kuban, M.E., Klassen, P., and Dickey, R. (2002). Retrospective self-reports of childhood accidents causing unconsciousness in phallometrically diagnosed paedophiles. *Arch. Sexual Behav.,* 31(6), 511–526.

Bogaert, A.F. (2001). Handedness, criminality and sexual offending. *Neuropsychologia,* 39(5), 465–469.

Cannon, T.D., Mednick, S.A., Parnas, J., Schulsinger, F., Praestholm, J., and Vestergaard, A. (1993). Developmental brain abnormalities in the offspring of schizophrenic mothers. I. Contributions of genetic and perinatal factors *Arch. Gen. Psychiatry,* 50(7), 551–564.

Comings, D.E. (1996). Both genes and environment play a role in antisocial behavior. *Politics Life Sci.,* 15, 84–86.

Da Costa, D.A. (1997). The role of psychosurgery in the treatment of selected cases of refractory schizophrenia, a reappraisal. *Schizophrenia Res.,* 28, 223–230.

Damasio, H., Grabowski, R., Frank, A., Galabunda, A., and Damasio, A.R. (1994). The return of Phineas Gage, clues about the brain from the skull of a famous patient. *Science,* 264, 1102–1105.

Davidson, G. and Neale, J. (1996). *Abnormal Psychology* (6th ed.). New York: Wiley.

Davidson, R.J., Putnam, K.M., and Larson, C.L. (2000). Dysfunction in the neural circuitry of emotion regulation — a possible prelude to violence. *Science,* 289(5479), 591–594.

Deckel, A.W., Bauer, L., and Hesselbrock, V. (1995). Anterior brain dysfunctioning as a risk factor in alcoholic behaviors. *Addiction,* 90, 1323–1334.

Deckel, W., Hesselbrock, V., and Bauer, L. (1996). Antisocial personality disorder, childhood delinquency, and frontal brain functioning, EEG and neuropsychological findings. *J. Clin. Psychology,* 52(6), 639–650.

Denno, D.W. (1990). *Biology and Violence, From Birth to Adulthood* (p. 218). Cambridge: Cambridge University Press.

Fehlow, P. (1989). Criminality and premature craniosynostosis in young people. *Arztliche Jugendkunde,* 80(4), 215–229.

Golden, C.J., Jackson, M.L., and Peterson, R.A. (1996). Neuropsychological correlates of violence and aggression. A review of the clinical literature. *Aggression Violent Behav.,* 1(1), 3–25.

Golden, Z.L. and Golden, C.J. (2001). Do early onset conduct disordered adolescents perform like brain injured or normal adolescents on cognitive tests?. *Int. J. Neurosci.,* 111(1–2), 109–121.

Green, M.F., Satz, P., and Christenson, C. (1994). Minor physical anomalies in schizophrenia patients, bipolar patients and their siblings. *Schizophrenia Bull.,* 20, 433–440.

Greene, A.F., Lynch, T.F., Decker, B., and Coles, C.J. (1997). A psychobiological theoretical characterization of interpersonal violence offenders. *Aggression Violent Behav.,* 2(3), 273–284.

Guy, J.D., Majorski, L.V., Wallace, C.J., and Guy, M.P. (1983). The incidence of minor physical anomalies in adult male schizophrenics. *Schizophrenia Bull.,* 9, 571–582.

Heinrichs, R.W. (1989). Frontal cerebral lesions and violent incidents in chronic neuropsychiatric patients. *Biol. Psych.,* 25, 174–178.

Jeffery, C.R., Del Carmen, R.V., and White, J.D. (1985). *Attacks on the Insanity Defense, Biological Psychiatry and New Perspectives on Criminal Behavior* (p. 238). Springfield, IL: Thomas.

Kalat, J.W. (1995). *Biological Psychology* (5th ed.). Pacific Grove, CA: Brooks/Cole.

León-Carrión, J. and Ramos, F.J.C. (2003). Blows to the head during development can predispose to violent criminal behavior, rehabilitation of consequences of head injury is a measure for crime prevention. *Brain Injury,* 17(3), 207–216.

Lewis, D.O. (1998). *Guilty by Reason of Insanity, A Psychiatrist Explores the Minds of Killers.* New York: Fawcett Columbine.

Lewis, D.O., Pincus, J.H., Bard, B., Richardson, E., Price, L.S., Feldman, M., and Yeager, C. (1988). Neuropsychiatric, psycho educational, and family characteristics of 14 juveniles condemned to death in the Chaptered States. *Am. J. Psych.,* 145(5), 584–589.

Lewis, D.O., Pincus, J.H., Bard, B., Richardson, E., Price, L.S., Feldman, M., and Yeager, C. (1986). Psychiatric, neurological and psycho-educational characteristics of 15 death row inmates in the Chaptered States. *Am. J. Psych.,* 143, 838–845.

Liddle, P.F. (1990). Prefrontal and subcortical dysfunction in schizophrenia. In Wellere, M. (Ed.), *International Perspectives in Schizophrenia, Biological, Social and Epidemiological Findings* (pp. 85–95). London: John Libbey.

LoPiccolo, P. (1996). Something snapped. *Tech. Rev.,* 99(7), 52–61.

Malhi, G.S. and Sachdev, P. (2002). Novel physical treatments for the management of neuropsychiatric disorders. *J. Psychosomatic Res.,* 53, 709–719.

Malizia, A.L. (1997). The frontal lobes and neurosurgery for psychiatric disorders. *J. Psychopharmacol.,* 11, 179–187.

Mark, V.H. and Ervin, F.R. (1970). *Violence and the Brain.* New York: Harper and Row.

Martell, D.A. (1996). Organic brain dysfunctions and criminality. In Schlesinger, L.B. (Ed.). *Explorations in Criminal Psychopathology. Clinical Syndromes with Forensic Implications* (pp. 170–186). Springfield, IL: Charles C Thomas.

Martell, D.A. (1992). Estimating the prevalence of organic brain dysfunction in maximum-security forensic psychiatric patients. *J. Forens. Sci.,* 37(3), 878–893.

Mashour, G.A., Walker, E.A., and Martuza, R.L. (2005). Psychosurgery, past, present and future. *Brain Res. Rev.,* 48(3), 409–419.

Mayer, A.R. and Kosson, D.S. (2000). Handedness and psychopathy. *Neuropsych. Neuropsychol. Behav. Neuro.,* 13(4), 233–238.

McKinley, W.W., Brooks, D.N., Bond, M.R., Martinage, D.P., and Marshall, M.M. (1981). The short-term outcome of severe blunt head injury, as reported by relatives of the injured persons. *J. Neurol. Neurosurg. Psych.,* 44, 285–293.

Miller, M.H. (1976). Dorsolateral frontal lobe lesions and behavior in the macaque, Dissociation of threat and aggression. *Cognitive Rehabilitation,* 8, 14–19.

Mills, S. and Raine, A. (1994). Neuroimaging and aggression. *J. Offender Rehabilitation*, 21(3/4), 145–158.

Milner, J.S. (Ed.). (1991). *Neuropsychology of Aggression* (pp. 167–180). Boston: Kluwer.

Moniz, E. (1936a). Essai d'un traitement chirurgical de certaines psychoses. *Bull. Acad. Natl. Med.*, 115, 385–392.

Moniz, E. (1936b). Les premieres tentatives operatoires dans le traitement de certaines psychoses. *Encephale*, 31, 1–29.

Moon, M.A. (2000). Mild concussion triggered kleptomania. *Clin. Psychiatry News*, 28(2), 30.

Myers, D.G. (1992). *Psychology.* New York: Worth.

Nachshon, I. (1991). Violence and cerebral lateralization. *Crime and Social Deviance*, 18, 514.

O'Callaghan, M.A.J. and Carroll, D. (1987). Psychosurgery and antisocial behavior. In Mednick, S., Moffitt, T., and Stack, S.A. (Eds.). *The Causes of Crime, New Biological Approaches* (pp. 312–328). Cambridge: University of Cambridge Press.

O'Callaghan, M.A. and Carroll, D. (1982). *Psychosurgery, A Scientific Analysis.* Lancaster: Medical and Technical Publishing.

Ommaya, A.K., Salazar, A.M., Dannenberg, A.L., Chervinsky, A.B., and Schwab, K. (1996). Outcome after traumatic brain injury in the US military medical system. *J. Trauma*, 41(6), 972–975.

Papez, J.W. (1937). Proposed mechanism of emotion. *Arch Neurol*, 38, 725–743.

*R. v. Delorey* [1997] C.J.E.D. No. 6056 (Ql, O. J.).

*R. v. Scott*, [1993] C.J.E.D. No. 3040 (Ql, Ont. C. A.).

Raine, A. (1993). Neuropsychology. *The Psychopathology of Crime, Criminal Behavior as a Clinical Disorder* (pp. 103–127). London: Academic Press.

Rosenbaum, A. and Hodge, S.K. (1989). Head injury and marital aggression. *Am. J. Psych.*, 146, 1048–1051.

Rosenbaum, A., Hoge, S.K., Adelman, S.A., Warnken, W.J., Fletcher, K.E., and Kane, R.L. (1994). Head injury in partner-abusive men. *J. Consulting Clin. Psychol.*, 62(6), 1187–1193.

Rosenfeld, J.V. (1999). Contemporary psychosurgery. *J. Clin. Neurosci.*, 6(2), 106–112.

Sebit, M.B., Acuda, W., and Chibanda, D. (1996). A case of the frontal lobe syndrome following head injury in Harare, Zimbabwe. *Central African J. Med.*, 42(2), 51–53.

Siegel, A. and Mirsky, A.F. (1990). The neurobiology of violence and aggression. In National Academy of Science's Conference on the Understanding and Control of Violent Behavior. Cited in Raine, 1993.

Singh, S.D. (1976). Sociometric analysis of the effect of bilateral lesions of frontal cortex on the social behavior of Rhesus Indian monkeys. *J. Psychol.*, 51, 144–160.

Stuss, D., Gow, C., and Hetherington, R. (1992). "No longer Gage." Frontal lobe dysfunction and emotion changes. *J. Consulting Clin. Psychol.*, 60(3), 349–359.

Swerdlow, R. and Burns, J. (2002). Brain tumor causes uncontrolled pedophilia. *New Scientist*, October 21.

Tardiff, K. (1998). Unusual diagnoses among violent patients. *Psych. Clinics N. Am.*, 21(3), 567–576.

Teichner, G., Golden, C.J., Van Hasselt, V.B., and Peterson, A. (2001). Assessment of cognitive functioning in men who batter. *Int. J. Neurosci.*, 11, 241–253.

Torrey, E.F. and Peterson, M.R. (1974). Schizophrenia and the limbic system. *Lancet*, 2, 942–946.

Volavka, J., Martell, D., and Convit, A. (1992). Psychobiology of the violent offender. *J. Forensic Sci.*, 37(1), 237–251.

Volkow, N.D. and Tancredi, L. (1987). Neural substrates of violent behavior A preliminary study with positron emission tomography. *Br. J. Psychiatry*, 151, 668–673.

Volkow, N.D., Fowler, J.S., and Wang, G.-J. (2003). Positron emission tomography and single-photon emission computed tomography in substance abuse research. *Sem. Nucl. Med.*, 33(2), 114–128.

Ward, A.C. (2000). Evidentiary Use of Biological Disorder. Ethics and Justice Honours thesis, School of Criminology. Simon Fraser University, Burnaby, B.C. (p. 61).

Wright, P., Nobrega, J., Langevin, R., and Wortzman, G. (1990). Brain density and symmetry in pedophilic and sexually aggressive offenders. *Ann. Sex Res.*, 3(3), 319–328.

Yeudall, L.T. (1977). Neuropsychological assessment of forensic disorders. *Canada's Mental Health*, 25, 7–16.

Yeudall, L.T., Fromm-Auch, D., and Davies, P. (1982). Neuropsychological impairment of persistent delinquency. *J. Nerv. Mental Dis*, 170, 257–265.

# Organic Brain Dysfunctions: Part II    10

## Introduction

As the brain is the seat of all behavior, it is not surprising to find that brain injury can affect behavior. As we have seen, this can occur through accidental trauma, birth trauma, child abuse, fetal alcohol spectrum disorder, or biochemical imbalances. However, to determine whether such trauma is present, we must be able to study the brain itself.

Medical advances in neurology have meant that our understanding of brain function has progressed rapidly in recent years. This chapter considers the methods used to analyze brain trauma and how specific types of deficits have been related to certain types of behavior. We will look more closely at CT scanning, MRI, PET, SPECT, and the increasing number of studies based on these technologies. Through these means, our ability to find more specific causes and regions of cause is increasing. We have found in previous chapters that learning disorders such as ADHD and predisposition to criminality can interact. Research has shown that even minor differences in brain function (e.g., ADHD) can have a major influence on future behavior. We are now able to study criminogenic behavior using the new techniques, and the promise of such imaging is exciting. The findings have a positive implication: with appropriate treatment, such behavior and many related problems can be alleviated or prevented.

## Brain Structure and Function

All behavior, whether criminal or otherwise, is controlled by the brain. To understand the basis for any behavior, one must understand how the brain functions. In the past, the brain was little understood, and the only way to study it was by examining the brains of the deceased. The information that could be derived from such examinations was obviously limited.

Today, there are several techniques available that allow us to see both the structure and the function of the brain in living conscious subjects. Modern techniques are sensitive and noninvasive enough that we can now zero in on tiny areas and learn both their structures and their functions while the subject is conscious. This has allowed us to learn more about the brain and behavior than was ever thought possible. These techniques provide direct measurements of the brain itself and its functions.

Techniques such as computer tomography (CT) and magnetic resonance imaging (MRI) are designed specifically to understand the *structure* of the brain. They were developed for medical reasons, to identify physical abnormalities such as a brain tumor, although they can be used to image other areas of the body such as a damaged knee joint. MRI and CT techniques are very valuable in showing structural changes or differences between people. However, they do not help us understand changes or differences in brain function.

To understand brain *function*, and to study functional deficits or changes, other techniques such as positron emission tomography (PET) and single photon emission computed tomography (SPECT) have been developed.

In medical tests, where a specific diagnosis is sought, the test chosen will reflect the specific problem. However, when a more general understanding of behavior itself is desired, more than one technique must often be used. Medical evidence has shown that a person with a physically damaged brain may have little or no obvious functional problems, and at the same time, many people may have severe functional issues with no obvious structural brain damage. To understand their behavior, we need to have a picture of both structural and functional deficits.

All these brain imaging techniques were designed for medical diagnoses, so there have been many studies that consider their use in medicine, and medically diagnostic "brain scans" are performed daily throughout the world. However, due to the expense involved in many of the tests, the astronomical costs of the machinery itself, and the fact that most hospitals and universities with such facilities concentrate on much-needed medical analyses, such techniques have not yet been used to their fullest extent in criminological studies. However, in recent years, this does appear to be changing.

The following describes the most common brain imaging techniques and some of the studies to date that have used these techniques in studying criminogenic behavior.

## Structural Brain Imaging

### Computer Tomography

Computer tomography (CT) is also sometimes referred to as computed axial tomography (CAT), computer-assisted tomography, or body section roentgenography. It is a medical diagnostic test that combines x-rays with computer technology. Extremely sophisticated x-ray equipment is used to obtain image information of the brain from every angle. The information is processed by computer to produce a three-dimensional image that can be examined at every plane, as if a cross-section were to be cut through the brain at any desired site. The technique can also be used on any other tissue, such as heart, lungs, and blood vessels. It is frequently used to diagnose cancers and spinal injuries.

The brain to be imaged is x-rayed first in one plane. The CT scanner measures the amount of radiation that passes through the organ, thus determining how much has been absorbed. The scanner rotates into a new position and the process is repeated; 160 locations are measured in that plane, and then the apparatus is rotated 1° and all the measurements are again repeated (Raine, 1993). This is continued through an entire 360°. The computer then digitizes the information and produces an exact three-dimensional image of the brain. Thus, a CT is somewhat like a three-dimensional x-ray. This technique creates a three-dimensional picture of whatever you scan. In forensic science, it is used to recreate a skull, which can then be used for facial reconstruction.

Of all the imaging techniques, CT is probably the cheapest to use; however, an obvious drawback is that the subject is exposed to x-rays, which can be damaging. As well, smaller brain structures may be difficult to individualize, although regular improvements in technique can eliminate this problem. Sometimes a bone artifact might be present where the brain meets the skull, making it difficult to resolve features at that juncture (Raine, 1993).

### Studies Using Computer Tomography

Many early studies used CT, as this was the most available and least expensive technique at the time. Raine (1993, pp. 134–141) reviewed eight early Canadian studies that used CT to study a range of offenders, including murderers, sex offenders, and pedophiles.

Four of the studies (Wright et al., 1990; Langevin et al., 1988; Hucker et al., 1988, Hucker et al., 1986) found structural differences in the brain between the study group and the controls. These differences included left and bilateral temporal horn dilation, right temporal horn abnormalities, and temporal and frontal lobe abnormalities (Raine, 1993). These studies compared pedophiles (Wright et al., 1990; Hucker et al., 1986), sadistic and nonsadistic rapists (Hucker et al., 1988), and incest offenders (Langevin et al., 1988) with control groups consisting of property offenders. In several studies, the same controls were utilized.

Four other studies, mostly by the same groups of researchers, did not show any significant differences in brain structure between murderers and assaulters (Langevin et al., 1987), aggressive people with temporal lobe epilepsy (Herzberg and Fenwick, 1988), pedophiles (Langevin et al., 1989a), and exhibitionists (Langevin et al., 1989b), as compared with property offenders. In one group (Herzberg and Fenwick, 1988), the controls were nonviolent sufferers of temporal lobe epilepsy.

Ordinarily, using a control group that is relatively similar to the experimentals reduces some possible variables, so the fact that the controls in these cases were, predominantly, offenders is good. However, the fact that the same control group was used in many of these studies may have had a confounding influence, especially if the control group was not an appropriate control. For example, this control group was found to have quite high levels of structural damage — in some cases, higher than the experimentals. This may suggest that property offenders are characterized by certain types of structural brain damage themselves (Raine, 1993, p. 137), making them an inappropriate control group. Obtaining such medical information from people is obviously not easy, and thus it is tempting to reuse the same control group. But by doing so, the researchers may have reduced the value of the studies.

It is interesting to note the pathology apparently seen in property offenders. If we think back to previous chapters on genetics, it was clear that there was a distinct difference in genetic heritability of the predisposition to commit property versus violent crime. The studies suggest that perhaps brain differences also exist.

It would have been interesting to also use a control group from the general population (with the usual caveats that this does not mean that the general population does not include all manner of uncaught offenders) to determine whether the high levels of structural damage seen in the property offender group was unusual. Specifically, it would be highly valuable to know the prevalence of all types of head injury in the general population. The incidence, as we have seen, of head injuries in the general population is considered to be between 5% (Blake et al., 1995) and 6% (Teichner et al., 2001). I suspect one would find that the number of people in the general population with some level of head injury would be higher. Consider all the contact sports children play and the number of times they could receive a blow to the head or even a mild concussion. Studies have shown that even mild head injuries in children can result in higher levels of behavioral problems, including aggressive and antisocial behavior, than in noninjured children (Andrews et al., 1998).

Raine (1993), who reviewed these early eight studies, suggests that frontal lobe damage may be associated with violent offending and rape, while temporal lobe dysfunction may have more relation to other types of sexual offenses, such as incest and pedophilia. However, he admits that the evidence thus far is not conclusive, and more data are required.

In a later study, 31 people either awaiting trial for murder, awaiting sentencing, or undergoing an appeal of a murder conviction were studied using CT as well as MRI and electroencephalogram (Blake et al., 1995). Some level of structural abnormality was seen in 20 of the 31 subjects, with several subjects having more than one diagnosis. Evidence of abnormalities in the frontal lobe was found in 64.5% of the sample and, in the temporal lobe, in 29%. However, no normal controls were included in the study, and the subjects themselves had a wide range of other conditions, including epilepsy, cerebral palsy, fetal alcohol spectrum disorder, and alcohol-induced dementia, so it is difficult to generalize the results. Nevertheless, the study does support a growing number of studies that indicate that brain injury and violent crime are frequently linked.

In a study of 77 male, maximum security hospital inmates in England, structural temporal changes were identified using CT in only the most violent of the patients (Wong et al., 1994). This was a blind study, so the researchers were unaware of the violence ratings of the individuals until after they were tested. The structural changes were particularly apparent in repeated violent offenders (Wong et al., 1994).

CT studies seem to be less popular today in the literature, probably due to the limits of resolution and other artifacts found with CT. When used in more modern studies, it is usually combined with MRI or a functional brain imaging method.

### Magnetic Resonance Imaging

Magnetic resonance imaging (MRI) is an advanced medical diagnostic technique that uses a very powerful magnet, radiofrequency waves, and computer imaging techniques to provide an image of the body's internal organs or structures. It can be used to image the brain, as well as any other structure. In the news, we frequently hear of sports figures awaiting results of the MRI of a recent injury to determine when and if they can return to their profession.

The development of the MRI was a tremendous step forward in the medical world. It allows a physician to see inside the body, from any angle, at any site, without invasive procedures, making the term "exploratory surgery" frequently a thing of the past.

The MRI machine creates a magnetic field, then sends radio waves into the body and subsequently measures the cellular response. Different tissues as well as diseased and normal tissue produce different resonance and thus can be distinguished at a very fine level. In particular, MRI gives clear images of soft tissue near and around bones so not only is it the technique of choice for examining spinal and joint injuries, but it also means that there is no bone artifact — a further advantage of MRI over CT, particularly when examining joints, or the brain. The technique is also safer because radio waves rather than x-rays are used.

MRI does have some limitations. As a powerful magnet is used, people with any metallic objects within their body cannot be imaged. These include people with any implants as well as pacemakers and heart clips. Also, the equipment required is extremely expensive and requires specialized technical support.

Both CT and MRI, although extremely valuable techniques, only provide structural information about the brain. Other techniques can measure metabolic activity in the brain and thus can provide information about brain function. Because such tests are performed on live, conscious patients, these functional tests allow doctors and researchers to study brain function while the subject performs tasks such as viewing images.

### Studies Using Magnetic Resonance Imaging

MRI studies now seem to outnumber CT studies, and MRI is now the technique of choice for studying structural brain deficits. Early studies looked at the brain as a whole, but more recent studies now focus in on very specific areas of interest.

In a study in Austria, several brain abnormalities were revealed by MRI between different groups of sex offenders (Eher et al., 1996). The 21 offenders were divided into two groups. The first group included offenders who had committed one or more aggressive sexual assaults with vaginal or anal penetration and had severely injured the victim. The second group included those who had raped but had not caused severe physical injury to the victim, or had attempted rape, or had exhibited nonviolent pedophilic or exhibitionist behavior (Eher et al., 1996). In a blind assessment, 75% of the first group, but only 18% of the second group, showed structural brain abnormalities. The groups were matched in areas such as age and general intelligence. These MRI abnormalities correlated well with clinical diagnoses and criminal records. The authors suggested that the structural abnormalities, which varied and included right ventricular enlargement, dilated right temporal horn, corticol atrophy, and a deep white matter lesion, were associated with the degree of physical violence exerted in the sexual offenses (Eher et al., 1996).

It is known that people who suffer from temporal lobe epilepsy (TLE) are more prone to sudden violent outbursts than non-epileptics, but only a small percentage of such epileptics are violent. A comparison of violent TLE individuals with nonviolent TLE individuals using CT showed no significant structural differences, as mentioned previously (Herzberg and Fenwick, 1988). However, the lack of findings may have been due to the lack of resolution in the CT. MRI has much greater resolution than CT, and a more recent study using MRI found that people with TLE and a history of unprovoked violent outbursts exhibited a decrease in gray matter in the left frontal lobe, in comparison with nonviolent TLE individuals and normal controls (Woermann et al., 2000).

MRI has been used to specifically measure the hippocampus, a horseshoe-shaped region of the temporal lobe, in 18 antisocial alcoholic offenders (Laakso et al., 2001). The MRIs were compared with the results of the offenders' psychological tests to measure psychopathic behavior. The researchers found a correlation between higher psychopathy scores and reduced volume in the posterior half of the hippocampus. The hippocampus is part of the limbic system and is responsible for memory, learning, emotional control, and regulation.

These researchers had previously shown that hippocampal volume is reduced in late-onset, nonviolent alcoholics, and this reduction continues as the person ages, indicating there is acquired damage over time (Laakso et al., 2000). However, in the more recent study, although the hippocampi were smaller than normal in antisocial alcoholic offenders, the size increased over time (Laakso et al., 2001). The authors suggested that there were major biological differences between antisocial alcoholics and nonviolent, late-onset alcoholics, and that the reduced posterior hippocampal volume in the violent alcoholics was due to factors other than alcohol abuse (Laakso et al., 2001).

Recently, Raine et al. (2004) compared hippocampal structure among 16 caught (unsuccessful) psychopaths, 12 uncaught (successful) psychopaths, and 23 normal controls. The researchers recruited men from the general public and assessed them using a structural MRI scan. All were then tested using the Pschopathy Checklist-Revised (PCL-R) (Hare, 1991). Self-report questionnaires and criminal conviction data were subsequently used to assess their criminal activity. Subjects were assessed as unsuccessful psychopaths (criminal convictions, scoring in top third of PCL-R scale), successful psychopaths (no criminal convictions, scoring in top third of PCL-R scale), and controls (no criminal convictions, scoring in the bottom third of the PCL-R scale). The unsuccessful psychopaths were found to have a significantly severe structural asymmetry between the left and right anterior parts of the hippocampus, in comparison with successful psychopaths and controls (Raine et al., 2004). The authors suggest that this reflects an interruption of some sort in the early childhood neural development process.

It is interesting that this asymmetry was found only in the unsuccessful psychopaths. Studies on psychopathic offenders (who are usually caught) have shown that such psychopaths have very poor fear conditioning, meaning that, as children, they did not respond normally to discipline, so did not learn to respond to environmental cues to avoid punishment for infractions.

The hippocampus is very important in memory and learning and thus is involved in retrieving memories of previously experienced unpleasant events, such as punishment (Raine et al., 2004). Therefore, if the hippocampus is impaired in any way, this could mean that childhood learning from normal disciplinary measures was prevented or disturbed. This might lead to higher crime rates in these unsuccessful individuals because they have no fear of being caught. Successful psychopaths may have had normal fear conditioning and thus are more aware of risk and therefore evade capture (Raine et al., 2004).

In another study, Raine et al. (2003) used MRI to study the corpus callosum region of the brain in psychopaths. The researchers found that psychopaths have an increased white matter volume as well as an increased callosal length, but reduction in thickness, with increased connectivity between the two hemispheres (Raine et al., 2003). The authors again felt that this reflected a disruption in early brain development.

Many offenders suffered from abuse or neglect as children. If the reported changes in brain development do relate back to a disturbance or interruption in neural development in childhood, then childhood abuse and neglect may well play a much bigger role in adult offending than is presently understood. It is often considered that an abusive environment during childhood may predispose the individual to later criminality, but perhaps the link is also related to biological damage caused by the abuse, rather than the environmental abuse alone.

Childhood abuse, both physical and sexual, has been linked to several changes in brain morphology, including reduced left hemisphere and left hippocampal development, a reduction in the size of the corpus callosum and amygdala, and reduced cortical integration between the left and right hemispheres (Teicher et al., 2004, 2003). A recent MRI study showed that neglect alone can have just as negative an effect on the development of the corpus callosum in boys as physical or sexual abuse, whereas girls were most negatively affected by sexual abuse (Teicher et al., 2004).

This would fit with Raine et al.'s hypothesis that asymmetry and hippocampal development relate to a disturbance of early neural development. Other studies, however, have not found asymmetry or reduced hippocampal size in young adults with a history of severe child abuse (Teicher et al., 2003) although this may be because the stress results in a gradual effect and thus is not discernable in young adults (Teicher et al., 2003). Stress can also influence hormone levels, which in turn can suppress the division of the glial cells that are involved in producing the sheath that surrounds and protects nerves (Teicher et al., 2003; Berrebi et al., 1988). The corpus callosum is myelinated so such stress could directly affect the development of the corpus callosum.

Teicher et al. (2003) have reviewed recent research on the effects of child-hood ill treatment on several regions of the brain. They have hypothesized that the impact is not direct damage or interruption of development of the neural pathways in childhood, but rather is a result of the young brain devel-oping along an alternative pathway in order to adapt and survive in an abusive life (Teicher et al., 2003). The brain is designed to develop and mature based on environment and experience. Experiences during the critical stages of development will affect the way the brain develops. Modifications that are induced by stress should allow the individual to adapt and withstand stress during life. The authors postulate that if a child experiences repeated, severe stress or abuse during the formative developmental period, the brain will develop along an alternative pathway, one that is evolutionarily designed to allow survival in an abusive world. Evolutionarily, this may have served an adaptive function, allowing the person to survive and eventually reproduce in a dangerous environment. Of course, such adaptation would be maladaptive in a more hospitable world (Teicher et al., 2003) and could predispose a person to aggression and over-reaction to stimuli where it was not appropriate.

MRIs are used to assess the structure of the brain, and these structural observations should be combined with other measures to determine whether structural deficits relate to a specific functional deficit. However, recent advances have resulted in an adaptation of the MRI to allow it to also assess function. This is termed a functional MRI (or fMRI) and allows mapping of brain activity. At the present time, fMRI may be one of the most sensitive techniques available for investigating many medical diseases, including tumors and strokes, as well as brain abnormalities. During an fMRI, brain activity can be observed while the subject is exposed to certain stimuli or sensations, to determine which part of the brain is stimulated under a given set of circumstances. No radioactive isotopes are required, as the fMRI directly measures blood flow. It is probable that fMRI will soon become the technique of choice in most brain imaging studies as it does not involve radioactivity, and thus is both cheaper and safer than PET or SPECT, and also has much greater resolution (Posse et al., 1996). However, at the moment, the technique is very new so PET and SPECT are seen more commonly in most studies.

In a Canadian fMRI study of psychopaths, eight psychopathic criminals were compared with eight nonpsychopathic criminals and eight noncriminal controls (Kiehl et al., 2001). Psychopaths, according to PCL-R, are charac-terized by extreme narcissism, lack of remorse, shallowness, manipulation, callousness, and superficial charm, so it is not surprising that they showed greatly reduced emotional response in several areas of the limbic region of the brain when responding to negative verbal stimuli (Kiehl et al., 2001). The limbic system is the primary region of the brain involved in emotion. They also exhibited over-activity in the frontal and temporal regions of the brain, which are involved in cognitive decision making and impulse control. The authors noted that the results were consistent with the belief that psychopaths process information differently from non-psychopaths, whether criminal or otherwise. No obvious structural deficits were noted. The limbic and prefrontal region of the brain has been shown to be involved in emotional and sexual self-regulation in normal subjects, so a defect in this system could have important implications (Beauregard et al., 2001).

## Functional Brain Imaging

### Positron Emission Tomography

Positron emission tomography (PET) was the first brain scanning technique developed that allowed doctors and researchers to study brain function rather than structure. PET measures the emission of positrons (anti-electrons) from the brain after a small amount of radioactive isotope is injected into the subject's bloodstream. The isotope used is a short-lived radioactive tracer that decays by emitting a positron. It is combined with a metabolically active molecule such as a sugar. Once injected, there is a short waiting period while the sugar becomes concentrated in the tissues being studied. The subject is placed in an imaging scanner, and the presence of the isotope in the tissues is detected as it decays, emitting positrons. This, therefore, shows the site of brain metabolism or function.

PET has been used extensively by doctors in efforts to understand which parts of the brain are involved in many different neurologic illnesses, including seizures, schizophrenia, and Parkinson's disease. PET has also been used to answer other interesting questions, such as which specific part or parts of the brain are involved in certain activities, such as solving mathematic problems, word puzzles, or cognitive tests.

PET is an excellent and direct measure of brain activity and can be used to determine brain function during various tasks or during cognitive tests. The resolution is excellent, and allows a physician or researcher to focus in on a very small region of the brain. If a dysfunction in a particular region is suspected, that area can be examined minutely while the subject is challenged with a task that is thought to be controlled in that area. The glucose metabolism can then be measured and compared with other areas.

There are, of course, several rather obvious drawbacks. The first is that the test is somewhat invasive, requiring the injection of a substance, followed by a series of blood tests. As well, the substance itself is radioactive, involving some risk to the subject and repeated tests on the same subject are not recommended. Perhaps the biggest drawback is the prohibitive cost of the cyclotron that is required to produce the isotope. Therefore, although PET is used in medical diagnoses, its utilization in research has been somewhat limited.

## Studies Using Positron Emission Tomography

Several studies have used PET to look at differences in brain function between control and offender groups.

In a series of articles, Raine and co-workers reported the results of their studies on those found not guilty of murder or attempted murder by reason of insanity in California compared with normal controls. The original experimental group consisted of 20 murderers and 2 attempted murderers (Raine et al., 1994). The controls were normal subjects and were carefully matched for sex and age, ethnicity, handedness, and even for mental illness, in that three individuals in the offender group were diagnosed schizophrenics and were matched with schizophrenic controls. All were tested in the same laboratory.

The subjects were examined using PET brain imaging with continuous performance challenge tasks. In all measurements, the results showed significantly reduced glucose metabolism in prefrontal areas in murderers, no matter which area of the frontal lobe was examined, indicating that they had less frontal lobe activity than the controls (Raine et al., 1994). The reduced brain activity in these murderers was very specific; it was found only in the frontal lobe and most specifically in the anterior or front region of the frontal lobe.

In most cases, these killers committed one homicide or attempted homicide and most were caught within hours or days of the offense. However, one killer had killed approximately 45 people before he was caught. This one individual showed a substantial level of frontal lobe activity (Raine et al., 1994). Frontal lobe damage can result in impulsivity, loss of self-control, irritability, violence, temper outbursts, and often results in poor organizational and planning skills (Golden et al., 1996). This would be consistent with a single murder, followed by a rapid arrest. The fact that the multiple murderer had good frontal lobe activity and was not caught for many years, whereas those murderers with poor frontal lobe activity were caught immediately, supports the role of the frontal lobe in cognitive thought processes such as careful planning and foresight.

All the offenders had been referred to the hospital in relation to their plea of not guilty by reason of insanity, so, as the authors point out, all were suspected of mental illness. Thus, it is difficult to know whether this study could be extended to other killers (Raine et al., 1994). As well, the controls, although certainly not murderers or criminals in any way, were not volunteers who received the PET as part of the experiment, but rather were patients who were referred for a PET scan, suggesting that they had some medical issue requiring assessment. However, the clear difference between the serial killer and the other killers suggests that different types of killers may show different results.

Raine et al. (1997) expanded their study to include 41 individuals in each group. The same result was obtained, with lower glucose metabolism in both lateral and medial prefrontal corticol areas. However, this study included a more detailed breakdown of the regions of the brain. This showed that the murderers had significantly lower brain activity in very specific regions of the brain. These included the prefrontal cortex, the superior lateral parietal gyrus, the left angular gyrus, and the corpus callosum (Raine et al., 1997). As well, they found less activity in the left hemisphere than in the right in the amygdala, hippocampus, thalamus, and medial temporal lobe (Raine et al., 1997). In the occipital region, higher glucose metabolism was seen in the murderers versus the controls. This study showed brain deficits in several regions of the brain, in particular the frontal lobe and the amygdala, both known to control behavior and emotion, as well as learning, memory, and attention (Raine et al., 1997).

This study also showed a distinct asymmetry between the two halves of the brain, which Raine suggests relates more to an early disturbance of brain development, either in the fetus or growing child, rather than a traumatic event later in life (Raine et al., 2004). This could also relate to early childhood stress because this has been shown to reduce normal development of the hippocampus (Andersen and Teicher, 2004; Teicher et al., 2003), and many offenders, and particularly psychopaths, have suffered from a severely abusive past (Raine et al., 2004).

In a further study, Raine et al. (1998a) used PET to study brain function in different types of murderers. They compared results from predatory murderers and impulsive murderers, and found that although both had abnormal PET scan results, the abnormalities were very different between the two groups. All individuals had pleaded not guilty by reason of insanity or were judged incompetent to stand trial. The controls were the same 41 controls as used by Raine et al. (1997).

What is particularly interesting here is that, although all the murderers showed some brain abnormalities, as compared with controls, the predatory murderers showed no significant abnormalities in the prefrontal cortex, although they did have excessive subcortical activity in the right hemisphere. Subcortical activity is related to aggression and violence, whereas frontal lobe activity is related to planning and foresight (Raine et al., 1998a). Therefore, it follows that predatory murderers would have good frontal lobe activity but would also have other brain abnormalities, whereas impulsive murderers, who were rapidly caught, had low frontal activity.

Both groups of murderers showed increased right hemisphere subcortical activity. This area of the brain is linked to negative mood, and the authors suggest that this excessive activity may contribute to an aggressive temperament in both types of killers (Raine et al., 1998a). However, the authors suggest that the reduced frontal lobe activity in the impulsive murderers resulted in little control over their impulses, while the predatory murderers were able to manage their aggressive behavior to fulfill their own needs (Raine et al., 1998a).

In an interesting follow-up study, Raine et al. (1998b) divided their group of impulsive murderers into those who had suffered psychosocial deprivation, such as child abuse and neglect, and those that had no such deprivation. Murderers who had undergone a relatively normal childhood had significantly lower prefrontal activity than those who had suffered from abuse or neglect in childhood (Raine et al., 1998b). This suggests that, in those individuals with both lower prefrontal activity and child abuse, it was the combination of these two factors that may have predisposed them to violence. The authors also suggested that in some killers, such as those without psychosocial deprivation, the brain abnormalities may be the stronger predisposition to violence than psychosocial issues (Raine et al., 1998b).

Wong et al. (1997) studied inmates in a maximum security mental hospital in England. In an earlier study, they had shown structural temporal changes in the most violent of inmates using CT (Wong et al., 1994). In the later study, Wong et al. (1997) considered violent repetitive and violent nonrepetitive schizophrenic and schizo-affected offenders using PET. They found that both groups showed low cortical activity in comparison with normal controls, but there was significantly lower metabolism or brain activity in the right anterior inferior temporal region among the nonrepetitive offenders.

In a study of perpetrators of domestic violence using PET, researchers found that some perpetrators of domestic violence showed lower metabolism in the right hypothalamus of the brain and a lesser correlation between cortical and sub-cortical brain structures (George et al., 2003). The authors believed that this was related to fear-induced aggression.

### Single Photon Emission Computed Tomography (SPECT)

Single photon emission computed tomography (SPECT) is used to study the regional cerebral blood flow (rCBF) as a measure of the metabolic rate of glucose in certain areas of the brain. Glucose is the only energy source utilized by the brain so measuring blood flow in different regions of the brain can be used to indicate levels of brain function.

SPECT can be used to produce a three-dimensional image of the rCBF, using gamma rays. The subject is injected with a gamma-emitting radio-pharmaceutical. Then a series of images are recorded by a gamma camera. The gamma camera revolves around the patient, recording images over a 360° rotation. The images are processed by a computer to produce the final three-dimensional image. The image can then be sliced in any plane.

This technique is not as precise as PET but it does not require a cyclotron, so it is easier and cheaper. There is also less exposure to radiation, although some is still required.

## Studies Using Single Photon Computed Emission Tomography

In a Swedish study of 21 persons convicted of impulsive violent crimes, the subjects were examined using both SPECT and MRI (Soderstrom et al., 2000). Eleven healthy subjects were used as controls. In 16 of the subjects, reduced activity was noted in the temporal and/or frontal lobes, although MRI showed no corresponding structural deficits. An increase in the rCBF in the parietal association cortices was also noted in the violent subjects. The results were not related to psychosis, medication, or substance abuse (Soderstrom et al., 2000).

In a later study, a new group of 32 violent offenders was assessed, using both SPECT and the Psychopathy Checklist-Revised (PCL-R) (Soderstrom et al., 2002). The PCL-R measures several aspects of psychopathy, including deceitful interpersonal style, affective unresponsiveness, and impulsive anti-social behavior (Cooke and Mitchie, 2001; Hare, 1991). All the offenders were incarcerated in the same facility and lived under the same conditions (Soderstrom et al., 2002). The authors found a strong relationship between reduced frontal and temporal lobe activity and high PCL-R scores, particularly in the areas of interpersonal features of psychopathy, such as callousness, domination seeking, affective unresponsiveness, and emotional detachment (Soderstrom et al., 2002). Two particular regions, the hippocampi and the head of the caudate nuclei, were most implicated (Soderstrom et al., 2002).

The results of this study, which combined brain function imaging with classic psychopathy measures, support previous structural brain imaging studies referred to earlier that implicated the frontal lobes (Raine, 1993) and the hippocampi (Laakso et al., 2001) in antisocial personality disorder and psychopathy, respectively.

An interesting case study suggested that, in at least this one case, some drinkers may be using alcohol in an effort to self-medicate their mental problems. In this case, a young man, who frequently became violent when drinking, was arrested during an armed robbery committed while the man was intoxicated (Amen, 1999). The author performed two SPECT exams on the man, one while sober and one after consuming the same quantity of alcohol as had been consumed on the night of the robbery. The scan performed when the individual was sober revealed hyperactivity in several regions of the brain, including areas of the frontal, parietal, and temporal lobes (Amen, 1999). When the individual was inebriated, the PET scan showed a reduction in abnormal activity in these regions, with only one region still exhibiting excess activity. However, although the hyperactivity was reduced, the alcohol resulted in reduced blood flow to both the temporal and frontal lobes (Amen, 1999). Reduced function in these areas can impair judgment and impulse control, and can increase the propensity for violence. The author concluded that the person may have been self-medicating an overactive brain, but in the process was increasing his level of violence (Amen, 1999).

## Conclusion

We have now looked at the results of many brain imaging studies (CT, MRI, fMRI, PET, SPECT). These have indicated that a variety of offenders show some structural and/or functional brain deficits or differences in comparison with non-offender populations. Most studies have related the temporal and frontal regions to deficits, which is not surprising because these areas are heavily involved with cognition, memory, learning, and emotion. The studies do not all agree, and some studies have found no differences, but the preponderance of studies that do show brain deficits in certain groups of offenders are in the majority.

Since first understanding that the brain controlled behavior, we have tried to link specific parts of the brain with specific actions. However, the brain is much more complicated than that, and each part of the brain affects many aspects of behavior. What is clear is that we are dramatically gaining an understanding of normal and abnormal brain functions. Brain imaging techniques that were thought miraculous just a few years ago are now becoming obsolete, with newer and more specific techniques emerging. It is probable that this is a research area that will provide many answers about biology and criminal behavior in a very short time.

At the moment, the studies are interesting. Most studies, by necessity, had a small sample size and often studied very specific offenders. We are still a long way from being able to generalize such results to a larger population of offenders. Larger studies are needed to give a better idea of the impact of brain deficits. As well, there are few data on the general population to give us a baseline for normal brain function and structure. At the moment, any differences between a small experimental and a small control group is considered exciting. However, it is very possible that quite normal, at least noncriminal, people do exhibit some type of brain deficit. It is certainly true that many people receive a variety of brain injuries, from mild to severe; and although they may exhibit behavioral differences, they certainly do not turn to crime or violence. Why, then, do some people with such damage become criminals? There is a lot we still do not understand, and we certainly cannot suppose that just because a person sustains a particular type of injury, he or she will develop a specific type of anti-social behavior.

There are many legal and ethical considerations related to brain injury. As discussed in Chapter 9, many incarcerated offenders, including the majority of death-row inmates in certain studies, have suffered from severe head injury that predated the offense. So the question becomes: what do we do with this information? Brain injury, like all other biological issues, does not cause a person to commit a crime. As with hormones or neurotransmitters, a brain injury or deficit may predispose a person to a behavior or condition that is more likely to result in a crime, such as a lack of remorse, or an increase in impulsivity.

Did the head injury relate to the offense? Should it be taken into account at trial? Should it be taken into account in sentencing and post-conviction? It is difficult to answer the first question. The brain injury did not cause the person to commit the offense, but it may have played a role in the person's behavior, which increased his/her propensity to commit the crime. This, however, is not a defense, just as being poor is not a defense for theft. The primary legal question would be whether the person did, at the time of the offense, understand that the behavior was wrong, because of a mental impairment. Even if brain imaging could indicate such a deficiency, it, like other analyses, cannot determine whether the person was not competent *at the time of the offense*.

If taken into account, it is likely that brain imaging assessment prior to trial would be valuable in determining whether a person is competent to stand trial or whether a plea of not guilty by reason of mental disorder should be entered.

Certainly, it would be valuable to assess offenders for brain damage when determining possible treatment options. Many problems related to brain injury can at least be ameliorated with appropriate treatment and routine. Therefore, offenders should be placed in appropriate facilities where they can receive treatment to alleviate their problems and prepare for a less confrontational life when they are released. Unfortunately, many incarcerated offenders are never assessed or treated for brain trauma, despite the fact that many studies have shown the high prevalence of such injuries in prison populations.

It is hoped that this is an area that will continue to be investigated by neurologists and biologists, but also that more criminologists and members of the criminal justice system, as well as the medical community, will begin to take more notice of such studies and to apply them. More in-depth medical follow-up of head trauma, in even mild cases, may help to ameliorate some of the side effects of brain trauma. As well, a better understanding of brain trauma in the criminal justice system may help in placing offenders in facilities where they can receive assistance.

## Questions for Further Study and Discussion

1. What are the limits of CT scans for studying criminogenic behavior?
2. Can we accept CT and MRI scan studies without reservation? What experimental design problems can you find in them?
3. Do the changes in brain structure and function due to child abuse or environmental deficits have an evolutionary advantage?
4. What legal implications can you find linked to these brain dysfunction studies? Do you think the courts will eventually have to recognize them?

## References

Amen, D.G. (1999). Regional cerebral blood flow in alcohol-induced violence, a case study. *J. Psychoactive Drugs,* 31(4), 389–393.

Andersen, S.L. and Teicher, M.H. (2004). Delayed effects of early childhood stress on hippocampal development. *Neuropsychopharmocology,* 29(11), 1988–1993.

Andrews, T.K., Rose, F.D., and Johnson, D.A. (1998). Social and behavioral effects of traumatic brain injury in children. *Brain Injury,* 12(2), 133–138.

Beauregard, M., Levesque, J., and Bourgouin, P. (2001). Neural correlates of conscious self-regulation of emotion. *J. Neurosci.,* 21, 1–6.

Berrebi, A.S., Fitch, R.H., Ralphe, D.L., Denenberg, J.O., Friedrich, V.L., and Denenberg, V.H. (1988). Corpus callosum, region-specific effects of sex, early experience and age. *Brain Res.,* 438(1), 216–224.

Blake, P.Y., Pincus, J.H., and Buckner, C. (1995). Neurologic abnormalities in murderers. *Neurology,* 45, 1641–1647.

Cooke, D.J. and Mitchie, C. (2001). Refining the construct of psychopathy, towards a hierarchial model. *Psychol. Assessment,* 13, 171–188.

Eher, R., Aigner, M., Wagner, E., and Gutierrez, K. (1996). Magnetic resonance tomography of the brain in 21 sex offenders. *European Psych.,* 11(4), 284.

George, D.T., Rawlings, R., Williams, W.A., Philips, M.J., Fong, G., Kerich, M., Momenan, R., Umhau, J.C., and Hommer, D. (2003). A select group of perpetrators of domestic violence, evidence of decreased metabolism in the right hypothalamus and reduced relationship between cortical/subcortical brain structures in positron emission tomography. *Psych. Res. Neuroimaging Section,* 130(1), 11–25.

Golden, C.J., Jackson, M.L., and Peterson, R.A. (1996). Neuropsychological correlates of violence and aggression. A review of the clinical literature. *Aggression Violent Behav.,* 1(1), 3–25.

Hare, R.D. (1991). *Manual for the Hare Psychopathy Checklist-Revised.* Toronto: Multi-Health Systems.

Herzberg, J.L. and Fenwick, P.B.C. (1988). The aetiology of aggression in temporal lobe epilepsy. *Br. J. Psychiatry*, 153, 50–55.

Hucker, S., Langevin, R., Wortzman, G., Bain, J., Handy, L.M., Chambers, J., and Wright, S. (1986). Neuropsychological impairment in pedophiles. *Can. J. Behav. Sci.*, 18, 440–448.

Hucker, S., Langevin, R., Wortzman, G., Dickey, R., Bain, J., Handy, L.M., Chambers, J., and Wright, S. (1988). Cerebral damage and dysfunction in sexually aggressive men. *Ann. Sex Res.*, 1, 33–47.

Kiehl, K.A., Smith, A.M., and Hare, R.D. (2001). Limbic abnormalities in affective processing by criminal psychopaths as revealed by functional magnetic resonance imaging. *Biol. Psychiatry*, 50(9), 677–684.

Laakso, M.P., Vaurio, O., Koivisto, L., Savolainen, M., Eronen, H.J., Aronen, P., Hakola, E., Repo, H., Soininen, H., and Tiihonen, J. (2001). Psychopathy and the posterior hippocampus. *Behav. Brain Res.*, 118(2), 187–193.

Laakso, M.P., Vaurio, O., Savolainen, M., Repo, H., Soininen, H., Aronen, P., and Tiihonen, J. (2000). A volumetric MRI study of the hippocampus in type 1 and type 2 alcoholism. *Behav. Brain Res.*, 109, 177–186.

Langevin, R., Ben-Aron, M., Wortzman, G., Dickey, R., and Handy, L. (1987). Brain damage, diagnosis, and substance abuse among violent offenders. *Behav. Sci. Law*, 5, 77–94.

Langevin, R., Wortzman, G., Wright, P., and Handy, L. (1989a). Studies of brain damage and dysfunction in sex offenders. *Ann. Sex Res.*, 2, 163–179.

Langevin, R., Lang, R.A., Wortzman, G., Frenzel, R.R., and Wright, P. (1989b). An examination of brain damage and dysfunction in genital exhibitionists. *Ann. Sex Res.*, 2, 77–94.

Langevin, R., Wortzman, G., Wright, P., and Handy, L. (1988). Neuropsychological impairment in incest offenders. *Ann. Sex Res.*, 1, 401–415.

Posse, S. Muller-Gartner, H.W., and Dager, S.R. (1996). Functional magnetic resonance studies of brain activation. *Sem. Clin. Neuropsychiatry*, 1, 76–88.

Raine, A. (1993). *The Psychopathology of Crime. Criminal Behavior as a Clinical Disorder* (pp. 129–155). San Diego: Academic Press.

Raine, A., Buchsbaum, M.S., and LaCasse, L. (1997). Brain abnormalities in murderers indicated by positron emission tomography. *Biol. Psychiatry*, 42, 495–508.

Raine, A., Buchsbaum, M.S., Stanley, J., Lottenberg, S., Abel, L., and Stoddard, J. (1994). Selective reductions in pre-frontal glucose metabolism in murders assessed with positron emission tomography. *Biol. Psychiatry*, 36, 365–373.

Raine, A., Ishikawa, S.S., Arce, E., Lencz, T., Knuth, K.H., Bihrle, S., LaCasse, L., and Colleti, P. (2004). Hippocampal structural asymmetry in unsuccessful psychopaths. *Biol. Psychiatry*, 55, 185–191.

Raine, A., Lencz, T., Taylor, K., Hellige, J.B., Bihrle, S., Lacasse, L., Lee, M., Ishikawa, S.S., and Colleti, P. (2003). Corpus callosum abnormalities in psychopathic antisocial individuals. *Arch. Gen. Psychiatry*, 60(11), 1134–1142.

Raine, A., Meloy, J.R., Bihrle, S., Stoddard, J., LaCasse, L., and Buchsbaum, M.S. (1998a). Reduced prefrontal and increased subcortical brain functioning assessed using positron emission tomography in predatory and affective murderers. *Behav. Sci. Law*, 16, 319–332.

Raine, A., Phil, D., Stoddard, J., Bihrle, S., and Buchsbaum, M.S. (1998b). Prefrontal glucose deficits in murderers lacking psychosocial deprivation. *Neuropsychiatry, Neuropsychol Behav. Neurol.*, 11(1), 1–7.

Soderstrom, H., Hultin, L., Tullberg, M., Wikkelo, C., Ekhom S., and Forsman, A. (2002). Reduced frontotemporal perfusion in psychopathic personality. *Psych. Res. Neuroimaging*, 114(2), 81–94.

Soderstrom, H., Tullberg, M., Wikkelo, C., Ekhom, S., and Forsman, A. (2000). Reduced cerebral blood flow in non-psychotic violent offenders. *Psych. Res. Neuroimaging Section*, 98, 29–41.

Teicher, M.H., Andersen, S.L., Polcari, A., Anderson, C.M., Navalta, C.P., and Kim, D.M. (2003). The neurobiological consequences of early stress and childhood maltreatment. *Neurosci. Biobehav. Res.*, 27, 33–44.

Teicher, M.H., Dumont, N.L., Ito, Y., Vaituzis, C., Gledd, J.N., and Andersen, S.L. (2004). Childhood neglect is associated with reduced corpus callosum. *Biol. Psychiatry*, 56, 80–85.

Teichner, G., Golden, C.J., Van Hasselt, V.B., and Peterson, A. (2001). Assessment of cognitive functioning in men who batter, *Int. J. Neurosci.*, 11, 241–253.

Woermann, F.G., van Elst, L.T., Koepp, M.J., Free, S.L., Thompson, P.J., Trimble, M.R., and Duncan, J.S. (2000). Reduction of frontal neocortical grey matter associated with affective aggression in patients with temporal lobe epilepsy, an objective voxel analysis of automatically segmented MRI. *J. Neurology, Neurosurgery, Psych.*, 68(2), 162–169.

Wong, M., Fenwick, P.B.C., Lumsden, J., Fenton, G.W., Maisey, M.N., Lewis, P., and Badawi, R. (1997). Positron emission tomography in male violent offenders with schizophrenia. *Psychiatry Res. Neuroimaging Section*, 68, 111–123.

Wong, M., Lumsden, J., Fenton, G.W., and Fenwick, P.B.C. (1994). Electroencephalography, computed tomography band violence ratings of male patients in a maximum security mental hospital — clinical and neuroimaging findings. *Med. Sci. Law*, 37, 150–160.

Wright, P., Nobrega, J., Langevin, R., and Wortzman, G. (1990). Brain density and symmetry in pedophilic and sexually aggressive offenders. *Ann. Sex Res.*, 3(3), 319–328.

# Diet, Toxins, and Food Additives

# 11

## Introduction

Chemical imbalances in the body have already been shown to influence behavior. Such imbalances are also and frequently the result of bad diet and can sometimes be rectified by correcting that diet. This chapter, therefore, will consider the effect of diet on behavior and on criminal behavior. Types of food, the body's ways of processing it, and sensitivities to food additives vary widely from person to person. Many people are allergic to some dietary components, and this alone can affect behavior. This variation between people is often biologically based, although the trigger, the food, is environmental. The objectives of this chapter are to consider various dietary components and to examine their effect on the body and subsequent behavior, with a view to finding if there are effects of diet on criminogenic behavior.

## Hypoglycemia (Low Blood Sugar)

One of the most researched areas that involves diet, as well as the body's ability to process that diet, is that of blood sugar levels. There have been many studies that link low blood sugar, or hypoglycemia, to violent or aggressive behavior (Raine, 1993). The human brain's sole source of energy is glucose, and normal functioning requires a very high level of glucose per minute. Any drop in glucose to the brain reduces the brain's ability to function normally, resulting in panic, irritability, nervousness, and aggression (Raine, 1993). When a person is irritable, he/she is much more likely to act without good emotional control. Reactive hypoglycemia, the most common form of low

257

blood sugar, results in symptoms occurring 2 to 4 hours after a meal, and drugs and alcohol will intensify the effect (Raine, 1993).

Many studies on humans and animals (reviewed in Venables and Raine, 1987) support the hypothesis that hypoglycemia is linked to aggression. Depending on eating habits, many people appear to have a low in their blood sugar around 11:00 to 11:30 a.m., and several studies have found that in prisons, this time period corresponds with the majority of cases of inmate violence (Raine, 1993). This is very suggestive, although not causal. In normal life, this time period often coincides with a break that usually includes a hot beverage and a snack such as a cookie or muffin. Even when totally absorbed in whatever one is doing, a person often feels a need for such a break mid-morning. This is the body telling the person that sugar levels are getting low and a snack would increase the sugar levels. In noninstitutionalized populations, a person can usually take a snack break whenever he/she feels the need, but such activities are controlled in an institutionalized population.

There are many empirical studies that do show a clear relationship between low sugar levels and aggression, such as those on violent offenders with a history of alcohol abuse. These studies indicate that such people frequently suffer from reactive hypoglycemia (Raine, 1993). This is interesting, but again, the studies have shown no causal link. There is also the question of what is the originating cause of the hypoglycemia. It might be the prior link to crime. The hypoglycemia could, for example, be a symptom of something such as poor diet, and it is thus the poor diet that is affecting the brain's chemical balance. Or, alcohol or drug usage might be the first instigator of the crime, and both can also result in hypoglycemia. So, is the hypoglycemia the problem, or is the problem whatever underlies the hypoglycemia?

A standard criticism leveled at these studies is that there have been no experiments to prove that the person was hypoglycemic during the commission of a crime. Because a blood test is not possible at this moment and because blood sugar levels vary dramatically over a 24-hour period, it appears highly unlikely that it would ever be possible to obtain such data.

Some people are more prone to hypoglycemia than others, feeling faint or ill when they do not eat; others show little effect. Thus, the effect of hypoglycemia will vary from person to person. Hypoglycemia is very easily rectified by eating. If a link between hypoglycemia and aggression is ever conclusively proven, then the simple act of giving prisoners a snack mid-morning may decrease violence in prisons. In fact, there is a lot of somewhat anecdotal evidence that suggests that this works very well. Many prison wardens in the United States have heard about these data and have added a snack break mid-morning to a prisoner's day and it has had remarkable effects.

Assault rates have decreased dramatically. Now, of course, these are not scientific studies and no proper controls are used, but they have been effective enough that word got out, and quite a few prison authorities are trying it as there is no harm in offering a snack; the anecdotal results are very encouraging. Some texts recommend a specific type of diet for prisoners that includes low levels of sugar and frequent snacks (Schauss, 1981).

It is probable that any effects of low blood sugar are interrelated with a number of other factors that *have* been causally related to violence and crime, such as alcohol usage, serotonin levels, EEG, and low heart rates. These have all been linked to hypoglycemia, and are themselves linked to violent offending. There is clear biological evidence indicating that serotonin, for example, plays an important role in the regulation of glucose metabolism. The exact mechanism by which it affects blood sugar is unknown but serotonin and its precursors cause the release of insulin and this, in turn, controls blood sugar. This has been shown to occur through *in vitro* and *in vivo* studies.

It is then possible that diet certainly could influence antisocial behavior through the many chemical balances in the body that influence behavior and that are maintained by correct diet. Diets very high in refined carbohydrates (that is, sugars) often result in extreme fluctuations in blood glucose levels as well as hypoglycemia. People often assume that eating a large quantity of sugar in a short period of time should lead to HYPERglycemia (high blood sugar) rather than HYPOglycemia. The reason that such an intake of sugar actually lowers blood sugar is due to one of the many feedback mechanisms in the human body. High-sugar foods are absorbed very easily and quickly by the gut, which of course means that you get a large and very rapid increase in sugar (glucose) in the bloodstream — briefly. This is not normal or good for the body, so it immediately responds by secreting a very large amount of insulin to quickly reduce the high sugar level. When we eat a normal, balanced diet, including carbohydrates, the body secretes insulin to keep the sugar levels at the optimum level. But when extremely high levels of carbohydrates are ingested, the body overreacts and thus secretes too much insulin and reduces the blood sugar level too much, so that, overall, the blood sugar level actually decreases (Raine, 1993). A healthy diet with a normal carbohydrate level allows a person to maintain a regular supply of sugar in the body, which is needed for energy. Increasing fiber, which slows down digestion, also helps to prevent sudden highs and, more importantly, sudden lows in blood sugar levels (Raine, 1993).

Biologically, it seems sound that hypoglycemia can lead to antisocial behavior because the brain is the organ that controls all human thought and all voluntary behavior, and the brain uses nearly 25% of all the available sugar in the body. Sugar, in the form of glucose, is the brain's only energy source, so anything that has an impact on sugar levels in the bloodstream will impact the brain and therefore affect the way the brain functions and ultimately affect behavior. For example, low sugar levels in the brain can result in symptoms that look just like chronic drunkenness (Raine, 1993).

There have been several studies claiming that changing the diet to reduce sugar levels has had dramatic positive results. In one study (Schoenthaler, 1983), the effects of a reduced sugar diet was studied over a 2-year period on incarcerated juvenile offenders aged 12 to 18 years. The study was conducted over a long time and was also double-blind, meaning that the researchers did not know which of the youths were getting the changed diet and which were still on the usual, high-sugar diet, until the end of the study. The researchers replaced soft drinks and junk food snacks with fruit juices and nutritious snacks, and eliminated high-sugar desserts and cereals. They found that this reduced antisocial behavior in the incarcerated juveniles by 48%. The percentage of well-behaved juveniles increased 71% and the percentage of chronic offenders decreased 56% (Schoenthaler, 1983). Of course, there are still problems with the study. One is the question of what else might have made the difference. Could there have been some other difference between the two groups? Also, can this be generalized to other settings? Even if the new diet reduced the recidivism rate *inside* the institution, will it also reduce it *outside*?

In another study, researchers found that even 1 month on a reduced sugar diet resulted in major improvements in paranoia and depression in male adult prisoners who were prone to hypoglycemia, in comparison with non-hypoglycemics and controls with no dietary changes (Fishbein and Thatcher, 1982). A large-scale study of more than 8000 juvenile inmates in 12 correctional institutions found that the youths exhibited 47% less antisocial behavior after their diet was changed by replacing high-fat and high-sugar foods with fruits, vegetables, and whole grains (Wolfgang et al., 1972). Most of these studies, however, have few, if any, true controls, so it is possible that other variables were the cause(s) of the change.

Although many criticisms have been leveled at such studies (Raine, 1993; Gray, 1986), thus making conclusions difficult to draw at the moment, the results are suggestive. Changing a person's diet from an unhealthy one, full of junk food high in refined carbohydrates, to a more balanced diet including high fiber, fruits, and vegetables, is unlikely to do any harm. Institutionalized populations that depend entirely on that institution for nutrition may particularly benefit. If inmates learn to like a good, healthy diet and can plan for it, the effects may last beyond incarceration.

As with almost all things that affect human biology, diet does not act in a vacuum. Researchers have shown that hyperactive children show a much better response to a change in diet when it is accompanied by a supportive and stable home environment (Rumsey and Rapoport, 1983). This again underlines the important protective value of a supportive, functioning environment and family. It also underscores the interactions involved; so clearly, diet and hypoglycemia should not be studied alone without considering all other factors (Raine, 1993).

## Glucose and Serotonin

We know that serotonin has been linked with aggression and impulsivity, and we also know that serotonin levels are affected by diet, so it follows that diet changes will impact serotonin levels and hence may impact behavior through serotonin levels. A large-scale study looked at the relationship between glucose metabolism, brain serotonin levels, and alcohol in a large sample of offenders in a psychiatric hospital in Finland (Virkkunen et al., 1994a). The control group was an age- and sex-matched group of healthy volunteers who also stayed as in-patients in the same psychiatric ward during the experiment. The glucose study was part of a very large research design that included many other themes (Virkkunen et al., 1996a), but this part of the study focused on violent, alcoholic offenders and impulsive fire-setters (Virkkunen and Linnoila, 1996). These people spent an average of 1 month on the psychiatric ward after being ordered there for psychiatric examination by their trial judges. They wore physical activity monitors on their wrists, which measured movement. They had lumbar punctures to test for levels of serotonin and were then tested by giving them either oral glucose or aspartame (a sugar substitute) in a double-blind system (so neither the experimenters nor the offenders knew what they had taken). Then they tested their blood (Virkkunen and Linnoila, 1996). Healthy volunteers with no history of drug or alcohol abuse or mental disorder were recruited by advertising and were paid for their participation. They stayed in the ward and were lumbar punctured, then wore the wrist motion monitors and also underwent a double-blind test of glucose or aspartame, then blood tests.

The researchers first found that the levels of serotonin (as measured by serotonin metabolites) were significantly lower among alcoholic, impulsive offenders versus alcoholic, nonimpulsive offenders (Virkkunen et al., 1996b, 1995, 1994a). The alcoholic, nonimpulsive offenders had significantly higher levels of serotonin than the controls. Among the alcoholic, impulsive offenders, those with antisocial personality and those with intermittent explosive disorder had similar average serotonin metabolite levels. Of the alcoholic, violent offenders, 25 had attempted suicide. Those who attempted suicide had lower mean serotonin metabolite levels than those who had not attempted suicide (Virkkunen and Linnoila, 1996). This, of course, is one of those things that has been reported several times before: that lower serotonin levels are observed in those who have attempted to kill themselves. These researchers have now found a difference in the tryptophan hydroxylase gene in those people who have lower serotonin levels and have attempted suicide (Nielsen et al., 1998; Virkkunen et al., 1996a). Remember that tryptophan is the precursor for serotonin, so a change in the tryptophan hydroxylase gene is going to impact how tryptophan is converted to serotonin and thus will change serotonin levels. This confirms that, at least in the suicide attempters studied by Virkkunen et al., these people have lower serotonin levels, and now we have a genetic reason for those lower levels. However, just as people kill for many different reasons, no doubt they also attempt/commit suicide for many reasons, so this may only apply to certain types of suicide attempters.

In normal people, serotonin levels fluctuate over the year, varying somewhat with the seasons. However, in previous studies, these workers had found that alcoholics did not show the same seasonal fluctuations. This was again confirmed in this study (Virkkunen and Linnoila, 1996). They also found that the alcoholic, impulsive offenders with intermittent explosive disorder had significantly lower mean blood glucose levels when given glucose, than did the healthy volunteers. There was no difference when the offenders just took the placebo of aspartame (Virkkunen and Linnoila, 1996). In another study by this group, a relationship was found between hypoglycemia and low serotonin levels. They found that when they measured both blood sugar and serotonin levels, they were able to predict which of their studied subjects were repeat, alcohol-abusing, violent offenders and impulsive fire-setters in 84.2% of cases (Virkkunen et al., 1989).

As an interesting aside, it was also noticed in the Finnish study that there were differences in physical activity levels between the groups (Virkkunen et al., 1994). Those alcoholics with antisocial personality disorder had much greater day and night-time activity than did the healthy volunteers. However, alcoholic, impulsive offenders with intermittent explosive disorder had the exact same activity patterns day and night (Virkkunen et al., 1994b). So in other words, alcoholic, impulsive offenders with intermittent explosive disorder show a major diurnal (day/night) disturbance to the normal rhythm or daytime activity and night-time inactivity. In rats, studies have shown that serotonin is important in training the brain to develop its daily activity patterns, based on light (Virkkunen and Linnoila, 1996). Thus, the brain is active when it is light and goes to sleep when it is dark. We know that serotonin has a role in sleep patterns and moods in people, so if it is also true that serotonin has an impact on training the brain to develop good activity patterns in people, then disturbed sleep might be related to low serotonin levels (Virkkunen and Linnoila, 1996). We all know that we get grumpy and irritable if we have a disturbed night's sleep, so this may just exacerbate any other problems.

However, the study also noted that about half of the alcoholic, impulsive offenders with antisocial personality disorder showed a difference between their night- and day-time activity patterns, despite the fact that they too had equally low serotonin levels (Virkkunen and Linnoila, 1996). On the other hand, compared with healthy volunteers, they still showed much higher night-time activity. The authors felt that this might be linked to a history of attention deficit disorder (ADD) and attention deficit hyperactivity disorder (ADHD), which is present in many alcoholic offenders with antisocial personality disorder because ADD and ADHD have been reported to be associated with increased diurnal physical activity (Virkkunen and Linnoila, 1996).

In this study, the researchers also checked testosterone levels and found that alcoholic, impulsive offenders with antisocial personality disorder had high mean CSF testosterone concentrations compared with the healthy volunteers (Virkkunen and Linnoila, 1996). The authors concluded that in their sample, a low CSF serotonin concentration was primarily associated with impulsivity and that high CSF testosterone concentration was associated with aggressiveness or interpersonal violence.

So, glucose levels have been linked with aggression, but are obviously interrelated with serotonin levels and alcoholism, and the full relationship among all of these is still not fully understood. Also, as discussed in a previous chapter, low serotonin levels imply many other imbalances, and the same is true of alcoholism and glucose metabolism.

## Dietary Tryptophan and Serotonin

It has already been clearly and repeatedly shown that there is a link between low serotonin levels and aggression (Coccaro, 1989). Low serotonin levels can be caused by many things, but for serotonin to be produced, the precursor must be present in good quantities. The precursor to serotonin is tryptophan, which is derived solely from the diet; thus, a diet low in tryptophan will result in a low-serotonin individual, even if that person has no other biological predisposition for low serotonin. An increase in dietary tryptophan could reverse the low serotonin levels.

In one human study, a significant increase in aggression was noted in normally healthy males after they consumed a tryptophan-free amino acid mixture and during a period where the subjects were on a low tryptophan diet (Moeller et al., 1996). CSF serotonin levels were not monitored but the results suggest that the increased aggression resulted from low serotonin levels.

In another study, tryptophan was used to treat psychiatric patients in a double-blind, placebo-controlled study (Volavka et al., 1990). The researchers treated patients either with tryptophan or a placebo, and repeatedly tested for tryptophan and other amino acids in the blood. There was a significant increase in tryptophan ratios in patients treated with tryptophan, as would be expected because they were being supplemented. Although the tryptophan treatment did not affect the number of violent incidents, the researchers felt that it did have an impact on violence because the need for injections of anti-psychotics and sedatives was reduced in the treated patients. The study thus provided indirect support for beneficial effects of tryptophan (Volavka et al., 1990).

In animal studies, rats fed diets low in tryptophan became more aggressive toward mice than controls (Fuller, 1996). Also, research on vervet monkeys found that tryptophan-free diets increased aggression in males, while high-tryptophan food reduced aggression in both males and females. Other studies have shown that using drugs such as fluoxetine, which increases uptake of tryptophan, decreases aggressive behavior in humans and animals (Fuller, 1996).

## Diet and Hormonal Changes

Diet can impact other body systems such as hormone production. Soy proteins are frequently substituted for other foods because they are considered healthy, and lactose-intolerant children are often fed soy milk. However, although soy may be beneficial in some quantities, some research has suggested that too much soy can influence behavior. Animal studies on male monkeys compared animals fed a soy-free diet with those fed a soy diet containing low levels of soy isoflavones, and those fed a soy diet high in soy isoflavones (Simon et al., 2004). Soy isoflavones are phytochemicals that are present in very high levels in soy. These isoflavones bind to estrogen receptors and thus mimic some of the effects of estrogen (Simon et al., 2004). The monkeys were fed the diet for 15 months and then assessed behaviorally. The monkeys fed the high soy diet exhibited markedly different behavior from the other two groups. Rates of aggression in this group increased by 67%; and rates of submission, in response to other aggression, increased by 203%. As well, monkeys fed the high soy diet were much less social than other monkeys, spending 68% less time in direct physical contact with the troop, and 50% less time in close proximity, spending 30% more time alone (Simon et al., 2004). The levels of isoflavones in the high soy diet were comparable to those found in many food supplements sold for human consumption. The authors believe that the high levels of isoflavones altered the male monkey's behavior by reducing the effects of one form of estrogen receptor, which in turn normally modulates a second receptor. This not only impacts hormonal levels, but also neurotransmitter levels, as this estrogen receptor indirectly relates to reduced serotonin function (Simon et al., 2004). Interestingly, despite the dramatic behavior changes, no effects could be seen on measured hormonal levels in the animals, suggesting that these changes may be very difficult to detect, and can impact behavior before other changes can be identified. The authors cautioned that a careful balance between benefit and side effects must be determined (Simon et al., 2004).

In another animal study, male hamsters fed a diet high in phytoestrogens reacted significantly more aggressively to a nonthreatening intruder than those fed a diet free of phytoestrogens (Moore et al., 2004). The testosterone levels were also higher in the experimental group. When the test was repeated on juvenile male hamsters, there was no significant difference between the two in aggression, but the experimental group still exhibited higher testosterone levels. Animals in both groups were sacrificed, and necropsy examination indicated a change in binding for vasopressin 1A receptors in both adult and juvenile male hamsters fed the phytoestrogens, indicating that the phytoestrogens resulted in aggressive behavior as well as changes in hormone levels and in the brain (Moore et al., 2004).

The human diet often contains things that are not intended to be ingested, but happen to be associated with our food. Studies on mice in Wisconsin have shown that common levels of insecticides, herbicides, and fertilizers in American groundwater can, in combination, affect mice behavior, immune system function, and hormone levels (Porter et al., 1999). The authors focused on the insecticide aldicarb, the herbicide atrazine, and nitrate, which is a chemical fertilizer. Exposure to the mixture had a much greater effect than each chemical alone, and increased aggression in the mice as well as altered their thyroid levels. These findings suggest that further study is required and that greater testing should be performed on such chemicals in combination, to determine safe levels (Porter et al., 1999). Aldicarb and atrizine are still widely used in the United States, but aldicarb was withdrawn from the Canadian market in 1996, and atrizine use was highly reduced. However, many chemicals can persist in the ground; and in tests in Wisconsin, aldicarb has been found 9 years after the last application.

## Influence of Lead as a Neurotoxin

There are many dangerous neurotoxins or nerve/brain poisons in the environment that often end up in food. Many of these neurotoxins are heavy metals and they can have major effects on the brain. Some researchers even believe that this may explain regional and geographical differences between crime rates (Stretesky and Lynch, 2001). The main neurotoxins include lead, cadmium, and manganese. In several studies, prison inmates have been found to have very high levels of all or any of these metals, and in two studies, lithium (which helps detoxify manganese) was very low. This might also explain why using lithium as a treatment can reduce aggression. There also seems to be a link with high heavy metals and alcoholism (Masters et al., 1998).

One of the most common neurotoxins is lead. Lead is a metallic neurotoxin and exposure to certain levels can cause brain damage (Nihei et al., 2000; Raine, 1993). Lead absorption lowers IQ and also disrupts cognitive development and social behavior (Nihei et al., 2000; Raine, 1993). One of the ways that lead may cause damage is by inhibiting brain receptors. Research in rats has shown that lead inhibits the NMDA receptors in the brain of rats, which are very important in learning and memory formation (Nihei et al., 2000). The NMDA receptors are triggered when they receive two incoming signals such as the visual sight of rain, together with the sensation of wet, which then initiate chemical changes in the brain that lead to forming a memory (Nihei et al., 2000). The authors believe that the mechanism of inhibition is related to reducing the entry of calcium into the nerve cell, which is extremely important because calcium is crucial in neuron function and in propagating a signal to the next neuron (Nihei et al., 2000).

We obtain lead from the air we breathe and the food we eat — it is everywhere. It has long been known that lead is bad for us, so we, as a society, have tried to reduce lead levels by banning lead in gasoline and in paint. Exposure to lead can cause brain damage, so it could, possibly, predispose humans to violence and crime. Most people feel that lead is no longer a problem in our society because we have removed many lead sources, such as leaded gasoline. However, lead levels are still very high throughout our environment. For example, drinking water was tested in the United States in 1992, and some cities were found to have greater than 14 times the recommended levels of lead in their drinking water alone (Raine, 1993). And that is not counting all the other ways that lead can enter the food chain, such as through food, air, and soil. As well, although gasoline no longer contains lead, there are still additives to gasoline that do contain lead. Such additives were banned in Canada some years ago but remain available in other countries. Today's paint no longer contains lead but much of the world is painted with older paint, meaning that the lead can still leach into the environment. An estimated 3 to 4 million American preschool children have blood lead levels above 10 micrograms/100mL, which is now known to be associated with subclinical neurologic impairment. As many as 68% of poor, minority children in U.S. inner cities may have unsafe lead levels (Landrigan and Todd, 1994).

There have been numerous studies that have shown that high lead levels in the environment of children are related to cognitive, learning, and attentional deficits, and that even relatively low lead levels can cause measurable deficits (Tuthill, 1996; Needleman et al., 1990). One study by Denno (1990) found that lead poisoning was the strongest predictor of disciplinary problems in school, which in turn were the strongest predictor of arrests between the ages of 7 and 22 years. Another study, of 501 boys in Edinburgh, Scotland, found that blood lead levels correlated strongly with measures of psychological deviance (Fulton et al., 1987).

Prolonged exposure to lead has been linked to the development of ADHD and ADD (Rice, 2000; Needleman et al., 1996; Landrigan and Todd, 1994). Studies have shown that even low lead levels that would not lead to medical attention, or recognition of sickness, can still lead to significant impairment in cognitive variables such as IQ and reaction times.

In one study, Needleman et al. (1996) followed 212 boys in the Pittsburgh public schools from age 7 through 11 years. None of the children had any obvious observable signs of lead toxicity, so they all seemed the same and any lead exposure was subclinical. The researchers calculated the boys' bone lead concentrations using a technique called K x-ray fluorescence, which measures cumulative exposure to lead. The study was conducted over 4 years, and during this time, teachers and parents periodically filled out questionnaires evaluating the children for aggression, delinquency, and other behavioral problems. In addition, the boys themselves were asked to report whether or not they had engaged in any antisocial behavior. So the study included both self-report and external evaluations of aggression.

Only a slight association between lead levels and behavior was seen at age 7. But by age 11, the children with elevated lead levels were judged by both parents and teachers to be more aggressive, have higher delinquent scores, and have more medical complaints than their low-lead counterparts, and the children themselves reported lead-related increases in antisocial acts (Needleman et al., 1996). Other problems associated with high lead levels included anxiety, depression, social problems, attention deficits, and somatic complaints (Needleman et al., 1996). Needleman and co-workers say that their findings agree with clinical observations linking lead poisoning to disturbed behavior, but their study extends the relationship to children who do not show any symptoms of high lead levels, but clearly are still affected.

The researchers also controlled for the effects of maternal intelligence, socioeconomic status, and quality of child rearing (Needleman et al., 1996). The researchers concluded that lead exposure is associated with increased risk for antisocial and delinquent behavior. They felt that if the study was representative of youth in the United States, then lead exposure could make a major contribution to delinquency. This is considered the first rigorous study to demonstrate a significant association between lead and antisocial behavior, although other studies have also shown the relationship (Raine, 1993). In a follow-up study, lead levels measured at age 7 years were found to predict both juvenile and adult crime. Also, high lead children were 7 times more likely to fail to graduate from high school than low lead children (Needleman et al., 1990). In Britain, researchers found significant relationships between lead levels assessed from blood in a large sample of over 500 children aged 6 to 9 years and teacher and parent ratings of aggressive and antisocial behavior (Thomson et al., 1989).

In another study, Tuthill (1996) found that even very slightly elevated lead levels were linked to attention deficit disorder, which in itself is a strong risk factor for criminal behavior. Tuthill analyzed lead levels in the hair of 277 first-graders from eight Massachusetts schools, and found a striking dose-response relationship between hair lead levels and symptoms of attention deficit disorder as reported by teachers. This relationship remained strong, he says, even after age, ethnicity, gender, and socioeconomic status were taken into account. An even stronger relationship existed between physician-diagnosed attention-deficit hyperactivity disorder and hair lead in the same children. Tuthill also found that there was no apparent "safe" threshold for lead, as even low exposure increased the likelihood of attention deficits. This is particularly disturbing considering the number of people who have mildly raised lead levels. This study also linked arsenic, mercury, cadmium, and aluminum concentrations in the hair of 80 elementary school children to teacher ratings of behavior (Tuthill, 1996). These metals were significantly related to acting-out behavior in the children; lead was the strongest individual predictor, while cadmium also interacted with lead in predicting acting-out behavior. Cadmium is also known to have effects on cognitive ability.

A large-scale, prospective study of a group of 195 children who were followed from pre-birth to adolescence showed a strong correlation between lead levels and delinquency (Dietrich et al., 2001). Maternal lead levels were measured during pregnancy, and then the children's lead levels were measured every 3 months until age 6 years. The children were then reassessed as teenagers. Adolescents with the highest lead levels at age 6 years reported an average of 4.5 times as many delinquent acts in the previous year as those with the lowest lead levels. The majority of the children were African-American and were equally divided between boys and girls. Exposure to lead correlated with antisocial behavior, even when other factors, such as socioeconomic status, parental IQ, birth weight, and quality of home environment were controlled for (Dietrich et al., 2001).

Although much lead is obviously ingested with food, some work has shown that dietary type can affect lead uptake. A study on inner-city pre-school children found a significant association between lead levels in the blood and both dietary fat and total calories, although researchers did not see an association with protein or carbohydrate intake levels (Lucas et al., 1996). The researchers felt that the lead/fat connection might stem from the role of bile (Lucas et al., 1996). The presence of bile, which is secreted when the body digests fats, results in an increased absorption of lead from the gastrointestinal tract. So the researchers postulated that a high fat diet might mean an increased level of lead absorption from the food. As many foods are slightly contaminated with lead, increased food intake may naturally result in increased lead intake. A poor diet is often one that is higher in fats, so this would suggest that those in a low socioeconomic bracket might be more likely to be affected by lead levels than others.

In a study that compared 194 convicted juvenile offenders with 146 control adolescents from high schools, bone lead levels were found considerably higher in the offender group in both Caucasians and African-Americans (Needleman et al., 2002). The offenders were four times more likely to have high lead levels. Of course, this study does not prove that the lead is causal, because there may be many other biological and environmental differences between the two groups that could result in both higher lead levels and higher offending rates. However, considering that lead has such a range of damaging effects on the brain and behavior, the study does suggest a relationship. These findings in children also appear to hold true in adult violent offenders. One recent study provides evidence that exposure to lead and cadmium is related to violent criminal behavior (Masters et al., 1998). These researchers examined levels of both lead and cadmium in the hair of 30 violent adult criminal offenders and 19 nonviolent psychiatrically disturbed controls. Violent offenders had significantly higher levels of lead and cadmium than the controls. A definite strength of this research was the use of controls who were nonviolent but still offenders, so the study looked at some type of specificity to violence (Masters et al., 1998).

Once more, the question arises of an interaction between environmental and biological causes. If there is a link between lead or other heavy metals and crime, is lead causing the problem, or do high lead levels tend to be found in those who are more socially disadvantaged, those coming from urban areas with high crime rates? Urban areas certainly have higher lead concentrations, and people in urban areas usually have higher levels of lead in their systems. As well, inner-city areas are the highest in lead. Is this yet another way that the poor in our communities are disadvantaged?

A recent study suggests an answer. It showed that high lead levels, although they correlate with homicide rates, are not just restricted to inner-city areas and that homicide rates correlate more with the lead levels than the urban areas (Stretesky and Lynch, 2001). Environmental Protection Agency data on air lead levels for 3111 counties in the 48 contiguous states were analyzed in relation to homicide rates (Stretesky and Lynch, 2001). The researchers controlled for factors such as county areas, percentage of county residents in the 16-to-29-year age range, poverty rates, educational levels, urbanization, county location, ethnic factors, and concentrations of other air pollutants (Stretesky and Lynch, 2001). They found that homicide levels were nearly 4 times higher in counties with maximum air lead concentrations than in the counties with the lowest levels. This is very exciting and, while the results do not prove a link, they are certainly suggestive. This is particularly interesting because the researchers controlled for whether the regions were urban or rural, so high homicide rates were not just related to inner cities but only to some inner cities with high lead pollution levels.

A classic case of the effects of lead poisoning can be found in the results of the ill-fated Franklin Expedition. The Franklin Expedition was intended to discover the Northwest Passage and set sail from England in 1845 (Beattie and Geiger, 1998). The ships were extremely well equipped for their time and contained one of the most modern inventions of the time, canned foods. Previous to the development of canning, long sea voyages were extremely difficult as food preservation techniques were very poor, with many sailors succumbing to diseases such as scurvy, caused by a deficiency in Vitamin C. Canning allowed large quantities of a variety of foods to be preserved for years. However, despite extensive planning, both ships disappeared and no one was ever seen alive again. Many searches were instigated but all that was ever found were the graves of three sailors who had died early on in the voyage and several cairns made of tin cans. The local people spoke of the last days of the sailors and told of acts of insanity, violence, and eventual cannibalism. Naturally, Victorian England refused to believe that such Englishmen could possibly have gone mad, and certainly no Englishman would ever, under any circumstances, eat another Englishman. So such rumors were ignored.

The true answers to the fate of the expedition were only discovered in the 1980s when Dr. Owen Beattie, a famous forensic anthropologist, conducted a research study on Beechy Island to exhume the only three bodies to be found (Beattie and Geiger, 1998). Beattie discovered enormously high levels of lead in all organs of the bodies. The source of the lead was found to be the canned food. The greatest pride of the expedition had been their undoing — the canned food. The lead solder used to seal the cans had leaked into the food. Some cans had simply exploded as the food rotted, but those that stayed sealed were very heavily laden with toxic layers of lead (Beattie and Geiger, 1998). It is suggested that the men died as a combination of starvation and lead poisoning. And with our understanding of lead poisoning and what it can do, especially at these extreme levels, it is entirely likely that the men became insane and, quite probably, did eat each other, Englishmen or not.

So lead solder brought down one of the greatest and most advanced expeditions of its time. A related question is what happened to the rest of the people in Europe who were just beginning to use cans and were quite convinced that it was the greatest invention ever made. However, buying canned goods was much too expensive for the average person, so it was the rich who could afford them. When we look back to the 1800s and 1900s, we are inclined to associate high crime rates and delinquency with the lower socioeconomic groups. But knowing what we know about lead and its effects on crime rates and delinquency, it would be interesting to note how many of those who ate canned food added to an increase in crime rates in comparison with the fresh (or even rotten) food eating people. Such a study might provide a whole new perspective on European crime rates of the time.

In light of these studies, Canada and other countries have initiated a proactive approach to reducing lead levels in the environment, indicating that the harmful effects of lead exposure are well recognized. Lead and other metals are easy to sample from hair, as hair stores all such toxins, and long hair has a perfect record of a person's exposure. This means that heavy metal levels can be easily detected in a noninvasive manner. Hair grows at about 2.5 cm (1 inch) per month, so a person with shoulder-length hair has at least a year's worth of data on their head, and long-haired people may have several years' worth of data.

## Manganese

Manganese (Mn) is another heavy metal implicated in criminogenic behavior. Manganese lowers the levels of serotonin and dopamine. These, of course, are the neurotransmitters associated with impulse control and planning functions. Even low exposure to manganese, if under stress, is related to loss of impulse control and outbursts of violent behavior (Masters et al., 1998). The mechanism of this is not well understood, but is thought to relate to altered levels of monoamine oxidase (MAO), another neurotransmitter, which has also been implicated in crime (Brunner, 1996). Severe exposure to manganese dust can result in a disease called "industrial manganism," which has symptoms similar to Parkinson's disease (Tran et al., 2002). Just like lead, manganese has subclinical effects on brain chemistry, causing learning disabilities, poor impulse control, and increased risk for aggressiveness (Masters et al., 1998).

There have been several reports to suggest that children with learning problems, attention deficits, and attention deficit hyperactivity disorder (ADHD) have elevated levels of manganese in their hair (Tran et al., 2002; Marlowe and Bliss, 1993). ADHD is one of the most commonly diagnosed childhood behavioral disorders, and several studies have linked ADHD with delinquency and adult crime (Eyestone and Howell, 1994; Moffitt, 1990; Zagar et al., 1989). Children with ADHD cannot sustain attention; are hyperactive and impulsive with a low frustration tolerance; and can have drastic, rapid mood swings. This frequently results in poor peer and familial relationships, academic failure, and low self esteem. It is probable that the link between delinquency and ADHD relates more to these "side effects" than to the disorder itself (Ward, 2000). Several genes that affect levels of the neurotransmitter dopamine have been implicated in the etiology of ADHD (Tannock 1998; Levy et al., 1997). Manganese is specifically toxic to the brain's dopamine systems so it is possible that higher manganese levels in ADHD children, as well as others with learning and attention deficits, is a reflection of this effect (Tran et al., 2002).

Manganese has a particularly severe effect on babies because their ability to detoxify and excrete it is very low (Tran et al., 2002). Breast milk is low in manganese, but it is much higher in baby formula, especially those that are soy based; and babies fed such formula may receive as much as 75 times as much manganese as breast-fed babies (Lönnerdal, 1994). In experiments on neonatal rats, high levels of dietary manganese resulted in damage to the dopamine system as well as behavioral deficits (Tran et al., 2002). In a concurrent study by the same authors, rats with the highest levels of manganese exposure had only 40% of the normal level of dopamine in the striatal structures of the brain, an area critical in problem solving and executive function tasks such as planning, impulse control, cognitive functioning, and goal-oriented behavior (Tran et al., 2002). Deficits in these regions are consistently seen in children with ADHD, as well as people with frontal lobe injury.

Manganese also interacts with other problems. For example, if the person has vitamin and mineral deficiencies, he/she will have problems in taking up calcium and will be more likely to retain manganese rather than excrete it. It has been shown that breast-fed babies have higher IQs than those who are bottle fed — this has been linked to the lower manganese in breast milk (Masters et al., 1998). Babies get high levels of manganese from baby formula, and it can even show up in other foods when crops absorb high levels from soil fertilizer.

A poor diet, which is low in essentials such as calcium and zinc, will result in an increased uptake of lead and manganese, so there is going to be a disproportionate effect on the people in the lower socioeconomic bracket. Also, in both cases, alcohol interacts with them to produce more physiological effects (Masters et al., 1998).

## Heavy Metals and Crime

There is a lot of evidence that shows scientific support for a heavy metal and crime link. Masters et al. (1998) performed a meta-analysis of five different lines of evidence that they felt could be analyzed to determine whether there is a relationship. Their conclusions are summarized as follows:

1. *Correlation.* Can we find a correlation between violent criminals and levels of toxic heavy metals? That is, do violent criminals have higher levels of toxic metals than non-criminals? Masters et al. (1998) looked at seven studies of prison inmates, and in each study they found that hair levels of either manganese or lead and cadmium were significantly higher in violent offenders than in nonviolent offenders or controls. As well, lithium, which detoxifies manganese, was abnormally low in two of the seven studies (Masters et al., 1998).

   There are also all the studies previously mentioned that link subclinical lead poisoning to learning disabilities and attention deficit disorder, which are both risk factors for deviant behavior. Also, extreme concentrations of manganese have been associated with violence in environments with mining operations or industrial exposure (Masters et al., 1998).

2. *Prediction.* Can we predict which people will come in conflict with the law based on their heavy metal levels as children? That is, are children with high toxin levels at increased risk for criminal behavior in later life? Needleman's work showed that lead levels at age 7 years were significantly predictive of juvenile delinquency or increased aggression in teenage years and early adulthood (Needleman et al., 1996). The largest and longest prospective study of lead effects on behavior was a longitudinal study of 1000 black Philadelphia residents who were studied from birth to age 22 years. In this study, they found that both high lead levels and anemia (low iron) at age 7 years were significant predictors of the number of juvenile offenses, seriousness of juvenile offenses, and number of adult offenses for males (Masters et al., 1998).

3. *Function.* Is it possible that heavy levels of these toxins actually could lead to criminal behavior? As already shown, clearly there are many ways in which these heavy metals can injure the brain and change the balance of crucial neurotransmitters. There also seems to be a catalytic effect with other substances, such as alcohol and drugs, which could multiply the effects overall. For example, excess lead in the brain damages cells called glia cells, which help detoxify harmful substances and are critical in behavioral inhibition (Masters et al., 1998). Other

heavy metals can also play a role. Too much copper in a young baby with a still developing brain can lead to abnormal development of the hippocampus, which is a brain structure that plays a critical role in learning. Too much manganese reduces brain levels of the neurotransmitters serotonin and dopamine, while increasing serotonin concentrations elsewhere in the body (Masters et al., 1998).

4. *Transmission.* Are people likely to be exposed to high levels of heavy metals? Clearly, the answer is yes because it has been shown that many people have high levels of heavy metals in their body. Despite the bans on leaded gasoline and paint, studies reveal that high levels of lead remain in the soil along heavily traveled urban routes. There are also many other sources of heavy metals, such as old public water systems, old water pipes inside homes, and old leaded paint (Masters et al., 1998).

Children are particularly susceptible to these toxins because they absorb up to 50% of the lead they ingest (as compared with 8% for adults) and because their brains are still developing (Masters et al., 1998). Baby formulas also affect manganese levels. Laboratory studies show that cellular uptake of manganese from cow's-milk formula is 5 times greater than from mother's milk, and the uptake from soy formula is 20 times greater (Masters et al., 1998). Thus, the practice of bottle-feeding a baby, which is apparently much more popular among poor, uneducated mothers than among wealthier mothers (possibly because they need go out and work early in the baby's life) is going to greatly increase their exposure (Masters et al., 1998).

Research also shows that when people or animals have nutritional deficiencies from a poor diet, this can increase the effects of the heavy metals (Masters et al., 1998). A good diet can be a protective factor against such toxins. Laboratory studies have shown that animals fed excessive amounts of manganese did not absorb it if their levels of calcium were normal but if their calcium levels were low (from a poor diet), then they absorbed the manganese and thus were affected (Masters et al., 1998). This can have a strong influence in real life because studies show that in the United States, black teenage males consume only about two thirds as much calcium as whites, and that calcium intakes of Hispanics, and of black women of child-bearing age, are also far lower than the white average (Masters et al., 1998). Thus, a poor diet with low levels of calcium would have a particularly bad impact during pregnancy and early childhood (Masters et al., 1998). As might be expected, the effects of heavy metals are magnified by alcohol usage. This can put people with poor diets and high alcohol consumption at particular risk (Masters et al., 1998).

5. *Ecology.* Do areas with high pollution levels have more crime? If heavy metals and violent crime are associated, then ecological measures of environmental pollution (controlling for other variables) should correlate with higher rates of violent crime. Masters et al. looked at all U.S. counties, integrating the U.S. Environmental Protection Agency's Toxic Release Inventory for lead and manganese, crime reports from the FBI, alcoholism statistics from the federal government, and socioeconomic and demographic data from the Census Bureau, and concluded that environmental pollution did have an effect on rates of violent crime. They controlled for variables such as income, population density, and ethnic composition (Masters et al., 1998). They found that counties with industrial lead pollution, industrial manganese releases, and higher than average rates of alcoholism have rates of violent crime over 3 times that of the national average (Masters et al., 1998). The later study by Stretesky and Lynch (2001) using a very large data set also showed an excellent correlation between environmental pollution and crime.

Whichever way you look at it, pollution, particularly with respect to heavy metals, can influence our behavior in a negative way. If we accept this as fact, then there are ways society might intervene. Masters et al. (1998) suggest several possible interventions:

- Allocate resources for parental training in child nutrition.
- Allocate resources for vitamin supplementation for children, either at home or at school (Masters et al., 1998). Vitamins are expensive, so possibly offering them free might help.
- Ensure that daycares, preschool, and elementary school programs feed balanced and healthy diets (Masters et al., 1998). It has been known for more than a century that a child (or an adult) cannot learn on an empty stomach, so school meals programs were developed. It now behooves us to realize that the nutritional quality of the food is just as important as quantity.
- Medically test offenders to determine which, if any, biochemical imbalances or toxins a person suffers from so that it can be corrected during their regular rehabilitation program (Masters et al., 1998). If basic imbalances are ignored, rehabilitation is less likely to be successful.
- Reduce environmental pollution. Although many attempts are made to reduce pollution, much more could be done. Not only would reduced pollution be beneficial health-wise, it might have long-term societal and economical gain if crime and delinquency can be reduced. Even minor damage can affect a child's cognitive abilities; so even if crime is not an issue, quality of life is.

Obviously, neurotoxicity is only one factor among many, probably functioning as some type of catalyst that, when added to other risk factors (such as poverty, social stress, alcohol or drug abuse, individual character, and other social factors) increases the likelihood that an individual will commit a violent crime. However, this is a risk we have perhaps a better chance at reducing, rather than other social ills such as poverty, so this is definitely an area that warrants further study. Reducing pollution is a global issue. However, if it was recognized that pollution itself might have an impact on crime, perhaps more funding would be directed toward it.

## Vitamins/Minerals

Everyone knows that a major part of a healthy diet includes consuming the appropriate vitamins and minerals. However, research has shown that proper vitamin supplementation can also influence delinquency in juveniles. Schoenthaler and Bier (2000) examined the effects of vitamin-mineral supplementation on juvenile delinquency among American schoolchildren. The researchers looked at 80 schoolchildren between the ages of 6 and 12 years in Phoenix, Arizona. The children were all those who had been disciplined in the previous semesters. The 80 children were disciplined 93 times during the fall and 115 times in the spring; 69 children were male. The researchers postulated that poor diet may have an effect on academic failure, and that this produces loss of self-esteem, frustration, depression, alienation, isolation, acting out, defiance, aggression, and retaliation, and thus could result in the need for discipline (Schoenthaler and Bier, 2000).

The children were given a vitamin tablet or a placebo daily for 4 months. The study was randomized and double-blind. The researchers measured the official school disciplinary records before and during the experiment as a way to determine whether there was a change in violent or antisocial behavior (Schoenthaler and Bier, 2000). The main finding from this study was that, among the 80 children who were disciplined during the school year, the 40 children who received active vitamins tablets were disciplined 47% less during the intervention period than the 40 children who received only the placebo (Schoenthaler and Bier, 2000). This indicates that the vitamins did have some effect, although it would have been nice to have had a nondisciplined group as a control as well.

The researchers concluded that the habitual child offender may have had sufficiently poor nutritional habits to cause low blood concentrations of water-soluble vitamins. It may sound as if they had a choice, but remember that these are children, so it is the parents, caregivers, or school staff members who are really responsible for the poor nutrition. When given supplemental vitamins, these low blood nutrient concentrations were corrected, which in turn corrected the impaired brain function. Once normal brain function resumed, according to the researchers, the children understood that their behavior was wrong and realized the consequences of their actions, and thus were able to correct their behavior (Schoenthaler and Bier, 2000). Although the results might seems simplistic, an important point to note here is that the research suggests that any brain dysfunction caused by the poor diet can be rectified and is reversible.

To determine whether the poor school performance seen in children without vitamin and mineral supplementation was due to reduced IQ Schoenthaler et al. (2000) compared the IQ levels of 245 children divided into two groups — one group received a vitamin-mineral supplement and the matched control group received only a placebo for 3 months. Overall, the researchers found a significant difference of 2.5 IQ points between the two groups, and a small group showed a massive 16-point gain in IQ. This is a highly significant increase. The authors report that the average high school graduate who enters a vocational school has an IQ of 100, whereas a university graduate entering graduate school has an IQ of 115 (Schoenthaler et al., 2000).

Shortly after these studies, research on learning-disabled students revealed that nutritional supplementation could dramatically improve learning-disabled students' school performance (Carlton et al., 2000). Significant academic and behavioral improvements were seen within weeks or months of nutritional supplementation, with some students gaining 3 to 5 years of reading comprehension and all children moving from special education to mainstream classes (Carlton et al., 2000). Not only did the children's academic performance improve, but so did their social lives and peer relationships. A cohort of 12 of the children were maintained on supplements for a further year, and 6 were maintained on supplements for 3 years. All continued to show improvement, including those who had been off the supplements for up to a year, at which point those still receiving supplements continued to improve, whereas those who had been off the supplements for over a year decreased dramatically in academic performance. The performance decreased to the extent that some were removed from the academic stream and placed in a vocational stream. Carlton et al. (2000) did not feel that the supplements increased the student's IQ directly, but rather that the supplementation allowed them to reach their full potential. The most beneficial supplements included magnesium, vitamin B6, ascorbic acid (vitamin C), thiamine, folic acid, and zinc.

Zinc supplementation has also been found to be beneficial for children with ADHD. In a double-blind, placebo-controlled study, researchers (Bilici et al., 2004) randomly assigned 400 ADHD students into two groups, one of which took a zinc supplement (150 mg zinc sulfate) and one that took a placebo, over a 3-month period. The students taking zinc showed reduced hyperactivity, reduced impulsivity, and increased sociability, but no improvement in attention deficits. Zinc is important in several areas. It is integral to the body's production of serotonin, so low zinc levels could result in low serotonin, which in turn is linked to impulsivity and aggression. It is also involved in regulating dopamine function, as it is needed for the production and modulation of melatonin, which is involved in dopamine function. ADHD is strongly linked to abnormal dopamine levels (Bilici et al., 2004). Zinc is also important in the metabolism of essential fatty acids, which are also involved in regulating dopamine and norepinephrine metabolism. Because such a dramatic effect was seen in these children in only 12 weeks with just one supplement, the researchers suggest that providing a range of supplements may have an even greater beneficial effect. In fact, in another study comparing ADHD children on conventional drug therapy (Ritalin) with those receiving no drugs, but instead receiving dietary supplements including vitamins, minerals, amino acids, essential fatty acids, and other nutrients, there was essentially no difference in the behavior of the children, and the supplementation was deemed just as successful as the drug therapy (Harding et al., 2003).

## Fat in the Diet

There have been several studies that have linked high and low fat diets to crime. Some studies have linked low serum cholesterol concentrations with the expression of aggressive or antisocial behavior in psychiatric and criminal populations.

In one study, researchers looked at the effects of fat and cholesterol on social behavior in monkeys (Kaplan et al., 1991). They fed a group of male monkeys either a luxury, high-fat, high-cholesterol diet or a prudent relatively low-fat, low-cholesterol diet. They looked at 30 male monkeys over 22 months on these diets. The monkeys were monitored for behavior and had serum lipid concentrations and body weight measured.

The researchers found that monkeys on the prudent diet (low fat, low cholesterol) initiated more contact aggression (such as slapping, grabbing, pushing, grappling, and biting) than did monkeys eating a relatively high-fat, high-cholesterol (luxury) diet The results are not conclusive, but are suggestive and are consistent with previous findings that relatively low serum cholesterol concentrations are common among persons who characteristically engage in violent behavior. However, this is not supported by the anecdotal studies that suggest that a healthier (i.e., lower fat) diet reduces aggression. Perhaps there is only a problem when the fat content in the diet is extremely low. In some studies, very low cholesterol levels have been linked to suicidal behavior (Engelberg, 1992). This link to suicide may, in turn, relate to the interaction between cholesterol and serotonin.

There may also be a direct link between dietary fat and serotonin because the same workers also observed that monkeys fed a chow diet (i.e., one relatively low in fat and cholesterol) had a significantly lower serum prolactin response to an enfluamine challenge (an indicator of low serotonin activity) than did monkeys consuming a relatively high-fat diet, which might link everything back to low serotonin levels (Kaplan et al., 1991).

In another study (Hilakivi-Clarke et al., 1996), a high-fat diet in adult mice and rats was found to increase aggression rather than reduce it. In this study, a high-fat diet elevated circulating estrogen levels, which in turn were associated with various nonreproductive behaviors such as male aggression. The time spent exhibiting aggression (in males) was longer in the males fed a high-fat diet. Serum levels of estradiol, a measure of estrogen, were elevated twofold in the male animals consuming a high-fat diet. These findings suggest that dietary fat can increase aggressive behavior in male mice and rats indirectly, possibly by elevating circulating estradiol levels (Hilakivi-Clarke et al., 1996).

## Fatty Acids

Omega-3 fatty acids are found in fish, leafy green vegetables, nuts, and flaxseed, and canola oils. In the past, early humans ate a diet that was very high in these fats, while modern humans eat a diet that is far lower in omega-3 fatty acids and far higher in the omega-6 fatty acids found in corn, soybean, cottonseed, safflower, and sunflower oils. As a result, many researchers have suggested that humans today are often deficient in several essential fatty acids that are obtained only by eating the correct foods (Anonymous, 1998). That is, we cannot synthesize them ourselves; we must include them in our diets. They are the building blocks of the synaptic membranes in the brain, which is the site of action of neurotransmitters. Without these in our diet, the neurotransmitter system will not work properly. They are also involved in eye and brain functioning, and supplementation has been found to result in improvements in dyslexics and in coordination and visual skills (Stordy, 2000).

Many studies suggest that omega-3 deficiencies are associated with aggression, other behavior problems, and several mental disorders; and preliminary trials of supplementation are very encouraging. A conference in 1998 reported the following findings (Anonymous, 1998):

1. The diets of people with bipolar disorder (manic depression) were supplemented with fish oil, which is high in omega-3 fatty acids. Nine of 14 patients taking fish oil responded well, compared with only 3 of 16 patients taking the placebo (Anonymous, 1998). Students were given capsules rich in the omega-3 fatty acid docosahexaenoic acid (DHA) or placebo capsules for 3 months (Hamazaki et al., 1996). The study started at the beginning of the semester, which was considered a non-stressful time and finished during a stressful time (i.e., final exams). Psychological tests were given throughout the trial to assess aggression and indicated that aggression toward others increased significantly in the nonsupplemented students when they were under stress, but not in supplemented students (Hamazaki et al., 1996). In another study (Horrocks and Yeo, 1999), DHA supplementation improved learning abilities and increased visual acuity in babies, whereas a reduction in DHA resulted in learning deficits.

2. Stevens et al. (1995) tested 53 boys with ADHD and 43 controls. They found that subjects with ADHD had significantly lower blood levels of major fatty acids than the controls. In a similar study, the same researchers found that in 6- to 12-year-old boys, the children with lower total omega-3 fatty acid concentrations had more behavioral problems, including temper tantrums, in comparison with children with normal levels. They also noted more learning and health problems in the experimental group. In a later study, Stevens et al. focused on a subset of hyperactive children, those who showed physical signs of low levels of long-chain polyunsaturated fatty acids, such as dry hair and excessive urination and drinking. The results suggested that this subset may have a disorder that prevents them from metabolizing fatty acid efficiently (Burgess et al., 2000). Tests showed that these children had a higher ratio of fatty acid precursors to fatty acid metabolites than controls or other ADHD children, suggesting that the children were not properly processing the fatty acid precursors (Burgess et al., 2000). Supplementing ADHD children with a combination of polyunsaturated fatty acids, including omega-3 fatty acids, did not result in an overall decrease in ADHD behaviors but did result in a decrease in disruptive behaviors (Stevens et al., 2003).

3. In another study (Hibbeln et al., 1998), it was found that people who had high levels of omega-3 fatty acids in their diet had greater concentrations of serotonin in the brain. This difference would obviously have an effect on behavior, but these results have not yet been confirmed in clinical trials. Preliminary studies on relationships between omega-3 fatty acids and serotonin and dopamine metabolites in healthy subjects, violent subjects, and early- and late-onset alcoholics

has shown that these relationships are significantly different in healthy subjects than in violent or early-onset-alcoholic subjects (Hibbeln et al., 1998).

4. A study (Hibbeln and Salem, 1998) of 18 patients with a history of suicide attempts showed that higher blood levels of the omega-3 fatty acid EPA correlated with a lower risk (as assessed by psychological tests) of future suicide attempts. The same researchers suggested that omega-3 fatty acid deficiencies might explain the reported link between lowered cholesterol levels and increased rates of suicide, homicide, and depression (Hibbeln and Salem, 1998). As the researchers point out, when a person is medically advised to reduce cholesterol, most people reduce their fat intake, but this can also result in a reduction of omega-3 fatty acids.

These findings are further supported by related research in other population segments. In a study of 3600 young urban adults, higher consumption of the omega-3 fatty acid docosahexaenoic acid (DHA), in either supplement form or as a part of diet, was significantly related to lower levels of hostility (Iribarren et al., 2004).

Fatty-acid levels in baby formula have also been studied (Birch et al., 2000). Birch et al. divided 56 newborn infants into three groups. One group received standard infant formula; the second group received a formula enriched with the essential fatty acid (DHA); and a third group received a formula enriched with both DHA and the essential fatty acid arachidonic acid (AA). At the end of the 4-month study, all three groups were put on standard formula. When the babies were 18 months old, researchers tested them using the Bayley Scales of Infant Development, which measures physical and mental development (Birch et al., 2000). Babies who had received the formula containing both DHA and AA during their first 4 months had an average IQ of 105.6, almost the same as the average of 106 in breast-fed babies. Infants receiving the formula with only DHA scored an average of 102, while those drinking only standard infant formula scored 98, which is slightly below the national average of 100 (Birch et al., 2000). This study is one of many reporting IQ gains in infants fed formulas enriched with essential fatty acids, nutrients that are currently included in infant formulas in 60 countries, although not yet in the United States.

Prematurely born children usually have lower IQs than babies who go to full term. However, a double-blind study showed that 424 premature babies fed fatty-acid-enriched formulas from birth for 1 month had verbal IQ scores that were an average of 12 points higher than comparable children who received standard formula as infants when the children were tested at age 8 years (Lucas et al., 1998). The greatest differences were seen in boys rather than girls. In a related study, full-term babies receiving enriched formula for 4 months performed better on a problem-solving test at 10 months of age than did other 10-month-olds who had received standard formula (Willatts et al., 1998).

## Food Additives

Much attention has been given to the subject of food additives and their possible impact on behavior — in particular, hyperactivity. Much of this interest began with the work of a pediatrician, named Feingold. Dr. Feingold, who believed that ADHD and other hyperactivity disorders in children were caused by problems in diet, most notably by additives such as preservatives and colorings. He developed a specific diet plan, believing that some people react more to these additives than do others. Proponents of the diet claim that it cures many behavioral problems, including bed-wetting (Feingold, 2006).

Feingold worked originally with adult patients with allergies to aspirin (salicylic acid). Some of these patients also appeared to react badly to other substances, so a special diet was developed to eliminate all salicylate-containing chemicals that occur naturally in some foods. The artificial food coloring tartrazine (FD and C Yellow #5) was also eliminated because it had been shown to produce the same allergic-like symptoms in some aspirin-sensitive patients. From this it was concluded that there could be many other additives in our diet that could cause adverse clinical responses. Therefore, the original diet was expanded to exclude artificial flavors and coloringss (Feingold, 2006). Because the symptoms of aspirin sensitivity could sometimes be behavioral, it was asserted that a diet high in additives could be responsible for the behavioral problems associated with learning disabilities and hyperactivity. Dr. Feingold has suggested that there is a causal relationship between an increase in the industrial use of artificial flavorings and colorings and an increase in hyperactivity or learning disability. It is a popular notion to blame all society's ills on food additives and mysterious food production. However, although there has been a significant increase in the awareness of hyperactivity disorders, there is no evidence whatsoever that hyperactivity or learning disabilities have actually increased in prevalence in the population.

Feingold's data are based entirely on clinical observations. He claims that 50% of hyperactive and learning-disabled children achieve a "full response," while 75% can be removed from drug management (Feingold, 2006). These results are very promising but there appears to be little research data to back them up. Clinical data are interesting but lack valid controls. It is also often difficult to determine what is actually an "additive," in that the chemical components of synthetic food flavourings are often identical to the chemicals contained in natural foods.

In response to Feingold's claims, a series of studies was conducted to determine the validity of the Feingold diet (Wender, 1986). In these studies, approximately 240 children were evaluated and, at most, only two or three childen (1%) demonstrated any consistent behavioral change in the expected direction. The 20 most hyperactive children performed less well on a laboratory learning task during a short period after the ingestion of a large dose of food coloring. However, no behavioral change was noted. More than 90% of the children studied showed no significant change of any kind when challenged with food colorings (Wender, 1986).

However, several more recent studies present empirical data to support the theory that some food additives may indeed have adverse effects on children's behavior, particularly in the area of hyperactivity. Kaplan et al. (1989) used a placebo-controlled, cross-over design to study 24 hyperactive boys and their responses to food additives. The study had three phases: (1) a baseline period during which the boys ate their usual home-cooked meals; (2) a placebo period when they ate pre-packaged meals that, unknown to the parents, actually contained the same levels of additives as their normal meals; and then (3) a one month period when the boys ate pre-packaged meals that were free of additives, artificial colorings, flavorings and preservatives, as well as chocolate, MSG, and caffeine. Children on the experimental diet exhibited fewer behavioral problems, including improved sleep patterns (Kaplan et al., 1989).

In a double-blind, placebo-controlled study of children challenged with the food coloring tartrazine (also known as Yellow #5), a strong association was recorded between adverse behavioral changes and the dye (Rowe and Rowe, 1994). The researchers gave either a placebo or tartrazine to three groups of children. The groups consisted of 23 hyperactive children who were thought by their parents to be allergic to food colorings, 11 hyperactive children whose parents were unsure of their children's sensitivity to food colorings, and 20 controls who were neither hypersensitive nor allergic. All were fed a diet free of any synthetic colorings for a period of time, then were randomly assigned to the tartrazine or the placebo group. Both parents and researchers were blind to the treatment that the children received. Parents stated that 19 of the hyperactive, allergic children, 3 of the hyperactive children with uncertain responses to colorings, and 2 of the control children clearly showed more hyperactive activity and behavioral disorders when taking the tartrazine. Younger children exhibited behaviors such as constant crying, temper tantrums, restlessness, sleep disturbances, and irritability; whereas, older children were more inclined to be aimless, to complain, lack self control, and be generally unhappy and irritable (Rowe and Rowe, 1994).

Even low doses of tartrazine had an impact, although the results were more intense at higher doses.

Research by Ward (1997) has linked hyperactivity (a strong risk factor for criminality) to nutritional deficiencies and food intolerance. Ward surveyed the parents of 486 hyperactive children and 172 nonhyperactive controls. The parents of the hyperactive children reported that more than 60% exhibited increased behavior problems when exposed to synthetic colorings and flavorings, preservatives, cow's milk, and certain chemicals. In contrast, only 12% of parents of the controls reported a connection between food additives or colorings and worsened behavior.

Ward (1997) identified a subgroup of hyperactive children with known sensitivities to synthetic food colorings and exposed the children to these chemicals. Of 23 exposed to the food coloring tartrazine, 18 responded by becoming overactive, 16 became aggressive, 4 became violent, and several developed eczema, asthma, poor speech, or poor coordination. In contrast, only one control subject showed minor behavioral changes after drinking tartrazine. Two other colorings, "sunset yellow" and amaranth, also caused significant behavioral effects in hyperactive subjects (Ward, 1997).

Ward (1997) uncovered one possible explanation for the food colorings' effects. The hyperactive children in the study had statistically lower zinc and iron levels than controls; and when hyperactive children known to be sensitive to the colorings tartrazine and "sunset yellow" were exposed to these chemicals, their blood serum zinc levels dropped markedly. Other studies have shown that animals deficient in zinc are more likely to be affected by stress and can be aggressive in comparison with normal cases, as well as links with tartrazine to hyperactivity (Ward, 1997).

Other research has also experimentally linked reactions to food additives with hyperactivity. Bateman et al. (2004) divided 277 preschool children into four groups: (1) those who exhibited symptoms of hyperactivity but no food additive allergies; (2) those who had allergies but not hyperactivity; (3) those with both conditions; and (4) those with neither condition. All children were placed on an additive-free diet and then exposed to either a placebo or a drink containing food additives and benzoate preservatives. The level of challenge was equivalent to a low to normal rate in a regular diet. The experiment was then reversed so that each child was challenged with either a placebo or the additive-containing drink. The children's behavior was ranked by parents and clinical observations in a double-blind test, with neither parents nor clinicians being aware of treatment group (Bateman et al., 2004). A substantial relationship between artificial food colorings and preservatives and hyperactivity was seen, indicating a general adverse effect of such additives on behavior (Bateman et al., 2004). These effects were only detectable by parents and not by clinical assessment, although parents observed the daily behavior of the children over a longer time period. However, the effects were seen not just in the allergic and hyperactive children, but also in perfectly normal children. Also, the effects of removing the additives and preservatives from the children's diet prior to commencing the experiment had a significant effect on the behavior of the hyperactive children, similar to that seen in drug treatment (Bateman et al., 2004).

## Food Allergies

Many people are allergic to or intolerant of certain food groups. In a study of 100 young offenders and 100 matched non-offenders, it was found that the offender group reported significantly higher rates of ill health than the nonoffender group. Offenders were, in general, far more likely than controls to report stomach aches, lethargy, eye and nose problems, poor sleep, abnormal thirst, poor concentration, and poor memory, and were more likely to be hyperactive (Bennett et al., 1998; Bennett and Brostoff, 1997).

The researchers noted that many symptoms exhibited by the offenders could be linked to food allergies or food intolerance, so they looked at this possibility in nine children between the ages of 7 and 16 years of age with histories of repetitive antisocial or criminal behaviors. The nine children had collectively committed 67 crimes, and all the subjects regularly displayed irrational aggression and violence (Bennett et al., 1998; Bennett and Brostoff, 1997).

Doctors identified nutrient deficiencies and food allergies in all nine subjects, and also found elevated levels of cadmium, a neurotoxic heavy metal, in four subjects. The researchers provided treatment for all subjects, including dietary restriction and allergy desensitization therapy. Coincidentally, this experiment was recorded by a television group producing a documentary. The television production team commented that the children showed uncontrolled, violent, competitive, and antisocial behavior before the intervention, but that afterward, were pleasant, controlled, cooperative, and generally very sociable. (Bennett et al., 1998; Bennett and Brostoff, 1997).

The researchers stated that the health and behavior of all nine subjects improved during treatment. Three children later discontinued the dietary intervention, and of those, two of them reoffended. Of the other children, two reoffended, but not as often or with the previous violence they had shown. In all, of nine subjects, five did not reoffend during the 2 years following the intervention (Bennett et al., 1998; Bennett and Brostoff, 1997). However, bear in mind that this study involved a small sample size and also that many children naturally grow out of petty crime as they mature.

## Diet and Overall Behavior

A study of children in the Mauritius Child Health Project showed that malnutrition at age 3 years had reduced verbal and cognitive abilities and by the age of 11 years had lower IQs, poorer reading ability, and both academic and neuropsychological deficits (Liu et al., 2003). The findings were unrelated to ethnicity or gender and were stable over time. In a follow-up study, the researchers were able to show that providing children with an improved diet, increased exercise, and an enriched early education could dramatically decrease the chances that they would develop antisocial behavioral problems or schizotypal symptoms in later adolescence or adulthood (Raine et al., 2003). The researchers compared 83 children in an experimental group with a group of several hundred matched children. Both groups were part of the Mauritius Child Health Project. The experimental group received a carefully designed kindergarten nutritional program that included a hot meal, salad, fruit juice, and milk every day, as opposed to the typical bread or rice meals served in the kindergarten. They also received extra outdoor activities, including free play, gymnastics, and sports, as well as an enhanced educational program that focused on increasing verbal skills, memory, perception, and coordination (Raine et al., 2003). The program began when the children were 3 years old and continued for 2 years. The control children were matched on a number of parameters, including temperament, nutritional status, and cognitive abilities.

The children were followed up at age 17 and 23 using self-report measures and criminal records for antisocial and criminal behavior as well as schizotypal symptoms. The results showed that the children in the enriched program had lower scores for schizotypal personality at age 17 years and for criminal behavior at age 23 (Raine et al., 2003). The effects were most obvious in children who had been malnourished at 3 years old, suggesting that nutrition played the larger role.

## Conclusion

The evidence strongly suggests that something as simple and ordinary as what we eat can have a major impact on our well-being and subsequent behavior. There are numerous components to our diet, and a simple deficiency may be enough to affect us. In some people who are more predisposed to other risk factors, the wrong diet may be the last straw. It would, therefore, seem common sense to ensure that children and pregnant mothers receive adequate diets and that offenders are assessed not just psychologically when placed in a corrections facility or detention center, but also medically to check for deficiencies or toxins. A dietary problem is so simple to correct but can have a major impact if left unchecked. It is also a very inexpensive solution to a very large problem.

## Questions for Further Study and Discussion

1. Discuss issues related to changing a child's diet in an effort to change their behavior.
2. Despite the fact that there is very little good experimental evidence (with good controls) to prove that a change in diet can reduce violence in prisons, why might it be valuable to change the diets of prisoners?
3. Many factors related to pollution are known to be bad for humans, and particularly for children. Discuss how this relates to crime, poverty, and other social factors, and how we might change this.

## References

Anonymous. (1998). Conference Report. Essential fatty acids predict biomarkers of aggression and depression. *Polyunsaturated Fatty Acids (PUFA) Newslett.*, 1(3).

Bateman, B., Warner, J.O., Hutchinson, E., Dean, T., Rowlandson, P., Grant, C., Grundy, J., Fitzgerald, C., and Stevenson, J. (2004). The effects of a double-blind, placebo-controlled, artificial food colorings and benzoate preservative challenge on hyperactivity in a general population sample of preschool children. *Arch. Dis. Child.*, 89(6), 506–511.

Beattie, O. and Geiger, J. (1998). *Frozen in Time, the Fate of the Franklin Expedition.* Vancouver: Greystone Books.

Bennett, C.P.W. and Brostoff, J. (1997). The health of criminals related to behavior, food, allergy and nutrition, a controlled study of 100 persistent young offenders. *J. Nutr. Environ. Med.*, 7, 359–366.

Bennett, C.P.W., McEwen, L.M., McEwen, H.C., and Rose, E.L. (1998). The Shipley Project, treating food allergy to prevent criminal behavior in community settings. *J. Nutr. Environ. Med.*, 8, 77–83.

Bilici, M., Yildirim, F., Kandil, S., Bekaroglu, M., Yildirimis, S., Deger, O., Ulge, M., Yildiran, A., and Aksu, H. (2004). Double-blind, placebo-controlled study of zinc sulfate in the treatment of attention deficit hyperactivity disorder. *Progr. Neuro-Psychopharm. Biol. Psych.*, 28(1), 181–190.

Birch, E., Garfield, S., Hoffman, D., Uauy, R., and Birch, D. (2000). A randomized controlled trial of early dietary supply of long chain polyunsaturated fatty acids and mental development in term infants. *Develop. Med. Child. Neurol.*, 42, 174–181.

Brunner, H.G. (1996). MAOA deficiency and abnormal behavior, perspectives on an association. *Ciba Found Symp.*, 194, 155–64.

Burgess, J.R., Stevens, J., Zhang, W., and Peck, L. (2000). Long-chain polyunsaturated fatty acids in children with attention deficit hyperactivity disorder. *Am. J. Clin. Nutr.*, 71(1), 327–330.

Carlton, R.M., Ente, G., Blum, L., Heyman, N., Davis, W., and Ambrosino, S. (2000). Rational dosages of nutrients have a prolonged effect on learning disabilities. *Alt. Therapies,* 6(3), 85–91.

Coccaro, E.F. (1989). Central serotonin and impulsive aggression. *Br. J. Psych.,* 155(Suppl. 8), 52–62.

Denno, D.W. (1990). *Biology and Violence, From Birth to Adulthood.* Cambridge: Cambridge University Press.

Dietrich, K.N., Douglas, R.M., Succop, P.A., Berger, O.G., and Bornschein, R.L. (2001). Early exposure to lead and juvenile delinquency. *Neurotoxicology Teratology,* 23(6), 511–518.

Engelberg, H. (1992). Low serum cholesterol and suicide. *Lancet,* 339(8795), 727–9.

Eyestone, L. and Howell, R. (1994). An epidemiological study of attention-deficit hyperactivity disorder and major depression in a male prison population. *Bull. Am. Acad. Psych. Law,* 22(2), 181–193.

Feingold, B.F. (2006). The Feingold Program Website and Dr. Feingold Biography. <http://www.feingold.org/us-pg.html> (Accessed April 27, 2006).

Fishbein, D.H. and Thatcher, R.W. (1982). Nutritional and electrophysiological indices of maladaptive behavior. MIT Conference on Research Strategies for Assessing the Behavioral Effects of Food and Nutrients, Cambridge, MA. Cited by Raine, 1993.

Fuller, R.W. (1996). The influence of fluoxetine on aggressive behavior [see comments]. *Neuropsychopharmacology,* 14(2), 77–81.

Fulton, M., Thomson, G., Hunter, R., Raab, G., Laxen, D., and Hepburn, W. (1987). Influence of blood lead on the ability and attainment of children in Edinburgh. *Lancet i,* 1221–1226.

Gray, G.E. (1986). Diet, crime and delinquency, a critique. *Nutr. Rev.,* 44(Suppl.) 89–94.

Hamazaki, T., Sawazaki, S., Itomura, M., Asoka, E., Nagao, Y., Nishimura, N., Yazawa, K., Kuwamori, T., and Kobayashi, M. (1996). The effect of docosahexaenoic acid on aggression in young adults, a placebo-controlled double-blind study. *J. Clin. Inv.,* 97, 1120–1133.

Harding, K.L., Judah, R.D., and Gant, C. (2003). Outcome-based comparison of Ritalin versus food-supplement treated children with ADHD. *Alt. Med. Rev.,* 8(3), 319–330.

Hibbeln, J.R., Umhau, J.C., Linnoila, M., George, D.T., Ragan, W., Shoaf, S.E., Vaughhan, M.R., Rawlings, R., and Salem, N.J. (1998). A replication study of violent and nonviolent subjects, cerebrospinal fluid metabolites of serotonin and dopamine are predicted by plasma essential fatty acids. *Biol. Psych.*, 44, 243–249.

Hibbeln, J.R. and Salem, N.J. (1998). Dietary polyunsaturated fatty acids and depression, when cholesterol does not satisfy. *Am. J. Clin. Nutr.*, 62(1), 1–9.

Hilakivi-Clarke, L., Cho, E., and Onojafe, I. (1996). High fat diet induces aggressive behavior in mice and rats. *Life Sciences*, 19, 1653–1660.

Horrocks, L.A. and Yeo, Y.K. (1999). Health benefits of docosahexaenoic acid (DHA). *Pharmacological Res.*, 40(3), 211–225.

Iribarren, C., Markovitz, J.H., Jacobs, D.R., Schreiner, P.J., Daviglus, M., and Hibbeln, J.R. (2004). Dietary intake of omega-3, omega-6 fatty acids and fish, relationship with hostility on young adults — the CARDIA study. *European J. Clin. Nutr.*, 58(1), 24–31.

Kaplan, J.R., Manuck, S.B., and Shively, C. (1991). The effects of fat and cholesterol on social behavior on monkeys. *Psychosomatic Med.*, 53, 634–642.

Kaplan, B.J., McNicol, J., Conte, R.A., and Moghadam, H.K. (1989). Dietary replacement in preschool-aged hyperactive boys. *Pediatrics*, 83(1), 7–17.

Landrigan, P.J. and Todd, A.C. (1994). Direct measurement of lead in bone, a promising biomarker. *J. Am. Med. Assoc.*, 274(3), 239–240.

Levy, F., Hay, D.A., McStephen, M., Wood, C., and Waldman, I. (1997). Attention-deficit hyperactivity disorder, a category or a continuum? Genetic analysis of a large-scale twin study. *J-Am. Acad. Child Adolesc. Psychiatry*, 36(6), 737–44.

Liu, J., Raine, A., Venables, P., Dalais, C., and Mednick, S.A. (2003). Malnutrition at age 3 years and lower cognitive ability at age 11 years. *Arch. Pediatric Adolescent Med.* 157, 593–600.

Lönnerdal, B. (1994). Manganese nutrition of infants. In Klimis-Tavantzis, D. (Ed.), *Manganese in Health and Disease* (pp. 175–191). Boca Raton, FL: CRC Press.

Lucas, A., Morley, R., and Cole, T.J. (1998). Randomised trial of early diet in preterm babies and later intelligence quotient. *Br. Med. J.*, 317, 1481–1487.

Lucas, S., Sexton, M., and Langenberg, P. (1996). Relationship between blood lead and nutritional factors in preschool children, a cross cultural study. *Pediatrics*, 97(1), 74–79.

Marlowe, M. and Bliss, L. (1993). Hair element concentrations and young children's behavior at school and home. *J. Orthomolecular Med.*, 9, 1–12.

Masters, R.D., Hone, B., and Doshi, A. (1998). Environmental pollution, neurotoxicity, and criminal violence. In Rose, J. (Ed.), *Environmental Toxicology*. Amsterdam: Gordon and Breach.

Moeller, G., Dougherty, D.M., Swann, M.C., Collins, D., Davis, C.M., and Cherek, D.R. (1996). Tryptophan depletion and aggressive responding in healthy males. *Psychopharmacology*, 126, 97–103.

Moffitt, T. (1990). Juvenile delinquency and attention deficit disorder. Boys' developmental trajectories from age 3 to age 15 child development. *Child Development*, 61, 893–910.

Moore, T.O., Karom, M., and O'Farrell, L. (2004). The neurobehavioral effects of phytoestrogens in male Syrian hamsters. *Brain Res.*, 1016(1), 102–110.

Needleman, H., McFarland, C., Ness, R.B., Fienberg, S.E., and Tobin, J. (2002). Bone lead levels in adjudicated delinquents. *Neurotoxicology Teratology*, 24(6), 711–717.

Needleman, H., Riess, J., Tobin, M., Biesecker, G., and Greenhouse, J. (1996). Bone lead levels and delinquent behavior. *J. Am. Med. Assoc.*, 275(5), 363–369.

Needleman, H., Schell, A., Bellinger, D., Leviton, A., and Allred, E. (1990). The long-term effects of exposure to low doses of lead in childhood, an 11-year follow-up report. *New Engl. J. Med.*, 322(2), 83–88.

Nielsen, D.A., Virkkunen, M., Lappalainen, J., Eggert, M., Brown, G.L., Long, J.C., Goldman, D., and Linnoila, M. (1998). A tryptophan hydroxylase gene marker for suicidality and alcoholism. *Arch. Gen. Psych.*, 55(7), 593–602.

Nihei, M.K., Desmond, J.L., McGlothan, J.L., Kuhlmann, A.C., and Guilarte, T.R. (2000). N-methyl-D-aspartate receptor subunit changes are associated with lead-induced deficits of long-term potentiation and spatial learning. *Neuroscience*, 99(2), 233–244.

Porter, W.P., Jaeger, J.W., and Carlson, I.H. (1999). Endocrine, immune and behavioral effects of aldicarb (carbamate), atrizine (triazine) and nitrate (fertilizer) mixtures at groundwater concentrations. *Tox. Indust. Hlth.*, 15(1–2), 133–150.

Raine, A. (1993). The Psychopathology of Crime. Criminal Behavior as a Clinical Disorder (pp. 191–214). London: Academic Press.

Raine, A., Mellingen, K., Liu, J., Venables, P., and Mednick, S.A. (2003). Effects of environmental enrichment at age 3–5 years on schizotypal personality and antisocial behavior at ages 17–23 years. *Am. J. Psychiatry*, 160(9), 1–9.

Rice, D.C. (2000). Parallels between attention deficit hyperactivity disorder and behavioral deficits produced by neurotoxic exposure in monkeys. *Env. Hlth. Perspectives*, 108(3), 405–408.

Rowe, K.S. and Rowe, K.J. (1994). Synthetic food coloring and behavior. A dose response effect in a double-blind, placebo-controlled repeated-measures study. *J. Pediatrics*, 125(5), 691–698.

Rumsey, J.M. and Rapoport, J.L. (Eds.) (1983). *Nutrition and the Brain*. New York: Raven Press.

Schauss, A. (1981). *Diet, Crime and Delinquency*. Berkeley, CA: Parker House.

Schoenthaler, S.J. (1983). Diet and crime, an empirical examination of the value of nutrition in the control and treatment of incarcerated juvenile offenders. *Int. J. Biosocial Res.*, 4, 25–39.

Schoenthaler, S.J. and Bier, I.D. (2000). The effect of vitamin-mineral supplementation on juvenile delinquency among American schoolchildren. A randomized, double-blind placebo-controlled study. *J. Alt. Compl. Med.*, 6(1), 7–17.

Schoenthaler, S.J., Bier, I.D., Young, K., Nichols, D., and Jansenns, S. (2000). The effect of vitamin-mineral supplementation on the intelligence of American school children, a randomized, double-blind placebo-controlled trial. *J. Alt. Compl. Med.*, 6(1), 19–29.

Simon, N.G., Kaplan, J.R., Hu, S., Register, T.C., and Adams, M.R. (2004). Increased aggressive behavior and decreased affiliative behavior in adult male monkeys after long-term consumption of diets rich in soy protein and isoflavones. *Hormones Behavior*, 45, 278–284.

Stevens, J., Zentall, S.S., Deck, J.L., Abate, M.L., Watkins, B.A., Lipp, S.R., and Burgess, J.R. (1995). Essential fatty acid metabolism in boys with attention deficit hyperactivity disorder. *American J. Clin. Nutr.*, 62(4), 761–768.

Stevens, L., Zhang, W., Peck, L., Kuczek, T., Grevstad, A., Mahon, A., Zentall, S.S., Arnold, L.E., and Burgess, J.R. (2003). EFA supplementation in children with inattention, hyperactivity and other disruptive behaviors. *Lipids*, 38(10), 1007–1021.

Stordy, B.J. (2000). Dark adaptation, motor skills, docosahexanoic acid, and dyslexia. *Am. J. Clin. Nutr.*, 71(1), 323–326.

Stretesky, P.B. and Lynch, M.J. (2001). The relationship between lead exposure and homicide. *Arch. Ped. Adolesc. Med.*, 155(5), 579–582.

Tannock, R. (1998). Attention deficit hyperactivity disorder. Advances in cognitive, neurobiological, and genetic research. *J. Child Psychol. Psych. Allied Disc.*, 39, 65–99.

Thomson, G.O., Raab, G., Hepburn, W.S., and Hunter, R. (1989). Blood levels and children behavior. Results from the Edinburgh lead study. *J. Child Psychol. Psych. Allied Disc.*, 30, 515–528.

Tran, T.T., Chowanadisai, W., Lonnendal, B., Le, L., Parker, M., Chicz-Demet, A., Crinella, F.M. (2002). Effects of neonatal dietary manganese exposure on brain dopamine levels and neurocognitive functions. *Neurotoxicology*, 145, 1–7.

Tuthill, R. (1996). Hair lead levels related to children's classroom attention-deficit behavior. *Arch. Env. Hlth.*, 51(3), 214–220.

Venables, P.H., Raine, A. (1987). Biological theory. In *Applying Psychology to Imprisonment: Theory and Practice*, McGurk, B., Thornton, D., Williams, M. (Eds.), London: Her Majesty's Stationary Office. pp. 3–28.

Virkkunen, M., De Jong, J., Bartko, J., Goodwin, F., and Linnoila, M. (1989). Relationship of psychobiological variables to revcidivism in violent offenders and impulsive fire setters. *Arch. Gen. Psych.*, 46, 600–603.

Virkkunen, M., Eggert, M., Rawlings, R., and Linnoila, M. (1996). A prospective follow-up study of alcoholic violent offenders and fire setters. *Arch. Gen. Psych.*, 53(6), 523–529.

Virkkunen, M., Goldman, D., and Linnoila, M. (Eds.) (1996). Serotonin in Alcoholic Violent Offenders. Genetics of Criminal and Antisocial Behavior. *Ciba Foundation Symposium*, John Wiley & Sons.

Virkkunen, M., Goldman, D., Nielsen, D.A., and Linnoila, M. (1995). Low brain serotonin turnover rate (low CSF 5-HIAA) and impulsive violence. *J. Psych. Neurosci.*, 20(4), 271–275.

Virkkunen, M., Kallio, E., Rawlings, R., Tokola, R., Poland, R.E., Guidotti, A., Nemeroff, C., Bissette, G., Kalogeras, K., and Karonen, S.L. (1994). Personality profiles and state aggressiveness in Finnish alcoholic, violent offenders, fire setters, and healthy volunteers. *Arch. Gen. Psych.*, 51(1), 28–33.

Virkkunen, M. and Linnoila, M. (1996). Serotonin and glucose metabolism in impulsively violent alcoholic offenders. In Stoff, D.M. and Cairns, R.B. (Eds.), *Aggression and Violence, Genetic, Neurobiological and Biosocial Perspectives* (pp. 87–99). Mahwah, NJ: Lawrence Erlbaum Associates.

Virkkunen, M., Rawlings, R., Tokola, R., Poland, R.E., Guidotti, A., Nemeroff, C., Bissette, G., Kalogeras, K., Karonen, S.L., and Linnoila, M. (1994b). CSF biochemistries, glucose metabolism, and diurnal activity rhythms in alcoholic, violent offenders, fire setters, and healthy volunteers. *Arch. Gen. Psych.*, 51(1), 20–27.

Volavka, J., Crowner, M., Brizer, D., Convit, A., Van Praag, H., and Suckow, R.F. (1990). Tryptophan treatment of aggressive psychiatric inpatients. *Biol. Psych.*, 28, 728–732.

Ward, N. (1997). Assessment of chemical factors in relation to child hyperactivity. *J. Nutr. Env. Med.*, 7, 333–342.

Ward, A.C. (2000). Evidentiary use of biological disorder, Ethics and Justice, MA thesis. School of Criminology, Simon Fraser University, Burnaby, B.C., Canada. 61pp.

Wender, E.H. (1986). The food additive-free diet in the treatment of behavior disorders,, a review. *Dev. Behva. Ped.*, 7, 35–42.

Willatts, P., Forsyth, J.S., DiModugno, M.K., Varma, S., and Colvin, M. (1998). Effect of long-chain polyunsaturated fatty acids in infant formula on problem solving at 10 months of age. *Lancet*, 352(9129), 1481–1487.

Wolfgang, M.E., Figlio, R.M., and Sellin, T. (1972*). Delinquency in a Birth Cohort.* Chicago: University of Chicago Press.

Zagar, R., Arbit, J., Hughes, J., Busell, R., and Busch, K. (1989). Developmental and disruptive behavior disorders among delinquents. *J. Am. Acad. Child Adolescent Psychiatry*, 28(3), 437–440.

# Epilogue

## Some Final Thoughts about Biological Influences on Criminal Behavior

Having covered myriad aspects of biology in this text, it should be clear that biology does impact behavior, because biology is the science of life; it must impact behavior, as it impacts everything about life. But biology does not and cannot act alone — our behavior is a complex mix of who we are, our experiences, *and* our genes, hormones, neurotransmitters, and even our diet. Nothing acts in a vacuum. Biology is not destiny any more than social experience is destiny.

Biology means much more than genetics, and many quite mundane facts such as hormone level or diet can influence our behavior. I hope to have made it clear that even if a person has a biological or, for that matter, a social predisposition to perform a behavior that might lead to a criminal act, that does not mean that the person will become a criminal — it is a predisposition only, a risk factor. The biological research included in this text has provided the best empirical evidence I know of to prove that the *environment* plays a major role in human behavior and has shown which environmental factors are protective. This research helps us gain an understanding of the best methods to use in any intervention.

Perhaps the most important information I hope you have gained from this text is that behavior can usually be modified, especially when it is biologically based. As you have seen, just small imbalances in the body's chemistry can cause dramatic mood and behavior shifts. With a proper understanding, in some cases, it could be a simple matter of shifting those balances.

Not only has this book highlighted the fact that any biological predisposition for an antisocial behavior can be ameliorated or treated much more easily than many social factors, I hope it is also clear that many problems can be prevented entirely with protective factors. Again and again, whether considering FASD, hormonal dysfunctions, neurotransmitter deficiencies, neural damage, or birth complications, the research studies show that a strong, supportive, and stable environment can dramatically reduce or eliminate the risks of criminal behavior. This same conclusion has been seen time and again, irrespective of country, researchers, or predisposition. Therefore, it is surely an area where more resources should be allocated. Many children come from unstable homes, but stability could be provided from the outside in the form of ongoing child mentors, better daycare, and school support. Such resources, clearly, would not be wasted.

Finally, I hope I have made it evident that considering biology as a potential explanation for certain aspects of crime is not a bad thing. It should *not* be taboo. It provides us with a vital understanding that may take us one step closer to understanding why people commit crime and how we can more intelligently intervene.

**Gail Anderson, 2006**

# Index

5-alpha-dihydrotestosterone (DHT), 140
5-HIAA, 133
    in suicidal individuals, 182
5-HTT gene
    legal defenses involving, 189
    short and long alleles, 183
5-Hydroxytryptamine (5-HT), and
    impulsive-aggressive behavior, 181

## A

Accidental death
    serotonin binding sites in, 186
    serotonin levels in, 182
Acetylcholine production, and FASD,
    163
Adaptation, 25, 26, 49
    aggression as, 68
    as compromise, 30–31
    and genetic variation, 57
Adolescent crime, 13. *See also* Juvenile
    crime
    and cheater theory, 45–46
    delinquency, 14–15
    and head injury, 217
Adoption studies, 95
    and aggression in rhesus monkeys,
      116–117
    Bohman's Stockholm adoption studies,
      110–112
    caveats to, 108–110
    of genetic predispositions, 105–106
    labeling by adoptive parents, 110

Mednick's Danish adoption studies,
    106–108
    time of adoption factor in, 109
Adoptive parents, criminal records of, 106
Adrenal glands
    cortisol regulation by, 145
    DHEAS secretion by, 140
Adrenalin, and criminal behavior, 147
Adult crime
    etiology relative to juvenile crime, 98
    genetic influence on, 100
Age
    decrease in criminal violence and
      testosterone with, 129–130
    of mother during pregnancy, 166
Age of onset of reproduction
    and criminal behavior, 47
    as indicator of parental investment, 46
Aggression
    and 5-HT, 181
    in alternate adaptation theory, 47–48
    and antisocial behavior, 117
    and body size, 196
    and dietary fat, 279
    and dopamine, 190
    due to head trauma, 231
    and frontal lobe injury, 216
    genetics of, 68–72, 116–118
    and hypoglycemia, 257
    inhibition by frontal lobe, 210
    and low fat/low cholesterol diets, 278
    and MOA, 191–193
    and natural testosterone levels, 129–133
    and norepinephrine, 189